CCSP Self-Study
CCSP SECUR
Exam Certification Guide

Greg Bastien
Christian Abera Degu

Cisco Press

Cisco Press
800 East 96th Street
Indianapolis, IN 46240 USA

CCSP Self-Study

CCSP SECUR Exam Certification Guide

Greg Bastien, Christian Abera Degu

Copyright© 2004 Cisco Systems, Inc.

Published by:
Cisco Press
800 East 96th Street
Indianapolis, IN 46240 USA

All rights reserved. No part of this book may be reproduced or transmitted in any form or by any means, electronic or mechanical, including photocopying, recording, or by any information storage and retrieval system, without written permission from the publisher, except for the inclusion of brief quotations in a review.

Printed in the United States of America 1 2 3 4 5 6 7 8 9 0

Library of Congress Cataloging-in-Publication Number: 2002109331

ISBN: 1-58720-072-4

First Printing December 2003

Warning and Disclaimer

This book is designed to provide information about selected topics for the Cisco SECUR exam for the CCSP certification. Every effort has been made to make this book as complete and as accurate as possible, but no warranty or fitness is implied.

The information is provided on an "as is" basis. The authors, Cisco Press, and Cisco Systems, Inc., shall have neither liability nor responsibility to any person or entity with respect to any loss or damages arising from the information contained in this book or from the use of the discs or programs that may accompany it.

The opinions expressed in this book belong to the author and are not necessarily those of Cisco Systems, Inc.

Trademark Acknowledgments

All terms mentioned in this book that are known to be trademarks or service marks have been appropriately capitalized. Cisco Press or Cisco Systems, Inc., cannot attest to the accuracy of this information. Use of a term in this book should not be regarded as affecting the validity of any trademark or service mark.

Corporate and Government Sales

Cisco Press offers excellent discounts on this book when ordered in quantity for bulk purchases or special sales. For more information, please contact: **U.S. Corporate and Government Sales   1-800-382-3419   corpsales@pearsontechgroup.com**

For sales outside of the U.S. please contact: **International Sales   1-317-581-3793   international@pearsontechgroup.com**

Feedback Information

At Cisco Press, our goal is to create in-depth technical books of the highest quality and value. Each book is crafted with care and precision, undergoing rigorous development that involves the unique expertise of members from the professional technical community.

Readers' feedback is a natural continuation of this process. If you have any comments regarding how we could improve the quality of this book or otherwise alter it to better suit your needs, you can contact us through e-mail at feedback@ciscopress.com. Please make sure to include the book title and ISBN in your message.

We greatly appreciate your assistance.

Publisher: John Wait

Editor-In-Chief: John Kane

Cisco Representative: Anthony Wolfenden

Cisco Press Program Manager: Nannette M. Noble

Executive Editor: Brett Bartow

Acquisitions Editor: Michelle Grandin

Production Manager: Patrick Kanouse

Senior Development Editor: Christopher Cleveland

Development Editor: Howard Jones

Copy Editor: Keith Cline

Technical Editors: Brad Dunsmore, Leon Katcharian, Inti Shah, John Stuppi

Team Coordinator: Tammi Barnett

Book and Cover Designer: Louisa Adair

Production Team: Octal Publishing, Inc.

Indexer: Eric Schroeder

Corporate Headquarters
Cisco Systems, Inc.
170 West Tasman Drive
San Jose, CA 95134-1706
USA
www.cisco.com
Tel: 408 526-4000
    800 553-NETS (6387)
Fax: 408 526-4100

European Headquarters
Cisco Systems International BV
Haarlerbergpark
Haarlerbergweg 13-19
1101 CH Amsterdam
The Netherlands
www-europe.cisco.com
Tel: 31 0 20 357 1000
Fax: 31 0 20 357 1100

Americas Headquarters
Cisco Systems, Inc.
170 West Tasman Drive
San Jose, CA 95134-1706
USA
www.cisco.com
Tel: 408 526-7660
Fax: 408 527-0883

Asia Pacific Headquarters
Cisco Systems, Inc.
Capital Tower
168 Robinson Road
#22-01 to #29-01
Singapore 068912
www.cisco.com
Tel: +65 6317 7777
Fax: +65 6317 7799

Cisco Systems has more than 200 offices in the following countries and regions. Addresses, phone numbers, and fax numbers are listed on the Cisco.com Web site at www.cisco.com/go/offices.

Argentina • Australia • Austria • Belgium • Brazil • Bulgaria • Canada • Chile • China PRC • Colombia • Costa Rica • Croatia • Czech Republic Denmark • Dubai, UAE • Finland • France • Germany • Greece • Hong Kong SAR • Hungary • India • Indonesia • Ireland • Israel • Italy Japan • Korea • Luxembourg • Malaysia • Mexico • The Netherlands • New Zealand • Norway • Peru • Philippines • Poland • Portugal Puerto Rico • Romania • Russia • Saudi Arabia • Scotland • Singapore • Slovakia • Slovenia • South Africa • Spain • Sweden Switzerland • Taiwan • Thailand • Turkey • Ukraine • United Kingdom • United States • Venezuela • Vietnam • Zimbabwe

Copyright © 2003 Cisco Systems, Inc. All rights reserved. CCIP, CCSP, the Cisco Arrow logo, the Cisco *Powered* Network mark, the Cisco Systems Verified logo, Cisco Unity, Follow Me Browsing, FormShare, iQ Net Readiness Scorecard, Networking Academy, and ScriptShare are trademarks of Cisco Systems, Inc.; Changing the Way We Work, Live, Play, and Learn, The Fastest Way to Increase Your Internet Quotient, and iQuick Study are service marks of Cisco Systems, Inc.; and Aironet, ASIST, BPX, Catalyst, CCDA, CCDP, CCIE, CCNA, CCNP, Cisco, the Cisco Certified Internetwork Expert logo, Cisco IOS, the Cisco IOS logo, Cisco Press, Cisco Systems, Cisco Systems Capital, the Cisco Systems logo, Empowering the Internet Generation, Enterprise/Solver, EtherChannel, EtherSwitch, Fast Step, GigaStack, Internet Quotient, IOS, IP/TV, iQ Expertise, the iQ logo, LightStream, MGX, MICA, the Networkers logo, Network Registrar, *Packet*, PIX, Post-Routing, Pre-Routing, RateMUX, Registrar, SlideCast, SMARTnet, StrataView Plus, Stratm, SwitchProbe, TeleRouter, TransPath, and VCO are registered trademarks of Cisco Systems, Inc. and/or its affiliates in the U.S. and certain other countries.

All other trademarks mentioned in this document or Web site are the property of their respective owners. The use of the word partner does not imply a partnership relationship between Cisco and any other company. (0303R)

Printed in the USA

About the Authors

Greg Bastien, CCNP, CCSP, CISSP, is currently a partner with Trinity Information Management Services, Inc., as a consultant to the federal government. He holds a position as adjunct professor at Strayer University, teaching networking and network security classes. He completed his undergraduate and graduate degrees at Embry-Riddle Aeronautical University while on active duty as a helicopter flight instructor in the U.S. Army.

Christian Abera Degu, CCNP, CCDP, CCSP, currently works for Veridian Networks/General Dynamics as a consulting engineer to the Federal Energy Regulatory Commission. He received his undergraduate degree from Strayer University and his graduate degree in computer information systems from George Mason University. He lives with his family in Alexandria, Virginia.

About the Technical Reviewers

Brad Dunsmore is a new product instructor with the Advanced Services group for Cisco Systems. He develops and deploys network solutions and training for Cisco Systems engineers, Cisco sales engineers, selected training partners, and customers. He specializes in SS7 offload solutions, WAN communication methods, and Cisco security products. He developed the Building Enhanced Cisco Security Networks course for Cisco and he currently holds the following industry certifications: CCNP, CCDP, CCSP, INFOSEC, MCSE+I, and MCDBA. He recently passed his written exam for the CCIE R/S certification and is currently working on his laboratory exam.

Leon Katcharian is an education specialist at Cisco Systems, Inc., where he develops and delivers training for Cisco network security products. He has more than 20 years of experience in the data-networking field, having been a technical support engineer, a technical instructor, and a course developer. Leon has worked as a technical support engineer or in an educational role for Motorola Information Systems Group, GeoTel Communications, ON Technology, Altiga Networks, and Cisco Systems. He holds a bachelor of science degree in business from Eastern Nazarene College along with several industry certifications. Leon is currently the lead course developer for the Securing Cisco IOS Networks (SECUR) curriculum.

Inti Shah has worked in the networking industry for more than 15 years in both enterprise and service provider environments. He has extensive expertise in designing and delivering large-scale networks, complex e-business solutions, intrusion detection, firewall, and VPN services. Inti currently works for Energis in the UK and holds the Cisco CCNA, CCNP, CCSP, CCIP Security, Check Point CCSA, and CCSE accreditations. He is currently pursuing his CCIE Security accreditation.

John Stuppi, CCIE No. 11154, is a network consulting engineer for Cisco Systems. John advises Cisco customers in the planning, design, and implementation of VPN and security related solutions, including IDS, IPSec VPNs, and firewall deployments. John is a CISSP and holds an Information Systems Security (INFOSEC) Professional certification. In addition, John has a BSEE from Lehigh University and an MBA from Rutgers University. John lives in Ocean Township, New Jersey with his wife, Diane, and his two wonderful children, Thomas and Allison.

Dedications

This book is dedicated to In Ho Park (February 27, 1973—December 16, 2001): CCNA, CCNP, and a good friend.

Acknowledgments

This book has been a very challenging, yet rewarding project. We sincerely appreciate the efforts of all those who helped to keep us focused throughout the process. We would especially like to thank Michelle Grandin, acquisitions editor, and the "development editor team" of Christopher Cleveland and Howard Jones for their guidance and encouragement. We would also like to thank the technical reviewers for their attention to detail, ability to decipher 2 a.m. techno-babble and offer up reasonable alternatives, and the sense of humor needed to hash through mountains of draft manuscripts. Last but not least, we would like to thank Andy and Mark for getting the ball rolling on the project.

Contents at a Glance

Foreword xxiii
Introduction xxiv

PART I **An Overview of Network Security** 2
Chapter 1 Network Security Essentials 5
Chapter 2 Attack Threats Defined and Detailed 23
Chapter 3 Defense in Depth 43

PART II **Managing Cisco Routers** 56
Chapter 4 Basic Router Management 59
Chapter 5 Secure Router Administration 79

PART III **Authentication, Authorization, and Accounting (AAA)** 98
Chapter 6 Authentication 101
Chapter 7 Authentication, Authorization, and Accounting 115
Chapter 8 Configuring RADIUS and TACACS+ on Cisco IOS Software 137
Chapter 9 Cisco Secure Access Control Server 157
Chapter 10 Administration of Cisco Secure Access Control Server 175

PART IV **The Cisco IOS Firewall Feature Set** 188
Chapter 11 Securing the Network with a Cisco Router 191
Chapter 12 Access Lists 203
Chapter 13 The Cisco IOS Firewall 219
Chapter 14 Context-Based Access Control (CBAC) 231
Chapter 15 Authentication Proxy and the Cisco IOS Firewall 251
Chapter 16 Intrusion Detection and the Cisco IOS Firewall 279

PART V	**Virtual Private Networks 300**
Chapter 17	Building a VPN Using IPSec 303
Chapter 18	Scaling a VPN Using IPSec with a Certificate Authority 339
Chapter 19	Configuring Remote Access Using Easy VPN 359
Chapter 20	Scaling Management of an Enterprise VPN Environment 379
PART VI	**Scenarios 400**
Chapter 21	Final Scenarios 403
Appendix	Answers to the "Do I Know This Already?" Quizzes and Q&A Sections 427

Glossary   463

Index   472

Contents

        Foreword   xxiii

        Introduction   xxiv

Part I   An Overview of Network Security   2

Chapter 1   Network Security Essentials   5

    "Do I Know This Already?" Quiz   5

    Foundation Topics   9

    Definition of Network Security   9

    Balancing Business Need with Security Requirement   9

    Security Policies   9

        Security Policy Goals   12

        Security Guidelines   13

            Management Must Support the Policy   13

            The Policy Must Be Consistent   13

            The Policy Must Be Technically Feasible   14

            The Policy Should Not Be Written as a Technical Document   14

            The Policy Must Be Implemented Globally Throughout the Organization   14

            The Policy Must Clearly Define Roles and Responsibilities   15

            The Policy Must Be Flexible Enough to Respond to Changing Technologies and Organizational Goals   15

            The Policy Must Be Understandable   15

            The Policy Must Be Widely Distributed   16

            The Policy Must Specify Sanctions for Violations   16

            The Policy Must Include an Incident Response Plan for Security Breaches   16

            Security Is an Ongoing Process   17

    Network Security as a Process   17

    Network Security as a Legal Issue   18

    Foundation Summary   19

    Security Policies   19

        Security Policy Goals   19

        Security Guidelines   20

    Network Security as a Process   20

    Q&A   21

Chapter 2   Attack Threats Defined and Detailed   23

    "Do I Know This Already?" Quiz   23

    Foundation Topics   27

    Vulnerabilities   27

        Self-Imposed Vulnerabilities   27

            Lack of Effective Policy   28

            Configuration Weakness   29

            Technology Weakness   30

    Threats 31
    Intruder Motivation 31
     Lack of Understanding of Computers or Networks *31*
     Intruding for Curiosity *32*
     Intruding for Fun and Pride *32*
     Intruding for Revenge *32*
     Intruding for Profit *32*
     Intruding for Political Purposes *33*
    Types of Attacks 33
     Reconnaissance Attacks *34*
     Access Attacks *34*
     DoS Attacks *36*
   Foundation Summary **37**
    Vulnerabilities 37
     Self-Imposed Vulnerabilities *37*
    Threats 38
     Intruder Motivation *38*
    Types of Attacks 39
   Q&A **40**

Chapter 3 Defense in Depth 43
   "Do I Know This Already?" Quiz 43
   Foundation and Supplemental Topics **46**
    Overview of Defense in Depth 46
     Components Used for Defense in Depth *47*
     Physical Security *51*
   Foundation Summary **52**
   Q&A **54**

Part II Managing Cisco Routers 56

Chapter 4 Basic Router Management 59
   "Do I Know This Already?" Quiz 59
   Foundation Topics **63**
    Router Configuration Modes 63
    Accessing the Cisco Router CLI 66
     Configuring CLI Access *68*
    Cisco IOS Firewall Features 69
   Foundation Summary **71**
    Router Configuration Modes 71
    Accessing the Cisco Router CLI 72
    Cisco IOS Firewall Features 72
   Q&A **75**

Chapter 5   Secure Router Administration   79

    "Do I Know This Already?" Quiz   79

    Foundation Topics   83

    Privilege Levels   83

    Securing Console Access   84

    Configuring the Enable Password   84

        enable secret   86

    service password-encryption   87

    Configuring Multiple Privilege Levels   87

    Warning Banners   89

    Interactive Access   90

    Securing vty Access   90

    Secure Shell (SSH) Protocol   91

        Setting Up a Cisco IOS Router or Switch as an SSH Client   91

    Port Security for Ethernet Switches   92

        Configuring Port Security   93

    Foundation Summary   95

    Q&A   96

Part III   **Authentication, Authorization, and Accounting (AAA)**   98

Chapter 6   Authentication   101

    "Do I Know This Already?" Quiz   101

    Foundation Topics   104

    Authentication   104

        Configuring Line Password Authentication   104

        Configuring Username Authentication   105

        Remote Security Servers   105

            TACACS Overview   106

            RADIUS Overview   107

            Kerberos Overview   109

    PAP and CHAP Authentication   109

        PAP   110

        CHAP   110

            MS-CHAP   111

    Foundation Summary   112

    Q&A   113

Chapter 7   Authentication, Authorization, and Accounting   115

    "Do I Know This Already?" Quiz   115

    Foundation Topics   119

    AAA Overview   119

        Authentication   119

        Authorization   120

        Accounting   120

Configuring AAA Services   120
  Configuring AAA Authentication   121
    Configuring Login Authentication Using AAA   122
    Enabling Password Protection at the Privileged Level   123
    Configuring PPP Authentication Using AAA   124
  Configuring AAA Authorization   125
  Configuring AAA Accounting   128
Troubleshooting AAA   130
Foundation Summary   133
Q&A   134

Chapter 8 Configuring RADIUS and TACACS+ on Cisco IOS Software   137

"Do I Know This Already?" Quiz   137
Foundation Topics   140
Configuring TACACS+ on Cisco IOS   140
  TACACS+ Authentication Examples   141
  TACACS+ Authorization Example   143
  TACACS+ Accounting Example   143
  AAA TACACS+ Troubleshooting   144
    debug aaa authentication   144
    debug tacacs   145
    debug tacacs events   145
Configuring RADIUS on Cisco IOS   146
  RADIUS Authentication and Authorization Example   148
  RADIUS Authentication, Authorization, and Accounting Example   148
  Testing and Troubleshooting RADIUS Configuration   150
Foundation Summary   153
Q&A   154

Chapter 9 Cisco Secure Access Control Server   157

"Do I Know This Already?" Quiz   157
Foundation Topics   161
Cisco Secure ACS for Windows   161
  Authentication   162
  Authorization   164
  Accounting   165
Administration   165
Cisco Secure ACS for Windows Architecture   166
  CSAdmin   167
  CSAuth   167
  CSDBSync   168
  CSLog   168
  CSMon   168
  CSTacacs and CSRadius   168
Cisco ACS for UNIX   169

Chapter 10 Administration of Cisco Secure Access Control Server   175

"Do I Know This Already?" Quiz   175
Foundation Topics   178
Basic Deployment Factors for Cisco Secure ACS   178
Hardware Requirements   178
Operating System Requirements   178
Browser Compatibility   179
Installing Cisco Secure ACS   179
Suggested Deployment Sequence   181
Troubleshooting Cisco Secure ACS for Windows   182
Authentication Problems   183
Troubleshooting Authorization Problems   183
Administration Issues   183
Foundation Summary   185
Q&A   186

Part IV The Cisco IOS Firewall Feature Set   188

Chapter 11 Securing the Network with a Cisco Router   191

"Do I Know This Already?" Quiz   191
Foundation Topics   194
Simple Network Management Protocol (SNMP)   194
Controlling Interactive Access Through a Browser   195
Disabling Directed Broadcasts   196
Routing Protocol Authentication   197
Small Server Services   198
Disabling Finger Services   198
Disabling Network Time Protocol (NTP)   199
Disabling Cisco Discovery Protocol (CDP)   199
Foundation Summary   200
Q&A   201

Chapter 12 Access Lists   203

"Do I Know This Already?" Quiz   203
Foundation Topics   207
What Are Access Lists   207
When to Configure Access Lists   208
Types of IP ACLs   208
  Standard IP ACLs   208
  Extended IP ACLs   212
  Reflexive ACLs   212
  Time-Based ACLs   213
Configuring ACLs on a Router   214

Foundation Summary   216
Q&A   217

Chapter 13   The Cisco IOS Firewall   219

"Do I Know This Already?" Quiz   219

Foundation Topics   222

The Cisco IOS Firewall Feature Set   222

Authentication Proxy   223
DoS Protection   224
Logging and Audit Trail   224
Intrusion Detection   224
Port-To-Application Mapping   225
  System-Defined Port Mapping   225
  User-Defined Port Mapping   227
  Host-Specific Port Mapping   227

Foundation Summary   228

Q&A   229

Chapter 14   Context-Based Access Control (CBAC)   231

"Do I Know This Already?" Quiz   231

Foundation Topics   235

Content-Based Access Control   235

DoS Detection and Protection   235
Alerts and Audit Trails   236
How CBAC Works   236
  UDP Sessions   237
  ACL Entries   238
CBAC Restrictions   238
Supported Protocols   238
Memory and Performance Impact   239

Configuring CBAC   239

Select an Interface   239
Configure IP ACLs at the Interface   240
Configure Global Timeouts and Thresholds   240
Define an Inspection Rule   241
  Configure Generic TCP and UDP Inspection   243
  Configure Java Inspection   243
Apply the Inspection Rule to an Interface   244

Verifying and Debugging CBAC   244

Debugging Context-Based Access Control   244
  Generic debug Commands   245
  Transport Level debug Commands   245
CBAC Configuration Example   245

Foundation Summary   247

Q&A   248

Chapter 15 Authentication Proxy and the Cisco IOS Firewall 251

"Do I Know This Already?" Quiz 251
Foundation Topics 255
Understanding Authentication Proxy 255
How Authentication Proxy Works 255
What Authentication Proxy Looks Like 256
Authentication Proxy and the Cisco IOS Firewall 258
Configuring Authentication Proxy on the Cisco IOS Firewall 258
Authentication Proxy Configuration Steps 259
Step 1: Configure AAA 260
Step 2: Configure the HTTP Server 261
Step 3: Configure the Authentication Proxy 261
Step 4: Verify the Authentication Proxy Configuration 262
Authentication Proxy Configuration Examples 263
Using Authentication Proxy with TACACS+ 266
Step 1: Complete the Network Configuration 267
Step 2: Complete the Interface Configuration 268
Step 3: Complete the Group Setup 269
Using Authentication Proxy with RADIUS 270
Limitations of Authentication Proxy 272
Foundation Summary 274
Q&A 276

Chapter 16 Intrusion Detection and the Cisco IOS Firewall 279

"Do I Know This Already?" Quiz 279
Foundation Topics 283
Cisco IOS Firewall IDS Features 283
Compatibility with the CSIDS 284
Cisco IOS Firewall IDS Configuration 285
Initialize the Cisco IOS Firewall IDS on the Router 286
Configuring the Notification Type 286
Configure the IOS Firewall IDS and Central Management Post Office Parameters 286
Define the Protected Network 288
Configure the Router Maximum Queue for Alarms 288
Configure Info and Attack Signatures 288
Create and Apply Audit Rules 290
Configure the Default Actions 290
Create the IDS Audit Rule 291
Create the IDS Audit Exclusions 291
Apply the IDS Audit Rule 292
Add the Cisco IOS Firewall IDS to the Centralized Management 292
Verifying the Cisco IOS Firewall IDS Configuration 292
Cisco IOS Firewall IDS Deployment Strategies 295

Foundation Summary   296
Q&A   298

Part V   Virtual Private Networks   300

Chapter 17   Building a VPN Using IPSec   303

"Do I Know This Already?" Quiz   303

Foundation Topics   307

Configuring a Cisco Router for IPSec Using Preshared Keys   309

How IPSec Works   309

Step 1: Select the IKE and IPSec Parameters   310

Define the IKE (Phase 1) Policy   311

Define the IPSec Policies   313

Verify the Current Router Configuration   317

Verify Connectivity   317

Ensure Compatible Access Lists   318

Step 2: Configure IKE   318

Enable IKE   319

Create the IKE Policy   319

Configure Preshared Key   319

Verify the IKE Configuration   320

Step 3: Configure IPSec   321

Create the IPSec Transform Set   322

Configure IPSec SA Lifetimes   323

Create the Crypto ACLs   323

Create the Crypto Map   324

Apply the Crypto Map to the Correct Interface   325

Step 4: Test and Verify the IPSec Configuration   326

Configuring Manual IPSec   328

Configuring IPSec Using RSA Encrypted Nonces   328

Configure the RSA Keys   329

Plan the Implementation Using RSA Keys   329

Configure the Router Host Name and Domain Name   330

Generate the RSA Keys   330

Enter Your Peer RSA Public Keys   330

Verify the Key Configuration   331

Manage the RSA Keys   332

Foundation Summary   333

Configure a Cisco Router for IPSec Using Preshared Keys   333

Verifying the IKE and IPSec Configuration   334

Explain the Issues Regarding Configuring IPSec Manually and Using RSA Encrypted Nonces   335

Q&A   336

Chapter 18   Scaling a VPN Using IPSec with a Certificate Authority   339

"Do I Know This Already?" Quiz   339

Foundation Topics 343

Advanced IPSec VPNs Using Cisco Routers and CAs 343
 Overview of Cisco Router CA Support 343
 Configuring the Cisco Router for IPSec VPNs Using CA Support 345
  Step 1: Select the IKE and IPSec Parameters 345
  Step 2: Configure the Router CA Support 346
  Step 3: Configure IKE Using RSA Signatures 353
  Step 4: Configure IPSec 354
  Step 5: Test and Verify the Configuration 355

Foundation Summary 356

Advanced IPSec VPNs Using Cisco Routers and CAs 356

Q&A 357

Chapter 19 Configuring Remote Access Using Easy VPN 359

"Do I Know This Already?" Quiz 359

Foundation Topics 362

Describe the Easy VPN Server 362
 Easy VPN Server Functionality 363
 Configuring the Easy VPN Server 364
  Prepare the Router for Easy VPN Server 365
  Configure the Group Policy Lookup 366
  Create the ISAKMP Policy for the Remote VPN Clients 366
  Define a Group Policy for a Mode Configuration Push 367
  Create the Transform Set 368
  Create the Dynamic Crypto Maps with Reverse Route Injection (RRI) 368
  Apply the Mode Configuration to the Dynamic Crypto Map 369
  Apply the Dynamic Crypto Map to the Interface 369
  Enable IKE DPD 370
  Configure xauth 370
 Easy VPN Modes of Operation 371

Foundation Summary 372

Describe the Easy VPN Server 372
 Easy VPN Server Functionality 372
 Configuring the Easy VPN Server 372
 Easy VPN Modes of Operation 375

Q&A 376

Chapter 20 Scaling Management of an Enterprise VPN Environment 379

"Do I Know This Already?" Quiz 379

Foundation Topics 383

Managing Enterprise VPN Routers 383
 CiscoWorks 2000 383
 VPN/Security Management Solution (VMS) 385
 Management Center for VPN Routers (Router MC) 385
 Concepts of the Router MC 386

           Supported Tunneling Technologies 388
           Router MC Integration with CiscoWorks Common Services 389
           Installation and Login to Router MC 389
           Connecting to the Router MC 392
           Router MC Workflow 392
    Foundation Summary 395
        Managing Enterprise VPN Routers 395
    Q&A 398

Part VI Scenarios 400

Chapter 21 Final Scenarios 403

        Task 1: Secure the Routers at All Locations 404
           Change All Administrative Access on All the Routers 405
           Configure Local Database Authentication Using AAA 406
           Configure a Secure Method for Remote Access of the Routers 406
           Disable Unnecessary Services 407
           Implement ACLs for Antispoofing Purposes 408
        Task 2: Secure Site-to-Site Connectivity 409
           Define VPN Configuration Parameters 409
           Configure the IKE Parameters 411
           Configure the IPSec Parameters 413
           Configure ACLs 414
           Create and Apply Crypto Maps 414
        Task 3: Configure CA Support 416
           Configure Host Name and Domain Name 416
           Configure NTP 417
           Enroll with the CA 418
        Task 4: Secure Remote Access 419
        Task 5: Secure the Enterprise Network 420
           Implement the Cisco IOS Firewall IDS 420
           Implement Authentication Proxy 423
           Implement CBAC 424

Appendix   Answers to the "Do I Know This Already?" Quizzes and Q&A Sections 427

    Chapter 1 427
        "Do I Know This Already?" Quiz 427
        Q&A 427
    Chapter 2 429
        "Do I Know This Already?" Quiz 429
        Q&A 430
    Chapter 3 432
        "Do I Know This Already?" Quiz 432
        Q&A 432

Chapter 4   433
  "Do I Know This Already?" Quiz   *433*
  Q&A   *433*
Chapter 5   435
  "Do I Know This Already?" Quiz   *435*
  Q&A   *435*
Chapter 6   437
  "Do I Know This Already?" Quiz   *437*
  Q&A   *437*
Chapter 7   438
  "Do I Know This Already?" Quiz   *438*
  Q&A   *438*
Chapter 8   440
  "Do I Know This Already?" Quiz   *440*
  Q&A   *440*
Chapter 9   441
  "Do I Know This Already?" Quiz   *441*
  Q&A   *442*
Chapter 10   443
  "Do I Know This Already?" Quiz   *443*
  Q&A   *443*
Chapter 11   444
  "Do I Know This Already?" Quiz   *444*
  Q&A   *445*
Chapter 12   446
  "Do I Know This Already?" Quiz   *446*
  Q&A   *446*
Chapter 13   448
  "Do I Know This Already?" Quiz   *448*
  Q&A   *448*
Chapter 14   449
  "Do I Know This Already?" Quiz   *449*
  Q&A   *449*
Chapter 15   451
  "Do I Know This Already?" Quiz   *451*
  Q&A   *451*
Chapter 16   452
  "Do I Know This Already?" Quiz   *452*
  Q&A   *453*
Chapter 17   454
  "Do I Know This Already?" Quiz   *454*
  Q&A   *454*

Chapter 18 456
  "Do I Know This Already?" Quiz 456
  Q&A 456
Chapter 19 457
  "Do I Know This Already?" Quiz 457
  Q&A 457
Chapter 20 458
  "Do I Know This Already?" Quiz 458
  Q&A 459

Glossary 463

Index 472

Icons Used in This Book

 Router

 Bridge

 Hub

 DSU/CSU

 Catalyst Switch

 Multilayer Switch

 ATM Switch

 ISDN/Frame Relay Switch

 Communication Server

 Gateway

 Access Server

Foreword

CCSP SECUR Exam Certification Guide is a complete study tool for the CCSP SECUR exam, enabling you to assess your knowledge, identify areas to concentrate your study, and master key concepts to help you succeed on the exams and in your daily job. The book is filled with features that help you master the skills needed to secure Cisco IOS Router networks. This book was developed in cooperation with the Cisco Internet Learning Solutions Group. Cisco Press books are the only self-study books authorized by Cisco for CCSP exam preparation.

Cisco and Cisco Press present this material in text-based format to provide another learning vehicle for our customers and the broader user community in general. Although a publication does not duplicate the instructor-led or e-learning environment, we acknowledge that not everyone responds in the same way to the same delivery mechanism. It is our intent that presenting this material via a Cisco Press publication will enhance the transfer of knowledge to a broad audience of networking professionals.

Cisco Press will present study guides on existing and future exams through these Exam Certification Guides to help achieve Cisco Internet Learning Solutions Group's principal objectives: to educate the Cisco community of networking professionals and to enable that community to build and maintain reliable, scalable networks. The Cisco career certifications and classes that support these certifications are directed at meeting these objectives through a disciplined approach to progressive learning. To succeed on the Cisco career certifications exams, as well as in your daily job as a Cisco-certified professional, we recommend a blended learning solution that combines instructor-led, e-learning, and self-study training with hands-on experience. Cisco Systems has created an authorized Cisco Learning Partner program to provide you with the most highly qualified instruction and invaluable hands-on experience in lab and simulation environments. To learn more about Cisco Learning Partner programs available in your area, please go to www.cisco.com/go/authorizedtraining.

The books Cisco Press creates in partnership with Cisco Systems will meet the same standards for content quality demanded of our courses and certifications. It is our intent that you will find this and subsequent Cisco Press certification and training publications of value as you build your networking knowledge base.

Thomas M. Kelly
Vice-President, Internet Learning Solutions Group
Cisco Systems, Inc.
August 2003

Introduction

This book is designed to help you prepare for the Cisco SECUR certification exam. The SECUR exam is the first in a series of five exams required for the Cisco Certified Security Professional (CCSP) certification. This exam focuses on the application of security principles with regard to Cisco IOS routers, switches, and virtual private network (VPN) devices.

Who Should Read This Book?

Network security is a very complex business. It is very important that you have extensive experience in and an in-depth understanding of computer networking before you can begin to apply security principles. The Cisco SECUR program was developed to introduce the security products associated with or integrated into Cisco IOS Software, explain how each product is applied, and explain how it can increase the security of your network. The SECUR program is for network administrators, network security administrators, network architects, and experienced networking professionals who are interested in applying security principles to their networks.

How to Use This Book

The book consists of 21 chapters. Each chapter tends to build upon the chapter that precedes it. The chapters that cover specific commands and configurations include case studies or practice configurations.

The chapters of the book cover the following topics:

- **Chapter 1, "Network Security Essentials"**—Chapter 1 is an overview of network security in general terms. This chapter defines the scope of network security and discusses the delicate "balancing act" required to ensure that you fulfill the business need without compromising the security of the organization. Network security is a continuous process that should be driven by a predefined organizational security policy.

- **Chapter 2, "Attack Threats Defined and Detailed"**—Chapter 2 discusses the potential network vulnerabilities and attacks that pose a threat to the network. This chapter provides you with a better understanding of the need for an effective network security policy.

- **Chapter 3, "Defense in Depth"**—Until recently, a network was considered to be secure if it had a strong perimeter defense. Network attacks are becoming much more dynamic and require a security posture that provides defense at many levels. Chapter 3 discusses the concepts that integrate all the security components into a single, very effective security strategy.

- **Chapter 4, "Basic Router Management"**—This chapter details the administration of the Cisco IOS router and discusses the IOS firewall feature set. This chapter focuses on the basics tasks that are required to manage an individual Cisco IOS router.

- **Chapter 5, "Secure Router Administration"**—This chapter explains how to secure the administrative access to the Cisco IOS router. It is important to secure this access to prevent unauthorized changes to the router.

- **Chapter 6, "Authentication"**—This chapter discusses the many different types of authentication and the advantages and disadvantages of each type.

- **Chapter 7, "Authentication, Authorization, and Accounting"**—AAA has become a key component of any security policy. AAA is used to verify which users are connecting to a specific resource, ensure that they are authorized to perform requested functions, and track which actions were performed, by whom, and at what time. Chapter 7 discusses the integration of AAA services into a Cisco IOS environment and how AAA can significantly impact the security posture of a network.

- **Chapter 8, "Configuring RADIUS and TACACS+ on Cisco IOS Software"**—TACACS+ and RADIUS are two key AAA technologies supported by Cisco IOS Software. Chapter 8 discusses the steps for configuring TACACS+ and RADIUS to communicate with Cisco IOS routers.

- **Chapter 9, "Cisco Secure Access Control Server"**—This chapter describes the features and architectural components of the Cisco Secure Access Control Server.

- **Chapter 10, "Administration of Cisco Secure Access Control Server"**—This chapter discusses the installation and configuration of the Cisco Secure Access Control Server on a Microsoft Windows 2000 Server.

- **Chapter 11, "Securing the Network with a Cisco Router"**—It is very important to restrict access to your Cisco IOS router to ensure that only authorized administrators are performing configuration changes. There are many different ways to access the Cisco IOS router. Chapter 11 describes how to ensure that all nonessential services have been disabled to reduce any chances of accessing the router by exploiting open ports or running services.

- **Chapter 12, "Access Lists"**—Access lists are used by the Cisco IOS router for basic traffic filtering. This chapter describes the different types of access lists and explains how each type is implemented.

- **Chapter 13, "The Cisco IOS Firewall"**—The Cisco IOS firewall feature set was an upgrade to the original Cisco IOS Software and allows for the integration of security functionality into a routing device. This chapter discusses the security features of the Cisco IOS firewall.

- **Chapter 14, "Context-Based Access Control (CBAC)"**—CBAC is a Cisco IOS firewall feature that enables you to filter data based on an inspection of the data packet. This is a key feature of the Cisco IOS firewall that is used to greatly increase the security of the network perimeter.

- **Chapter 15, "Authentication Proxy and the Cisco IOS Firewall"**—Authentication proxy is a function that enables users to authenticate when accessing specific resources. The Cisco IOS firewall is designed to interface with AAA servers using standard authentication protocols to perform this function. This functionality enables administrators to create a very granular and dynamic per-user security policy.

- **Chapter 16, "Intrusion Detection and the Cisco IOS Firewall"**—Intrusion detection is a key component of any network security design. Intrusion detection systems (IDSs) enable security administrators to detect and react to potentially malicious activity on the network. The key difference between firewall and IDS activity is that firewalls just apply rules to network traffic while IDSs normally scan the traffic and react to content within the packet. In addition, a firewall may drop the traffic and add an entry in the firewall logs, whereas an IDS normally generates an alarm and can react in other ways to malicious traffic. It is most common on enterprise networks to use a combination of firewalls and IDSs. This chapter discusses the Cisco IOS firewall IDS.

- **Chapter 17, "Building a VPN Using IPSec"**—Prior to the creation of VPN technology, the only way to secure communications between two locations was to purchase a "dedicated circuit." To secure communications across an enterprise would be tremendously expensive and securing communications with remote users was simply cost prohibitive. VPN technology enables you to secure communications that travel across the public infrastructure (that is, the Internet). VPN technology allows organizations to interconnect their different locations without having to purchase dedicated lines, greatly reducing the cost of the network infrastructure.

- **Chapter 18, "Scaling a VPN Using IPSec with a Certificate Authority"**—Cisco IOS devices are designed with a feature called CA Interoperability Support, which allows them to interact with a certificate authority (CA) when deploying IPSec. This functionality allows for a scalable and manageable enterprise VPN solution.

- **Chapter 19, "Configuring Remote Access Using Easy VPN**—Cisco Easy VPN is a client/server application that allows for VPN security parameters to be "pushed out" to the remote locations that connect using Cisco SOHO/ROHO products. The server portion is a component of Cisco IOS Release 12.2(8)T, and the client portion is available for the 800 to 1700 series routers, PIX 501 Firewall, 3002 VPN Hardware Client, and Easy Remote VPN Software Client 3.x.

- **Chapter 20, "Scaling Management of an Enterprise VPN Environment"** — Administration of any enterprise network can be a very difficult objective. The sheer size of a network and diverse range of components used on that network can make centralized administration an insurmountable task. Cisco has developed tools that enable administrators to organize, configure, and effectively monitor Cisco VPN routers deployed throughout the enterprise.

- **Chapter 21, "Final Scenarios"** — This chapter provides a practical overview of topics discussed throughout the book. It consists of a scenario for an organization that requires your expertise with Cisco products to meet their constantly evolving business needs.

Each chapter follows the same format and incorporates the following tools to assist you by assessing your current knowledge and emphasizing specific areas of interest within the chapter.

- **Do I Already Know This Quiz?** — Each chapter begins with a quiz to help you assess your current knowledge of the subject. The quiz is broken down into specific areas of emphasis that enable you to best determine where to focus your efforts when working through the chapter.

- **Foundation Topics** — The foundation topics are the core sections of each chapter. They focus on the specific protocols, concepts, or skills that you must master to successfully prepare for the examination. The foundation topics map directly to the exam objectives published by Cisco.

- **Foundation Summary** — Near the end of each chapter, the foundation topics are summarized into important highlights from the chapter. In many cases, the foundation summaries are broken into charts, but in some cases the important portions from each chapter are just restated to emphasize their importance within the subject matter. Remember that the foundation portions are in the book to assist you with your exam preparation. It is very unlikely that you will be able to successfully complete the certification exam by just studying the foundation topics and foundation summaries, although they are a good tool for last-minute preparation just before taking the exam.

- **Q&A** — Each chapter ends with a series of review questions to test your understanding of the material covered. These questions are a great way to ensure that you not only understand the material, but that you also exercise your ability to recall facts.

Figure I-1 depicts the best way to navigate through the book. If you think that you already have a sufficient understanding of the subject matter in a chapter, test yourself with the "Do I Know This Already?" Quiz. Based on you score, you should determine whether to complete the entire chapter or to move on to the "Foundation Summary" and then on to the "Q&A" sections.

Figure I-1 *Completing the Chapter Material*

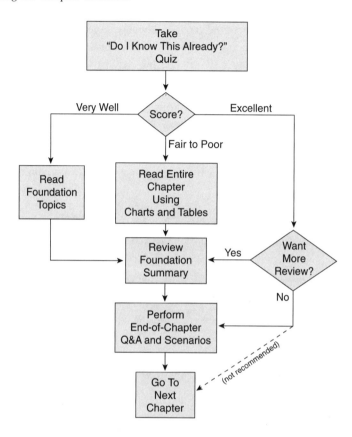

- **CD-ROM-based practice exam**—This book includes a CD-ROM containing several interactive practice exams. It is recommended that you continue to test your knowledge and test-taking skills by using these exams. You will find that your test-taking skills will improve just by continued exposure to the test format. Keep in mind that the potential range of exam questions is limitless. Therefore, your goal should not be to "know" every possible answer but to have a sufficient understanding of the subject matter that you can figure out the correct answer with the information provided.

The Certification Exam and This Preparation Guide

The questions for each certification exam are a closely guarded secret. The truth is that if you had the questions and could only pass the exam, you would be in for quite an embarrassment as soon as you arrived at your first job that required these skills. The point is to know the material, not just to successfully pass the exam. We do know what topics you must know to successfully complete this exam because they are published by Cisco. Coincidently, these are the same topics required for you to be proficient when configuring Cisco IOS routers. It is also very important to understand that this book is a "static" reference, whereas the course objectives are dynamic. Cisco can and does change the topics covered on certification exams often. This exam guide should not be your only reference when preparing for the certification exam. There is a wealth of information available at Cisco.com that covers each topic in painful detail. The goal of this book is to prepare you as well as possible for the SECUR exam. Some of this is completed by breaking a 500-page (average) implementation guide into a 20-page chapter that is easier to digest. If you think that you need more detailed information on a specific topic, feel free to surf. We have broken these topics down into foundation topics and covered each topic throughout the book. Table I-1 lists each foundation topic along with a brief description.

Note that because security vulnerabilities and preventative measures continue apace, Cisco Systems reserves the right to change the exam objectives without notice. Although you may refer to the list of exam objectives listed in Table I-1, always check on the Cisco Systems web site to verify the actual list of objectives to be sure you are prepared before taking an exam. You can view the current exam objectives on any current Cisco certification exam by visiting their website at Cisco.com, clicking **Learning & Events>Career Certifications and Paths**. Note also that, if needed, Cisco Press may post additional preparatory content on the web page associated with this book at www.ciscopress.com/1587200724. It's a good idea to check the website a couple of weeks before taking your exam to be sure that you have up-to-date content.

Table I-1 *SECUR Foundation Topics and Descriptions*

Reference Number	Exam Topic	Description
1	Secure Administrative Access for Cisco Routers	To ensure that your network is not compromised, it is important to ensure that administrative access to your devices is properly secured. There are several ways to ensure that administrative access to Cisco IOS routers is limited to only authorized administrators. The topic is discussed in Chapters 4, 5, and 11.
2	Describe the Components of a Basic AAA Implementation	A successful AAA implementation requires many components. The implementation of AAA is discussed in Chapters 7 and 8.

continues

Table I-1 *SECUR Foundation Topics and Descriptions (Continued)*

Reference Number	Exam Topic	Description
3	Test the Perimeter Router AAA Implementation Using Applicable **debug** Commands	AAA implementation and troubleshooting are explained in Chapters 7 and 8.
4	Describe the Features and Architecture of CSACS 3.0 for Windows	The Cisco Secure Access Control Server is discussed in Chapters 9 and 10.
5	Configure the Perimeter Router to Enable AAA Processes to Use a TACACS Remote Service	The implementation of AAA protocols (TACACS+ and RADIUS) are described in Chapters 7 and 8.
6	Disable Unused Router Services and Interfaces	The most effective way to secure the Cisco IOS router is to disable services and interfaces that are not necessary for the operation of the router. The correct steps for disabling the administrative interfaces are covered in Chapter 5. Disabling unnecessary services is discussed in Chapter 11.
7	Use Access Lists to Mitigate Common Router Security Threats	Access lists are a relatively simple way to filter malicious traffic. The different access list types and configuration steps for each are discussed in Chapter 12.
8	Define the Cisco IOS Firewall and CBAC	CBAC is the basis of the Cisco IOS firewall. Chapters 13 and 14 discuss CBAC in great detail and outline the features of the IOS firewall feature set.
9	Configure CBAC	The configuration of CBAC is explained in Chapter 14.
10	Describe How Authentication Proxy Technology Works	Authentication proxy is a service that enables administrators to proxy user authentication at the firewall. This IOS firewall feature is covered in Chapter 15.
11	Configure AAA on a Cisco IOS Firewall	There are many different aspects that all involve AAA. The configuration of AAA is discussed in Chapters 7, 8, and 9.
12	Name the Two Types of Signature Implementations Used by the Cisco IOS Firewall IDS	The Cisco IDS features on the Cisco IOS firewall are referenced in Chapter 16.
13	Initialize a Cisco IOS Firewall IDS Router	Configuration of the Cisco IOS router IDS is discussed in Chapter 16.

Table I-1 *SECUR Foundation Topics and Descriptions (Continued)*

Reference Number	Exam Topic	Description
14	Configure a Cisco Router for IPSec Using Preshared Keys	VPNs using IPSec and Cisco IOS firewalls are discussed in Chapter 17.
15	Verify the IKE and IPSec Configuration	The steps required to verify the configuration of IKE and IPSec are referenced in Chapter 17.
16	Explain the issues Regarding Configuring IPSec Manually and Using RSA-Encrypted Nonces	The implementation of IPSec using RSA-encrypted nonces is discussed in Chapter 17.
17	Advanced IPSec VPNs Using Cisco Routers and CAs	Configuring VPNs using a certificate authority for peer authentication is a very scalable method for building multiple VPNs. This type of configuration is discussed in Chapter 18.
18	Describe the Easy VPN Server	The Easy VPN Server is defined in Chapter 19. The configuration steps for building VPNs using Easy VPN Server are also covered in this chapter.
19	Managing Enterprise VPN Routers	The products used to centrally manage an enterprise-level VPN using Cisco VPN routers are discussed in Chapter 20.

Overview of the Cisco Certification Process

The network security market is currently in a position where the demand for qualified engineers vastly surpasses the supply. For this reason, many engineers consider migrating from routing/networking over to network security. Remember that "network security" is just "security" applied to "networks." This sounds like an obvious concept, but it is actually a very important one if you are pursuing your security certification. You must be very familiar with networking before you can begin to apply the security concepts. Although a previous Cisco certification is not required to begin the Cisco security certification process, it is a good idea to at least complete the CCNA certification. The skills required to complete the CCNA will give you a solid foundation that you can expand into the network security field.

The security certification is called Cisco Certified Security Professional (CCSP) and consists of the following exams:

- **CSVPN**—Cisco Secure Virtual Private Networks (642-511)
- **CSPFA**—Cisco Secure PIX Firewall Advanced (642-521)
- **SECUR**—Securing Cisco IOS Networks (642-501)

- **CSIDS**—Cisco Secure Intrusion Detection System (642-531)
- **CSI**—Cisco SAFE Implementation (642-541)

The requirements for and explanation of the CCSP certification are outlined at the Cisco Systems website. Go to Cisco.com, click **Learning & Events>Career Certifications and Paths**.

Taking the SECUR Certification Exam

As with any Cisco certification exam, it is best to be thoroughly prepared before taking the exam. There is no way to determine exactly what questions are on the exam, so the best way to prepare is to have a good working knowledge of all subjects covered on the exam. Schedule yourself for the exam and be sure to be rested and ready to focus when taking the exam.

The best place to find out the latest available Cisco training and certifications is http://www.cisco.com/en/US/learning/index.html.

Tracking CCSP Status

You can track your certification progress by checking https://www.certmanager.net/~cisco_s/login.html. You will need to create an account the first time you log on to the site.

How to Prepare for an Exam

The best way to prepare for any certification exam is to use a combination of the preparation resources, labs, and practice tests. This guide has integrated some practice questions and labs to help you better prepare. If possible, you want to get some hands-on time with the Cisco IOS routers. There is no substitute for experience, and it is much easier to understand the commands and concepts when you can actually work with the Cisco IOS router. If you do not have access to a Cisco IOS router, you can choose from among a variety of simulation packages available for a reasonable price. Last, but certainly not least, Cisco.com provides a wealth of information about the Cisco IOS Software, and all the products that operate using Cisco IOS Software and the products that interact with Cisco routers. No single source can adequately prepare you for the SECUR exam unless you already have extensive experience with Cisco products and a background in networking or network security. At a minimum you will want to use this book combined with the Technical Assistance Center (http://www.cisco.com/public/support/tac/home.shtml) to prepare for this exam.

Assessing Exam Readiness

After completing a number of certification exams, I have found that you don't really know if you're adequately prepared for the exam until you have completed about 30 percent of the questions. At this point, if you aren't prepared it's too late. The best way to determine your readiness is to work through the "Do I Know This Already?" portions of the book, the review questions in the "Q&A"

sections at the end of each chapter, and the case studies/scenarios. It is best to work your way through the entire book unless you can complete each subject without having to do any research or look up any answers.

Cisco Security Specialist in the Real World

Cisco has one of the most recognized names on the Internet. You cannot go into a data center or server room without seeing some Cisco equipment. Cisco-certified security specialists are able to bring quite a bit of knowledge to the table due to their deep understanding of the relationship between networking and network security. This is why the Cisco certification carries such clout. Cisco certifications demonstrate to potential employers and contract holders a certain professionalism and the dedication required to complete a goal. Face it, if these certifications were easy to acquire, everyone would have them.

Cisco IOS Software Commands

A firewall or router is not normally something to play with. That is to say that once you have it properly configured, you will tend to leave it alone until there is a problem or you need to make some other configuration change. This is the reason that the question mark (**?**) is probably the most widely used Cisco IOS Software command. Unless you have constant exposure to this equipment it can be difficult to remember the numerous commands required to configure devices and troubleshoot problems. Most engineers remember enough to go in the right direction but will use the **?** to help them use the correct syntax. This is life in the real world. Unfortunately, the question mark is *not* always available in the testing environment. Many questions on this exam require you to select the best command to perform a certain function. It is extremely important that you familiarize yourself with the different commands and their respective functions.

This book follows the Cisco Systems, Inc., conventions for citing command syntax:

- **Boldface** indicates the command or keyword that is entered by the user literally as shown
- *Italics* indicate arguments for the command or option for which the user supplies a value.
- Vertical bars/pipe symbol (|) separate alternative, mutually exclusive, command options. That is, the user can enter one and only one of the options divided by the pipe symbol.
- Square brackets ([ ]) indicate optional elements for the command
- Braces ({ }) indicate a required option for the command. The user must enter this option
- Braces within brackets ([{ }]) indicate a required choice if the user implements the optional element for the command.

Rules of the Road

We have always found it very confusing when different addresses are used in the examples throughout a technical publication. For this reason we are going to use the address space depicted in Figure I-2 when assigning network segments in this book. Note that the address space we have selected is all reserved space per RFC 1918. We understand that these addresses are not routable across the Internet and are not normally used on outside interfaces. Even with the millions of IP addresses available on the Internet, there is a slight chance that we could have chosen to use an address that the owner did not want published in this book.

Figure I-2 *Addressing for Examples*

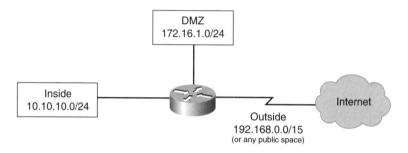

It is our hope that this will assist you in understanding the examples and the syntax of the many commands required to configure and administer Cisco IOS routers.

Exam Registration

The SECUR exam is a computer-based exam, with multiple-choice, fill-in-the-blank, list-in-order, and simulation-based questions. You can take the exam at any Pearson VUE (http://www.pearsonvue.com) or Prometric (http://www.2test.com) testing center. Your testing center can tell you the exact length of the exam. Be aware that when you register for the exam, you might be told to allow a certain amount of time to take the exam that is longer than the testing time indicated by the testing software when you begin. This is because VUE and Prometric want you to allow for some time to get settled and take the tutorial about the testing engine.

Book Content Updates

Because Cisco Systems will occasionally update exam objectives without notice, Cisco Press may post additional preparatory content on the web page associated with this book at http://www.ciscopress.com/1587200899. It's a good idea to check the website a couple of weeks before taking your exam, to review any updated content that may be posted online. We also recommend that you periodically check back to this page on the Cisco Press website to view any errata or supporting book files that may be available.

PART I: An Overview of Network Security

Chapter 1   Network Security Essentials

Chapter 2   Attack Threats Defined and Detailed

Chapter 3   Defense in Depth

Although Cisco has not defined specific exam objectives that apply to this part of the book, it is imperative that you have an in-depth understanding of network security principles. This part is designed to give you the foundation you need to fully grasp the topics covered remaining parts of the book.

This chapter covers the following subjects:

- Definition of Network Security

- Balancing Business Need with Security Requirement

- Security Policies

- Network Security as a Process

- Network Security as a Legal Issue

CHAPTER 1

Network Security Essentials

The term *network security* defines a broad range of complex subjects. To understand the individual subjects and how they relate to each other, it is important for you to first look at the big picture and get an understanding of the importance of the entire concept. Ask yourself why you lock the door to your home. The answer is likely that you do not want someone to walk in and steal your stuff. You can think of network security in much the same fashion. Security is applied to your network to prevent unauthorized intrusions and theft or damage of property. In this case the "property" is "data." In this information age, data has become a very valuable commodity with both public and private organizations making the security of their assets a very high priority.

"Do I Know This Already?" Quiz

The purpose of the "Do I Know This Already?" quiz is to help you decide whether you really need to read the entire chapter. If you already intend to read the entire chapter, you do not necessarily need to answer these questions now.

The 11-question quiz, derived from the major sections in the "Foundation Topics" portion of the chapter, helps you determine how to spend your limited study time.

Table 1-1 outlines the major topics discussed in this chapter and the "Do I Know This Already?" quiz questions that correspond to those topics.

Table 1-1 *"Do I Know This Already?" Foundation Topics Section-to-Question Mapping*

Foundation Topics Section	Questions Covered in This Section
Definition of Network Security	11
Balancing the Business Need with the Security Requirement	9
Security Policies	1, 2, 3, 5, 6, 7, 10
Network Security as a Process	4
Network Security as a Legal Issue	8

> **CAUTION** The goal of self-assessment is to gauge your mastery of the topics in this chapter. If you do not know the answer to a question or are only partially sure of the answer, you should mark this question wrong for purposes of the self-assessment. Giving yourself credit for an answer you correctly guess skews your self-assessment results and might provide you with a false sense of security.

1. Which of the following should be included in the security policy?
    a. Capabilities of the firewall
    b. Manufacturer of the firewall
    c. User responsibilities
    d. Sanctions for violating the policy
    e. A network diagram
    f. Routing protocols used

2. Which of the following employees should have access to a copy of the security policy?
    a. Managers
    b. Network engineers
    c. Human resources
    d. Temporary employees
    e. All employees

3. Which of the following is true about a security policy?
    a. The policy should require testing.
    b. The policy should not be revealed to the general public.
    c. Cisco equipment should be specified.
    d. The policy is a business document, not a technical document.
    e. The policy should be changed every six months.

4. Which of the following are acts directed by "the security wheel"?
    a. Configuring
    b. Securing
    c. Implementation
    d. Testing
    e. Monitoring and responding

5. Which of the following are benefits of a security policy?

    a. Leads to stability of the network

    b. Allows management to bypass security efforts

    c. Allows the technical team to have an unlimited budget

    d. Enables users to know the consequences of their actions

    e. Informs the user of how to break into systems

6. What are reasons for implementing a security policy?

    f. Enables management to judge the effectiveness of security efforts

    g. Enables the technical team to understand their goals

    h. Enables users to browse the web without fear of getting a virus

    i. Enables management to justify a larger technical team

    j. Lessens costs due to network downtime

7. True or False: The security policy is a document that is designed to allow the business to participate in certain electronic communications?

    a. True

    b. False

8. Choose the six main goals of security policy:

    a. Guides the technical team in purchasing equipment

    b. Guides the technical team in choosing their equipment

    c. Guides the technical team in configuring the equipment

    d. Gains management approval for new personnel

    e. Defines the use of the best-available technology

    f. Defines the responsibilities for users and administrators

    g. Defines sanctions for violating the policies

    h. Provides a Cisco-centered approach to security

    i. Defines responses and escalations to recognized threats

9. What is the determining factor when evaluating the business need against the security posture?

   a. Security is always the most important.

   b. The business need overrides security.

   c. You have to factor security with the Bell-LaPadula Security Model.

   d. Security isn't important unless your business is big enough to sue.

   e. None of the above.

10. What IETF RFC governs the *Site Security Handbook*?

    a. RFC 1918

    b. RFC 2196

    c. RFC 1700

    d. RFC 1500

11. True or False: Network security can be achieved by having consultants install firewalls at your network perimeter.

    a. True

    b. False

The answers to the "Do I Know This Already?" quiz are found in the appendix. The suggested choices for your next step are as follows:

- **8 or less overall score**—Read the entire chapter. This includes the "Foundation Topics" and "Foundation Summary" sections and the "Q&A" section.

- **9 or 10 overall score**—If you want more review on these topics, skip to the "Foundation Summary" section and then go to the "Q&A" section. Otherwise, move on to the next chapter.

Foundation Topics

Network security covers a very broad range of topics that differ for nearly every organization depending upon their business function, size, and structure. This chapter defines network security as it applies to this test and addresses the security policy, its goals and benefits, how it should be developed and by whom, how the policy should be implemented and maintained, and how to ensue that the policy remains effective as the organization continues to change.

Definition of Network Security

Network security is the implementation of security devices, policies, and processes to prevent the unauthorized access to network resources or the alteration or destruction of resources or data. Security policies are defined later in this chapter and are the basis for the security implementation. The security devices and processes implemented are simply used to enforce the security policy.

Balancing Business Need with Security Requirement

It is important to recognize that there is a trade-off between a completely secure network and the needs of business. The only way to completely secure a computer is to physically disconnect it from the network and perhaps lock it in a secure area. Of course this solution would greatly reduce your ability to use whatever resources were to be shared on that system. The goal is to identify the risks and make an informed decision about how to address them.

Security Policies

Security policies are created based upon the security philosophy of the organization. The technical team uses the security policy to design and implement the corporate security structure. The corporate *security policy* is a formal statement that specifies a set of rules users must follow while accessing the corporate network.

The security policy is not a technical document; it is a business document that lays out the permitted and prohibited activities as well as the efforts and responsibilities regarding security. As defined in RFC 2196 *Site Security Handbook*, the security policy does not dictate how the business is operated. Rather, the business needs dictate the scope and depth of the security policy. Normally, a security policy is divided into several documents that each addresses a specific topic. These "usage policy statements" define the acceptable use of the network and the users roles and responsibilities with respect to the network. The depth and scope of the security policy documents depend on the size of the organization but should normally address the following topics.

- **Acceptable use of corporate assets**—This policy defines what is considered to be acceptable use of the corporate network. It should address such items as use of e-mail and Internet access. Acceptable use must be defined so that employees know what they can and cannot do.

- **Server and workstation configuration policy**—This policy defines what applications are to be configured on the network and should designate a specific build for each system. This policy is key to ensuring that all systems on the network adhere to a standard configuration, greatly reducing the time required for troubleshooting configuration problems. The definition of testing procedures for configuration/change management may be included in this policy or there may be a separate policy dedicated to that topic.

- **Patch management policy**—The patch management policy defines how systems are upgraded and should outline how new patches are tested before being applied in the production environment. After a patch is approved for use in the production environment, it is added to the standard build to ensure that all new systems are configured with the approved system patch.

- **Network infrastructure policy**—The network infrastructure policy defines how the infrastructure is to be managed and who is responsible for maintenance. This policy should address the following items:
    — Network addressing scheme
    — Naming convention
    — Configuration/change management
    — Quality of service
    — Management and monitoring of systems
    — Log consolidation and processing

- **User account policy**—The user account policy defines what users should be assigned which account permissions. It is recommended that you limit user permissions to ensure that users adhere to the workstation configuration policy.

- **Other policies**—The number and scope of policies depends on the organization. Other policies can address such items as data handling, backup, use of encryption, password requirements (length, type, and lifetime), and remote access.

Cisco recommends that three steps be implemented when establishing a security policy:

- **Preparation**—When establishing a security policy, you should first create your general-usage statements or a rough draft of the previously listed policy documents. This will give you a good starting point. Next you need to perform a risk analysis to determine what risks you need to guard against and to define a level of acceptable risk. Risk levels are normally broken into high, medium, and low risk, but what is considered to be a risk must be defined for each organization. The final preparation item should be the designation of security team personnel and the definition of their duties.

- **Prevention**—This step defines how changes to you security posture are evaluated and implemented. Additionally, this step outlines how the security of the network should be managed and monitored. This should include the handling of log data, correlation and trending of log data, log data archive, and so on.
- **Response**—This step defines what actions are taken in the event of a problem on the network. It defines the individual responsibilities of members of the security team and addresses the following topics:
    - Reaction to an attempted security breach
    - How to isolate and handle a compromised system
    - Evidence gathering and handling of log data
    - Working with law enforcement authorities
    - Network and system restoration
    - Policy review to ensure that any newly discovered vulnerabilities are compensated for

Creating the security policy is not normally a task for a single individual. A security policy team should include members from management, legal, and technical. The security policy must have the full support of management and must be enforceable based on applicable laws and regulations. Finally, the policy must be technically feasible.

Some people question the need for a policy. There is really only one reason to have a written security policy: cost savings. The cost savings can come in a variety of forms, including the following:

- **Savings through not having data corrupted**—Preventing unauthorized users from accessing your data greatly reduces the chances of that data being corrupted. The cost of having to restore corrupted data can be tremendous.
- **Savings through not being devastated by a denial-of-service (DoS) attack**—Although it is impossible to prevent a DoS attack, it is not too difficult to mitigate the attack by preventing access at multiple points on your network and at the Internet service provider. This type of defense requires significant coordination and cannot be implemented at the last minute.
- **Savings through not having data manipulated**—Restricting access to only authorized users greatly reduces the risk of intentional data manipulation. Data manipulation is normally done to embarrass an organization and can have a lasting affect on their public image.
- **Savings through increased efficiencies**—An organization that standardizes its operations and clearly defines its practices will function as a more efficient unit.
- **Savings through reduced "unknown" problems on the network**—"Unknown" problems on the network can be the result of the introduction of untested systems, configurations, or applications into the environment. By thoroughly testing and validating all practices, procedures, applications, and configurations prior to implementing them in a production environment, you will greatly reduce the changes of creating these types of issues.

Security Policy Goals

The first goal of the security policy is to guide the technical team in choosing their equipment, not to specify the equipment for the technical team. Because the security policy is not a technical document, a good policy does not dictate the exact equipment or configurations employed. For example, a good policy does not state that a Cisco PIX 515E Firewall will be used. Instead, the policy needs to define the minimum requirements for perimeter security, such as using a stateful inspection or proxy firewall.

A second goal of the policy is to guide the technical team in configuring the equipment. For example, a security policy may state that the technical team should use their best efforts to ensure that users cannot view pornographic sites. However, the policy should not state specific sites that are allowed or disallowed.

The third goal of the security policy is to define the responsibilities for users and administrators. Clearly defined responsibilities allow management and technicians to measure performance in security efforts. When people know what is expected of them, they usually respond accordingly. Much of this would be addressed in the organizations acceptable-use policy.

The fourth goal of a security policy is to define consequences for violating the policies. If the security policy states that no programs will be downloaded from the Internet, for example, there must be a stated penalty for violating that policy. This allows users to understand that there are consequences for their actions.

The fifth goal of a good policy is to define responses and escalations to recognized threats. Knowing how a threat is to be dealt with enables personnel to plan for the event. Failure to plan for a threat results in confusion should that threat ever become a reality. Additionally, it is important to define escalation procedures for problems that are more difficult to pinpoint on the network. It is important that each member of the organization understand what steps to take in the event of a problem on the network.

In general, the goals of the security policy can be summarized as follows: The security policy is a guideline to be used by administrators in planning security efforts and responses. Responsibilities and sanctions for users and administrators are defined, as well as a planned response when the employed measures are unsuccessful.

Now that the general goals of the security policy have been discussed, it's time to consider some guidelines for a successful policy.

Security Guidelines

For a security policy to succeed, the following minimum guidelines should be followed:

- Management must support the policy.
- The policy must be consistent.
- The policy must be technically feasible.
- The policy should not be written as a technical document.
- The policy must be implemented globally throughout the organization.
- The policy must clearly define roles and responsibilities.
- The policy must be flexible enough to respond to changing technologies and organizational goals.
- The policy must be understandable.
- The policy must be widely distributed.
- The policy must specify sanctions for violations.
- The policy must include a response plan for security breaches.
- Security is an ongoing process.

The next sections explore each of guidelines.

Management Must Support the Policy

As in most business endeavors, unless management actively supports a policy, it will not be effective. A policy that restricts a business function or is considered to lack flexibility but addresses a critical need requires the full support of management; otherwise, it will not be followed. Remember that any security policy is going to restrict someone from performing a task that he thinks is necessary. The security policy is designed to weigh the good of the organization before the needs of the individual.

The Policy Must Be Consistent

An effective policy must be consistent. Few things frustrate and confuse users more than inconsistent policies. Consistency of the policy refers to the application of the policy, not equal access for all employees within the organization. Access for each user should be determined by job function and need for such access.

However, policies need to be consistent in scope and goal. For example, you should not have one group of employees that do not use passwords just because the manager of that group does not see the need. Likewise, managers should be required to maintain the same security precautions as the average user. When one group of users needs additional resources, these resources should be allocated with the same care as any other access.

Inconsistent policies are very difficult to implement and, by their nature, demonstrate a lack of consistency within the organization. Inconsistent or vague policies are also open to interpretation and may cause a debate as to which policy applies to a particular situation.

The Policy Must Be Technically Feasible

This should be common sense. It is important to understand that the creation of a security policy is a management function. The security administrator should review the policy with management and ensure that they are advised as to its technical feasibility. The security administrator should recommend solutions that meet the business need without compromising the security of the organization. The policy must also be feasible for the users. This is to say that the policy should not be so complicated that the user disregards it.

The Policy Should Not Be Written as a Technical Document

Writing the security policy in a nontechnical manner has a number of advantages. First, it is usually easier to understand than a technical document for the average employee. Second, because this document will be widely distributed, it is important that those receiving this document be able to understand it.

Making the policy a nontechnical document allows for the security concepts to be distributed without revealing the specific technologies used to accomplish the goals. For example, an administrator should be reluctant to distribute any document that specifies the make and model of firewall to be used or that specifies exactly how systems will be monitored. Making public such specific information can increase the vulnerability of an organization because a good cracker will use this information to form his or her attack strategy. Of course some portions (or documents) will be more technical than others. Whereas acceptable-use policies will be very nontechnical, the server and workstation configuration document will be more technical due to the nature of the topic.

The implementation plan is a section of the security policy where specific hardware and application information is defined. Access to the implementation plan must be restricted to authorized personnel only. Normally this includes the security team members and anyone involved in the implementation of the security plan.

The Policy Must Be Implemented Globally Throughout the Organization

Because most organizations with more than one office location interconnect via private Frame Relay networks, virtual private networks (VPNs), or other similar means, it is critical that all sites have the same emphasis on security. Although a good security design will limit and authenticate access between sites, a security hole at a single site poses a threat to the entire organization.

The Policy Must Clearly Define Roles and Responsibilities

Users need to be aware of what is allowed and prohibited. One can hardly blame a user for downloading music, for instance, if no policies prohibit such action.

Administrators must know their security goals and responsibilities if they are to be effective in accomplishing these goals. Management must also be aware of the role they are to play within the security efforts if these efforts are to be accomplished.

The Policy Must Be Flexible Enough to Respond to Changing Technologies and Organizational Goals

The security policy should be specific enough to define all requirements but not so inflexible that it does not account for changes in technology, growth within the organization, or infrastructure changes. The information technology field is ever evolving and system and infrastructure upgrades and improvements occur constantly. The security policy is a living document and should constantly be reviewed and modified as necessary to ensure its relevance for the organization.

The Policy Must Be Understandable

Often nontechnical employees have difficulty understanding technical terms and concepts. Therefore, it is imperative that the policy be clear and concise so that employees understand what is expected of them. Avoiding the use of terms that are unnecessarily ambiguous or technology specific ensures that the nontechnical reader understands his or her responsibilities. Many organizations present the policy to new employees during an orientation seminar and require them to acknowledge the training prior to receiving their network logon.

For example, a policy may address the issue of installing software in the following manner:

> Software Installation: The Information Systems department is responsible for ensuring that all computers operate efficiently and effectively. To this end the Information Systems department will configure all systems within the organization with approved software. Downloading any software onto any computer is prohibited for all users except when specifically approved by the Information Systems department. Failure to abide by this policy is subject to disciplinary action as described in Section X.

The preceding statement starts by explaining the reasoning behind the policy. Following this is a statement defining who is responsible for installing applications. The reader is also directed to another part of the policy that lists the disciplinary actions that may be taken if this policy is disregarded.

Notice that the policy does not specifically state what applications are allowed or not allowed. This allows the Information Systems department to determine the appropriateness of applications without the need to rewrite the policy.

The Policy Must Be Widely Distributed

Many organizations publish their security policies on the Internet. This can be a valuable resource when starting to write your company's policies. Most of the large colleges and universities are a good source of sample policies.

Because the policy should not reveal any of your technical specifics, there is no reason for this policy not to be released to all employees. Distributing the policy to everyone within the organization and having each employee acknowledge receipt makes it easier to enforce the policy.

The Policy Must Specify Sanctions for Violations

Employees should be made aware of the policy and understand that violations of the policy have consequences. However, these sanctions should also be constructed in a way that does not limit the company to a specific action.

Because the rights of employees vary by city, state, and country, it is very important to ensure that security team members from human resources and legal are involved when creating any policies that deal with disciplinary measures. The following policy is meant as an example only:

> Sanctions for Violating the Corporate Security Policy: Management may impose any disciplinary action it sees fit for any violations of the corporate security policies. These actions, while not limited to the following, may include verbal counseling, written letter of counseling, written letter of reprimand, or termination.

The Policy Must Include an Incident Response Plan for Security Breaches

Any network has the potential of being compromised. Complex networks are more difficult to protect and can be more difficult to monitor. It is important to identify when your network is under attack and when the attack has resulted in a system or network breach. It is also very important to develop an incident response plan so that the security personnel know how to react to the compromise. Although the ultimate goal is to discover all breaches, some may go unnoticed. The policy must state what actions to take if a breach is discovered. Most policies differentiate between breaches occurring from within the organization and those originating from the Internet. The difference is because it is normally less difficult to identify the offender as long as the attack originated from within the network and not from an internal resource that was exploited by an external source.

A sample policy section follows:

> Response to Internal Denial-of-Service (DoS) Attacks: Upon discovery of a DoS attack originating within the local-area network (LAN), the administrator will record and document the discovery for future forensics use. A secure machine should be utilized to track all packets originating from the source computer.
>
> The administrator will attempt to isolate the offending machine from the LAN. Next, the network segment where the attack is originating will be isolated.

Security Is an Ongoing Process

Security is a recurring process, not a single implementation effort. Figure 1-1 depicts what is commonly referred to as *the security wheel*. This figure, and many similar to it, are shown throughout security documentation. It is used to illustrate the recurring efforts that must be made to effectively implement security within a corporation. These recurring efforts are referred to as the *security posture assessment* (SPA).

Network Security as a Process

The security wheel demonstrates the ongoing process to ensure that networks are secured and remain secure. The driving force at the center of the SPA is the security policy. The security policy states how often testing and monitoring must occur, what areas are tested, and how new security initiatives are implemented.

Figure 1-1 *The Security Wheel*

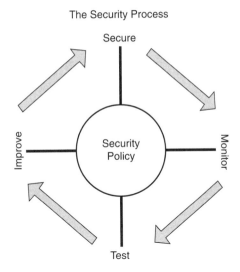

Four steps must considered while implementing a security policy. Keep in mind that this is not a single process that is completed after one round. This is an ongoing process that should continue, thus allowing the network to evolve and constantly improve as new threats arise. Generally, each step continues as an ongoing process of its own with each step relying on the other for input and improvement. The four steps of the security wheel are as follows:

- **Secure**—This step is used in the actual implementation of a device or configuration. Adding firewalls, intrusion detection systems, or AAA servers all fall under this step.

- **Monitor/Respond**—When an implementation has occurred, the next step is to monitor that implementation. Monitoring enables the security administrators to better understand the challenges facing them. Monitoring should occur at all times, with new monitoring being implemented after changes to the network. Any issues discovered while monitoring the system need to be resolved as they are found (return input to the "secure" step).

- **Test**—Testing is a critical step to the SPA because without testing there is no definitive feedback to determine the effectiveness of the implementations. Whereas the time between testing varies by company, all companies need to test to determine the effectiveness of their security efforts. Testing should always occur after significant changes to the network.

- **Manage/Improve**—Management of all systems and of the process is very important. It is also key to make improvements as necessary to systems, processes, policies, and so on. Whether these improvements involve new equipment or configuration changes, they are a result of previous testing and a prelude to more efforts to secure the network.

Network Security as a Legal Issue

Consider the following scenario: An employee of Company X uses his computer (without authorization) to scan the Internet and eventually finds a server that belongs to Company Y that he is able to take control of using a documented exploit. The employee then uses that server to break into the database server at Insurance Company Z and steals the medical records of a celebrity containing very sensitive and potentially damaging personal information. The stolen information is later distributed to the public. Who is responsible? Of course the employee is ultimately responsible, but probably lacks the financial resources that makes it worthwhile for the celebrity to seek legal recourse. However, Companies X, Y, and Z will all probably become involved in legal action as a result of this theft.

Just as a person expects that a bank would take "reasonable steps" to ensure that her money is kept secure, organizations are expected to ensure that personal information is kept secure from public access. Many of the definitions for reasonable care are being created today and these definitions constantly change in this fast-paced and very fluid environment. The security policy mentioned earlier in this chapter is defined by RFC 2196, also known as the Internet Engineering Task Force's (IETF) *Site Security Handbook*.

Foundation Summary

The "Foundation Summary" section of each chapter lists the most important facts from the chapter. Although this section does not list every fact from the chapter that will be on your exam, a well-prepared candidate should at a minimum know all the details in each "Foundation Summary" section before going to take the exam.

Security Policies

The following list outlines the key points for and advantages of having a security policy:

- Security policies are created based upon the security philosophy of the organization.
- The technical team uses the security policy to design and implement the corporate security structure.
- The security policy is not a technical document.
- Read the *Site Security Handbook* (RFC 2196).
- The security policy should be developed by the security team consisting of members from management, legal, human relations, and technical staff.
- Having a good security policy saves in the following areas:
    - Savings through not having data corrupted
    - Savings through not being devastated by a DoS attack
    - Savings through not having data manipulated
    - Savings through increased efficiency due to a standardized configurations
    - Savings through reduced "unknown" problems on the network because only tested and approved configurations are allowed on the network

Security Policy Goals

Many goals are achieved by implementing a strong yet balanced security policy. The following list outlines these goals:

- Guides the technical team in choosing their equipment
- Guides the technical team in configuring the equipment
- Defines the responsibilities for users and administrators
- Defines sanctions for violating the policies
- Defines responses and escalations to recognized threats

Security Guidelines

The following list outlines the guidelines for developing and implementing a security policy:

- Management must support the policy.
- The policy must be consistent.
- The policy must be technically feasible and not so complex that users have difficulty understanding and following it.
- The policy should not be written as a technical document or documents.
- The policy must be implemented globally throughout the company.
- The policy must clearly define responsibilities for users, administrators, and management.
- The policy must be flexible enough to respond to changing technologies and company goals.
- The policy must be understandable.
- The policy must be widely distributed.
- The policy must specify sanctions for violations.
- The policy must contain an incident response plan.
- Security must be viewed as an ongoing process.

Network Security as a Process

The SPA is driven by the security policy. The security wheel demonstrates the four ongoing steps used to continuously improve the security of a network.

- **Secure**—Implement the equipment and processes and secure your system configurations to reduce your network exposure.
- **Monitor/Respond**—Monitor the network to determine how changes have affected your network and look for additional threats and respond to any newly discovered issues.
- **Test**—Test the current network and system configurations to determine whether any vulnerabilities exist.
- **Manage/Improve**—Manage the process and make continuous improvements based on the results of your testing and vulnerabilities noted during the network monitoring or based on normal component upgrades and improvements.

Q&A

As mentioned in the section, "How to Use this Book," in the Introduction to this book, you have two choices for review questions. The questions that follow next give you a bigger challenge than the exam itself by using an open-ended question format. By reviewing now with this more difficult question format, you can exercise your memory better and prove your conceptual and factual knowledge of this chapter. The answers to these questions are found in the appendix.

For more practice with exam-like question formats, including questions using a router simulator and multiple choice questions, use the exam engine on the CD-ROM.

1. Why is consistency important in a network policy?
2. Why is it so important that management accept the policy?
3. How often should testing occur?
4. When should monitoring occur?
5. Why is it necessary to even have a written security policy?
6. Why is it important to specify sanctions for failing to abide by the security policy?
7. Why is it not a security risk to publish the security policy on a public website?
8. Why is the security policy shown in the center of the security wheel?
9. Why should a policy be implemented globally? Why not just implement it at one site?
10. Why is flexibility important in a security policy?
11. What organization published the *Site Security Handbook*?

This chapter covers the following subjects:

- Vulnerabilities
- Threats
- Intruder Motivation
- Types of Attacks

CHAPTER 2

Attack Threats Defined and Detailed

This chapter discusses the potential network vulnerabilities and attacks that pose a threat to the network and provides you with a better understanding of the need for an effective network security policy.

"Do I Know This Already?" Quiz

The purpose of the "Do I Know This Already?" quiz is to help you decide whether you really need to read the entire chapter. If you already intend to read the entire chapter, you do not necessarily need to answer these questions now.

The 10-question quiz, derived from the major sections in the "Foundation Topics" portion of the chapter, helps you determine how to spend your limited study time.

Table 2-1 outlines the major topics discussed in this chapter and the "Do I Know This Already?" quiz questions that correspond to those topics.

Table 2-1 *"Do I Know This Already?" Foundation Topics Section-to-Question Mapping*

Foundation Topics Section	Questions Covered in This Section
Vulnerabilities	1, 5
Threats	10
Intruder Motivation	4, 6
Types of Attacks	2, 3, 7, 8, 9

CAUTION The goal of self-assessment is to gauge your mastery of the topics in this chapter. If you do not know the answer to a question or are only partially sure of the answer, you should mark this question wrong for purposes of the self-assessment. Giving yourself credit for an answer you correctly guess skews your self-assessment results and might provide you with a false sense of security.

1. Your boss insists that it is fine to use his wife's name as his password, despite the fact that your security policy states that this is not a sufficient password. What weaknesses are revealed?

    a. This shows a lack of an effective security policy (policy weakness).

    b. This shows a technology weakness.

    c. This shows a protocol weakness.

    d. This shows a configuration weakness.

    e. This shows that your boss is an idiot.

2. You receive a call from a writer for a computer magazine. They are doing a survey of network security practices. What form of attack could this be?

    a. Reconnaissance

    b. Unauthorized access

    c. Data manipulation

    d. Denial of service

    e. None of the above

3. Walking past a programmer's desk, you see that he is using a network analyzer. What category of attack should you watch for?

    a. Reconnaissance

    b. Unauthorized access

    c. Data manipulation

    d. Denial of service

    e. None of the above

4. Looking at the logs, you notice that your manager has erased some system files from your NT system. What is the most likely motivation for this?

    a. Intruding for political purposes

    b. Intruding for profit

    c. Intruding through lack of knowledge

    d. Intruding for fun and pride

    e. Intruding for revenge

5. Your new engineer, who has very little experience working in your corporate environment, has added a new VPN concentrator onto the network. You have been too busy with another project to oversee the installation. What weakness do you need to be aware of concerning his implementation of this device?

   a. Lack of effective policy
   b. Technology weakness
   c. Lack of user knowledge
   d. Operating system weakness
   e. Configuration weakness

6. Statistically, what is the most likely launch site for an attack against your network?

   a. From poor configurations on the firewall
   b. From the Internet over FTP
   c. From the Internet through e-mail
   d. From within your network
   e. None of the above

7. Your accountant claims that all the electronic funds transfers from the previous day were incorrect. What category of attack could this be caused by?

   a. Reconnaissance
   b. Unauthorized access
   c. Denial of service
   d. Data manipulation
   e. None of the above

8. Your logs reveal that someone has attempted to gain access as the administrator of a server. What category of attack could this be?

   a. Reconnaissance
   b. Unauthorized access
   c. Denial of service
   d. Data manipulation
   e. None of the above

9. Your firewall and IDS logs indicate that a host on the Internet scanned all of your public address space looking of connections to TCP port 25. What type of attack does this indicate?

   a. Reconnaissance attack, vertical scan
   b. Reconnaissance attack, block scan
   c. Reconnaissance attack, horizontal scan
   d. Reconnaissance attack, DNS scan
   e. Reconnaissance attack, SMTP scan

10. True or False: A "script kiddie" that is scanning the Internet for "targets of opportunity" represents a structured threat to an organization?

    a. True
    b. False

The answers to the "Do I Know This Already?" quiz are found in the appendix. The suggested choices for your next step are as follows:

- **8 or less overall score**—Read the entire chapter. This includes the "Foundation Topics" and "Foundation Summary" sections and the "Q&A" section.

- **9 or 10 overall score**—If you want more review on these topics, skip to the "Foundation Summary" section and then go to the "Q&A" section. Otherwise, move on to the next chapter.

Foundation Topics

Computer systems have become a fundamental component of nearly every organization today. Large corporations and government organizations devote a tremendous amount of their assets to maintaining their networks, and even the smallest organization is likely to use a computer for maintaining their records and financial information. Because these systems are able to perform functions rapidly and accurately and because they make it very easy to facilitate communication between organizations, computer networks continue to grow and become more interconnected. Any organization that wants to provide some public access to their network maintains a connection to the Internet. This access does not come without certain risks. This chapter defines some of the risks to networks and explains how an ineffective security policy can further increase the chance of a network security breach.

Vulnerabilities

To understand cyberattacks you must remember that computers, no matter how advanced, are still just machines that operate based on predetermined instruction sets. The operating systems and other software packages are just compiled instruction sets that the computer uses to transform input into output. A computer has no capability to determine the difference between authorized and unauthorized input unless this information is written into the instruction sets. Any point in a software package that enables a user to alter the software or gain access to a system (that was not specifically designed into the software) is called a *vulnerability*. In most cases, a cracker can gain access to a network or computer by exploiting a vulnerability if that user does not already have authorized access. (See the section "Internal Threats" later in this chapter.) It is possible to remotely connect to a computer on any of 65,535 ports. As hardware and software technology continues to advance, the "other side" continues to search for and discover new vulnerabilities. For this reason, most software manufacturers continue to produce patches for their products as vulnerabilities are discovered.

Self-Imposed Vulnerabilities

All networks contain a combination of public and private data. A properly implemented security scheme protects all of the data on the network yet allows some data to be accessed from outside entities, usually without the ability to change that data. One example of this may be the corporate website. Other data, such as payroll information, should not be made available to the public and should be restricted to only specific users within the organization. Network security, properly implemented, secures the corporate data, reduces the effectiveness of hacking attempts, and ensures that systems are used for their intended purposes. Networks designed to be freely available to the public need to be secured to ensure accuracy of the information and availability to the public if the network is to be useful. Additionally, properly securing a network ensures that the network is not used as an attack point against other networks.

Security attacks can become effective and damage networks for the following three main reasons:

- Lack of effective policy
- Configuration weakness
- Technology weakness

Lack of Effective Policy

Because a network security policy directs the administrators regarding how communications should be enabled and implemented, this is the basis for all security efforts. Security policies have weaknesses for a number of reasons, including the following:

- **Politics**—Politics within an organization can cause a lack of consistency within the policies or, worse, a lack of uniformly applying the policies. Many policies make so many exceptions for management and business owners that the policies become meaningless.

- **Lack of a written policy**—The lack of a written policy is essentially the same as not having any policy. Publishing and widely distributing the security policy prevents confusion about it within the organization.

- **Lack of continuity**—When personnel change too frequently, there is often a loosening in the care people take to ensure that policies are enforced. When a system administrator leaves a position, for example, all the passwords used by that administrator should be changed. In an organization that changes administrators several times each year, there is a natural reluctance to change the passwords because users knows they will be changed again very shortly due to administrator turnover.

- **Lack of disaster recovery planning**—A good disaster recovery plan must include contingencies for security breaches. The resulting confusion after a disaster can prevent forensic efforts from being successful because administrators are not careful in their recovery efforts.

- **Lack of patch management within the security policy**—A good security policy allows for frequent hardware and software upgrades. A detailed procedure for implementing new hardware and software ensures that security does not become forgotten while implementing new equipment.

- **Lack of monitoring**—Failure to monitor logs and intrusion detection systems appropriately exposes many organizations to attack without any knowledge that those attacks are occurring.

- **Lack of proper access controls**—Unauthorized network access is made easier when poorly designed access controls are implemented on the network. Improper password length, infrequent password changes, passwords written on notes attached to monitors, and freely shared passwords are items that have the potential to lead to security breaches.

Configuration Weakness

As network devices become increasingly complex, the knowledge base required to configure systems correctly grows. This can be more of an issue in smaller organizations where a single administrator is responsible for the LAN, WAN, servers, and workstations. Configuration weaknesses can be classified into one of the following:

- **Misconfigured equipment**—A simple misconfiguration can cause severe security issues. Whether the error is caused through lack of knowledge or is just a typo, the consequences can still lead to an insecure network. Some areas that are susceptible to this are access lists, SNMP settings, and routing protocols.

- **Weak or exposed passwords**—Passwords that are too short, are easily guessed, or consist of common words make it easy for an intruder to gain access to resources. A "strong" password should consist of at least eight characters and should include upper- and lowercase, numbers, and special characters. Additionally, using the default password on administrator accounts is an especially poor practice. It is also important that users don't create a password that is too complex to remember. In such a scenario, the user will tend to write down the password, defeating the purpose for the password in the first place. One common method for creating and remembering passwords is the "vanity plate" method: Think of a word or phrase and convert it into the characters used on a vanity license plate, then change the case of a letter or two, and substitute one or more numbers for letters. Here is an example: In Virginia, for instance, a Honda owner is apparently not fond of mayonnaise. The Honda owner's license plate reads IH8 Mayo. You can drop in an underscore and an exclamation point and you get IH8_Mayo!. Not too fancy and very easy to remember.

- **Misconfigured Internet services**—Java applets, Java script, FTP security settings, and IP can all be configured in ways that are considered unsafe. Knowing exactly what services are required and what services are running ensures that Internet services do not create potential security breaches.

- **Using default settings**—The default settings on a great number of products were designed for assisting in the configuration of a device and placing it in a production environment. For example, the default filters for the Cisco 3000 Series VPN concentrators are insufficient protection for use in a production network. By default, there are no access lists limiting telnet access on routers; if telnet is enabled, you must ensure the access is limited to only authorized IP addresses (from your management network). These are just two examples of how the default settings are insufficient for production use.

Technology Weakness

All technologies have intrinsic weaknesses. These weaknesses can reside in the operating system, within the protocol, or within networking equipment. Each of these items is discussed further in the following sections:

- **Operating system weakness**—This was discussed earlier in this chapter under the heading "Vulnerabilities." Operating systems are simple, coded instructions written for the computer. If an intruder is able to inject additional instructions into the system by exploiting a vulnerability within the operating system, he or she may be able to affect how that system functions. It is extremely important to keep operating systems patched to reduce system vulnerabilities.

- **Protocol weakness**—Some protocols suites, such as TCP/IP, were designed without an emphasis on security aspects. Some of the security weaknesses of protocols are detailed in the following list:

    — Network File System (NFS) is used by Novell and UNIX servers. There are no provisions for authentication or encryption. Additionally, because NFS uses a random selection of ports, it can be difficult for an administrator to limit access.

    — The TCP/IP suite consists of ICMP, UDP, and TCP and has several inherent weaknesses. For example, the header and footer on an IP packet can be intercepted and modified without leaving evidence of the change. ICMP packets are routinely used in DoS attacks, as discussed later in this chapter.

    — AppleTalk is used by older Macintosh systems. Using this protocol raises a number of issues regarding security. Lack of encryption, a random port selection, and lack of authentication raise security concerns when using this protocol. MacOS now fully supports the TCP/IP suite and is not commonly used.

- **Application weaknesses**—Many applications are written without regard to security. The primary objective when developing applications is functionality. Service packs, upgrades, and patches are normally released by the application developer as vulnerabilities are identified. As technology continues to develop, however, security is becoming a greater priority and is now being written into newly created applications as they are designed.

- **Network equipment weakness**—Although all manufacturers strive to produce the best product possible, any system of sufficient complexity is prone to configuration errors or system design vulnerabilities. Additionally, all systems have their particular strengths and weaknesses. One product may be very efficient and secure when it processes a specific protocol or traffic for a specific application, for example, but may be weak or not support a different protocol or application. It is very important to focus on exactly what type of network traffic you need to support and ensure that you implement the correct device in the correct location on the network. Additionally, you should always test your systems to ensure that they perform their functions as expected. An administrator who knows the strengths and weaknesses of his equipment can overcome these shortcomings through the proper deployment and configuration of equipment.

Threats

Potential threats are divided into the following two categories, but their motivations fall into much larger categories, detailed in the section "Intruder Motivation," which follows:

- **Structured threats**—A structured threat is an organized effort to breach a specific target. This can be the most dangerous threat because of its organized nature. This is a preplanned attack by a person or group that is seeking a specific target.
- **Unstructured threat**—Unstructured threats are by far the most common. These are usually a result of scanning of the Internet by persons seeking targets of opportunity. Many different types of scanning files or "scripts" are available for download on the Internet and can be used to scan a host or network for vulnerabilities.

Intruder Motivation

Several motivations prompt someone to intrude on another's network. Although no text can list all the reasons that someone would choose to steal or corrupt data, some common themes become evident when looking at the motivations of previous intruders. To refine the discussion of intruder motivations, it is first necessary to define some terms. In the context of this chapter, the word *intruder* can be defined as someone who attempts to gain access to a network or computer system without authorization. Intruders can be further classified as *crackers*, *hackers*, or *script kiddies*:

- **Cracker**—Someone who uses an advanced knowledge of networking and the Internet to compromise network security without proper authorization. Crackers are usually thought of as having a malicious intent.
- **Hacker**—Someone who investigates the integrity or security of a network or operating system. Usually relying on advanced programming techniques, the hacker's motivations are not always malicious. The ethical hacker is a term used for security consultants; the hacker may be hired by a company to test an organization's current defenses and expose weaknesses.
- **Script kiddie**—This is a commonly used slang term for a novice hacker who relies heavily on publicly available scripts to test the security of a network and scan for vulnerabilities.

The reasons that someone attempts to access, alter, or disrupt a network are as different as the intruders themselves. Some of the most common motivations are discussed in the following sections.

Lack of Understanding of Computers or Networks

Sometimes a user initiates a security breach through a lack of understanding. For example, an uneducated user with administrative rights on a Windows NT system can easily remove or change critical settings, resulting in an unusable system. Having too much trust combined with a lack of understanding can be equally dangerous. It is not uncommon for an administrator to open up their whole network to someone when access to a single machine is all that is required. A poorly trained administrator of a firewall can easily open connectivity to the point that the firewall becomes ineffective. Another possibility is that a temporary firewall opening becomes a permanent opening because there are no procedures in place to ensure that temporary openings are closed after the need for them has been removed. Although a good security policy can help prevent these examples, some security breaches occur without any malicious intent.

Intruding for Curiosity

Sometimes people are just curious regarding the data contained in a system or network. One incident typical of this type is a 14-year-old boy who broke into a credit card company's system to look around. When asked the reason for breaking into the system, he replied that simple curiosity was the motivation. Sometimes an employee, for example, may attempt to break into a payroll system just to see whether he or she is receiving pay in accordance with coworkers. Alternatively, an employee may be curious regarding the financial status of the company or wondering whether there is anything interesting within the personnel record. Despite the focus of the curiosity, the common theme among those intruding out of curiosity is that there is usually little or no damage to the data.

Intruding for Fun and Pride

Some intruders enjoy the challenge of being able to bypass security measures. Many times, the more sophisticated the security measures, the greater the challenge. Whether these intruders are hackers, crackers, or script kiddies, their motivation is fun, pride, or a combination of the two. When George Leigh Mallory was asked why he wanted to climb Mount Everest, his reply was, "Because it is there." This seems to be the motivation for a number of intruders. There are several bulletin boards and discussion groups where members list their latest conquests and the challenges posed to breaking into the systems. The members of these groups applaud successful attempts and provide guidance to those who are unsuccessful. These are good places for a security administrator to monitor for information on the latest techniques used for breaking into systems.

Intruding for Revenge

Revenge can be powerful motivation. Disgruntled or former employees who have a good understanding of the network and know what assets they want to target can cause substantial problems for an organization. It is always advisable to change passwords and disable accounts whenever key personnel leave the company and ensure that you monitor the network for attacks that target specific assets.

Intruding for Profit

Profit is another powerful motivator for breaking into systems. Credit card information, unauthorized bank transfers, and manipulation of billing information can be extremely profitable if successful. However, not all intrusions for profit are based on money. In November 2002, a prominent news agency was accused of breaking into a Swedish company's computer system to steal data related to financial performance. The news agency was accused of obtaining this information to release it before the official announcement, thereby beating all the other news agencies to the story. At the time of this writing, there has been no determination whether this accusation has any merit. This example shows how profit may not always be directly related to transferring funds or obtaining credit card information. Of course, the theft of corporate secrets could provide a competitor with a significant advantage in the marketplace.

Intruding for Political Purposes

The fact that economies depend largely upon electronic transactions makes those economies vulnerable to disruptions by an attacker. Cyber-warfare does exist and can pose a real threat to any economy. If disruption of an economy is desired, doing so through electronic means may become the chosen method due to a number of factors. Among these factors are the ability to launch an attack from virtually any location, low equipment cost, low cost of connectivity, and a lack of sufficient protection. In November 2002, a number of the primary DNS servers on the Internet were attacked through a distributed denial-of-service (DDoS) attack and were rendered inoperable for a number of hours. Although we cannot guess the motivation for this attack, a more sophisticated version could dramatically affect Internet traffic and disrupt many organizations that communicate via the Internet. Another more common political motivation is known as *hactivism*, which is the act of targeting an organization and defacing their websites for political purposes.

Types of Attacks

Before discussing the characteristics of specific attacks, it's necessary to categorize the different types of attacks. Attacks are defined by the goal of the attack rather than the motivation of the attacker. There are three major types of network attacks, each with its own specific goal:

- **Reconnaissance attacks**—An attack designed not to inflict immediate damage to a system or network but only to map out the network to discover which address ranges are used, which systems are running, and which services are on those systems. One must "access" a system or network to some degree to perform reconnaissance, but normally one does not cause any damage at that time.
- **Access attacks**—An attack designed to exploit a vulnerability and to gain access to a system on a network. Once access is gained, the user can do the following:
    — Retrieve, alter, or destroy data
    — Add, remove, or change network resources, including user access
    — Install other exploits that can be used at a later date to gain access to the network
- **DoS attacks**—A DoS attack is designed solely to cause an interruption to a computer or network.

Reconnaissance Attacks

The term *reconnaissance* attack is misleading. The goal of this type of attack is actually to perform reconnaissance of a computer or network, and the goal of the reconnaissance is to determine the makeup of the targeted computer or network and to search for and map any vulnerabilities. A reconnaissance attack can be an indicator of the potential for other more invasive attacks. Many reconnaissance attacks have been written into scripts that enable novice hackers or script kiddies to launch attacks on networks with a few mouse clicks. The following list identifies the more common reconnaissance attacks:

- **DNS whois queries**—A whois query of the DNS provides the unauthorized user with such information as what address space is assigned to a particular domain and who owns that domain.

- **Ping sweep**—The output from a ping sweep can tell the unauthorized user the number of hosts that are active on the network.

- **Vertical scans**—Vertical scans scan the service ports of a single host and request different services at each port. This method enables the unauthorized user to determine which type of operating system is running and what services are running on the computer.

- **Horizontal scans**—Horizontal scans scan an address range for a specific port or service. A very common horizontal scan is the FTP sweep. This is scanning a network segment looking for replies to connection attempts on port 21.

- **Block scan**—A block scan is a combination of the vertical and horizontal scans. In other words, it scans a network segment and attempts connections on multiple ports of each host on that segment.

Access Attacks

As the name implies, the goal of an access attack is to gain access to a computer or a network. Having gained access, the user can perform many different functions. These functions can be broken into three distinct categories:

- **Interception**—If the unauthorized user is able to capture traffic going from the source to the destination, that user can store that data for later use. The data could be anything that is crossing the network segment that is connected to the sniffer and could include confidential data such as personnel records, payroll, or research and development projects. If network management data is crossing the network, it is possible to acquire passwords for specific components and take control of that equipment. The methods used for intercepting traffic vary but usually require physical connectivity with the network. Upgrading from hub to switching technology greatly reduces the amount of traffic that can be captured by a network sniffer. The most effective way to protect your sensitive data is to save it in an encrypted format or to send it via an encrypted connection. This prevents the intruder from being able to read the data. Figure 2-1 depicts how interception may occur.

Figure 2-1 *Interceptions Can Occur if Data Is Sent in an Unencrypted Format*

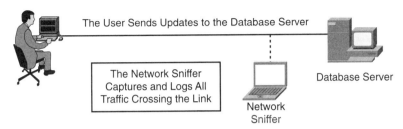

- **Modification**—Having access, the unauthorized user can now alter the resource. This not only includes altering file content, it also includes system configurations, unauthorized system access, and unauthorized privilege escalation. Unauthorized system access is completed by exploiting a vulnerability in either the operating system or another software package running on that system. *Unauthorized privilege escalation* refers to a user with a low level but authorized account attempting to gain higher-level or more privileged user account information to increase the unauthorized user's privilege level. This enables the intruder to have greater control of the target system or network.

- **Fabrication**—With access to the target system or network, the unauthorized user can create false objects and introduce them into the environment. This could include altering data or inserting packaged exploits such as a virus, a worm, or a Trojan horse that can continue to attack the network from within.

  — **Virus**—Computer viruses range from annoying to destructive. They consist of computer code that attaches itself to other software running on the computer. This way, each time the attached software opens the virus reproduces and can continue to grow until it wreaks havoc on the infected computer.

  — **Worm**—A worm is a virus that exploits vulnerabilities on networked systems to replicate itself. A worm scans a network looking for a computer with a specific vulnerability. When it finds a host, it copies itself to that system and begins scanning from there as well.

  — **Trojan horse**—A Trojan horse is a program that usually claims to perform one function (such as a game) but does something completely different (such as corrupting data on your hard disk). Many different types of Trojan horses get attached to systems, and the effects of these programs range from a minor irritation for the user to total destruction of the computer file system. Trojan horses are sometimes used to exploit systems by creating user accounts on systems that enable unauthorized users to gain access or upgrade their privilege level. Some Trojan horses capture data from the host system and send it back to a location where it can be accessed by the attacker. Others enable the attacker to take control of the system and enlist it in a DDoS attack; this is a very common use of the Trojan horse.

DoS Attacks

A DoS attack is designed to deny user access to computers or networks. These attacks usually target specific services and attempt to overwhelm them by making numerous requests concurrently. If a system is not protected and cannot react to a DoS attack, it can be very easy to overwhelm that system by running scripts that generate multiple requests. It is possible to greatly increase the magnitude of a DoS attack by launching the attack from multiple systems against a single target. This practice is referred to as a *distributed denial-of-service* (DDoS) attack. The use of Trojan horses in a DDoS was discussed in the previous section.

Foundation Summary

The "Foundation Summary" section of each chapter lists the most important facts from the chapter. Although this section does not list every fact from the chapter that will be on your SECUR exam, a well-prepared candidate should at a minimum know all the details in each "Foundation Summary" before going to take the exam.

Vulnerabilities

A vulnerability is anything that can be exploited to gain access to or gain control of a host or network.

Self-Imposed Vulnerabilities

An organization can create its own vulnerabilities by not ensuring that the following issues are resolved through process or procedure:

- The lack of a effective and consistent security policy due to any of the following conditions:
    - **Politics**—Politics within an organization can cause a lack of consistency within the policies or a lack of uniform application of policies.
    - **Lack of a written policy**—The lack of a written policy is essentially the same as not having any policy.
    - **Lack of continuity**—When personnel change too frequently, there is often a loosening in the care people take to ensure that policies are enforced.
    - **Lack of disaster recovery planning**—The resultant confusion after a disaster often results in virtually all security efforts being dropped if the administrators are not careful in their recovery efforts.
    - **Lack of upgrade plans within the security policy**—A detailed procedure for implementing new hardware and software ensures that security does not become forgotten while implementing new equipment.
    - **Lack of monitoring**—Failure to monitor logs and intrusion detection systems appropriately exposes many organizations to constant attack without any knowledge that those attacks are occurring.
    - **Lack of proper access controls**—Improper password length, infrequent password changes, passwords written on notes attached to monitors, and freely shared passwords are all items that can lead to security breaches.

- Configuration weakness within a organization can result in significant vulnerability exposure.
  - **Misconfigured equipment**—A simple misconfiguration can cause severe security issues.
  - **Insufficient passwords**—Passwords that are too short, are easily guessed, or consist of common words, especially when transmitted over the Internet, are cause for concern.
  - **Misconfigured Internet services**—Knowing exactly which services are required and which services are running ensures that Internet services do not create potential security breaches.
  - **Using default settings**—The default settings on a great number of products are designed to assist in their configuration and are placed in a production environment.
- All technologies have intrinsic weaknesses. These weaknesses can reside in the operating system, within the protocol, or within networking equipment.
  - All operating systems have weaknesses. You must take proper measures to make these systems as secure as possible.
  - Certain protocols can be exploited because of the way they were written and the functionality that was written into the protocol.
- Although all manufacturers strive to make the best product possible, any system of sufficient complexity is prone to human and mechanical errors. Additionally, all systems have their particular strengths and weaknesses. Knowing the nuances of your particular equipment is the best way of overcoming technology weaknesses.

Threats

There are two different types of threats to computer networks:

- Structured threats are an organized effort to attack a specific target.
- Unstructured threats are not organized and do not target a specific host, network, or organization.

Intruder Motivation

- There are three different names for potential intruders, categorized by their skill level and intent:
  - **Cracker**—More advanced and usually part of a structured threat
  - **Hacker**—Can be involved in both structured and unstructured threats.
  - **Script kiddie**—Novice hacker using script files that perform most of the scanning and hacking functions

- The motivations for intruders vary but generally fit into one of the following categories:
  - Intruding through lack of knowledge
  - Intruding for curiosity
  - Intruding for fun and pride
  - Intruding for revenge
  - Intruding for profit
  - Intruding for political purposes

Types of Attacks

There are three major types of network attacks, each with its own specific goal:

- **Reconnaissance attacks**—An attack designed to gather information about a system or a network. The goal is to map the network, identify the systems and services, and to identify vulnerabilities that can be exploited at a later time.
- **Access attacks**—An attack designed to exploit a vulnerability and to gain access to a system on a network. After access has been gained, the user can do the following:
  - Retrieve, alter, or destroy data
  - Add, remove, or change network resources, including user access
  - Install other exploits that can be used at a later date to gain access to the network
- **DoS attacks**—A DoS attack is designed solely to cause an interruption to a computer or network.

Q&A

As mentioned in the section, "How to Use This Book," in the Introduction to this book, you have two choices for review questions. The questions that follow next give you a bigger challenge than the exam itself by using an open-ended question format. By reviewing now with this more difficult question format, you can exercise your memory better and prove your conceptual and factual knowledge of this chapter. The answers to these questions are found in the appendix.

For more practice with exam-like question formats, including questions using a router simulator and multiple choice questions, use the exam engine on the CD-ROM.

1. An application that is supposed to monitor your network and alert you in the event of an outage is being considered by your manager. You begin testing the product and discover that it requires a management connection to every network component (each requiring a password) but maintains these nonencrypted (clear-text) connections. This would require that the system send clear-text passwords to every network component that you want to manage. Would you consider this product for you network and why?

2. How many TCP ports can a system communicate over if no ports are blocked and a service is listening on every available port?

3. What are three "self-imposed vulnerabilities"?

4. Can a system misconfiguration be a security vulnerability?

5. Why would you not want to install security devices using the default settings?

6. How does NFS make network connections and why can it be difficult to secure?

7. Why is it difficult to determine whether IP traffic is spoofed?

8. What is a structured threat?

9. Which type of threat is more common: structured or unstructured?

10. Why should your security administrator be well trained and very familiar with the product that she is using?

11. What is the goal of a reconnaissance attack?

12. What is a "vertical scan"?

13. What is a "worm"?

14. What is a DDoS attack?

This chapter covers the following subjects:

- Overview of Defense in Depth

CHAPTER 3

Defense in Depth

As technology continues to advance, network perimeters are becoming very difficult to define. This chapter looks at the combination of security devices, policies, and procedures required to secure today's networks.

"Do I Know This Already?" Quiz

The purpose of the "Do I Know This Already?" quiz is to help you decide whether you really need to read the entire chapter. If you already intend to read the entire chapter, you do not necessarily need to answer these questions now.

The eight-question quiz, derived from the major sections in the "Foundation Topics" portion of the chapter, helps you determine how to spend your limited study time.

Table 3-1 outlines the major topics discussed in this chapter and the "Do I Know This Already?" quiz questions that correspond to those topics.

Table 3-1 *"Do I Know This Already?" Foundation Topics Section-to-Question Mapping*

Foundation and Supplemental Topics Section	Questions Covered in This Section
Overview of Defense in Depth	1–8

CAUTION The goal of self-assessment is to gauge your mastery of the topics in this chapter. If you do not know the answer to a question or are only partially sure of the answer, you should mark this question wrong for purposes of the self-assessment. Giving yourself credit for an answer you correctly guess skews your self-assessment results and might provide you with a false sense of security.

1. What is the major concern with having a compromised host on the internal network?
   a. It will make the security administrator look bad.
   b. Data on that host can be copied.
   c. Data on that host can be corrupted.
   d. The host can be used to launch attacks against other hosts on the network.
   e. None of the above.

2. What are some advantages in implementing AAA on the network? (Choose all that apply.)
   a. It limits access to only authorized users.
   b. It allows for single sign-on.
   c. It provides encrypted connections for user access.
   d. It restricts users to only authorized functions.
   e. All of the above.

3. Which devices can be used to segment a network? (Choose all that apply.)
   a. Firewalls
   b. Routers
   c. Switches
   d. Address scheme
   e. All of the above

4. Where does a host-based IDS reside?
   a. At the network layer
   b. At the data link layer
   c. At the presentation layer
   d. As an add-on to the system processor
   e. None of the above

5. What is the advantage of an anomaly-based IDS?
   a. They protect against unknown attacks.
   b. They protect against known attacks.
   c. They can restart a Windows server after a system crash.
   d. They stop and restart services when needed.
   e. They are very cost effective.

6. How does a signature-based IDS determine whether it is under attack?

   a. It compares the traffic to previous traffic.

   b. It compares traffic to predefined signatures.

   c. It correlates logs from numerous devices.

   d. All of the above.

   e. None of the above.

7. Why is it important to monitor system logs?

   a. To determine the state of the network

   b. To determine whether your systems are running properly

   c. To pick a needle from the haystack

   d. To determine whether you are under attack

   e. To determine whether you can figure out what they mean

8. What is the advantage of using correlation and trending?

   a. Most packages print out graphs that you can use for presentations.

   b. They enable you to consolidate log data from multiple sources into a readable format.

   c. They enable you to correlate log data from multiple sources to get a better understanding of the situation.

   d. They enable you to delete traffic that does not apply to your network.

   e. None of the above.

The answers to the "Do I Know This Already?" quiz are found in the appendix. The suggested choices for your next step are as follows:

- **6 or less overall score**—Read the entire chapter. This includes the "Foundation Topics" and "Foundation Summary" sections and the "Q&A" section.

- **7 or 8 overall score**—If you want more review on these topics, skip to the "Foundation Summary" section and then go to the "Q&A" section. Otherwise, move on to the next chapter.

Foundation and Supplemental Topics

Overview of Defense in Depth

The term *internetworking* refers to the task of connecting different networks so they can communicate, share resources, and so on. Many organizations consider their perimeter to be the connection to the Internet; however, with the liberal use of intranet, extranet, and remote user connections, the true perimeter has faded and is difficult to determine. This issue is further complicated by the organizations on the far end of your intranet, extranet, and remote user connections. It is no longer possible to secure your network by just placing security devices (such as firewalls) at the Internet gateway.

Think of the network as a fortress that is under siege. You need to implement multiple layers of defense and try to use different types of defense at each layer. Doing so will enable you to handle a more diverse range of attacks. A common example of this would be an attack that successfully penetrates the firewalls and gets to the targeted server but is terminated by host-based intrusion detection/prevention systems installed on the server. Network attacks are becoming more complex and can now target multiple areas of the network. Table 3-2 describes some of the many targets on a network.

Table 3-2 *Potential Targets*

Target	Description
Routers	The type of attack used against a router depends upon the attacker's intent. An access attack is used if the intent is to gain access to the router or network. A DoS or DDoS is used to bring the router down and deny access to the network.
Firewalls	The attacks against firewalls are virtually the same as routers. The techniques may differ depending on the size and type of firewall being attacked.
Switches	Any attack on a network component will effect how traffic flows across that segment. Because network traffic concentrates at the switches, it is very important to ensure that switches are very secure.
Networks	Traffic flow on the network can be drastically affected by successful attacks against routers, firewalls, and switches.
Hosts	A host can be compromised and used to launch attacks against other network resources. Hosts are often attacked just because the attacker has discovered a vulnerability on that host and wants to exploit that vulnerability.
Applications	An attacker will normally exploit a vulnerability within an application to compromise a host. As technologies advance, the number and type of attacks increase.

Table 3-2 *Potential Targets (Continued)*

Target	Description
Data	Data can be intercepted and manipulated, but the data itself does not have any vulnerabilities. Normally attacks are launched to access specific data. When access is gained, that data may be copied, altered, or destroyed.
Management components	Because management components are used to manage the different network components, it is important to ensure that they are secured to prevent an attacker from gaining control of the entire network.

Components Used for Defense in Depth

The number and combination of different components used to secure today's networks changes continuously as new threats and threat-mitigation techniques arise. The following list identifies some of the many components used for a defense in-depth strategy:

- **Security policy**—An effective security policy is the centerpiece of any organization's security implementation. As described in Chapter 1, "Network Security Essentials," and Chapter 2, "Attack Threats Defined and Detailed," the security policy defines the who, what, when, where, why, and how of every aspect of an organization's operations. Although many aspects are not defined in technical detail, the overall functionality is defined in the policy. All the following elements are merely the implementation of the security policy.

- **Use of authentication, authorization, and accounting (AAA)**—The implementation of AAA helps ensure that only authorized users access resources necessary to perform their job functions. Additionally, accounting and audit logs can be used to determine whether users are performing tasks that expose the network to unnecessary security risks.

- **VPN connectivity**—VPN technology is normally considered to be a cost-saving measure because it allows organizations to interconnect offices across the Internet. The use of VPN technology is not limited to the Internet and is normally determined by the organization, its business function, the type and value of its data, and the perceived threat. Many organizations that maintain very sensitive data use VPN technology to secure dedicated circuits between their offices even though both endpoints are known. The use of VPN technology is a major cost-saving factor for many organizations because it enables them to get rid of expensive dedicated connections and securely interconnect their different offices across public networks. Another significant advantage is the ability to secure connections for remote users. With the increase in the availability of broadband Internet connectivity, many users are able to work from home using an encrypted connection to their corporate network.

48 Chapter 3: Defense in Depth

- **Network segmentation**—A jewelry store owner does not normally leave his most valuable merchandise in an unlocked cabinet in the front of the store. The best way to protect assets is to segregate them by their value and restrict access to specific users, groups, and so on. Network segmentation can be completed with firewalls, routers, and switches by the effective implementation of access lists, VLANs, and address/port translation.

  Assets that require specific access from a specific audience can be grouped together and placed on the same network segments. (For instance, all servers that host websites for public access should reside on a public DMZ segment, should be assigned public address space [non-RFC 1918], and should allow access from the Internet via the standard HTTP ports.) Assets that require limited access should be placed further within the network and can use RFC 1918 addressing to prevent access from the Internet. Access to these assets can be restricted to specific sources and include the use of nonstandard ports by using Network Address Translation (NAT) and Port Address Translation (PAT). Figure 3-1 depicts a simplified version of network segmentation.

Figure 3-1 *Network Segmentation*

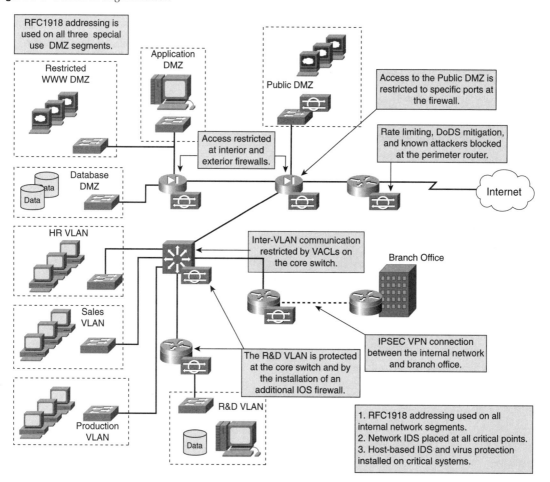

As Figure 3-1 illustrates, all network resources are segregated by type and value. Assets with a greater value to the organization are located further within the network and are, therefore, protected at multiple layers within the network. The use of RFC 1918 addressing on the internal networks prevents attacks that originate from the Internet unless those segments are NAT'd at the network perimeter. Additionally, network intrusion detection systems (IDS) should be implemented liberally at all critical points of the network, and host-based IDS and virus protection should be implemented on *all* hosts.

NOTE This access "from the Internet" does not include known hostile hosts and networks. Known hostile entities are addresses that have performed reconnaissance or other attacks and are identified by firewall and IDS log correlation and trending. These addresses are normally blocked at the perimeter. Chapter 2 discussed motivations of the intruder. Some organizations will identify organizations that have an agenda contrary to their own as "hostile" and either monitor them very closely or block their access altogether.

- **Dynamic perimeter security**—It would not be wise to think that a statically configured firewall or router could protect your network against attacks in an environment that is as dynamic as today's Internet. A statically configured device can only protect against known attacks. Because technology continues to change at such a rapid pace, the challenge is to protect against the unknown. The most effective way to do this is through the effective use of firewalls/routers and IDS. This topic is discussed in greater detail in Chapter 16, "Intrusion Detection and the Cisco IOS Firewall."

- **Host-based defense**—The prelude to any host-based defense is for the host to be as secure as possible. The developers of operating systems and applications produce service packs and patches as soon as a vulnerability has been identified. To limit the number of vulnerabilities that can be exploited by an attacker, it is very important to ensure that all systems are up to the recommended patch level. If an attacker were able to penetrate multiple lines of defense to get to the target host, the attack would still be ineffective if the attacker were unable to access their target. Host-based IDS are installed between the operating system and the kernel and can detect and prevent unauthorized activity on the host system. Additionally, these systems normally generate an alarm to identify that the system is under attack. There are two different types of host-based IDS:

    — **Signature based**—Signature-based IDS watch the system and match instruction sets with the signatures of known attack profiles.

    — **Anomaly based**—Anomaly-based IDS require time to establish a baseline of approved activities. Any instruction that is not part of the approved baseline is considered to be an attack and is blocked. Of course, you can configure the anomaly-based IDS to perform specific functions when it encounters instructions that are not within the baseline instead of just blocking the instruction. The major advantage of anomaly-based IDS is that it enables you to protect against the known and unknown threat.

- **Effective monitoring**—Why do burglar alarms normally include a siren? So people will know that someone is trying to break in. Firewalls, routers, switches, IDS, and virtually every other piece of network equipment produce an incredible amount of log data. It is very important that critical systems are monitored to accurately determine the state of the network.

- **Correlation and trending**—This is the next step in effective monitoring. Correlation and trending enable you to determine what is "normal." By identifying what is normal, you can determine what is not normal and what you need to react to. Additionally, correlation products enable you to correlate data from multiple devices to get a better picture of the situation. This enables you to see the data from a possible attack from many different sources (firewall/router, IDS, and so on).

- **Effective security process**—Remember that the process is the effective implementation of the policy. The process is ongoing and is the driving force behind the constant improvement of your security posture. The security wheel discussed in Chapter 1 depicts how potential threats are identified and mitigated as part of the ongoing evolution of the network. This ongoing process is discussed in Chapter 1 along with the security wheel, that includes four steps:

    Step 1 **Secure**—Secure the network against all known vulnerabilities by implementing equipment, processes, and system configurations.

    Step 2 **Monitor and Respond**—Monitor the network to ensure that the preceding changes have the desired result and respond to any adverse effects or newly discovered issues.

    Step 3 **Test**—Test the network to verify that the components, processes, and configuration changes have secured the network.

    Step 4 **Manage/Improve**—Continue to manage the network and implement improvements as necessary.

The use of defense in depth enables you to move from the old analogy of the network being a chain and only being as strong as the weakest link. Today's networks should function more as vines that are constantly growing and improving. The vines are dynamic and can adapt to changing environments, which is exactly how a secure network should function. All the components of defense in depth are discussed in great detail in the Cisco "SAFE: A Security Blueprint for Enterprise Networks," which can be found at http://www.cisco.com/en/US/netsol/ns110/ns170/ns171/ns128/networking_solutions_package.html.

It is estimated that approximately 70 percent of network attacks originate from within the network. This fact, and the relatively new threat of dynamic attacks, is the driving force behind the concept of multiple layers of defense. It is crucial to ensure that your core networks are adequately protected from all attacks without regard to the source of the attack.

Physical Security

Much of this chapter is dedicated to logically securing your networks and systems. If an attacker is able to gain physical access to your systems, the amount of damage the attack could cause is only limited by the amount of time available. Physical access to facilities and networks should always be restricted to authorized personnel within the organization or personnel who have a business function within the organization.

Foundation Summary

The "Foundation Summary" section of each chapter lists the most important facts from the chapter. Although this section does not list every fact from the chapter that will be on your SECUR exam, a well-prepared candidate should at a minimum know all the details in each "Foundation Summary" before going to take the exam.

In today's very dynamic environment, it is not enough just to secure the network perimeter. With the increasing use of intranets, extranets, remote users, and wireless technology, it is becoming very difficult to determine where the network perimeter is actually located. Attackers now have more potential points of access and a greater selection of tools at their disposal when trying to breach a network. The best possible solution is to implement a defense in-depth concept with multiple layers of defense that each compensates for a possible weakness of another layer. The key to defense in depth is that all components work together; failure of a single component does not necessarily mean that the attack was a success, because the attack can be mitigated at many different points.

Anything on the network, including the network itself, can be considered the target of a potential attack. There are several components that combine to form defense in depth, shown in Table 3-3.

Table 3-3 *Defense In-Depth Components*

Term	Definition
Security policy	The centerpiece of an organization's implementation. Defines everything about who/what is allowed on the network, how systems are to be protected, and who is responsible for which functions. The security policy is a policy document and does not include specific technical information.
Use of AAA	Enables you to ensure that only authorized users access network resources and provides accounting information for trend analysis.
VPN WAN connectivity	Ensures secure connectivity between locations and network segments.
Network segmentation	Enables you to separate resources by asset value and type. Provides for multiple layers of security for resources of greater value. Includes the use of RFC 1918 addressing with NAT/PAT.
Dynamic perimeter security	Dynamic configurations that require the use of firewalls/routers with network-based IDS. This combination allows the perimeter to detect and respond to attacks.
Host-based defense	The last line of defense. In the event that an attacker is able to breach the network and get to his target. the attacker's actions will be terminated by host-based IDS. Anomaly-based IDS can prevent unknown attacks because it reacts to anything that deviates from the allowed baseline.

Table 3-3 *Defense In-Depth Components (Continued)*

Term	Definition
Effective monitoring	It is very important to ensure that you monitor the log output from your various network devices to spot a network attack.
Correlation and trending	Correlation and trending enable you to effectively manage the large amounts of log data that are produced by the many network devices. Additionally, you can correlate the data from different devices (for instance, a firewall and IDS) to get a better picture of the attack.
Effective security process	This is an ongoing process that drives constant improvement, greater accuracy, and a greater understanding of the environment.

Q&A

As mentioned in the section, "How to Use This Book," in the Introduction to this book, you have two choices for review questions. The questions that follow next give you a bigger challenge than the exam itself by using an open-ended question format. By reviewing now with this more difficult question format, you can exercise your memory better and prove your conceptual and factual knowledge of this chapter. The answers to these questions are found in the appendix.

For more practice with exam-like question formats, including questions using a router simulator and multiple choice questions, use the exam engine on the CD-ROM.

1. Define the term *internetworking*.
2. How does the use of RFC 1918 addressing on internal networks help prevent attacks that originate from the Internet?
3. What is a major limitation of a statically configured firewall?
4. What type of IDS uses a system baseline for acceptable behavior?
5. What processes enable you to look at events on the network from different views?
6. What is the goal of the security process?

PART II: Managing Cisco Routers

Chapter 4   Basic Router Management

Chapter 5   Secure Administration

This part of the book addresses the following exam objectives as posted at Cisco.com:

- Secure administrative access for Cisco routers
- Disable unused router services and interfaces

This chapter covers the following subjects:

- Router Configuration Modes
- Accessing the Cisco Router CLI
- IOS Firewall Features

CHAPTER 4

Basic Router Management

The Cisco IOS router and Cisco IOS firewall are actually the same hardware. The difference is a low-cost, advanced firewall feature set that was integrated into Cisco Internet Operating System (Cisco IOS). All the basic functionality of Cisco IOS Software remains on the IOS firewall with additional features added, called the *firewall feature set*. The Cisco IOS router is commonly referred to as the IOS firewall if any of the firewall feature set components are used. This chapter discusses access to and management of the Cisco IOS firewall.

"Do I Know This Already?" Quiz

The purpose of the "Do I Know This Already?" quiz is to help you decide whether you really need to read the entire chapter. If you already intend to read the entire chapter, you do not necessarily need to answer these questions now.

The 10-question quiz, derived from the major sections in the "Foundation Topics" portion of the chapter, helps you determine how to spend your limited study time.

Table 4-1 outlines the major topics discussed in this chapter and the "Do I Know This Already?" quiz questions that correspond to those topics.

Table 4-1 *"Do I Know This Already?" Foundation Topics Section-to-Question Mapping*

Foundation Topics Section	Questions Covered in This Section
Router Configuration Modes	1, 3, 4, 5–8
Accessing the Cisco Router CLI	9, 10
IOS Firewall Features	2

CAUTION The goal of self-assessment is to gauge your mastery of the topics in this chapter. If you do not know the answer to a question or are only partially sure of the answer, you should mark this question wrong for purposes of the self-assessment. Giving yourself credit for an answer you correctly guess skews your self-assessment results and might provide you with a false sense of security.

Chapter 4: Basic Router Management

1. What router configuration mode do you enter by default when connecting to a router?

    a. Console

    b. ROM monitor

    c. User EXEC

    d. Privileged EXEC

    e. None of the above

2. Which IOS firewall feature enables you to inspect traffic at multiple layers of the ISO model?

    a. Multilayer inspection

    b. Context-based access control

    c. Stateful inspection

    d. Extended access control lists

    e. Connection-based access control

3. Which configuration mode is considered the path to the global configuration mode?

    a. User EXEC

    b. Line configuration

    c. Interface configuration

    d. Subinterface configuration

    e. None of the above

4. What configuration mode are you in when you see the following prompt on RouterA?
   RouterA%

    a. User EXEC

    b. Global configuration

    c. Privileged EXEC

    d. Unable to determine because the prompt has been changed

    e. None of the above

5. What configuration mode must you be in to configure telnet access?

  a. Line configuration
  b. Interface configuration
  c. Telnet configuration
  d. Global configuration
  e. Connection configuration
  f. None of the above

6. What is the default symbol for the global configuration mode?

  a. hostname#
  b. hostname(config)%
  c. router(config)>
  d. hostname (global)>
  e. hostname(config)#

7. What command do you use to exit the privileged EXEC mode?

  a. **Ctrl-Z**
  b. **disable**
  c. **enable**
  d. **exit**
  e. **end**

8. What are you most likely doing in the subinterface configuration mode?

  a. Changing the telnet password
  b. Binding additional IP addresses to an interface
  c. Changing the system password
  d. Configuring system monitoring
  e. Adding the default gateway

9. What access port would you use when connecting a modem?

   a. Console port

   b. Telnet port

   c. Dialup port

   d. Secure Shell

   e. Auxiliary port

10. What clear-text protocol is not recommended for managing routers from external network segments?

    a. Telnet

    b. Secure Shell

    c. RSH

    d. SNMP

    e. SMTP

The answers to the "Do I Know This Already?" quiz are found in the appendix. The suggested choices for your next step are as follows:

- **8 or less overall score**—Read the entire chapter. This includes the "Foundation Topics" and "Foundation Summary" sections and the "Q&A" section.

- **9 or 10 overall score**—If you want more review on these topics, skip to the "Foundation Summary" section and then go to the "Q&A" section. Otherwise, move on to the next chapter.

Foundation Topics

Router Configuration Modes

Before jumping into the command-line interface (CLI) of the Cisco router, it is important to understand the different command modes available. Consider the command mode to be a level where you are able to perform specific functions. If you are not at the correct level, you cannot perform the correct function (to configure the router). This is a very simplified explanation but will make more sense as each mode is discussed. The following are command modes on a Cisco router:

- **ROM monitor mode**—The ROM monitor mode is the mode the router boots to if it cannot find a valid system image. You only need to use this mode if you need to change the system boot parameters to include resetting the system password. If the router has a working image installed, you need to press the Break key during the first 60 seconds of the router boot sequence.

- **User EXEC mode**—The user EXEC mode is the mode that you connect to by default. If the router is configured with a password, you are prompted for the password and given three attempts to provide the correct password. You will know that you are in the user EXEC mode because the router displays the host name followed by a right-angle bracket (>) symbol.

    ```
    RouterA>
    ```

    In the user EXEC mode, you can perform limited functions to check the status of the router but cannot change the router configuration. To exit the user EXEC mode, use the command **logout**.

- **Privileged EXEC mode**—To get from the user EXEC mode to privileged EXEC mode, use the **enable** command. If an enable password (or better yet, enable secret password) has been configured (and it should have), you are again prompted for a password and given three attempts. In this mode, the router displays its host name followed by the hash (#) symbol.

    ```
    RouterA> enable
    RouterA#
    ```

    In the privileged EXEC mode, you can perform all the functions that were available in the user EXEC mode but still cannot make any configuration changes. You do, however, have access to **show** and **debug** commands that are not available in the user EXEC mode. The privileged EXEC mode is the path to the global configuration mode. To return to the user EXEC mode, use the command **disable**.

    ```
    RouterA# disable
    RouterA>
    ```

- **Configuration modes and submodes**—There are many different configuration modes. Each of these makes changes to the device configuration. To ensure that those configuration changes are not lost if the router reboots, you must copy the running configuration to the startup configuration. The type and number of configuration submodes depends on the type of router, the IOS version, and the components installed on the router.
  - **Global configuration mode**—The command for accessing the global configuration mode is **configure terminal**. In the global configuration mode, the router continues to display its host name followed by (config) and the # symbol.

    ```
    RouterA# configure terminal
    RouterA(config)#
    ```

    The global configuration mode is where you can make "global" changes to the configuration of the router. A very common example of a global configuration is the creation of an access list. From the global configuration mode, you can move to a position that enables you to configure specific components of the router, such as the router interfaces, VPN components (isakmp, crypto, and so on), CLI connections (line), AAA server groups, and many more. To exit to the privileged global configuration mode, use the key combination **Ctrl-Z** or type the command **end**.

    ```
    RouterA(config)# end
    RouterA#
    ```

  - **Interface configuration mode**—From the global configuration mode, the command for accessing the interface configuration submode is **interface** *interface-type interface-number*. The router displays its host name followed by (config-if) indicating that it is in the interface configuration mode.

    ```
    RouterA(config)# interface Ethernet 0
    RouterA(config-if)#
    ```

    At this point, you are ready to configure the interface that you have selected. If you are configuring subinterfaces, you need to use the same command to enter the subinterface configuration mode.

    ```
    RouterA(config)# interface Ethernet 0.1
    RouterA(config-subif)#
    ```

    It is also possible to enter the subinterface configuration mode from the interface configuration mode due to a backward command link.

    ```
    RouterA(config-if)# interface Ethernet 0.1
    RouterA(config-subif)#
    ```

— **Line configuration mode**—Another configuration submode that must be configured is the line configuration. This is the mode used to configure the CLI access to the router. The command for accessing the line configuration mode from the global configuration mode is **line** *type number*.

```
RouterA(config)# line con 0
RouterA(config-line)#
```

To exit the configuration mode and return to the privileged EXEC mode, use the key combination **Ctrl-Z** or type the command **end**.

```
RouterA(config-subif)# end
RouterA#
```

To return to the global configuration mode, type the command **exit**. (This command works for both interface configuration and subinterface configuration modes.)

```
RouterA(config-subif)# exit
RouterA(config)#
```

> **NOTE** The command prompts used in these examples are the default prompts. It is possible to change the system prompt (>, #) by using the **prompt** command while in the global configuration mode.

For a list of the available commands in each configuration, you can use the question mark (**?**). This is perhaps the most useful command written into the Cisco IOS Software. In the event that you are not completely familiar with the correct syntax of a command, it is possible to input a portion of the command followed by **?**. The router then provides you with the correct syntax. Table 4-2 shows how to navigate between modes when configuring the router.

Table 4-2 *Configuration Modes on the Cisco Router*

Command	Description
`Router> enable` `Password: ********`	Enter the router in the user EXEC mode. Use the **enable** command and the correct password to enter the privileged EXEC mode.
`Router# configure terminal`	Enter the global configuration mode.
`Router# (config) ip routing`	Enable IP routing on the router.
`Router# (config) hostname RouterA`	Configure the router host name to RouterA.

continues

Table 4-2 *Configuration Modes on the Cisco Router (Continued)*

Command	Description
`RouterA# (config) interface Ethernet 0/0`	Enter the interface configuration mode.
`RouterA# (config) ip address 10.10.10.254 255.255.255.0`	Configure eth0/0 for 10.10.10.254/24.
`RouterA# (config) no shutdown`	The **no shutdown** command ensures that the interface is enabled.
`RouterA# (config) exit`	Configuration complete, exit to global configuration mode.

`RouterA# (config) end`
 	
or
 	
`RouterA# (config) Ctrl-Z`
	Configuration complete, exit to privileged EXEC mode.

NOTE Some commands change depending upon the router series and Cisco IOS Software version.

Accessing the Cisco Router CLI

You can access the Cisco router CLI via any of three methods:

- **Console**—The console connection requires a direct connection to the console port of the router using a rollover cable normally from the serial interface of a computer. This is considered to be the most secure method for administration of the router because it requires a physical connection to the router. This method can be very impractical for enterprise networks.
- **Auxiliary**—The auxiliary connection is normally a remote dialup connection completed by connecting a modem to the aux port of the router. The administrator just dials in to the attached modem to initiate the connection to the modem. This method is commonly used for administering large networks or as a backup method to telnet.
- **Telnet**—The telnet connection occurs via the network interface. Telnet connections can be completed using telnet or Secure Shell (SSH). Telnet is a clear-text protocol and should be restricted to internal (protected) network segments only. SSH is a protocol that uses encryption and can be used for remote management across public networks. This is the most common method for remote administration because it allows for administration of an entire enterprise from a central location. Additional steps are required to configure the router to accept SSH connections:

— **Enable the SSH server**—To enable the SSH server on the router, you must enter the global configuration mode and configure the domain name for the device. The domain name is important because it is used when generating the SSH key, which is used to authenticate the router when making the connection.

```
RouterA(config)# ip domain-name secur-example.com
```

Next you should use the **crypto key generate rsa** command followed by the key length.

— **Configure the SSH parameters on the router**—The optional command **ip ssh** {[**timeout** *seconds*]|[**authentication-retries** *interger*]} enables you to configure the authentication *parameters* for the SSH connection to the router. It tells the router how long to wait for a response from the client and how many attempts to allow before terminating the connection.

— If you want to restrict the router to only SSH connections, you must add the command **transport input ssh** from the global configuration mode.

The implementation of SSH is discussed in greater detail in Chapter 5 "Secure Router Administration."

NOTE SSH requires IOS versions that support DES (56 bit) or 3DES (168 bit) encryption.

Figure 4-1 depicts the CLI connections to a Cisco 2600 series router.

Figure 4-1 *CLI Connections to a 2600 Router*

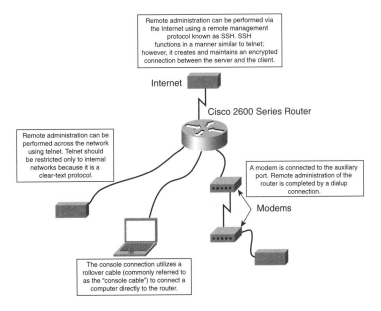

Configuring CLI Access

A new router is delivered without passwords. You must configure passwords for the access method that you intend to use and disable the methods that you do not intend to use. There are different ways to complete the initial configuration of a router. The autoinstall feature installs a configuration on the router that is sufficient to get the router on the network and allow telnet connections to complete the configuration. The other configuration methods usually require a physical connection to the router using a console cable. After connecting with the router, you need to enter the line configuration mode and to configure the CLI access. After connecting to the router, you must configure the passwords for each type of connection. It is a good idea to configure a different password for each connection type.

Example 4-1 shows the configuration of RouterA for a console connection using the password N3wY0rk$$.

Example 4-1 *Configuring the Console Password*

```
RouterA> enable
RouterA# configure terminal
RouterA(config)# line con 0
RouterA(config-line)# login
RouterA(config-line)# password N3wY0rk$$
RouterA(config-line)# end
RouterA#
```

Example 4-2 shows the configuration of RouterA for an auxiliary connection using the password B0stoN&!.

Example 4-2 *Configuring the Auxiliary Password*

```
RouterA> enable
RouterA# configure terminal
RouterA(config)# line aux 0
RouterA(config-line)# login
RouterA(config-line)# password B0stoN&!
RouterA(config-line)# end
RouterA#
```

Example 4-3 shows the configuration of RouterA for a telnet or virtual terminal (vty) connection using the password Ch1cag0!. Remember that you can use SSH to complete a telnet connection as long as the SSH server has been enabled on the router.

Example 4-3 *Configuring the vty Password*

```
RouterA> enable
RouterA# configure terminal
RouterA(config)# line vty 0 4
RouterA(config-line)# login
RouterA(config-line)# password Ch1cag0!
RouterA(config-line)# exit
RouterA(config)# transport input ssh      << This is an optional command to disallow telnet
  and only permit SSH connections
RouterA(config)# end
RouterA#
```

Cisco IOS Firewall Features

As mentioned in the beginning of this chapter, the Cisco IOS firewall feature is an enhancement to the Cisco IOS Software that incorporates additional security-related features. The Cisco IOS firewall provides an additional level of security for the network without the expense of purchasing dedicated hardware. The Cisco IOS firewall feature set was first introduced as *CiscoSecure Integrated Software* (CSIS). The Cisco IOS firewall overview lists the following features:

- **Standard and extended access lists**—The router can be configured to perform basic traffic filtering by using standard or extended access lists.

- **Dynamic access lists**—Dynamic access lists are used to configure lock-and-key traffic filtering. This is the capability to generate dynamic temporary access through the firewall for specific predefined circumstances. This feature provides a more flexible method for filtering network access.

- **Reflexive access lists**—Reflexive access lists only allow specific traffic to maintain state. In other words, traffic that is generated on an internal network is allowed through the firewall only until the initial session state has terminated. Reflexive access lists are used only if context-based access control (CBAC) is not implemented.

- **System auditing**—The firewall maintains a record of all transactions in an orderly format that can be used for detailed reports.

- **TCP intercept**—TCP intercept is used to prevent a type of denial-of-service (DoS) attack known as the TCP SYN flood. This feature is used only if CBAC is not implemented.

- **Java blocking**—The firewall scans Java code and can block code that is unsigned or determined to be malicious.

- **Context-based access control**—CBAC examines traffic passing through the firewall at all layers (up to the application layer). CBAC is used to generate dynamic access lists.

- **Cisco IOS firewall IDS**—The Cisco IOS firewall IDS is a signature-based IDS that can be configured to take the following actions when an intrusion is detected:
  - Send an alarm to the director
  - Drop the packet
  - Send a TCP reset
- **DoS mitigation**—The system is designed to detect and react to DoS attacks.
- **Authentication proxy**—Authentication proxy is used to proxy authentication requests to a AAA server. This allows authentication to occur on a per-user basis.
- **Port-to-application mapping (PAM)**—PAM enables administrators to specify which ports can be used for which services. This allows for the configuration of services on nonstandard ports when traversing the firewall.
- **Security server support**—The Cisco IOS firewall supports the following AAA servers:
  - TACACS+
  - RADIUS
  - Kerberos
- **Network Address Translation (NAT)**—The Cisco IOS firewall supports NAT and Port Address Translation (PAT). NAT enables administrators to translate RFC 1918 addressing to public addressing on a one-for-one basis, and PAT enables administrators to hide an entire internal network behind a single public address. The Cisco IOS firewall supports the use of both NAT and PAT on the same device.
- **IPSec network security**—The Cisco IOS firewall supports all the standard IPSec protocols. This allows for the configuration of VPNs.
- **Neighbor router authentication**—The Cisco IOS firewall can authenticate its peer routers to ensure that all routing updates are legitimate.
- **Event logging**—The Cisco IOS firewall logs all error messages and system events to the console terminal by default. These messages can be redirected to a syslog server for easy storage and recovery. The system logs are commonly used for troubleshooting connection issues and for network forensics.
- **User authentication and authorization**—Integration with AAA servers allows for authentication and authorization on a per-user basis. This functionality enables administrators to designate specific permissions for users and groups.
- **Real-time alerts**—The firewall can be configured to perform alert functions in the event of a known attack or other event that is determined to be a severe security risk.

Foundation Summary

The "Foundation Summary" section of each chapter lists the most important facts from the chapter. Although this section does not list every fact from the chapter that will be on your SECUR exam, a well-prepared candidate should at a minimum know all the details in each "Foundation Summary" before going to take the exam.

Router Configuration Modes

Table 4-3 lists the configuration modes of the Cisco router along with a brief description. It is important to understand that except for the ROM monitor mode you must navigate from one mode to another to view and edit different components of the router configuration.

> **NOTE** The terms *specific configuration mode* and *very specific configuration mode* in Table 4-3 are not actual Cisco terms but are used to describe how the configuration of each component becomes more granular on the router.

Table 4-3 *Router Configuration Modes*

Configuration Mode	Description
ROM monitor	The ROM monitor mode is used to change the system boot configuration only.
User EXEC	The user EXEC mode is the mode entered by default. It is possible to view the general condition of the router in this mode.
Privileged EXEC	The privileged EXEC mode is entered by using the **enable** command. It is possible to view much of the router configuration but changes cannot be made.
Global configuration	General configuration changes are made in the global configuration mode. The command **configure terminal** is used to enter this mode.

continues

Table 4-3 *Router Configuration Modes (Continued)*

Configuration Mode	Description
Specific configuration	Multiple specific items must be configured, each in its own configuration mode. Examples of specific configuration items include but are not limited to the following: 1. Router interfaces 2. Line configuration 3. Crypto map 4. ISAKMP policy 5. Modem pool For a list of specific configuration modes available, just enter the **?** when in the global configuration mode.
Very specific configuration	Some configuration items require even more specific configuration. A common example is the subinterface configuration mode, which is used to bind additional virtual interfaces to a single physical interface.

Accessing the Cisco Router CLI

Table 4-4 describes the three connection methods used for management of the router and the command used to enter the line configuration mode to configure each access method.

Table 4-4 *CLI Connection Methods*

Connection Method	Connection Type	Command
Console port	Direct connection from a computer to the router using a console cable.	**line con 0**
Auxiliary port	Dialup connection. The receiving modem is connected to the router auxiliary port.	**line aux 0**
Telnet	Connection across the network, accessing the router via the network interface.	**line vty 0 4**

Cisco IOS Firewall Features

Table 4-4 lists the features that differentiate the Cisco router from the Cisco IOS firewall. It is important to note that all of these features are software based and are available in the current version of Cisco IOS Software.

Table 4-5 *IOS Firewall Features*

Feature	Explanation
Standard and extended access lists	Standard and extended access lists are used for static filtering of traffic passing through the firewall.
Dynamic access lists	Dynamic access lists are used to temporarily open ports to allow specific traffic through the firewall. These ports are closed as soon as the session is completed.
Reflexive access lists	Reflexive access lists only allow access as long as the connection state remains active. Reflexive access lists cannot be used in conjunction with CBAC.
System auditing	The Cisco IOS firewall maintains an audit log of all changes made to the router.
TCP intercept	TCP intercept is used to prevent a SYN flood attack. It cannot be used in conjunction with CBAC.
Java blocking	The Cisco IOS firewall can detect and block malicious Java code.
Context-based access control	CBAC inspects traffic up to the application layer and can affect the traffic based on the configured policy.
Cisco IOS firewall IDS	Cisco IOS firewall IDS compares traffic to predefined attack signatures to detect and react to malicious traffic. The firewall IDS can react in any of the following manners: • Send an alert • Drop the packet • Reset the connection
DoS mitigation	The Cisco IOS firewall can detect and react to potential DoS attacks.
Authentication proxy	Authentication proxy is used to proxy authentication requests to a AAA server. This allows for per-user or per-group policies.
Port-to-application mapping (PAM)	Port-to-application mapping enables administrators to configure applications to pass through the firewall using nonstandard ports.
Security server support	The Cisco IOS firewall supports the following AAA servers: • TACACS+ • RADIUS • Kerberos
Network Address Translation (NAT)	The Cisco IOS firewall can translate source and destination addresses. This allows for the use of RFC 1918 addresses on internal and DMZ segments, greatly reducing the attacker's ability to route attacks across public networks.

continues

Table 4-5 *IOS Firewall Features (Continued)*

Feature	Explanation
IPSec network security	The Cisco IOS firewall supports IPSec standards and can be used to configure VPNs.
Neighbor router authentication	Neighbor router authentication is used to ensure that the Cisco IOS firewall receives updated routing information from only authenticated sources.
Event logging	The Cisco IOS firewall can be configured to log all traffic that passes through it. The firewall logs can be very helpful for troubleshooting and network forensics.
User authentication and authorization	Authentication and authorization allow for the configuration of per-user and per-group policies.
Real-time alerts	The Cisco IOS firewall can generate alerts in real time. This greatly increases the ability to react to an attempted attack.

Q&A

As mentioned in the section, "How to Use This Book," in the Introduction to this book, you have two choices for review questions. The questions that follow next give you a bigger challenge than the exam itself by using an open-ended question format. By reviewing now with this more difficult question format, you can exercise your memory better and prove your conceptual and factual knowledge of this chapter. The answers to these questions are found in the appendix.

For more practice with exam-like question formats, including questions using a router simulator and multiple choice questions, use the exam engine on the CD-ROM.

1. You have just started work at a new facility and need to configure an old unused router. Unfortunately you cannot find the current password for the router. What router configuration mode would you need to enter to change the password?

2. Place the following configuration modes in the correct order:

    a. Privilege EXEC

    b. Global configuration

    c. User EXEC

    d. Subinterface configuration

    e. Interface configuration

3. What is the best way to ensure that your configuration changes are not lost if the router is rebooted?

4. If it has not been changed using the **prompt** command, what will the prompt for RouterA look like in the global configuration mode?

5. What is the difference between the **end** and **exit** commands?

6. What command enables you to see the available commands in your current configuration mode?

7. How do you configure CBAC to implement reflexive access lists?

8. What type of cable is required to complete a telnet connection to the router via Ethernet 0/0 interface.

9. What type of router management is considered to be the most secure, yet the most difficult to use for enterprise networks? (Explain your answer.)

10. What command generates the key used for SSH on the IOS router?

11. What Cisco IOS firewall feature enables administrators to configure access to services on nonstandard ports?

12. What AAA server types can interact with the IOS firewall?

13. How does the Cisco IOS firewall ensure that routing updates are valid?

This chapter covers the following subjects:

- Privilege Levels
- Securing Console Access
- Configuring the Enable Password
- The **service password-encryption** Command
- Configuring Multiple Privilege Levels
- Warning Banners
- Interactive Access
- Securing vty Access
- Secure Shell (SSH) Protocol
- Port Security for Ethernet Switches

CHAPTER 5

Secure Router Administration

The Cisco IOS firewall helps secure the trusted network from unauthorized users. The security of the network also involves the security of the Cisco IOS firewall itself. In addition to physical security of the Cisco IOS firewall, it is important to secure administrative accesses to interfaces on the Cisco IOS firewall. This chapter discusses the different methods that are available in securing the administrative access to the Cisco IOS firewall.

"Do I Know This Already?" Quiz

The purpose of the "Do I Know This Already?" quiz is to help you decide whether you really need to read the entire chapter. If you already intend to read the entire chapter, you do not necessarily need to answer these questions now.

The 10-question quiz, derived from the major sections in "Foundation Topics" section of the chapter, helps you determine how to spend your limited study time.

Table 5-1 outlines the major topics discussed in this chapter and the "Do I Know This Already?" quiz questions that correspond to those topics.

Table 5-1 *"Do I Know This Already?" Foundation Topics Section-to-Question Mapping*

Foundation Topics Section	Questions Covered in This Section
Secure Administrative Access for Cisco Routers	1–10

CAUTION The goal of self-assessment is to gauge your mastery of the topics in this chapter. If you do not know the answer to a question or are only partially sure of the answer, you should mark this question wrong for purposes of the self-assessment. Giving yourself credit for an answer you correctly guess skews your self-assessment results and might provide you with a false sense of security.

Chapter 5: Secure Router Administration

1. What are some of the steps that can be taken to secure the console interface on a router or switch device?

   a. Administratively shut down the console interface.

   b. Physically secure the device.

   c. Apply an access list using the **access-class** command.

   d. Configure a console password.

2. How many characters can you have in an enable password?

   a. 256

   b. 32

   c. 25

   d. 12

3. Which of the following is the least restrictive privilege level?

   a. 0

   b. 22

   c. 15

   d. 17

4. The **service password-encryption** command does which of the following?

   a. Encrypts the configuration on the router

   b. Stores passwords in an encrypted manner in the router configuration

   c. Only encrypts the telnet password in the Cisco IOS configuration

   d. Is only available on PIX Firewall

5. Which of the following choices has the correct configuration for encrypting the enable password?

   a. Router(config)#**enable secret gr3twhite**

   b. Router#**enable encryption gr3twhite**

   c. Router#**enable secret gr3twhite**

   d. Router#(config)**enable encryption t gr3twhite**

6. Which of the following commands are associated with privilege level 0?

   a. disable
   b. configure terminal
   c. enable
   d. logout

7. Which of the following configurations displays a login banner when a router is accessed?

   a. Router# **banner exec** *d If you are not an authorized user disconnect immediately message d*
   b. Router(config)# **banner login** *d If you are not an authorized user disconnect immediately d*
   c. Router(config)#**banner exec** *d If you are not an authorized user disconnect immediately d*
   d. Router# **banner login** *d If you are not an authorized user disconnect immediately d*

8. For maintaining confidentiality and integrity in accessing a router, _____ is recommended over telnet.

   a. SSH
   b. AH
   c. Secure telnet
   d. VPN

9. How do you secure the Ethernet port on a switch? (Select two.)

   a. Disable unused ports.
   b. Configure port security.
   c. Set access list.
   d. Security cannot be configured on the port.

10. In the event of a security violation, what is the default response of the port?

    a. Switches into restrictive mode
    b. Switches into a temporary shutdown mode
    c. Switches into permanent shutdown mode
    d. Switches into a temporary restrictive mode

The answers to the "Do I Know This Already?" quiz are found in the appendix. The suggested choices for your next step are as follows:

- **8 or less overall score**—Read the entire chapter. This includes the "Foundation Topics" and "Foundation Summary" sections and the "Q&A" section.

- **9 or 10 overall score**—If you want more review on these topics, skip to the "Foundation Summary" section and then go to the "Q&A" section. Otherwise, move on to the next chapter.

Foundation Topics

One of the important elements to securing the network is preventing unauthorized users from gaining access to router and switch administrative access interfaces. If an intruder were to gain console or terminal access into a networking device, such as a router, switch, or network access server, that person could do significant damage to your network—perhaps by reconfiguring the device, or even by just viewing the device's configuration information.

Typically, you want administrators to have access to your networking device; you do not want other users on your LAN or those dialing in to the network to have administrative access to the router.

Steps can be taken to securely configure your administrative access to your network devices. Password protection enables you to restrict access to a network or a network device. Privilege levels enable you to define what commands users can issue after they have logged in to a network device.

Privilege Levels

By default, the Cisco IOS Software command-line interface (CLI) has two levels of access to commands:

- User EXEC mode (level 1)
- Privileged EXEC mode (level 15)

However, you can configure additional levels of access to commands, called *privilege levels*, to meet the needs of your users while protecting the system from unauthorized access. Up to 16 privilege levels can be configured, from level 0, which is the most restricted level, to level 15, which is the least restricted level.

Access to each privilege level is enabled through separate passwords, which you specify when configuring the privilege level. If you want a certain set of users to be able to configure only certain interfaces, but not allow them access to other configuration options, for instance, you could create a separate privilege level for only specific interface configuration commands and distribute the password for that level to those users.

Securing Console Access

The console administrative interface is primarily accessed by attaching a terminal (for instance, a laptop) directly to a router. Physical security has to be put in place for the router to prevent unauthorized users from gaining access to routers the console interface. You also have to configure the router to require a password when users try to access it via the console port. The router or switch can authenticate users locally or via a remote security database such as Cisco Secure Access Control Server (CSACS).

The console password can have from 1 to 25 uppercase and lowercase alphanumeric characters. Example 5-1 shows the configuration of a console password for a router.

Example 5-1 *Simple Console Interface Configuration for a Router*

```
Router(config)#line console 0
Router(config-line)#login
Router(config-line)#password Mer0n!
```

After you enter the password for the console interface you will be in EXEC mode with the greater than sign (>) after the router name, as shown in Example 5-2.

Example 5-2 *Accessing the EXEC Mode*

```
User access Verification
Password:Mer0n!
Router>
```

However, you cannot make configuration changes to the router unless you are in the privilege mode. The privilege mode is accessed by typing in the **enable** command and the enable password if one is configured.

Configuring the Enable Password

To set a local password to control access to various privilege levels, use the enable password command in global configuration mode.

```
enable password [level level] {password | [encryption-type] encrypted-password}
```

Table 5-2 shows the different options that the **enable** command has.

Table 5-2 **enable** *Command Options*

level level	Level for which the password applies. You can specify up to 15 privilege levels, using numbers 1 through 15. This is an optional parameter that provides not only authentication but also authorization.
password	Password users type this to enter enable mode.
encryption-type	Cisco-proprietary algorithm used to encrypt the password. Currently the only encryption type available is 7.
encrypted-password	Encrypted password you enter.

(This table has been reproduced by Cisco Press with the permission of Cisco Systems Inc. Copyright © 2003 Cisco Systems, Inc. All Rights Reserved.)

The use of the privilege level in the **enable** command helps administrators/managers better manage user access to the routers. After you specify the level and the password, give the password to the users who need to access this level. Use the **privilege level** configuration command to specify commands accessible at various levels.

You will not ordinarily enter an encryption type. Typically you enter an encryption type only if you copy and paste into this command a password that has already been encrypted by a Cisco router.

CAUTION   If you specify an encryption type and then enter a clear-text password, you will not be able to reenter enable mode. You cannot recover a lost password that has been encrypted by any method. However, you can enter the router in ROMMON mode. Use **configreg 0x2142** (depending on the router) and change the enable password but do not recover the old password.

You can enable or disable password encryption with the **service password-encryption** command.

An enable password is defined as follows:

- It must contain from 1 to 25 uppercase and lowercase alphanumeric characters.
- It must not have a number as the first character.
- It can have leading spaces, but they are ignored. However, intermediate and trailing spaces are recognized.
- It can contain the question mark (?) character if you precede the question mark with the key combination Crtl-V when you create the password; for example, to create the password gen?X, do the following:

Step 1   Enter **gen**.

Step 2   Press **Crtl-V**.

Step 3   Enter **?X**.

When the system prompts you to enter the enable password, you need not precede the question mark with the Ctrl-V; you can just enter **gen?X** at the password prompt. The following example enables the password Mer0n for privilege level 4:

```
enable password level 4 Mer0n
```

enable secret

The **enable secret** command provides better security by storing the enable secret password using a nonreversible cryptographic function. The added layer of security encryption provides proves useful in environments where the password crosses the network or is stored on a TFTP server.

```
enable secret [level level] {password | [encryption-type] encrypted-password}
```

You will not ordinarily enter an encryption type. Typically you enter an encryption type only if you paste into this command an encrypted password that you copied from a router configuration file.

If you use the same password for the **enable password** and **enable secret** commands, you receive an error message warning that this practice is not recommended, but the password is accepted. By using the same password, however, you undermine the additional security the **enable secret** command provides.

> **NOTE** After you set a password using the **enable secret** command, a password set using the **enable password** command works only if the enable secret is disabled or an older version of Cisco IOS Software is being used, such as when running an older rxboot image. In addition, you cannot recover a lost password that has been encrypted.

An enable password is defined as follows:

- It must contain from 1 to 25 uppercase and lowercase alphanumeric characters
- It must not have a number as the first character.
- It can have leading spaces, but they are ignored. However, intermediate and trailing spaces are recognized.
- It can contain the question mark (?) character if you precede the question mark with the key combination Crtl-V when you create the password.

Example 5-3 specifies the enable secret password of ladyhawk

Example 5-3 *Enable Secret Password Configuration*

```
Router(config)#enable secret ladyhawk
```

After you specify an enable secret password, users must enter this password to gain access. Any passwords set through enable password will no longer work.

In addition to the enable secret password, the **username secret** command provides an additional layer of security over the username password. It also provides better security by encrypting the password using nonreversible Message Digest 5 (MD5) encryption and storing the encrypted text. The added layer of MD5 encryption proves useful in environments in which the password crosses the network or is stored on a TFTP server. This command was introduced in Cisco IOS Software Release 12.0(18)S. The syntax to encrypt a user password with MD5 is as follows:

```
username name secret {[0] password | 5 encrypted-secret}
```

Example 5-4 illustrates the use of the **username secret** command

Example 5-4 *The* **username secret** *Command*

```
Router(config)# username Aida secret 0 ysf600
```

service password-encryption

The **service password-encryption** command stores passwords in an encrypted manner in router configuration.

```
Router(config)#service password-encryption
```

The actual encryption process occurs when the current configuration is written or when a password is configured. Password encryption is applied to all passwords, including username passwords, authentication key passwords, the privileged command password, console and virtual terminal line access passwords, and BGP neighbor passwords. This command is primarily useful for keeping unauthorized individuals from viewing your password in your configuration file and it does not provide the highest level of network security. When password encryption is enabled, the encrypted form of the passwords is displayed.

Configuring Multiple Privilege Levels

To configure a new privilege level for users and associate commands with a privilege level, use the **privilege** command syntax as follows:

```
privilege mode [all] {level level | reset} command-string
```

Table 5-3 shows the different options that the privilege command provides.

Table 5-3 **privilege** *Command Options*

Option	Description
all	(Optional) Changes the privilege level for all the suboptions to the same level.
level *level*	Specifies the privilege level you are configuring for the specified command or commands. The level argument must be a number from 0 to 15.
reset *command-string*	Resets the privilege level of the specified command or commands to the default and removes the privilege level configuration from the running-config file.

The password for a privilege level defined using the **privilege** command is configured using the **enable secret** command.

Level 0 can be used to specify a more-limited subset of commands for specific users or lines. For example, you can allow user user1 to use only the **show users** and **exit** commands

> **NOTE** Five commands are associated with privilege level 0: **disable**, **enable**, **exit**, **help**, and **logout**. If you configure AAA authorization for a privilege level greater than 0, these five commands are not included.

When you set the privilege level for a command with multiple words, note that the commands starting with the first word will also have the specified access level. If you set the **show ip route** command to level 15, for example, the **show** commands and **show ip** commands are automatically set to privilege level 15—unless you set them individually to different levels. This is necessary because you can't execute, for instance, the **show ip** command unless you have access to **show** commands.

To change the privilege level of a group of commands, use the **all** keyword. When you set a group of commands to a privilege level using the **all** keyword, all commands that match the beginning string are enabled for that level, and all commands that are available in submodes of that command are enabled for that level. If you set the **show ip** keywords to level 5, for example, **show** and **ip** are changed to level 5 and all the options that follow the **show ip** string (such as **show ip accounting**, **show ip aliases**, **show ip bgp**, and so on) are available at privilege level 5.

Example 5-5 shows how to set axsforL14 as the password users must enter to use level 14 commands.

Example 5-5 *Sample Configuration Showing Different Passwords Set for Different Privilege Levels*

```
enable secret level 14 axsforL14
```

Example 5-6 shows how to set the **show** and **ip** keywords to level 6. The suboptions coming under **ip** are also allowed to users with privilege level 6 access.

Example 5-6 *Assignment of the Command* **show ip** *with the Privilege Level 6*

```
Router(config)# privilege exec all level 6 show ip
```

Warning Banners

In some jurisdictions, civil and criminal prosecution of crackers who break into your systems is made much easier if you provide a banner informing unauthorized users that their use is in fact unauthorized. In other jurisdictions, you may be forbidden to monitor the activities of even unauthorized users unless you have taken steps to notify them of your intent to do so. One way to provide this notification is to put it into a banner message configured with the Cisco IOS **banner login** command.

Legal notification requirements are complex and vary in each jurisdiction and situation. Even within jurisdictions, legal opinions vary, and this issue should be discussed with your own legal counsel. In cooperation with counsel, consider which of the following information should be put into your banner:

- A notice that the system is to be logged in to or used only by specifically authorized personnel, and perhaps information about who may authorize use.
- A notice that any unauthorized use of the system is unlawful and may be subject to civil and criminal penalties.
- A notice that any use of the system may be logged or monitored without further notice, and that the resulting logs may be used as evidence in court.
- Specific notices required by specific local laws.

From a security, rather than a legal, point of view, your login banner usually should not contain any specific information about your router, its name, its model, what software it's running, or who owns it; such information may be abused by crackers.

The banner messages can be displayed when a user enters privileged EXEC mode, upon line activation, on an incoming connection to a virtual terminal, or as a message of the day. To create a banner message, use the following command:

```
banner {exec | incoming | login | motd} d message d
```

Table 5-4 shows the different command options of the banner command.

Table 5-4 banner *Command Options*

Command Syntax	Description
exec	Specifies a messages to be displayed when an EXEC process is created.
incoming	Specifies a banner displayed when an incoming connection to a line (asynchronous) from a host on the network is made.
login	Identifies a message to be displayed during a login before the username and password login prompts.
motd	Specifies the display of the message of the day (MOTD) banner. This banner is displayed at the login and is useful for sending messages that affect all network users.
d	You must use a delimiting character of your choice, such as a pound sign (#). You cannot use the delimiting character in the banner message.
message	The actual message text.

Interactive Access

Besides those already discussed, there are additional ways to get interactive connections to routers. Cisco IOS Software, depending on the configuration and software version, may support connections via telnet; rlogin; SSH; non-IP–based network protocols such as LAT, MOP, X.29, and V.120 and possibly other protocols as well as via local asynchronous connections and modem dial-ins. More protocols for interactive access are always being added. Interactive telnet access is available not only on the standard telnet TCP port (port 23) but on a variety of higher-numbered ports as well.

All interactive access mechanisms use the IOS TTY abstraction (in other words, they all involve sessions on "lines" of one sort or another). Local asynchronous terminals and dialup modems use standard lines, known as *TTYs*. Remote network connections, regardless of the protocol, use virtual TTYs, or *vtys*. The best way to protect a system is to make certain that appropriate controls are applied on all lines, including both vty lines and TTY lines.

Because it's difficult to be certain that all possible modes of access have been blocked, you should usually make sure that logins on all lines are controlled using some sort of authentication mechanism, even on machines that are supposed to be inaccessible from untrusted networks. This is especially important for vty lines and for lines connected to modems or other remote-access devices.

Securing vty Access

Any vty should be configured to accept connections only with the protocols actually needed. You can do this with the **transport input** command. A vty expected to receive only telnet sessions could be configured with **transport input telnet**, for example, whereas a vty permitting both telnet and

SSH sessions would have **transport input telnet ssh**. Not configuring a transport input for vty access is also an option if you want to disable the service.

One way to reduce this exposure is to configure an access list on all vty lines. This will restrict the router to accept connections only from a single, specific administrative workstation. Example 5-7 shows a sample configuration of an access list configured on a vty line.

Example 5-7 *Access List Configured on a vty Line*

```
Router(config)#access-list 10 permit 192.168.100.0 0.0.0.255
Router(config)#line 1 5
Router(config-line)#access-class 10 in
```

Another useful tactic is to configure vty timeouts using the **exec-timeout** command. This prevents an idle session from consuming a vty indefinitely. Although its effectiveness against deliberate attacks is relatively limited, it also provides some protection against sessions accidentally left idle.

The password that is sent over a telnet session is in clear text. This makes telnet an insecure method. SSH is a more secure method of interactive access to the router.

Secure Shell (SSH) Protocol

SSH was originally intended to replace telnet and the UNIX **r-** commands. Both of these session types have vulnerabilities such as spoofing, man-in-the-middle attacks, and session hijacking, which SSH addresses and mitigates for the most part. For maintaining confidentiality and integrity in accessing a router, it is recommended to deploy SSH rather than telnet.

SSH protects against the following:

- Attacks from machines pretending to be another server, router, or a domain name server
- IP spoofing, where a remote host sends out packets that pretend to come from another trusted host
- IP source routing, where a host can pretend that an IP packet comes from another trusted host
- DNS spoofing, where an attacker forges name server records
- Interception of clear-text passwords or data on the network
- Manipulation of data by people in control of intermediate hosts

Setting Up a Cisco IOS Router or Switch as an SSH Client

Before you start with the SSH configuration, download the required image on your router. The SSH server requires you to have an IPSec (DES or 3DES) encryption software image from Cisco IOS

Software Release 12.1(1)T downloaded on your router. The SSH client requires you to have an IPSec (DES or 3DES) encryption software image from Cisco IOS Software Release 12.1(3)T downloaded on your router.

To enable SSH support on a Cisco IOS router, follow these four steps:

Step 1   Configure the **hostname** command.

Step 2   Configure the DNS domain.

Step 3   Generate the SSH key to be used.

Step 4   Enable SSH transport support for the vty.

```
Router(config)#hostname JAH
JAH(config)#aaa new-model
JAH(config)#username haile password 0 selassie
JAH(config)#ip domain-name secure-exam.org
JAH(config)#cry key generate rsa
JAH(config)#ip ssh time-out 60
JAH(config)#ip ssh authentication-retries 3
JAH(config)#line vty 0 4
JAH(config-line)#transport input SSH
```

Port Security for Ethernet Switches

The port security feature enables you to block input to an Ethernet, Fast Ethernet, or Gigabit Ethernet port when the MAC address of the station attempting to access the port is different from any of the MAC addresses specified for that port. This also is referred to as *MAC address lockdown*.

The global resource for the system is 1024 MAC addresses. In addition to this global resource space, there is space for one default MAC address per port to be secured. The total number of MAC addresses that can be specified per port is limited to the global resource of 1024 plus one default MAC address. The total number of MAC addresses on any port cannot exceed 1025.

The maximum number of MAC address for each port is determined by your network configuration. The following combinations are examples of valid allocations:

- 1025 (1 + 1024) addresses on 1 port and 1 address each on the rest of the ports
- 513 (1 + 512) each on 2 ports in a system and 1 address each on the rest of the ports
- 901 (1 + 900) on 1 port, 101 (1 + 100) on another port, 25 (1 + 24) on the third port, and 1 address each on the rest of the ports

After you allocate the maximum number of MAC addresses on a port, you can either specify the secure MAC address for the port manually or you can have the port dynamically configure the MAC address of the connected devices. Out of an allocated number of maximum MAC addresses on a port, you can manually configure all, allow all to be autoconfigured, or configure some manually and allow the rest to be autoconfigured. After addresses have been manually configured or autoconfigured, they are stored in NVRAM and maintained after a reset.

After you allocate a maximum number of MAC addresses on a port, you can specify how long addresses on the specified port will remain secure. After the age time expires, the MAC addresses on the port become insecure. By default, all addresses on a port are secured permanently.

In the event of a security violation, you can configure the port to go into shutdown mode or restrictive mode. The *shutdown mode* option enables you to specify whether the port is permanently disabled or disabled for only a specified time. The default is for the port to shut down permanently. The *restrictive mode* option enables you to configure the port to remain enabled during a security violation and drop only packets that are coming in from insecure hosts.

When a secure port receives a packet, the source MAC address of the packet is compared to the list of secure source addresses that were manually configured or autoconfigured (learned) on the port. If a MAC address of a device attached to the port differs from the list of secure addresses, the port shuts down permanently (default mode), shuts down for the time you have specified, or drops incoming packets from the insecure host. The port's behavior depends on how you configure it to respond to a security violation.

When a security violation occurs, the link LED for that port turns orange, and a link-down trap is sent to the SNMP manager. An SNMP trap is not sent if you configure the port for restrictive violation mode. A trap is sent only if you configure the port to shut down during a security violation.

Configuring Port Security

Consider the following when configuring port security:

- You cannot configure port security on a trunk port.
- You cannot enable port security on a SPAN destination port and vice versa.
- You cannot configure dynamic, static, or permanent CAM entries on a secure port.
- When you enable port security on a port, any static or dynamic CAM entries associated with the port are cleared; any currently configured permanent CAM entries are treated as secure.

NOTE The following port security configuration is for Catalyst OS (CatOS) — it differs for switches running native IOS (for example, Cat 3550 and 2950XL).

Example 5-8 shows how to enable port security using the learned MAC address on a port and verify the configuration.

Example 5-8 *Enabling Port Security on Port 2/19*

```
ATL-SWITCH> (enable) set port security 2/19 enable
Port 2/19 port security enabled with the learned mac address.
Trunking disabled for Port 2/19 due to Security Mode
ATL-SWITCH> (enable) show port 2/19
Port  Name              Status      Vlan       Level  Duplex Speed Type
----- ----------------- ----------  ---------- ------ ------ ----- ------------
 2/19                   connected   2          normal full   100   100BaseTX

Port  Security Secure--Addr     Last-Src-Addr       Shutdown Trap     IfIndex
----- -------- ----------------- ----------------- -------- -------- -------
 2/19 enabled  00-90-2b-03-CC-08 00-90-2b-03-CC-08 No       disabled 1081
Port   Broadcast-Limit Broadcast-Drop
-----  --------------- --------------
 2/19         -              0
Port  Align-Err  FCS-Err   Xmit-Err  Rcv-Err   UnderSize
----- ---------- --------- --------- --------- ---------
 2/19      0         0         0         0         0
Port  Single-Col Multi-Coll Late-Coll Excess-Col Carri-Sen Runts     Giants
----- ---------- ---------- ---------- --------- --------- --------- ---------
 2/19      0         0         0         0         0         0         0
Last-Time-Cleared
--------------------------
Fri June 8 2003, 19:31:10
```

Example 5-9 shows how to enable port security on a port and manually specify the secure MAC address.

Example 5-9 *Manually Assigning a MAC Address to a Port*

```
ATL-SWITCH> (enable) set port security 3/8 enable 00-A0-3C-03-2D-03
Port 3/8 port security enabled with 00-A0-3C-03-2D-03 as the secure mac address
Trunking disabled for Port 3/8 due to Security Mode
ATL-SWITCH> (enable)
ATL-SWITCH> (enable) show port security 3/8
Port  Security Violation Shutdown-Time Age-Time Max-Addr Trap     IfIndex
----- -------- --------- ------------- -------- -------- -------- -------
 3/8  enabled  shutdown       300          60       5    disabled   921
Port   Num-Addr Secure--Addr      Age-Left Last-Src-Addr      Shutdown/Time-Left
-----  -------- ----------------- -------- ----------------- ------------------
 3/8      1     00-A0-3C-03-2D-03   60     00-A0-3C-03-2D-03 no          -
```

Foundation Summary

The "Foundation Summary" section of each chapter lists the most important facts from the chapter. Although this section does not list every fact from the chapter that will be on your exam, a well-prepared candidate should at a minimum know all the details in each "Foundation Summary" section before going to take the exam.

Securing the administrative accesses to the Cisco router is one of the many tasks that have to be completed to secure the network. Administrative access points, such as the console and vty access, should require at minimum a password. Creating privilege levels on the Cisco routers for the type of commands authenticated users can execute provides an additional level of security.

Q&A

As mentioned in the section, "How to Use This Book," in the Introduction to this book, you have two choices for review questions. The questions that follow next give you a bigger challenge than the exam itself by using an open-ended question format. By reviewing now with this more difficult question format, you can exercise your memory better and prove your conceptual and factual knowledge of this chapter. The answers to these questions are found in the appendix.

For more practice with exam-like question formats, including questions using a router simulator and multiple choice questions, use the exam engine on the CD-ROM.

1. How many levels of command access does the CLI have?
2. What are some of the characteristics of the enable password?
3. What are the commands associated with privileged level 0?
4. What is the **banner login** command used for?
5. Give one of example of telnet vulnerability?
6. Give two advantages of using SSH for connecting to your device?
7. What is maximum number of MAC addresses allowed on a port?
8. What does the **service password-encryption** command do?
9. What is the advantage of using the **enable secret** command over **enable password** command?
10. What are the steps required to configure SSH on a Cisco IOS router?

PART III: Authentication, Authorization, and Accounting (AAA)

Chapter 6 Authentication

Chapter 7 Authentication, Authorization, and Accounting

Chapter 8 Configuring RADIUS and TACACS+ on Cisco IOS Software

Chapter 9 Cisco Secure Access Control Server

Chapter 10 Administration of Cisco Secure Access Control Server

This part of the book addresses the following exam objectives as posted at Cisco.com:

- Describe the components of a basic AAA implementation
- Test the perimeter router AAA implementation using applicable debug commands
- Describe the features and architecture of CSACS 3.0 for Windows
- Configure the perimeter router to enable AAA processes to use a TACACS remote service
- Configure AAA on a Cisco IOS Firewall

This chapter covers the following subjects:

- Authentication

- PAP and CHAP Authentication

CHAPTER 6

Authentication

The identification and verification of users requesting access to a device or network is one of the core objectives of security. Although several methods of authentication are available, it is essential that one or a combination of authentication be used to secure the device or network. This chapter provides an introduction to the different types of authentication methods that you can use for Cisco devices and networks.

"Do I Know This Already?" Quiz

The purpose of the "Do I Know This Already?" quiz is to help you decide whether you really need to read the entire chapter. If you already intend to read the entire chapter, you do not necessarily need to answer these questions now.

The eight-question quiz, derived from the major sections in "Foundation Topics" section of the chapter, helps you determine how to spend your limited study time.

Table 6-1 outlines the major topics discussed in this chapter and the "Do I Know This Already?" quiz questions that correspond to those topics.

Table 6-1 *"Do I Know This Already?" Foundation Topics Section-to-Question Mapping*

Foundation Topics Section	Questions Covered in This Section
TACACS	5
RADIUS	7
CHAP and PAP	6, 8
Configuring Line Authentication	4
Authentication	1, 2, 3

Chapter 6: Authentication

> **CAUTION** The goal of self-assessment is to gauge your mastery of the topics in this chapter. If you do not know the answer to a question or are only partially sure of the answer, you should mark this question wrong for purposes of the self-assessment. Giving yourself credit for an answer you correctly guess skews your self-assessment results and might provide you with a false sense of security.

1. Which of the following is true? (Choose two.)

    a. Authentication provides a method for verifying the identity of users.

    b. NAS cannot provide authentication.

    c. Usernames and passwords can be stored on NAS.

    d. Cisco does not support RADIUS.

2. Which of the following is the least secure method of authentication? (Choose two.)

    a. Username/password static

    b. Username/password aging

    c. Session key one-time password

    d. Token cards

3. Which of the following security protocols is not supported by Cisco network devices?

    a. TACACS+

    b. RADIUS

    c. Kerberos

    d. TLS

4. Which of the following command syntax is correct for creating a username and password locally on the NAS?

    a. Router(config)#**username** *meron* **password** *k0nj0*

    b. Router#**username** *meron* **password** *k0nj0*

    c. Router(config)#**set username** *meron* **set password** *k0nj0*

    d. Router#**set username** *meron* **password** *k0nj0*

5. Which port is reserved for TACACS+?

   a. UDP 1645

   b. TCP 1645

   c. TCP 49

   d. UDP 49

6. Password Authentication Protocol (PAP)_____

   a. Involves a two-way handshake where the username and password are sent across the link in clear text.

   b. Sends username and passwords in encrypted format.

   c. Involves a one-way handshake.

   d. Is not supported by Cisco network devices.

7. Which of the following port does RADIUS use?

   a. UDP 49

   b. TCP 1645

   c. TCP 49

   d. UDP 1645

8. The CHAP authentication protocol _____

   a. Involves a three-way handshake.

   b. Involves a one-way handshake.

   c. Is not supported by Cisco network devices.

   d. Sends password in clear text.

The answers to the "Do I Know This Already?" quiz are found in the appendix. The suggested choices for your next step are as follows:

- **6 or less overall score**—Read the entire chapter. This includes the "Foundation Topics" and "Foundation Summary" sections and the "Q&A" section.

- **7 or 8 overall score**—If you want more review on these topics, skip to the "Foundation Summary" section and then go to the "Q&A" section. Otherwise, move on to the next chapter.

Foundation Topics

Authentication

Authentication provides the method for verifying the identity of users and administrators who are requesting access to network resources, through username and password dialog boxes, challenge and response, token cards, and other methods.

Various types of authentication methods are available today. They range from the simple username and password databases to stronger implementation of token cards and one-time passwords (OTPs). Table 6-2 lists the authentication methods, from the strongest and most complex methods to the weakest and easy methods.

Table 6-2 *Authentication Methods*

Method	Description
Token cards and soft tokens	Token cards are small electronic devices. A PIN is given to users. The user authenticates with a combination of the token card and the PIN.
One-time passwords	OTP systems are based on a secret pass-phrase that generates passwords. These are only good for one-time use, and thus guard against eavesdropping attacks, playback attacks, and password attacks.
Username and passwords (with expiration date)	The user must change the password because it expires (usually every 30–60 days).
Static username and password database	The password is the same unless changed by the system administrator. Vulnerable to password-cracking programs and other password attacks.
No username and password	This is usually an open invitation to hackers who discover the access method to gain access to the network system.

Configuring Line Password Authentication

You can provide access control on a terminal line by entering the password and establishing password checking. To do so, use the following commands in line configuration mode:

```
Router(config) line console 0
Router(config-line)# password password
```

The password checker is case-sensitive and can include spaces; for example, the password Secret is different from the password secret, and you can use two words for an acceptable password. You can disable line password verification by disabling password checking. To do so, use the following command in line configuration mode:

```
Router(config-line)# no login authentication
```

> **NOTE** A password for a vty line has to be configured for telnet access to work.

Configuring Username Authentication

You can create a username-based authentication system, in which a user is prompted for a username and password when attempting to access the network access server (NAS) or router. The username and password database is stored locally on the Cisco NAS device.

To establish username authentication, use the following commands in global configuration mode

```
Router(config)# username name [nopassword | password password |
    password encryption-type encrypted-password]
```

The following example shows the creation of a user named Meron with a password D0wnUnd3r.

```
Router(config)# username Meron password D0wnUnd3r
```

> **NOTE** Passwords display in clear text in your configuration unless you enable the **service password-encryption** command.

Local username and password works very well for administrative access authentication. For remote-access dial-in users, however, using an external database to do authentication may be a good choice.

Remote Security Servers

A remote security database provides uniform remote-access security policies throughout the enterprise. It centrally manages all remote user profiles. Cisco network devices support the following three primary security server protocols:

- TACACS+
- RADIUS
- Kerberos

TACACS Overview

Terminal Access Controller Access Control System (TACACS) provides a way to centrally validate all users individually before they can gain access to a router or access server. TACACS was derived from the United States Department of Defense and is described in RFC 1492. TACACS is an open protocol and can be ported to most username or password databases. Figure 6-1 shows a TACACS+ server supporting a dialup client.

Figure 6-1 *TACACS+ Server Supporting a Dialup User*

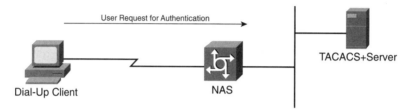

The Cisco IOS Software implements TACACS to allow centralized control over who can access routers and access servers. Authentication also can be provided for Cisco IOS administration tasks on the routers' and access servers' user interfaces. With TACACS enabled, the router and access server prompts the user for a username and a password. Then the router or access server queries a TACACS server to determine whether the user provided the correct corresponding password. TACACS was originally designed to run on UNIX workstations but can now run on Windows too. The three current versions of TACACS security server application are as follows:

- **TACACS**—An older access protocol, incompatible with the newer TACACS+ protocol. It provides password checking and authentication and notification of user actions for security and accounting purposes.
- **XTACACS**—An extension to the older TACACS protocol, supplying additional functionality to TACACS. Extended TACACS provides information about protocol translator and router use. This information is used in UNIX auditing trails and accounting files.
- **TACACS+**—An improved protocol providing detailed accounting information and flexible administrative control over authentication and authorization processes. TACACS+ is facilitated through AAA and can be enabled only through AAA commands.

The TACACS and XTACACS protocols in Cisco IOS Software are officially considered end-of-maintenance and are no longer maintained by Cisco for bug fixes or enhancement.

TACACS+ provides for separate and modular authentication, authorization, and accounting facilities. TACACS+ allows for a single access control server (the TACACS+ daemon) to provide authentication, authorization, and accounting services independently. Each service can be tied into its own database to take advantage of other services available on that server or on the network, depending on the capabilities of the daemon.

The TACACS+ protocol provides authentication between the NAS and the TACACS+ daemon, and it ensures confidentiality because all protocol exchanges between a NAS and a TACACS+ daemon are encrypted, typically using Message Digest 5 (MD5) algorithms. TACACS+ can forward the password types for ARA, SLIP, PAP, CHAP, and standard telnet. Therefore, clients can use the same username password for different protocols. TCP port 49 is reserved for TACACS+.

RADIUS Overview

RADIUS is a distributed client/server protocol that secures networks against unauthorized access. RADIUS includes two pieces: an authentication server and client protocols. A NAS operates as a client of RADIUS. The client is responsible for passing user information to designated RADIUS servers, and then acting on the response that is returned. RADIUS servers are responsible for receiving user connection requests, authenticating the user, and then returning all configuration information necessary for the client to deliver service to the user. The RADIUS servers can act as proxy clients to other kinds of authentication servers. RADIUS uses UDP as the communication protocol between the client and the server on port UDP 1645. Figure 6-2 shows a RADIUS server supporting a dialup client.

Figure 6-2 *Dialup Client Supported by a RADIUS Server*

RADIUS encrypts only the password in the access-request packet, from the client to the server. The remainder of the packet is unencrypted. Other information, such as username, authorized services, and accounting, could be captured by a third party.

The RADIUS server supports a variety of methods to authenticate a user. When it is provided with the username and original password given by the user, it can support PPP, PAP, CHAP, UNIX login, and other authentication mechanisms.

RADIUS combines authentication and authorization. The access-accept packets sent by the RADIUS server to the client contain authorization information. This makes it difficult to decouple authentication and authorization. RADIUS does perform accounting separately.

When a user attempts to log in and authenticate to an access server using RADIUS, the following steps occur:

1. The user is prompted for and enters a username and password.
2. The username and encrypted password are sent over the network to the RADIUS server.
3. The user receives one of the following responses from the RADIUS server:
   - **ACCEPT**—The user is authenticated.
   - **REJECT**—The user is not authenticated and is prompted to reenter the username and password, or access is denied.
   - **CHALLENGE**—A challenge is issued by the RADIUS server. The challenge collects additional data from the user.
   - **CHANGE PASSWORD**—A request is issued by the RADIUS server, asking the user to select a new password.

The ACCEPT or REJECT response is bundled with additional data that is used for EXEC or network authorization. You must first complete RADIUS authentication before using RADIUS authorization

Table 6-3 shows a brief comparison between TACACS+ server and RADIUS.

Table 6-3 *Features of TACACS+ and RADIUS Protocols*

Functionality	TACACS+	RADIUS
AAA support	Authentication, authorization, and accounting services are separate.	Authentication and authorization are combined, but accounting services are separate.
Transport protocol	TCP port 49.	UDP Port 1645—Authentication/Authorization UDP Port 1646—Accounting Above are the original RFC ports (still supported) New (additional) ports are UDP Port 1812—Authentication/Authorization UDP Port 1813—Accounting
Challenge/response	Bidirectional.	Unidirectional.
Protocol support	Multiproctocol support.	No NetBEUI, ARA.

Table 6-3 *Features of TACACS+ and RADIUS Protocols (Continued)*

Functionality	TACACS+	RADIUS
Data integrity	The entire TACACS+ packet is encrypted in MD5.	Only the user password is encrypted.
Accounting	Limited.	Extensive.

Kerberos Overview

The Kerberos protocol was designed by the Massachusetts Institute of Technology to provide strong authentication for client/server applications by using secret-key cryptography. Kerberos keeps a database of its clients and their private keys. The private key is a large number known only to Kerberos and the client it belongs to. In the case that the client is a user, it is an encrypted password. Network services requiring authentication register with Kerberos, as do clients wanting to use those services. The private keys are negotiated at registration.

Because Kerberos knows these private keys, it can create messages that convince one client that another is really who it claims to be. Kerberos also generates temporary private keys, called *session keys*, which are given to two clients and no one else. A session key can be used to encrypt messages between two parties.

Kerberos provides three distinct levels of protection. The application programmer determines which is appropriate, according to the requirements of the application. For example, some applications require only that authenticity be established at the initiation of a network connection and can assume that further messages from a given network address originate from the authenticated party.

Other applications require authentication of each message, but do not care whether the content of the message is disclosed. For these, Kerberos provides safe messages. Yet a higher level of security is provided by private messages, where each message is not only authenticated but also encrypted. Private messages are used, for example, by the Kerberos server itself for sending passwords over the network.

You can find more information on Kerberos at http://web.mit.edu/kerberos/www/.

PAP and CHAP Authentication

Traditionally, remote users dial in to an access server to initiate a PPP session. PPP is the standard encapsulation protocol for the transport of different network protocols across ISDN, serial, or Public Switched Telephone Network (PSTN) connections.

PPP currently supports two authentication protocols: PAP and CHAP. Both are specified in RFC 1334 and are supported on synchronous and asynchronous interfaces. Authentication via PAP or CHAP is equivalent to typing in a username and password when prompted by the server. CHAP is considered to be more secure because the remote user's password is never sent across the connection.

PAP

Password Authentication Protocol (PAP) involves a two-way handshake where the username and password are sent across the link in clear text. When PAP is enabled, the remote client attempting to connect to the access server is required to send an authentication request. If the username and password specified in the authentication request are accepted, the access server sends an authentication acknowledgment. Figure 6-3 shows the two-handshake process of PAP.

Figure 6-3 *Two-Handshake Process of PAP*

An example of a PAP authentication on a NAS follows:

```
Router(config-if)# ppp authentication pap
```

PAP provides no protection from playback and password attacks. A protocol analyzer could easily capture the password. Although a lot of vendors support PAP, CHAP is the preferred method of authentication because it is more secure.

CHAP

Challenge Handshake Authentication Protocol (CHAP) is a more secure authentication method than PAP because the password is never sent over the wire. CHAP periodically verifies the identity of the peer using a three-way handshake. This is done upon initial link establishment and may be repeated any time after the link has been established. Figure 6-4 shows the three-way handshake of CHAP.

Figure 6-4 *Three-Way Handshake of CHAP*

After the link establishment phase is complete, the access server sends a "challenge" message to the remote peer. The remote peer responds with a value calculated using a "one-way hash" function (typically MD5). The access server checks the response against its own calculation of the expected hash value. If the values match, the authentication is acknowledged.

CHAP provides protection against playback attacks through the use of an incrementally changing identifier and a variable challenge value. The use of repeated challenges is intended to limit the time of exposure to any single attack. The access server is in control of the frequency and timing of the challenges.

MS-CHAP

Microsoft Challenge Handshake Authentication Protocol (MS-CHAP) is the Microsoft version of CHAP and is an extension of RFC 1994. Like the standard version of CHAP, MS-CHAP is used for PPP authentication; in this case, authentication occurs between a PC using Microsoft Windows NT or Microsoft Windows 95 and a Cisco router or access server acting as a NAS.

MS-CHAP differs from the standard CHAP as follows:

- MS-CHAP is enabled by negotiating CHAP algorithm 0x80 in LCP option 3, Authentication Protocol.
- The MS-CHAP response packet is in a format designed to be compatible with Microsoft Windows. This format does not require the authenticator to store a clear or reversibly encrypted password.
- MS-CHAP provides an authenticator-controlled authentication retry mechanism.
- MS-CHAP provides an authenticator-controlled change-password mechanism.
- MS-CHAP defines a set of reason-for-failure codes returned in the failure packet's Message field.

Foundation Summary

The "Foundation Summary" section of each chapter lists the most important facts from the chapter. Although this section does not list every fact from the chapter that will be on your exam, a well-prepared candidate should at a minimum know all the details in each "Foundation Summary" before going to take the exam.

- Authentication methods vary from strong to weak:
    - One-time passwords using token cards
    - One-time passwords using token cards
    - The session key one-time password (OTP) systems
    - Expiring or aging username and passwords
    - Static username and password
    - No username and password
- TACACS+ separates authentication, authorization, and accounting services. RADIUS combines authentication and authorization but separates accounting services.
- CHAP periodically verifies the identity of the peer using a three-way handshake.
- PAP involves a two-way handshake where the username and password are sent across the link in clear text. PAP provides no protection from playback and password attacks.

Q&A

As mentioned in the introduction, "How to Use This Book," you have two choices for review questions. The questions that follow next give you a bigger challenge than the exam itself by using an open-ended question format. By reviewing now with this more difficult question format, you can exercise your memory better and prove your conceptual and factual knowledge of this chapter. The answers to these questions are found in the appendix.

For more practice with exam-like question formats, including questions using a router simulator and multiple choice questions, use the exam engine on the CD-ROM.

1. Which port is reserved TACACS+ use?

2. Why is PAP considered insecure compared to other authentication protocols such CHAP and MS-CHAP?

3. What type of encryption algorithm does CHAP uses during the three-way handshake?

4. Who developed and designed the Kerberos authentication protocol?

5. Give one difference between CHAP and MS-CHAP?

6. Which versions of the TACACS protocol in Cisco IOS Software have officially reached end-of-maintenance?

7. What command is used to disable the console password for a network access server?

8. Which two popular authentication methods does PPP support?

9. In the RADIUS security architecture, what is the network access server?

This chapter covers the following subjects:

- AAA Overview
- Configuring AAA Services
- Troubleshooting AAA

CHAPTER 7

Authentication, Authorization, and Accounting

An access control system has to be in place to manage and control access to network services and resources. Authentication, authorization, and accounting (AAA) network security services provide the primary framework through which you set up access control on your router or network access server (NAS).

"Do I Know This Already?" Quiz

The purpose of the "Do I Know This Already?" quiz is to help you decide whether you really need to read the entire chapter. If you already intend to read the entire chapter, you do not necessarily need to answer these questions now.

The 10-question quiz, derived from the major sections in "Foundation Topics" section of the chapter, helps you determine how to spend your limited study time.

Table 7-1 outlines the major topics discussed in this chapter and the "Do I Know This Already?" quiz questions that correspond to those topics.

Table 7-1 *"Do I Know This Already?" Foundation Topics Section-to-Question Mapping*

Foundation Topics Section	Questions Covered in This Section
Configure AAA on Cisco IOS Firewall	1–6, 9, 10
Test the Perimeter Router AAA Implementation Using Applicable debug Commands	7, 8

CAUTION The goal of self-assessment is to gauge your mastery of the topics in this chapter. If you do not know the answer to a question or are only partially sure of the answer, you should mark this question wrong for purposes of the self-assessment. Giving yourself credit for an answer you correctly guess skews your self-assessment results and might provide you with a false sense of security.

Chapter 7: Authentication, Authorization, and Accounting

1. Which of the following best describes AAA authentication?

   a. Authentication is last defense against hackers.

   b. Authentication can only work with firewalls.

   c. Authentication is the way a user is identified prior to being allowed into the network.

   d. Authentication is a way to manage what a user can do on a network.

   e. Authentication is way to track what a user does once logged in.

2. Which of the following best describes AAA authorization?

   a. Authorization cannot work without accounting.

   b. Authorization provides the means of tracking and recording user activity on the network.

   c. Authorization is the way a user is identified.

   d. Authorization determines which resources the user is permitted to access and what operation the user is permitted to perform.

3. Which of the following best describes AAA accounting?

   a. Accounting is the way that users are identified before they log in to the network.

   b. Accounting enables you to track the services users are accessing as well as the amount of network resources they are consuming.

   c. Accounting cannot be used for billing.

   d. Accounting is a way to curtail where users can go on a network access server.

   e. AAA accounting is used only to track users logging on to the network.

4. What is the command that enables AAA on a network access server or a router?

   a. **aaa in**

   b. **aaa on**

   c. **aaa new-model**

   d. **enable aaa**

   e. **start aaa services**

5. Which of the following is the correct syntax to specify RADIUS as the default method for a user authentication during login?

   a. **authentication radius login**

   b. **login radius aaa authentication**

c. aaa login authentication group radius

   d. aaa authentication login default group radius

   e. radius authentication login

6. Which of the following authorization methods does AAA not support?

   a. TACACS+

   b. RADIUS

   c. SQL

   d. NDS

   e. Cisco

7. What command enables you to troubleshoot and debug authentication problems?

   a. **debug authentication**

   b. **debug aaa authentication**

   c. **authentication debug aaa**

   d. **show authentication**

   e. **show aaa authentication**

8. How do you track user activity on your network access server?

   a. You cannot track user activities on your NAS.

   b. Use AAA authorization only.

   c. Use AAA authentication only.

   d. A and B.

   e. Configure AAA accounting.

9. Which of the following commands requires authentication for dialup users via async or ISDN connections?

   a. **ppp authentication default radius**

   b. **aaa authentication ppp default local**

   c. **authentication line isdn**

   d. **aaa authentication login remote**

   e. **aaa ppp authentication radius**

10. After an authentication method has been defined, what is the next step to make AAA authentication work on the access server?

   a. Set up AAA accounting.

   b. Do nothing.

   c. Apply the authentication method to the desired interface.

   d. Reload the router or NAS.

The answers to the "Do I Know This Already?" quiz are found in the appendix. The suggested choices for your next step are as follows:

- **8 or less overall score**—Read the entire chapter. This includes the "Foundation Topics" and "Foundation Summary" sections and the "Q&A" section.

- **9 or 10 overall score**—If you want more review on these topics, skip to the "Foundation Summary" section and then go to the "Q&A" section. Otherwise, move on to the next chapter.

Foundation Topics

AAA Overview

Access control is the cornerstone in ensuring the integrity, confidentiality, and availability of a network and its resources. Enforcing identification and verification of users, permitting, and then reporting or auditing their activity provides a solid framework for security. You can think of it as accessing some secure buildings today. When you first walk in front door, you are asked to provide your identification. Your name is logged in and then you are permitted to go beyond the lobby into the building. After you have access through the front door, it does not necessarily mean that you are permitted to access all the floors or offices within the building. You only have access to the rooms and floors to which you are given permission. At the end of the day when you leave, your departure from the building will be logged.

Now that is a high level overview of what you would like to accomplish with users accessing your network and resources. You would like to first identify and verify who they are, then give them permission to only some of resources on the network, and also have the capability to audit their activity while they are in your network. You can accomplish these functions by configuring authentication, authorization, and accounting (better as known as AAA) on the Cisco IOS Software.

AAA provides a modular way to perform the authentication, authorization, and accounting through the use of method lists, as discussed in the following sections.

Authentication

Authentication is the verification that the user's claimed identity is a valid. Mechanisms used to verify authentication include usernames and passwords, challenge and response, and token cards. Chapter 6, "Authentication," discusses these mechanisms in more detail.

Most Cisco products support AAA authentication that uses local authentication (for instance, on the router) or that uses a remote security server database such as a Cisco access control server or RADIUS server. The local authentication method is an effective solution for a small user community, whereas the separate remote security server is scalable and appropriate for a larger community of users.

AAA authentication service is implemented by first defining the authentication method, also known as *method list*, and then applying the method list to the interface desired. Having more than one method of authentication ensures a continuity of the authentication service should one of the authentication methods fail. In addition to defining the type of authentication to be performed, a method list also defines the sequence in which the authentication will be performed. If no method lists are defined for an interface, the default method list applies. With the exception of local, line password, and enable password, all authentication methods must be defined through AAA.

> **NOTE** When a user submits an incorrect username and password combination, a FAIL response occurs. On the other hand, an ERROR occurs when the security server fails to respond to an authentication request. Secondary and tertiary authentication method lists are used only when an ERROR is detected and not when a FAIL response occurs.

Authorization

Authorization determines which resources the user is permitted to access and which operations the user is permitted to perform after being successfully authenticated. Just like AAA authentication, authorization information for each user is either stored locally on the routers or remotely on TACACS+ RADIUS security servers. AAA authorization works by comparing attributes that describe the authorization of the user to information stored in the database. Like AAA authentication method lists, authorization method lists have to be first defined and then applied to the desired interface. All authorization methods must be defined through AAA.

Accounting

User activity reporting, such as start and stop times, executed commands, number of packets, user identities, and number of bytes, are logged by the AAA accounting service. Information collected, including the amount of resources consumed by users, can be used for billing and auditing.

Configuring AAA Services

AAA configuration includes four mandatory steps and two optional steps. It involves enabling AAA, providing security server information, defining the method list, and then applying the method list to the interface of interest. The following steps describe the configuration process:

Step 1 Activate AAA services by using the **aaa new-model** command.

Step 2 Select the type of security protocols (for instance, RADIUS, TACACS+, or Kerberos).

Step 3 Define the method list's authentication by using an **aaa authentication** command.

Step 4 Apply the method list to a particular interface or line, if required.

Step 5 (Optional) Configure authorization using the **aaa authorization** command.

Step 6 (Optional) Configure accounting using the **aaa accounting** command.

Configuring AAA Authentication

Administrative and remote LAN network access to routers and network access servers can be secured using AAA. To configure AAA authentication, perform the following steps:

Step 1 Activate AAA by using the **aaa new-model** command.

Step 2 Create a list name or use default. A list name is alphanumeric and can have one to four authentication methods.

Step 3 Specify the authentication method lists for the **aaa authentication** command. You may specify up to four.

Step 4 Apply the method list to an interface (for example, sync, async, and virtual-configured PPP, SLIP, and NASI) or to lines (for example, vty, tty, console, aux, and async lines).

There are several **aaa authentication** commands available in Cisco IOS Software Release 12.2, including the following:

- **aaa authentication arap**
- **aaa authentication login**
- **aaa authentication ppp**
- **aaa authentication enable**
- **aaa authentication banner**
- **aaa authentication username-prompt**
- **aaa authentication fail-message**
- **aaa authentication nasi**

The following sections discuss these three **aaa authentication** commands:

- **aaa authentication login**
- **aaa authentication ppp**
- **aaa authentication enable**

Configuring Login Authentication Using AAA

Multiple login authentication methods are available in the AAA security services. The **aaa authentication login** command is used to enable AAA authentication. With this command, you create one or more lists of authentication methods that are tried at login. These lists are then applied to interfaces you are interested in. Table 7-2 describes the steps for applying the **aaa authentication login** command.

Step 1 Enable AAA.

```
Router(config)#aaa new-model
```

Step 2 Create a local authentication list.

```
Router(config)# aaa authentication login {default | list-name} method1 [method2...]
```

Step 3 Apply the authentication list to a line or set of lines.

```
Router(config-line)# login authentication {default | list-name}
```

The *list-name* argument can be any name that you give to describe the list. The *method* argument is the name of the method the authentication algorithm tries. The additional methods of authentication are used only if the preceding method returns an error. The **none** argument lets the authentication succeed if all the authentication methods return an error.

Table 7-2 lists the supported login authentication.

Table 7-2 *Supported login authentication*

Keyword	Description
default	Uses the listed authentication methods that follow this argument as the default list of methods when a user logs in.
list-name	Character string used to name the list of authentication methods activated when a user logs in.
method	Specifies at least the following keywords.
enable	Uses the enable password for authentication.
krb5-telnet	Uses the Kerberos 5 telnet authentication protocol when using telnet to connect to the router.
line	Uses the line password for authentication.
local	Uses the local username database for authentication.
local-case	Uses case-sensitive local username authentication.
none	Uses no authentication.

Table 7-2 *Supported login authentication (Continued)*

Keyword	Description
group radius	Uses the list of all RADIUS servers for authentication.
group tacacs+	Uses the list of all TACACS+ servers for authentication.
group *group-name*	Uses a subset of RADIUS or TACACS+ servers for authentication as defined by the **aaa group server radius** or **aaa group server tacacs+** command.

(This table has been reproduced by Cisco Press with the permission of Cisco Systems Inc. Copyright © 2003 Cisco Systems, Inc. All Rights Reserved.)

Example 7-1 shows use the local username database as the method of user authentication at the console interface.

Example 7-1 *Sample Configuration for Console Interface Access Using AAA Authentication Login*

```
Router(config)#aaa new-model
Router(config)#username meron password abc123
Router(config)#aaa authentication login conaccess local
Router(config)#line console 0
Router(config-line)#login authentication conaccess
```

Enabling Password Protection at the Privileged Level

Use the **aaa authentication enable default** command to create a series of authentication methods that are used to determine whether a user can access the privileged EXEC command level. The following shows the syntax for **aaa authentication enable**:

```
Router(config)# aaa authentication enable default method1 [method2...]
```

Table 7-3 shows **aaa authentication enable default** methods.

Table 7-3 **aaa authentication enable default** *Methods*

Keyword	Description
enable	Uses the enable password authentication.
line	Uses the line password for authentication.
none	Uses no authentication.
group radius	Uses the list of all RADIUS hosts for authentication.
group tacacs+	Uses the list of all TACACS+ hosts for authentication.
group *group-name*	Uses a subset of RADIUS or TACACS+ servers for authentication as defined by the **aaa group server radius** or **aaa group server tacacs+** command.

Example 7-2 shows a configuration for privileged EXEC access authentication using AAA.

Example 7-2 *Configuring Privileged EXEC Access Authentication Using AAA*

```
Router(config)#aaa new-model
Router(config)#aaa authentication enable default enable
```

Configuring PPP Authentication Using AAA

Users who dial in to your network need to be authenticated. Dialup configuration (PPP ARA) is typically configured on serial interfaces on your router. AAA provides a range of authentication methods for use on the serial interfaces configured for PPP. The **aaa authentication ppp** command enables AAA authentication. The syntax for **aaa authentication ppp** is as follows:

```
aaa authentication ppp {default | list-name} method1 [method2...]
```

Table 7-4 shows **aaa authentication ppp** methods.

Table 7-4 **aaa authentication ppp** *Methods*

Keyword	Description
if-needed	Does not authenticate if user has already been authenticated on tty line.
krb5	Uses Kerberos 5 for authentication (can only be used for PAP authentication).
local	Uses the local username database for authentication.
local-case	Uses case-sensitive local username authentication.
none	Uses no authentication.
group radius	Uses the list of all RADIUS servers for authentication.
group tacacs+	Uses the list of all TACACS+ servers for authentication.
group *group-name*	Uses a subset of RADIUS or TACACS+ servers for authentication as defined by the **aaa group server radius** or **aaa group server tacacs+** command.

(This table has been reproduced by Cisco Press with the permission of Cisco Systems Inc. Copyright © 2003 Cisco Systems, Inc. All Rights Reserved.)

The following steps outline the configuration procedure for AAA authentication methods for serial lines using PPP:

Step 1   Enable AAA globally.

   Router(config)# **aaa new-model**

Step 2   Create a local authentication list.

   Router(config)# **aaa authentication ppp** {default | list-name} method1 [method2...]

Step 3 Enter the configuration mode for the interface to which you want to apply the authentication list.

```
Router(config)#interface interface-type interface-number
```

Step 4 Apply the authentication list to a line or set of lines.

```
Router(config-if)# ppp authentication {protocol1[protocol2...]} [if-needed]
    {default | list-name}[callin] [one-time]
```

The configuration shown in Example 7-3 has AAA authentication configured for PPP connections to use the local username database as the default method for user authentication.

Example 7-3 *Configuration of* **aaa authentication ppp**

```
Router(config)#aaa new-model
Router(config)#username meron password abc123
Router(config)#aaa authentication ppp default local
```

Configuring AAA Authorization

You can restrict the type of operation users can perform or the network resources they can access by using the AAA authorization service. After AAA authorization is enabled and configured, user profiles are stored on the local database or in a remote security server. From information in these profiles, users' sessions are configured after they have been authenticated.

AAA supports five different methods of authorization:

- **TACACS+**—User profile information is stored on a remote security server that has TACACS+ services running. The network access server communicates with the TACACS+ service to configure the user's session.
- **If-authenticated**—Successful authentication is required first before the user is allowed to access the requested function.
- **None**—Authorization is not performed over this line or interface.
- **Local**—User information is stored locally on the router or access server
- **RADIUS**—User profile information is stored on a remote security server. The router or access server requests authorization information from the RADIUS security server.

AAA authorization controls the user's activity by permitting or denying access to what type of network access a user can start (PPP, SLIP, ARAP), what type of commands the user can execute, and more. The seven types of AAA authorization supported on the Cisco IOS Software are as follows:

- **Auth-proxy**—Applies specific security policies on a per-user basis.
- **Commands**—Applies to the EXEC mode commands a user issues. Command authorization attempts authorization for all EXEC mode commands, including global configuration commands, associated with a specific privilege level.

- **EXEC**—Applies to a user EXEC terminal session.
- **Network**—Applies to network connections. This can include a PPP, SLIP, or ARAP connection.
- **Reverse access**—Applies to reverse telnet sessions.
- **Configuration**—Applies to downloading configurations from the AAA server.
- **IP mobile**—Applies to authorization for IP mobile services.

The syntax for the **aaa authorization** command is as follows:

```
Router(config)# aaa authorization {auth-proxy | network | exec | commands level |
   reverse-access | configuration | ipmobile} {default | list-name}
   [method1 [method2]]
```

Table 7-5 shows **aaa authorization** command parameters.

Table 7-5 aaa authorization *Command Parameters*

Keyword	Description
network	Enables authorization for all network-related service requests, including SLIP, PPP, PPP NCPs, and ARAP.
auth-proxy	Enables authorization that applies specific security policies on a per-user basis. For detailed information on the authentication proxy feature, see Chapter 15, "Authentication Proxy and the Cisco IOS Firewall."
exec	Enables authorization to determine whether a user is allowed to run an EXEC shell.
commands	Enables authorization for specific, individual EXEC commands associated with a specific privilege level. This enables you to authorize all commands associated with a specified command level from 0 to 15.
reverse-access	Enables authorization for reverse telnet functions.
configuration	Downloads the configuration from the AAA server.
default	Uses the listed authentication methods that follow this argument as the default list of methods for authorization.
level	Specific command level that should be authorized, from 0 through 15.
list-name	Character string used to name the list of authentication methods.
method	Specifies at least one of the keywords that follow.
group *group-name*	Uses a subset of RADIUS or TACACS+ servers for authentication as defined by the **aaa group server radius** or **aaa group server tacacs+** command.

(This table has been reproduced by Cisco Press with the permission of Cisco Systems Inc. Copyright © 2003 Cisco Systems, Inc. All Rights Reserved.)

Configuring AAA Services

The following steps outline the configuration procedure for AAA authorization methods:

Step 1 Create an authorization method list for a particular authorization type and enable authorization.

```
Router(config)# aaa authorization {auth-proxy | network | exec | commands level |
    reverse-access | configuration | ipmobile} {default | list-name}
    [method1 [method2...]]
```

Step 2 Enter the line configuration mode for the lines to which you want to apply the authorization method list.

```
Router(config)# line [aux | console | tty | vty]line-number [ending-line-number]
```

Step 3 Apply the authorization list to a line or set of lines.

```
Router(config-line)# authorization {arap | commands level | exec | reverse-access}
    {default | list-name}
```

Example 7-4 shows a sample configuration of a NAS (enabled for AAA and communication with a RADIUS security server) for AAA services to be provided by the RADIUS server. If the RADIUS server fails to respond, the local database is queried for authentication and authorization information.

Example 7-4 *Configuring a NAS for AAA Services Provided by the RADIUS Server*

```
Router(config)#aaa new-model
Router(config)#aaa authentication login admins local
Router(config)#aaa authorization network la-users group radius local
Router(config)#username mark password whatisthema7r1x
Router(config)#radius-server host 10.2.1.17
Router(config)#radius-server key ToPs3cret
Router(config)#interface group-async 1
Router(config-line)#group-range 1 16
Router(config-line)#encapsulation ppp
Router(config-line)#ppp authentication chap admins
Router(config-line)#ppp authorization la-users
Router(config)#line 1 16
Router(config-line)#autoselect ppp
Router(config-line)#modem dialin
```

The lines in this sample RADIUS AAA configuration are defined as follows:

- The **aaa new-model** command enables AAA network security services.

- The **aaa authentication ppp dialins group radius local** command defines the authentication method list dialins, which specifies that RADIUS authentication and then (if the RADIUS server does not respond) local authentication is used on serial lines using PPP.

- The **aaa authorization network la-users group radius local** command defines the network authorization method list named la-users, which specifies that RADIUS authorization will be used on serial lines using PPP. If the RADIUS server fails to respond, local network authorization is performed.
- The **username** command defines the username and password to be used for the PPP Password Authentication Protocol (PAP) caller identification.
- The **radius-server host** command defines the name of the RADIUS server host.
- The **radius-server key** command defines the shared secret text string between the NAS and the RADIUS server host.
- The **interface group-async** command selects and defines an asynchronous interface group.
- The **ppp authentication chap dialins** command selects Challenge Handshake Authentication Protocol (CHAP) as the method of PPP authentication and applies the dialins method list to the specified interfaces.
- The **ppp authorization la-users** command applies the la-users network authorization method list to the specified interfaces.

Configuring AAA Accounting

Enabling AAA accounting feature of AAA helps you log user activity, including network resource utilization, which could be used for billing and auditing. Like authentication and authorization, the AAA accounting feature has method lists. The two methods used by the AAA accounting feature are RADIUS and TACACS+.

The following six types of accounting can be configured on the Cisco IOS Software:

- **Network**—Provides information for all PPP, SLIP, or ARAP sessions, including packet and byte counts.
- **EXEC**—Provides information about user EXEC terminal sessions of the NAS.
- **Commands**—Provides information about the EXEC mode commands that a user issues. Command accounting generates accounting records for all EXEC mode commands, including global configuration commands, associated with a specific privilege level.
- **Connection**—Provides information about all outbound connections made from the NAS, such as telnet.
- **System**—Provides information about system-level events.
- **Resource**—Provides start and stop records for calls that have passed user authentication, and provides stop records for calls that fail to authenticate.

The syntax for the **aaa accounting** command is as follows:

```
aaa accounting {auth-proxy | system | network | exec | connection | commands level}
     {default | list-name} {start-stop | stop-only | none} [broadcast] group groupname
```

Table 7-6 explains the keywords and arguments for the **aaa accounting** command.

Table 7-6 aaa accounting *Command Syntax Explanation*

Keywords	Description
auth-proxy	Provides information about all authenticated proxy user events.
system	Performs accounting for all system-level events not associated with users, such as reloads.
network	Runs accounting for all network-related service requests, including SLIP, PPP NCPs, and ARAP.
exec	Runs accounting for EXEC shell session. This keyword might return user profile information such as what is generated by the **autocommand** command.
connection	Provides information about all outbound connections made from the NAS, such as telnet, LAT, TN3270, PAD, and rlogin.
commands *level*	Runs accounting for all commands at the specified privilege level. Valid privilege level entries are integers from 0 through 15.
Default	Uses the listed accounting methods that follow this argument as the default list of methods for accounting services.
list-name	Character string used to name the list of at least one of the accounting methods.
start-stop	Sends a "start" accounting notice at the beginning of a process and a "stop" accounting notice at the end of a process.
stop-only	Sends a "stop" accounting notice at the end of the requested user process.
none	Disables accounting services on this line or interface.
broadcast	(Optional) Enables sending accounting records to multiple AAA servers. Simultaneously sends accounting records to the first server in each group. If the first server is unavailable, failover occurs using the backup servers defined within that group.
group *groupname*	**radius** or **tacacs+**.

The following example shows **aaa accounting** configuration for users accessing the NAS via PPP.

```
Router(config)#aaa new-model
Router(config)#aaa authentication login neteng group radius local
Router(config)#aaa authentication ppp default group radius local
Router(config)#aaa authorization exec neteng group radius
Router(config)#aaa authorization network neteng group radius
Router(config)#aaa accounting exec neteng start-stop group radius
Router(config)#aaa accounting network neteng start-stop group radius
```

Troubleshooting AAA

After AAA services are configured, you must test and monitor your configuration. The **debug** command is a very useful command to troubleshoot and test your AAA configuration. The following **debug** commands enable you to troubleshoot and test your AAA configuration:

- **debug aaa authentication**
- **debug aaa authorization**
- **debug aaa accounting**

Example 7-5 provides sample output of the **debug aaa authentication** command. A single EXEC login that uses the default method list and the first method, TACACS+, is displayed. The TACACS+ server sends a GETUSER request to prompt for the username, then a GETPASS request to prompt for the password, and finally a PASS response to indicate a successful login. The number 35149617 is the session ID, which is unique for each authentication. Use this ID number to distinguish different authentications if several are occurring concurrently.

Example 7-5 *debug aaa authentication Command Output*

```
Router# debug aaa authentication
2:13:51: AAA/AUTHEN: create_user user='' ruser='' port='tty19'
  rem_addr='192.168.100.14' authen_type=1 service=1 priv=1
2:13:51: AAA/AUTHEN/START (0): port='tty19' list='' action=LOGIN service=LOGIN
2:13:51: AAA/AUTHEN/START (0): using "default" list
2:13:51: AAA/AUTHEN/START (35149617): Method=TACACS+
2:13:51: TAC+ (35149617): received authen response status = GETUSER
2:13:51: AAA/AUTHEN (35149617): status = GETUSER
2:13:51: AAA/AUTHEN/CONT (35149617): continue_login
2:13:51: AAA/AUTHEN (35149617): status = GETUSER
2:13:51: AAA/AUTHEN (35149617): Method=TACACS+
2:13:51: TAC+: send AUTHEN/CONT packet
2:13:51: TAC+ (35149617): received authen response status = GETPASS
2:13:51: AAA/AUTHEN (35149617): status = GETPASS
2:13:51: AAA/AUTHEN/CONT (35149617): continue_login
2:13:51: AAA/AUTHEN (35149617): status = GETPASS
```

Example 7-5 debug aaa authentication *Command Output (Continued)*

```
2:13:51: AAA/AUTHEN (35149617): Method=TACACS+
2:13:51: TAC+: send AUTHEN/CONT packet
2:13:51: TAC+ (35149617): received authen response status = PASS
2:13:51: AAA/AUTHEN (35149617): status = PASS
```

Example 7-6 shows sample output from the **debug aaa authorization** command. In this display, an EXEC authorization for user Howard is performed. On the first line, the username is authorized. On the second and third lines, the attribute value (AV) pairs are authorized. The **debug** output displays a line for each AV pair that is authenticated. Next, the display indicates the authorization method used. The final line in the display indicates the status of the authorization process, which, in this case, has failed.

Example 7-6 debug aaa authorization *Command Output*

```
Router# debug aaa authorization
12:41:21: AAA/AUTHOR (0): user='Howard'
12:41:21: AAA/AUTHOR (0): send AV service=shell
12:41:21: AAA/AUTHOR (0): send AV cmd*
12:41:21: AAA/AUTHOR (642335165): Method=TACACS+
12:41:21: AAA/AUTHOR/TAC+ (642335165): user=Chris
12:41:21: AAA/AUTHOR/TAC+ (642335165): send AV service=shell
12:41:21: AAA/AUTHOR/TAC+ (642335165): send AV cmd*
12:41:21: AAA/AUTHOR (642335165): Post authorization status = FAIL
```

The **aaa authorization** command causes a request packet containing user profile information to be sent to the TACACS+ services daemon as part of the authorization process. The service responds in one of the following three ways:

- Accepts the request as is
- Makes changes to the request
- Refuses the request, thereby refusing authorization

Example 7-7 demonstrates sample output from the **debug aaa accounting** command.

Example 7-7 debug aaa accounting *Command Output*

```
Router# debug aaa accounting
16:49:21: AAA/ACCT: EXEC acct start, line 10
16:49:32: AAA/ACCT: Connect start, line 10, glare
16:49:47: AAA/ACCT: Connection acct stop:
task_id=70 service=exec port=10 protocol=telnet address=172.31.3.78
  cmd=glare bytes_in=308 bytes_out=76 paks_in=45 paks_out=54 elapsed_time=14
```

The information displayed by the **debug aaa accounting** command is independent of the accounting protocol used to transfer the accounting information to a server. You also can use the **show accounting** command to step through all active sessions and to print all the accounting records for actively accounted functions.

The **show accounting** command enables you to display the active accountable events on the system. It provides systems administrators a quick look at what is happening and may also prove useful for collecting information in the event of a data loss of some kind on the accounting server.

Foundation Summary

The "Foundation Summary" section of each chapter lists the most important facts from the chapter. Although this section does not list every fact from the chapter that will be on your SECUR exam, a well-prepared candidate should at a minimum know all the details in each "Foundation Summary" before going to take the exam.

To configure security on a Cisco router or access server using AAA, follow these steps:

Step 1 Activate AAA services by using the **aaa new-model** command.

Step 2 Select the type of security protocols (for instance, RADIUS, TACACS+, or Kerberos).

Step 3 Define the method list's authentication by using an **aaa authentication** command.

Step 4 Apply the method lists to a particular interface or line, if required.

Step 5 (Optional) Configure authorization using the **aaa authorization** command.

Step 6 (Optional) Configure accounting using the **aaa accounting** command.

- **debug aaa authentication**—Displays debugging messages on authentication functions
- **debug aaa authorization**—Displays debugging messages on authorization functions
- **debug aaa accounting**—Displays debugging messages on accounting functions

Q&A

As mentioned in the section, "How to Use This Book," in the Introduction to this book, you have two choices for review questions. The questions that follow next give you a bigger challenge than the exam itself by using an open-ended question format. By reviewing now with this more difficult question format, you can exercise your memory better and prove your conceptual and factual knowledge of this chapter. The answers to these questions are found in the appendix.

For more practice with exam-like question formats, including questions using a router simulator and multiple choice questions, use the exam engine on the CD-ROM.

1. What command enables AAA on a router/NAS?
2. Which of the AAA services can be used for billing and auditing?
3. What are the seven types of AAA authorization supported on the Cisco IOS Software?
4. What AAA command would you use to configure authentication for login to an access server?
5. Name *two* authorization methods supported by AAA?
6. What command enables you to troubleshoot a AAA authorization problem?
7. How many authentication methods can you specify in AAA configuration?
8. What is the difference between a FAIL response and an ERROR response in a AAA configuration?
9. How would you display all the accounting records for actively accounted functions?
10. What command disables AAA functionality on your access server?

This chapter covers the following subject:

- Configure the perimeter router to enable AAA processes to use a TACACS remote service

CHAPTER 8

Configuring RADIUS and TACACS+ on Cisco IOS Software

TACACS+ and RADIUS provide a way to centrally validate users attempting to gain access to a router or access server. This chapter discusses the basic configuration of a network access server (NAS) and router to work with TACACS+ and RADIUS servers.

"Do I Know This Already?" Quiz

The purpose of the "Do I Know This Already?" quiz is to help you decide whether you really need to read the entire chapter. If you already intend to read the entire chapter, you do not necessarily need to answer these questions now.

The eight-question quiz, derived from the major sections in the "Foundation Topics" portion of the chapter, helps you determine how to spend your limited study time.

Table 8-1 outlines the major topics discussed in this chapter and the "Do I Know This Already?" quiz questions that correspond to those topics.

Table 8-1 *"Do I Know This Already?" Foundation Topics Section-to-Question Mapping*

Foundation Topics Section	Questions Covered in This Section
Configure the Network Access Server to Enable AAA Processes to Use a TACACS Remote Service	1–8

CAUTION The goal of self-assessment is to gauge your mastery of the topics in this chapter. If you do not know the answer to a question or are only partially sure of the answer, you should mark this question wrong for purposes of the self-assessment. Giving yourself credit for an answer you correctly guess skews your self-assessment results and might provide you with a false sense of security.

Chapter 8: Configuring RADIUS and TACACS+ on Cisco IOS Software

1. Which of the following is the command to specify the TACACS+ server on the access server?

   a. **tacacs-server host**

   b. **tacacs host**

   c. **server tacacs+**

   d. **server host**

2. Which is the default port that is reserved for TACACS?

   a. UDP 49

   b. TCP 49

   c. UDP 1046

   d. TCP 1046

3. Which of the following commands enables you to verify or troubleshoot a RADIUS configuration on a network access server?

   a. **show radius**

   b. **debug radius**

   c. **debug radius-server**

   d. **verify radius**

4. What is the significance of the **tacacs-server key** command?

   a. It specifies an encryption key that will be used to encrypt all exchanges between the access server and the TACACS+ server.

   b. It is used to specify a special text when the user logs in to the access server.

   c. It is an optional configuration and not required in the TACACS+ configuration.

   d. It uniquely identifies the TACACS+ server.

5. Which of the following commands identifies a RADIUS server in a RADIUS configuration?

   a. **radius-server host**

   b. **radius-host**

   c. **server radius+**

   d. **server host**

6. Which of the following are the basic steps that are required to configure RADIUS on Cisco IOS Software?

   a. Enable AAA.

   b. Create an access list.

   c. Identify RADIUS server.

   d. Define the method list using AAA authentication.

7. Which of the following commands deletes the RADIUS server with IP address 10.2.100.64 from a router configuration?

   a. **del radius-server host 10.2.100.64**

   b. **remove radius-server host 10.2.100.64**

   c. **no radius-server host 10.2.100.64**

   d. **disable radius-server host 10.2.100.64**

8. Which of the following is the default port used by RADIUS?

   a. TCP 1685

   b. UDP 1645

   c. TCP 1645

   d. UDP 1685

The answers to the "Do I Know This Already?" quiz are found in the appendix. The suggested choices for your next step are as follows:

- **6 or less overall score**—Read the entire chapter. This includes the "Foundation Topics" and "Foundation Summary" sections and the "Q&A" section.

- **7 or 8 overall score**—If you want more review on these topics, skip to the "Foundation Summary" section and then go to the "Q&A" section. Otherwise, move on to the next chapter.

Foundation Topics

Configuring TACACS+ on Cisco IOS

To configure the Cisco access server to support TACACS+, you must perform the following steps:

Step 1 Enable AAA. Use the **aaa new-model** command to enable AAA.

Step 2 Identify the TACACS+ server. Use the **tacacs-server host** command to specify the IP address or name of one or more TACACS+ servers.

Step 3 Configure AAA services. Use the **aaa authentication** command to define method lists that use TACACS+ for authentication.

Step 4 Apply the method lists to the interfaces. Use **line** and **interface** commands to apply the defined method lists to various interfaces.

If needed, you can configure authorization using the **aaa authorization** command to authorize user-specific functions. Unlike authentication, which can be configured per line or per interface, authorization is configured globally for the entire network access server. Similarly, accounting can be configured using the **aaa accounting** command to enable accounting for TACACS+ connections.

The **tacacs-server host** command enables you to specify the names of the IP host or hosts maintaining a TACACS+ server. Because the TACACS+ software searches for the hosts in the order specified, this feature can prove useful for setting up a list of preferred servers. The following syntax is used to specify a TACACS server :

```
tacacs-server host host-name [single-connection] [port integer] [timeout integer]
  [key string]
```

Table 8-2 shows the command parameters and the description of the **tacacs-server host** command.

Table 8-2 *The Parameters for the* **tacacs-server host** *Command*

Parameter	Description
hostname	Name or IP address of the host.
single-connection	(Optional) Used to specify a single connection. Rather than have the router open and close a TCP connection to the daemon each time it must communicate, the **single-connection** option maintains a single open connection between the router and the daemon. This is more efficient because it allows the daemon to handle a higher number of TACACS operations.

Table 8-2 *The Parameters for the* **tacacs-server host** *Command*

Parameter	Description
port	(Optional) Used to identify the server port number. If this option is used, it overrides the default, which is port 49.
timeout	(Optional) Specify a timeout value. This overrides the global timeout value set with the **tacacs-server timeout** command for this server only.
key	(Optional) Specify an authentication and encryption key. This must match the key used by the TACACS+ daemon. Specifying this key overrides the key set by the global command **tacacs-server key** for this server only.
string	(Optional) Character string specifying authentication and encryption key.

Table source: Cisco.com

It is also possible to configure the encryption key used for TACACS+ separately using the **tacacs-server key** command. Specifying the encryption key with the **tacacs-server host** command overrides the default key set by the global configuration **tacacs-server key** command for this server only.

The following example specifies a TACACS+ server with an IP address of 192.168.1.10:

```
NAS(config)#tacacs-server host 192.168.1.10
```

The following example specifies that, for authentication, authorization, and accounting (AAA) confirmation, the access server consults the TACACS+ server with IP address 192.168.1.10 on port number 49. The timeout value for requests on this connection is three seconds; the encryption key is **seferea**.

```
NAS(config)#tacacs-server host 192.168.1.10 port 49 timeout 3 key seferea
```

TACACS+ Authentication Examples

Example 8-1 shows a sample configuration for TACACS+ to be used for PPP authentication. Figure 8-1 shows a remote client being authenticated via the TACACS+ server.

Figure 8-1 *A TACACS+ Server Being Used as a Security Server for AAA Authentication*

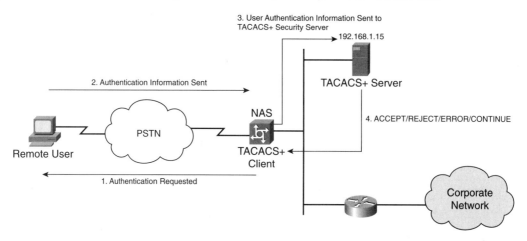

Example 8-1 *Sample Configuration for PPP Authentication Using TACACS+*

```
NAS(config)#aaa new-model
NAS(config)#aaa authentication ppp meist tacacs+ local
NAS(config)#tacacs-server host 192.168.1.15 key meron
NAS(config)#interface serial 0
NAS(config-if)#ppp authentication chap  meist
```

In this example:

- The **aaa new-model** command enables the AAA services globally.

- The **aaa authentication** command defines a method list, meist, to be used on serial interfaces running PPP. The keyword **tacacs+** means that authentication will be done through TACACS+. If TACACS+ returns an error of some sort during authentication, the keyword **local** indicates that authentication will be attempted using the local database on the network access server.

- The **tacacs-server host** command identifies the TACACS+ server as having an IP address of 192.168.1.15. The **tacacs-server key** command defines the shared encryption key to be meron.

- The **interface** command selects the line, and the **ppp authentication** command applies the test method list to this line.

NOTE The local database is chosen if the TACACS+ server does not respond; it is not used if authentication does not pass because of incorrect username/password combination.

TACACS+ Authorization Example

Example 8-2 shows a sample TACACS+ configuration to be used for PPP authentication using the default method list and network authorization.

Example 8-2 *Sample Configuration for PPP AAA Authentication and Network Authorization*

```
NAS(config)#aaa new-model
NAS(config)#aaa authentication ppp default if-needed tacacs+ local
NAS(config)#aaa authorization network tacacs+
NAS(config)#tacacs-server host 192.168.1.15 key meron
NAS(config)#interface serial 0
NAS(config-if)#ppp authentication default
```

In this example:

- The **aaa new-model** command enables the AAA security services.

- The **aaa authentication** command defines a method list, default, to be used on serial interfaces running PPP. The keyword **default** means that PPP authentication is applied by default to all interfaces. The **if-needed** keyword means that if the user has already authenticated by going through the ASCII login procedure, PPP authentication is not necessary and can be skipped. If authentication is needed, the keyword **tacacs+** means that authentication will be done through TACACS+. The keyword **local** indicates that local authentication will be used using the local database if the TACACS+ returns an error (that is, if the TACACS+ server is not accessible).

- The **aaa authorization** command configures network authorization via TACACS+. Unlike authentication lists, this authorization list always applies to all incoming network connections made to the network access server.

- The **tacacs-server host** command identifies the TACACS+ server as having an IP address of 192.168.1.15. The **tacacs-server key** command defines the shared encryption key to be meron.

- The **interface** command selects the line, and the **ppp authentication** command applies the default method list to this line.

TACACS+ Accounting Example

Example 8-3 shows a sample TACACS+ configuration to be used for PPP authentication using the default method list and accounting.

Example 8-3 *Sample Configuration for AAA Authentication and Accounting with TACACS+ Security Server*

```
NAS(config)#aaa new-model
NAS(config)#aaa authentication ppp default if-needed tacacs+ local
NAS(config)#aaa accounting network stop-only tacacs+
NAS(config)#tacacs-server host 192.168.1.15
```

Example 8-3 *Sample Configuration for AAA Authentication and Accounting with TACACS+ Security Server (Continued)*

```
NAS(config)#tacacs-server key meron
NAS(config)#interface serial 0
NAS(config-if)#ppp authentication default
```

In this example:

- The **aaa new-model** command enables the AAA security services.
- The **aaa accounting** command configures network accounting via TACACS+. In this example, accounting records describing the session that just terminated will be sent to the TACACS+ server whenever a network connection terminates.
- The **tacacs-server host** command identifies the TACACS+ daemon as having an IP address of 192.168.1.15. The **tacacs-server key** command defines the shared encryption key to be meron.
- The **interface** command selects the line, and the **ppp authentication** command applies the default method list to this line.

AAA TACACS+ Troubleshooting

Verifying and testing TACACS+ configuration is accomplished using the following commands:

- **debug aaa authentication**
- **debug tacacs**
- **debug tacacs events**

The following examples show sample outputs from the commands listed in the preceding sections.

debug aaa authentication

Example 8-4 shows a sample output from the **debug aaa authentication** command for a TACACS login attempt that was successful. The information indicates that TACACS+ is the authentication method used.

Example 8-4 *Sample Output from a* **debug aaa authentication** *Command Showing a Successful Authentication*

```
NAS# debug aaa authentication
17:42:03: AAA/AUTHEN (182481354): Method=TACACS+
17:42:03: TAC+: send AUTHEN/CONT packet
17:42:03: TAC+ (182481354): received authen response status = PASS
17:42:03: AAA/AUTHEN (182481354): status = PASS
```

There are three possible results of an AAA session: PASS, FAIL, or ERROR.

debug tacacs

Example 8-5 shows a sample output from the **debug tacacs** command for a TACACS login attempt that was successful, as indicated by the status PASS.

Example 8-5 *Sample Output from a* **debug tacacs** *Command Showing a Successful Authentication*

```
NAS# debug tacacs
18:03:33: TAC+: Opening TCP/IP connection to 192.168.1.15 using source 10.100.14.184
18:03:33: TAC+: Sending TCP/IP packet number 858503507-1 to 192.168.1.15 (AUTHEN/START)
18:03:33: TAC+: Receiving TCP/IP packet number 858503507-2 from 192.168.1.15
18:03:33: TAC+ (858503507): received authen response status = GETUSER
18:03:34: TAC+: send AUTHEN/CONT packet
18:03:34: TAC+: Sending TCP/IP packet number 858503507-3 to 192.168.1.15 (AUTHEN/CONT)
18:03:34: TAC+: Receiving TCP/IP packet number 858503507-4 from 192.168.1.15
18:03:34: TAC+ (858503507): received authen response status = GETPASS
18:03:38: TAC+: send AUTHEN/CONT packet
18:03:38: TAC+: Sending TCP/IP packet number 858503507-5 to 192.168.1.15 (AUTHEN/CONT)
18:03:38: TAC+: Receiving TCP/IP packet number 858503507-6 from 192.168.1.15
18:03:38: TAC+ (858503507): received authen response status = PASS
18:03:38: TAC+: Closing TCP/IP connection to 192.168.1.15
```

debug tacacs events

Example 8-6 shows a sample output from the **debug tacacs events** command. This example shows the opening and closing of a TCP connection to a TACACS+ server (192.168.100.24), the bytes read and written over the connection, and the TCP status of the connection.

Example 8-6 *Sample Output from a* **debug tacacs events** *Command*

```
NAS# debug tacacs events
13:22:21: TAC+: Opening TCP/IP to 192.168.100.24/1049 timeout=15     <--
13:22:21: TAC+: Opened TCP/IP handle 0x48A87C to 192.168.100.24/1049
13:22:21: TAC+: periodic timer started
13:22:21: TAC+: 192.168.100.24 req=3BD868 id=-1242409656 ver=193
  handle=0x48A87C (ESTAB)
expire=14 AUTHEN/START/SENDAUTH/CHAP queued
13:22:22: TAC+: 192.168.100.24 ESTAB 3BD868 wrote 46 of 46 bytes
13:22:27: TAC+: 192.168.100.24 CLOSEWAIT read=12 wanted=12 alloc=12 got=12
13:22:27: TAC+: 192.168.100.24 CLOSEWAIT read=61 wanted=61 alloc=61 got=49
13:22:27: TAC+: 192.168.100.24 received 61 byte reply for 3BD868
13:22:27: TAC+: req=3BD868 id=-1242409656 ver=193 handle=0x48A87C (CLOSEWAIT)
  expire=9
AUTHEN/START/SENDAUTH/CHAP processed
13:22:27: TAC+: periodic timer stopped (queue empty)
```

continues

Example 8-6 *Sample Output from a* **debug tacacs events** *Command (Continued)*

```
13:22:27: TAC+: Closing TCP/IP 0x48A87C connection to 192.168.100.24/1049
13:22:27: TAC+: Opening TCP/IP to 192.168.100.24/1049 timeout=15
13:22:27: TAC+: Opened TCP/IP handle 0x489F08 to 192.168.100.24/1049
13:22:27: TAC+: periodic timer started
13:22:27: TAC+: 192.168.100.24 req=3BD868 id=299214410 ver=192 handle=0x489F08
  (ESTAB)
expire=14 AUTHEN/START/SENDPASS/CHAP queued
00:03:23: TAC+: 192.168.100.24 ESTAB 3BD868 wrote 41 of 41 bytes
00:03:23: TAC+: 192.168.100.24 CLOSEWAIT read=12 wanted=12 alloc=12 got=12
00:03:23: TAC+: 192.168.100.24 CLOSEWAIT read=21 wanted=21 alloc=21 got=9
00:03:23: TAC+: 192.168.100.24 received 21 byte reply for 3BD868
00:03:23: TAC+: req=3BD868 id=299214410 ver=192 handle=0x489F08 (CLOSEWAIT)
  expire=13
AUTHEN/START/SENDPASS/CHAP processed
00:03:23: TAC+: periodic timer stopped (queue empty)
```

Among the messages shown in Example 8-6 are the following:

- Line 1 indicates that a TCP open request to host 192.168.100.24 on port 1049 will time out in 15 seconds if it gets no response.
- Line 2 indicates a successful open operation and provides the address of the internal TCP handle for this connection.
- Line 7 indicates that all 46 bytes were written to address 192.168.100.24 for request 3BD868.
- Line 8 indicates that 12 bytes were read in reply to the request.
- Line 26 indicates that the TACACS+ server helper process switched itself off when it had no more work to do.

The **debug tacacs events** command generates a substantial amount of output and has to be used with caution. For more detailed information, refer to the "Debug Command Reference" documentation from Cisco.

Configuring RADIUS on Cisco IOS

To configure RADIUS on your Cisco router or access server, you must perform the following steps:

Step 1   Enable AAA. Use the **aaa new-model** global configuration command to enable AAA.

Step 2   Identify the RADIUS server. Use the **radius-server host** command to specify the IP address. Use the **radius-server key** command to specify an encryption key that will be used to encrypt all exchanges between the network access server and the RADIUS server.

Step 3 Configure AAA services. Use the **aaa authentication** global configuration command to define method lists that use RADIUS for authentication.

Step 4 Apply the method lists to the interfaces. Use **line** and **interface** commands to apply the defined method lists to various interfaces.

If needed, you can configure authorization using the **aaa authorization** command to the network access server. Similarly, you can configure accounting using the **aaa accounting** command to enable accounting for RADIUS connections.

To configure RADIUS to use the AAA security commands, you must specify the host running the RADIUS server and a secret text string that it shares with the access server. To specify a RADIUS server host and shared secret text string, use the following commands in global configuration mode:

```
radius-server host {hostname | ip-address} [auth-port port-number]
    [acct-port port-number] [timeout seconds] [retransmit retries] [key string]
    [alias {hostname | ip-address}]
```

Table 8-3 shows the radius-server host command parameters and their description.

Table 8-3 *Parameters for the* **radius-server host** *Command*

Parameter	Description
*hostname	ip-address*	Name or IP address of the RADIUS server host.
auth-port *port-number*	(Optional) Specifies the UDP destination port for authentication requests. The default port number is 1645.
acct-port *port-number*	(Optional) Specifies the UDP destination port for accounting requests. The default port number is 1646.
timeout *seconds*	(Optional) The time interval (in seconds) that the router waits for the RADIUS server to reply before retransmitting. This setting overrides the global value of the **radius-server timeout** command. If no timeout value is specified, the global value is used. Enter a value in the range 1 to 1000.
retransmit *retries*	(Optional) The number of times a RADIUS request is re-sent to a server, if that server is not responding or responding slowly. This setting overrides the global setting of the **radius-server retransmit** command.
key *string*	(Optional) Specifies the authentication and encryption key used between the router and the RADIUS daemon running on this RADIUS server. This key overrides the global setting of the **radius-server key** command. If no key string is specified, the global value is used. The key is a text string that must match the encryption key used on the RADIUS server.
alias	(Optional) Allows up to eight aliases per line for any given RADIUS server.

RADIUS Authentication and Authorization Example

Example 8-7 shows a sample configuration to authenticate and authorize using RADIUS

Example 8-7 *Sample Configuration Using RADIUS*

```
NAS(config)#aaa new-model
NAS(config)#radius-server host 192.168.100.15
NAS(config)#radius-server key ladyhawk
NAS(config)#username meron password k0nj0
NAS(config)#aaa authentication login test radius local
NAS(config)#aaa authentication ppp test if-needed radius
NAS(config)#aaa authorization exec radius
NAS(config)#aaa authorization network radius
```

The configuration lines in this sample RADIUS authentication and authorization configuration are defined as follows:

- The **aaa authentication login test radius local** command configures the router to use RADIUS for authentication at the login prompt. If RADIUS returns an error, the user is authenticated using the local database. In this example, test is the name of the method list, which specifies RADIUS and then local authentication.

- The **aaa authentication ppp test if-needed radius** command configures the Cisco IOS Software to use RADIUS authentication for lines using PPP if the user has not already been authenticated. If the EXEC facility has authenticated the user, RADIUS authentication is not performed. In this example, test is the name of the method list defining RADIUS as the if-needed authentication method.

- The **aaa authorization exec radius** command sets the RADIUS information that is used for EXEC authorization, autocommands, and access lists.

- The **aaa authorization network radius** command sets RADIUS for network authorization, address assignment, and access lists.

RADIUS Authentication, Authorization, and Accounting Example

Example 8-8 is a general configuration using RADIUS with the AAA command set. This configuration is shown in Figure 8-2.

Figure 8-2 *General Configuration Using RADIUS*

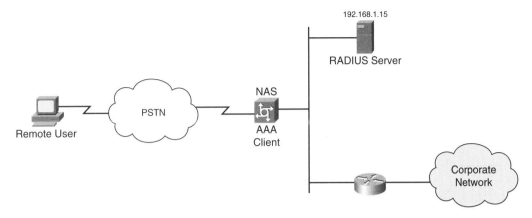

Example 8-8 *Sample RADIUS Configuration*

```
NAS(config)#aaa new-model
NAS(config)#radius-server host 192.168.100.15
NAS(config)#radius-server key ladyhawk
NAS(config)#username meron password k0nj0
NAS(config)#aaa authentication ppp test1 radius local
NAS(config)#aaa authorization network radius local
NAS(config)#aaa accounting network start-stop radius
NAS(config)#aaa authentication login admins local
NAS(config)#aaa authorization exec local
NAS(config)#line 1 8
NAS(config-line)#login authentication admins
NAS(config)#interface group-async 1
NAS(config-line)#ppp authentication pap test1
```

The lines in this example RADIUS authentication, authorization, and accounting configuration are defined as follows:

- The **radius-server host** command defines the IP address of the RADIUS server host.
- The **radius-server key** command defines the shared secret text string between the network access server and the RADIUS server host.
- The **aaa authentication ppp test1 radius** local command defines the authentication method list, test1, which specifies that RADIUS authentication, then (if the RADIUS server does not respond) local authentication will be used on serial lines using PPP.

- The **ppp authentication pap test 1** command applies the **test 1** method list to the lines specified.

- The **aaa authorization network radius local** command is used to assign an address and other network parameters to the RADIUS user.

- The **aaa accounting network start-stop radius** command tracks PPP usage.

- The **aaa authentication login admins local** command defines another method list, admins, for login authentication.

- The **login authentication admins** command applies the admins method list for login authentication to lines 1–8.

Testing and Troubleshooting RADIUS Configuration

The commands that are used for RADIUS configuration testing and configuration are very similar to ones used by TACACS and AAA.

- **debug radius**
- **debug aaa authentication**
- **debug aaa authorization**
- **debug aaa accounting**
- **show accounting**

Example 8-9 shows a sample output from the **debug radius** command.

Example 8-9 *Sample Output from the* **debug radius** *Command*

```
NAS# debug radius
Radius protocol debugging is on
Radius packet hex dump debugging is off
Router#
14:51:04: RADIUS: ustruct sharecount=3
14:51:04: Radius: radius_port_info() success=0 radius_nas_port=1
14:51:04: RADIUS: Initial Transmit ISDN 0:D:23 id 0 192.168.100.64:1824,
  Accounting-Request, len 358
14:51:04: RADIUS: NAS-IP-Address [4] 6 10.100.10.0
14:51:04: RADIUS: Vendor, Cisco [26] 19 VT=02 TL=13 ISDN 0:D:23
14:51:04: RADIUS: NAS-Port-Type [61] 6 Async
14:51:04: RADIUS: User-Name [1] 12 "7358827539"
14:51:04: RADIUS: Called-Station-Id [30] 7 "74762"
14:51:04: RADIUS: Calling-Station-Id [31] 12 "7358827539"
14:51:04: RADIUS: Acct-Status-Type [40] 6 Start
14:51:04: RADIUS: Service-Type [6] 6 Login
14:51:04: RADIUS: Vendor, Cisco [26] 27 VT=33 TL=21 h323-gw-id=5300_43.
14:51:04: RADIUS: Vendor, Cisco [26] 55 VT=01 TL=49
```

Example 8-9 *Sample Output from the* **debug radius** *Command (Continued)*

```
      h323-incoming-conf-id=8F3A3163 B4980003 0 29BD0
14:51:04: RADIUS: Vendor, Cisco [26] 31 VT=26 TL=25 h323-call-origin=answer
14:51:04: RADIUS: Vendor, Cisco [26] 32 VT=27 TL=26 h323-call-type=Telephony
14:51:04: RADIUS: Vendor, Cisco [26] 57 VT=25 TL=51
   h323-setup-time=*13:14:02.222 EST sun mar 22 2003
14:51:04: RADIUS: Vendor, Cisco [26] 46 VT=24 TL=40 h323-conf-id=8F3A3163
   B4980003 0 29BD0
14:51:04: RADIUS: Acct-Session-Id [44] 10 "00000004"
14:51:04: RADIUS: Delay-Time [41] 6 0
```

Example 8-10 is sample output from the **debug aaa accounting** command.

Example 8-10 *Sample Output from the* **show accounting** *Command*

```
NAS# debug aaa accounting
08:22:12 : AAA/ACCT: EXEC acct start, line 10
08:22:22: AAA/ACCT: Connect start, line 10, glare
08:22:37: AAA/ACCT: Connection acct stop:
task_id=11 service=exec port=10 protocol=telnet address=192.168.100.17 cmd=glare
   bytes_in=283 bytes_out=84 paks_in=32 paks_out=41 elapsed_time=12
```

The **show accounting** command enables you to display the active accountable events on the network. It provides system administrators with a quick look at what is going on, and it also can help collect information in the event of a data loss on the accounting server. (Refer to Example 8-11.)

Example 8-11 *Sample Output of the* **show accounting** *Command*

```
NAS# show accounting
Active Accounted actions on Interface Serial4:16, User meron Priv 1
Task ID 27, Network Accounting record, 00:00:13 Elapsed
task_id=27 timezone=EDT service=ppp mlp-links-max=4 mlp-links-current=4
protocol=ip addr=192.168.100.12 mlp-sess-id=6
Active Accounted actions on Interface Serial4:17, User meron Priv 1
Task ID 29, Network Accounting record, 00:00:44 Elapsed
task_id=29 timezone=EDT service=ppp mlp-links-max=4 mlp-links-current=4
protocol=ip addr=192.168.100.12mlp-sess-id=1
Active Accounted actions on Interface Serial4:18, User meron Priv 1
Task ID 17, Network Accounting record, 00:01:19 Elapsed
task_id=17 timezone=EDT service=ppp mlp-links-max=4 mlp-links-current=4
protocol=ip addr=192.168.100.12mlp-sess-id=1
Active Accounted actions on Interface Serial4:20, User meron Priv 1
Task ID 14, Network Accounting record, 00:01:03 Elapsed
task_id=14 timezone=EDT service=ppp mlp-links-max=4 mlp-links-current=4
mlp-sess-id=1 protocol=ip addr=192.168.100.12
```

continues

Example 8-11 *Sample Output of the* **show accounting** *Command (Continued)*

```
Active Accounted actions on , User (not logged in) Priv 0
Task ID 1, Resource-management Accounting record, 04:32:21 Elapsed
task_id=1 timezone=EDT rm-protocol-version=1.0
service=resource-management
protocol=nas-status event=nas-start reason=reload
Overall Accounting Traffic
Starts Stops Updates Active Drops
Exec 0 0 0 0 0
Network 8 4 0 4 0
Connect 0 0 0 0 0
Command 0 0 0 0 0
R-mgmt 1 0 0 1 0
System 0 0 0 0 0
User creates:21, frees:9, Acctinfo mallocs:15, frees:6
Users freed with accounting unaccounted for:0
Queue length:0
```

Foundation Summary

The "Foundation Summary" section of each chapter lists the most important facts from the chapter. Although this section does not list every fact from the chapter that will be on your SECUR exam, a well-prepared candidate should at a minimum know all the details in each "Foundation Summary" before going to take the exam.

The following are the steps required to configure TACACS+ or RADIUS server on a router.

Step 1 Enable AAA. Use the **aaa new-model** global configuration command to enable AAA.

Step 2 Identify the server. Use the **radius-server host** or **tacacs-server host** command to specify the IP address. Use the **radius-server key** or **tacacs-server key** command to specify an encryption key that will be used to encrypt all exchanges between the router and authentication servers.

Step 3 Configure AAA services. Use the **aaa authentication** global configuration command to define method lists that use RADIUS for authentication.

Step 4 Apply the method lists to the interfaces. Use **line** and **interface** commands to apply the defined method lists to various interfaces.

If needed, you can configure authorization using the **aaa authorization** command for the network access server. Similarly, you can configure accounting using the **aaa accounting** command to enable accounting for RADIUS connections.

The following troubleshooting commands enable you to test and verify RADIUS and TACACS+ server configuration:

- **debug radius**
- **debug aaa authentication**
- **debug tacacs**
- **debug tacacs events**

Q&A

As mentioned in the section, "How to Use This Book," in the Introduction to this book, you have two choices for review questions. The questions that follow next give you a bigger challenge than the exam itself by using an open-ended question format. By reviewing now with this more difficult question format, you can exercise your memory better and prove your conceptual and factual knowledge of this chapter. The answers to these questions are found in the appendix.

For more practice with exam-like question formats, including questions using a router simulator and multiple choice questions, use the exam engine on the CD-ROM.

1. What is the command that specifies a TACACS server?
2. Give two commands to test and verify your RADIUS configuration?
3. What is the purpose of the **tacacs-server key** command?
4. What is the purpose of the keyword **local** in the following configuration line?

    aaa authentication ppp test1 tacacs local

5. Is it possible to change the default port used by RADIUS authentication?
6. What is the command to delete the RADIUS server configuration?
7. What is the command to enable network-level authorization to use a TACACS+ server?
8. Which testing and verifying command used for TACACS+ produces a substantial amount of output?
9. What is the default port that is reserved for TACACS?
10. Is it possible to have both RADIUS and TACACS configuration on a single router/NAS?

This chapter covers the following subjects:

- Cisco Secure ACS for Windows
- Cisco Secure ACS for Windows Architecture
- Cisco Secure ACS for UNIX

CHAPTER 9

Cisco Secure Access Control Server

Cisco Secure Access Control Server (Cisco Secure ACS) provides AAA services for dialup access, dial-out access, wireless, VLAN access, firewalls, VPN concentrators, administrative controls, and more. The list of external databases supported has also continued to grow, and the use of multiple databases, as well as multiple Cisco Secure ACSs, has become more common.

This chapter describes the features and architectural components of the Cisco Secure ACS.

"Do I Know This Already?" Quiz

The purpose of the "Do I Know This Already?" quiz is to help you decide whether you really need to read the entire chapter. If you already intend to read the entire chapter, you do not necessarily need to answer these questions now.

The 10-question quiz, derived from the major sections in "Foundation Topics" section of the chapter, helps you determine how to spend your limited study time.

Table 9-1 outlines the major topics discussed in this chapter and the "Do I Know This Already?" quiz questions that correspond to those topics.

Table 9-1 *"Do I Know This Already?" Foundation Topics Section-to-Question Mapping*

Foundation Topics Section	Questions Covered in This Section
Describe the Features and Architecture of Cisco Secure ACS	1–10

CAUTION The goal of self-assessment is to gauge your mastery of the topics in this chapter. If you do not know the answer to a question or are only partially sure of the answer, you should mark this question wrong for purposes of the self-assessment. Giving yourself credit for an answer you correctly guess skews your self-assessment results and might provide you with a false sense of security.

1. Which of the following devices are supported by Cisco Secure ACS?

    a. Cisco PIX firewall

    b. Cisco Network Access Servers (NAS)

    c. Cisco 412

    d. Cisco 550

2. Which of the following is true about Cisco Secure ACS?

    a. Centralizes access control and accounting

    b. Centralizes configuration management for routers and switches

    c. Is a distributed security application only for firewalls

    d. Only supports Cisco products

3. Which of the following user repository systems are supported by Cisco?

    a. Windows NT/2000 user database

    b. Generic LDAP

    c. Novell NetWare Directory Services (NDS)

    d. CipherTec database

4. Which of the following password protocols is not supported by Cisco Secure ACS?

    a. EAP-CHAP

    b. EAP-TLS

    c. LEAP

    d. ERTP

5. Which of the following is a feature of the Cisco Secure ACS authorization feature?

    a. Denying logins based on time of day and day of week

    b. Denying access based on operating system of the client

    c. Permitting access based on packet size

    d. Permitting access based on the type of encryption used

6. Which of the following are the types of accounting logs that can be generated by Cisco Secure ACS?

   a. Administrative accounting

   b. PAP accounting

   c. TACACS+ accounting

   d. RADIUS accounting

7. Which of the following is not part of the main services/modules that are installed for Cisco Secure ACS for Windows?

   a. CSMon

   b. CSAdmin

   c. CSAuth

   d. CSACS

8. What does the CSMon services do?

   a. Provides logging services for both accounting and system activity

   b. Provides the HTML interface for administration

   c. Provides recording and notification of Cisco Secure ACS performance.

   d. Monitors firewall activities

9. Authentication and authorization function is handled by which service in the Cisco Secure ACS for Windows?

   a. CSAdmin

   b. CSAuthen

   c. CSAuth

   d. SecureAuthen

10. Under which condition(s), using the Cisco Secure user database, are users forced to change their password?

    a. After a specified number of days

    b. After a specified number of logins

    c. The first time a new user logs in

    d. Never

The answers to the "Do I Know This Already?" quiz are found in the appendix. The suggested choices for your next step are as follows:

- **8 or less overall score**—Read the entire chapter. This includes the "Foundation Topics" and "Foundation Summary" sections and the "Q&A" section.

- **9 or 10 overall score**—If you want more review on these topics, skip to the "Foundation Summary" section and then go to the "Q&A" section. Otherwise, move on to the next chapter.

Foundation Topics

Cisco Secure ACS for Windows

Cisco Secure ACS is a highly scalable, access control server that operates as a centralized RADIUS server or TACACS+ server system and controls the authentication, authorization, and accounting (AAA) of users who access corporate resources through a network.

Cisco Secure ACS for Windows provides authentication, authorization, and accounting services to network devices that function as AAA clients, such as a network access servers, PIX firewalls, and routers. The AAA client in Figure 9-1 represents any such device that provides AAA client functionality and uses one of the AAA protocols supported by Cisco Secure ACS.

Figure 9-1 *A AAA Client Being Supported by a Cisco Secure ACS*

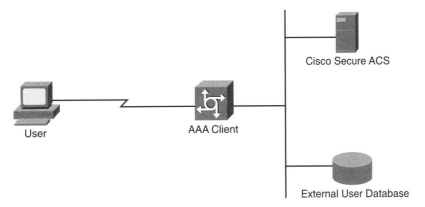

Cisco Secure ACS supports a broad set of networking access products, including all Cisco IOS routers, VPN access products, voice-over-IP (VoIP) solutions, cable broadband access, content networks, wireless solutions, storage networks, and 802.1x-enabled Cisco Catalyst switches. It also supports third-party devices that can be configured with TACACS+ or RADIUS. Cisco Secure ACS treats all such devices as AAA clients.

Cisco Secure ACS centralizes access control and accounting. With Cisco Secure ACS, network administrators can quickly administer accounts and globally change levels of service offerings for entire groups of users. Although the external user database shown in Figure 9-1 is optional, support for many popular user repository implementations enables companies to put to use the working knowledge gained from and the investment already made in building their corporate user repositories such as Windows Active Directory.

To maintain reliability and security in your network, the AAA features of the Cisco Secure ACS application help you monitor and control the following:

- **Authentication**—Who is logging in to the system
- **Authorization**—Whether a particular user should be using the requested service
- **Accounting**—What each user has been doing

The network access server directs all dial-in user access requests for authentication and authorization to Cisco Secure ACS using the TACACS+ or RADIUS protocol. If the user's request is authenticated, Cisco Secure ACS sends the user's authorizing attributes and the accounting function is then started. Figure 9-2 shows an overview of how Cisco Secure ACS for Windows works.

Figure 9-2 *Cisco Secure ACS Overview*

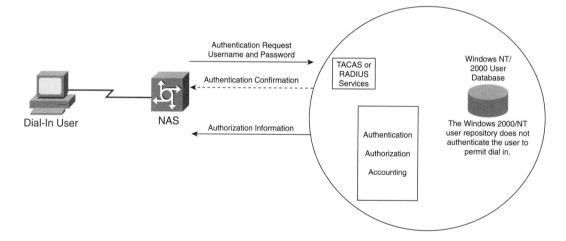

Authentication

Cisco Secure ACS supports a variety of user databases for authentication. It supports the Cisco Secure user database and the following external user databases:

- Windows NT/2000 user database
- Generic LDAP
- Novell NetWare Directory Services (NDS)

- Open Database Connectivity (ODBC)-compliant relational databases
- CRYPTOCard token server
- SafeWord token server
- PassGo token server
- RSA SecureID token server
- AXENT
- LEAP proxy agent
- Safeword
- ActivCard token server
- Vasco token server

You can configure Cisco Secure ACS to forward authentication of users to one or more external user databases, which means that different levels of security can be concurrently used with Cisco Secure ACS for different requirements. The basic user-to-network security level is Password Authentication Protocol (PAP). Although it represents the unencrypted security, PAP does offer convenience and simplicity for the client. PAP allows authentication against the Windows NT/2000 database. With this configuration, users need to log in only once.

CHAP allows a higher level of security than PAP for encrypting passwords when communicating from an end-user client to the AAA client. You can use CHAP with the Cisco Secure user database. AppleTalk Remote Access Protocol (ARA Protocol) support is included to support Apple clients.

Cisco Secure ACS supports many common password protocols including EAP-CHAP, EAP-TLS, LEAP, ARA Protocol, ASCII/PAP, CHAP, MS-CHAP.

With Cisco Secure ACS you can choose whether and how you want to use password aging. Control for password aging may reside either in the Cisco Secure user database or in a Windows NT/2000 user database. Each password-aging mechanism differs as to requirements and setting configurations.

The password-aging feature controlled by the Cisco Secure user database enables you to force users to change their passwords under any of the following conditions:

- After a specified number of days
- After a specified number of logins
- The first time a new user logs in

The Windows NT/2000-based password-aging feature enables you to control the following password-aging parameters:

- Maximum password age in days
- Minimum password age in days

The methods and functionality of Windows password aging differ according to whether you are using Windows NT or Windows 2000 and whether you use Active Directory (AD) or Security Accounts Manager (SAM).

Authorization

Cisco Secure ACS can send user profile policies to a AAA client to determine the network services the user can access. You can configure authorization to give different users and groups different levels of service. For example, standard dialup users might not have the same access privileges as premium customers and users. You can also differentiate by levels of security, access times, and services.

The Cisco Secure ACS access-restrictions feature enables you to permit or deny logins based on time of day and day of week. For example, you could create a group for temporary accounts that can be disabled on specified dates. This would make it possible for a service provider to offer a 14-day free trial. The same authorization could be used to create a temporary account for a consultant with login permission limited to Monday through Friday, 9 a.m. to 5 p.m.

You can restrict users to a service or combination of services such as PPP, ARA, or Serial Line Internet Protocol (SLIP), or EXEC. After a service is selected, you can restrict Layer 2 and Layer 3 protocols, such as IP and IPX, and you can apply individual access lists. Access lists on a per-user or per-group basis can restrict users from reaching parts of the network where critical information is stored or prevent them from using certain services such as FTP or SNMP.

Cisco Secure ACS can provide information to the network device for a specific user to configure a secure tunnel through a public network such as the Internet. The information can be for the access server (such as the home gateway for that user) or for the home gateway router to validate the user at the customer premises. In either case, Cisco Secure ACS can be used for each end of the virtual private dialup network (VPDN).

Additional authorization-related features of Cisco Secure ACS features include the following:

- Group administration of users, with support for up to 500 groups
- The capability to map a user from an external user database to a specific Cisco Secure ACS group

- Restricting access by time-of-day and day-of-week access
- Support for VoIP, including configurable logging of accounting data
- Disabling an account after a number of failed attempts, specified by the administrator
- Disabling an account on a specific date
- Restricting network access based on remote address caller line identification (CLID) and dialed number identification service (DNIS)
- Per-user and per-group TACACS+ or RADIUS attributes
- Define usage quotas by duration or total number based on daily, monthly, or weekly periods

Accounting

AAA clients use the accounting functions provided by the RADIUS and TACACS+ protocols to communicate relevant data for each user session to the AAA server for recording. Cisco Secure ACS writes accounting records to a comma-separated value (CSV) log file or ODBC database, depending on your configuration. You can easily import these logs into popular database and spreadsheet applications for billing, security audits, and report generation. You can generate the following types of accounting:

- **Administrative accounting**—Lists commands entered on a network device with TACACS+ command authorization enabled
- **RADIUS accounting**—Lists when sessions stop and start; records AAA client messages with username; provides CLID information; records the duration of each session
- **TACACS+ Accounting**—Lists when sessions start and stop; records AAA client messages with username; provides CLID information; records the duration of each session

The Cisco Secure ACS provides the following accounting features:

- Configurable supplementary user ID fields for capturing additional information in logs
- Centralized logging, allowing several Cisco Secure ACS servers to forward their accounting data to a remote Cisco Secure ACS server
- Customizable logs, enabling you to capture as much information as needed

Administration

The web administration interface is platform independent so that it can configure, maintain, and protect its AAA functionality. Almost all the configuration of the Cisco ACS server is done via the web interface post installation. The HTML interface enables you to easily modify Cisco Secure ACS configuration from any connection on your LAN or WAN.

The administration interface primarily uses HTML, along with some Java functions, to enhance ease of use. This design keeps the interface responsive and straightforward. The inclusion of Java requires that the browser used for administrative sessions supports Java.

Through the web interface, you can do the following:

- View and edit user and group information
- Restart services
- Add remote administrators
- View reports from anywhere on the network
- Back up the system
- Change AAA client information

The Cisco Secure ACS provides the following administrative capabilities:

- Define different privileges per administrator
- Log administrator activities
- View a list of logged-in users
- Restore Cisco Secure ACS configuration, user accounts, and group profiles from a backup file
- CSMon service, providing monitoring, notification, logging, and limited automated failure response
- Replication of Cisco Secure user database components to other Cisco Secure ACS servers
- Automatic configuration of users, groups, network devices, and custom RADIUS vendor-specific attributes (VSAs)
- Scheduled and on-demand Cisco Secure ACS system backups

Cisco Secure ACS for Windows Architecture

Cisco Secure ACS is modular and flexible to fit the needs of both simple and large networks. Cisco Secure ACS for Windows operates as a set of Windows 2000 services and controls the authentication, authorization, and accounting of users accessing networks.

When you install Cisco Secure ACS on your server, the installation adds several Windows services. These services provide the core of the Cisco Secure ACS functionality and are as follows:

- **CSAdmin**—Provides the HTML interface for administration of Cisco Secure ACS
- **CSAuth**—Provides authentication and authorization services

- **CSDBSync**—Provides synchronization of the Cisco Secure user database with an external RDBMS application
- **CSLog**—Provides logging services, both for accounting and system activity
- **CSMon**—Provides monitoring, recording, and notification of Cisco Secure ACS performance, and includes automatic response to some scenarios
- **CSTacacs and CSRadius**—Provides communication between RADIUS or TACACS+ AAA clients and the CSAuth service

Figure 9-3 shows the cores services in the Cisco ACS for Windows.

Figure 9-3 *The Core Services of Cisco ACS for Windows*

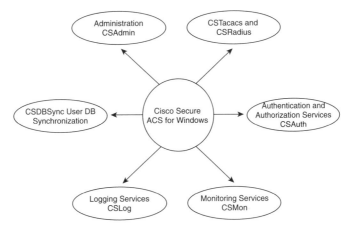

CSAdmin

CSAdmin provides the web server for the Cisco Secure ACS HTML interface. After Cisco Secure ACS is installed, you must configure it from its HTML interface; therefore, CSAdmin must be running when you configure Cisco Secure ACS.

Cisco Secure ACS has a built-in web server for ACS administration. The web server uses port 2002 rather than the standard port 80 usually associated with HTTP traffic. CSAdmin is multithreaded, which enables several Cisco Secure ACS administrators to access it at the same time. Therefore, CSAdmin is well-suited for distributed, multiprocessor environments.

CSAuth

CSAuth is the authentication and authorization service. It permits or denies access to users by processing authentication and authorization requests. CSAuth determines whether access should be granted and defines the privileges for a particular user. It is the Cisco Secure ACS database manager.

To authenticate users, Cisco Secure ACS can use the internal user database or one of many external databases. When a request for authentication arrives, Cisco Secure ACS checks the database that is configured for that user. If the user is unknown, Cisco Secure ACS checks the database configured for unknown users.

When a user has authenticated, Cisco Secure ACS obtains a set of authorizations from the user profile and the group to which the user is assigned. This information is stored with the username in the Cisco Secure user database. Some of the authorizations included are the services to which the user is entitled, such as IP over PPP, IP pools from which to draw an IP address, access lists, and password-aging information. The authorizations, with the approval of authentication, are then passed to the CSTacacs or CSRadius modules to be forwarded to the requesting device.

CSDBSync

CSDBSync is the service used to synchronize the Cisco Secure ACS database with third-party relational database management systems (RDBMSs). CSDBSync synchronizes AAA client, AAA server, network device groups, and proxy table information with data from a table in an external relational database.

CSLog

CSLog is the service used to capture and place logging information. CSLog gathers data from the TACACS+ or RADIUS packet and CSAuth and then manipulates the data to be placed into the comma-separated value (CSV) files. CSV files can be imported into spreadsheets that support this format.

CSMon

CSMon is a service that helps minimize downtime in a remote-access network environment. It provides monitoring, recording, and notification of Cisco Secure ACS performance and includes automatic responses to some scenarios. CSMon works for both TACACS+ and RADIUS and automatically detects which protocols are in use. You can use the Cisco Secure ACS HTML interface to configure the CSMon service. The Cisco Secure ACS Active Service Management feature provides the options for configuring CSMon behavior.

CSTacacs and CSRadius

The CSTacacs and CSRadius services communicate between the CSAuth module and the access device that is requesting authentication and authorization services. CSTacacs is used to communicate with TACACS+ devices and CSRadius to communicate with RADIUS devices. Both services can run at the same time. When only one security protocol is used, only the applicable service needs to be running; however, the other service does not interfere with normal operation and does not need to be disabled.

Cisco ACS for UNIX

Cisco Secure ACS for UNIX incorporates a multiuser, web-based Java configuration and management tool that simplifies server administration. Security services can be managed by several system administrators located in multiple location simultaneously.

Cisco Secure ACS for UNIX supports Sybase and Oracle relational databases. The Cisco Secure ACS includes SQLAnywhere from Sybase. Although this version of the database does not have client/server support, it is optimized to perform the essential AAA services with the Cisco Secure ACS.

The Cisco Secure ACS for UNIX is designed to provide for easy expansion of AAA services in a NAS. It uses relational enterprise databases, allowing an environment in which any number of Cisco Secure ACSs can be distributed among many locations.

The distributed databases provide the necessary replication of data among the Cisco Secure ACSs, especially for organizations that have several sites. This solution allows for redundancy, user-entry scalability, and performance scalability.

The distributed architecture of the Cisco Secure ACS enables you to scale your performance. In a dial-in network with multiple dial-in port banks located in different regions, you can scale network performance by installing separate Cisco Secure ACSs to support each region.

Features of Cisco Secure ACS 2.3 for UNIX products include the following:

- Web-page–based interface to do the following:
    - Manage TACACS+-enabled and RADIUS-enabled Cisco Secure ACSs
    - Set up and manage remote connections to VPDNs
    - Administer Secure Computing token card users
    - Manage TACACS+-enabled and RADIUS-enabled NAS clients
    - Configure a default profile to accommodate guest users or users logging in through a client NAS but who are authorized by some other control system to access the network
    - Assign mid-level group administration privileges
    - Configure token caching for all users logging in through a token server
- UNIX CLI support
- Profile data caching (for enhanced authentication performance)
- Support for database replication among multiple Oracle or Sybase database sites that contain the profile data for multiple Cisco Secure ACS sites

Cisco Secure ACS for UNIX can be used with the both the TACACS+ protocol and RADIUS protocol. Although some AAA features are supported by both protocols, other features are protocol dependent, as shown on Table 9-2.

Table 9-2 *AAA Features Supported by the TACACS+ and RADIUS Protocols for the UNIX Cisco Secure ACS Version*

AAA Feature	TACACS+ Support	RADIUS Support
Web-based administration	Yes	Yes
Encrypted password transactions	Yes	Yes
Solaris 2.5 or greater support	Yes	Yes
Option to disable accounts after failed login attempt count exceeded	Yes	Yes
User group membership support	Yes	Yes
Accounting support	Yes	Yes
Session key authentication support	Yes	Yes
Option to specify maximum sessions per user	Yes	Yes
Support for use of common token card servers (CRYPTOCard, Secure Computing, and Security Dynamics, Inc.)	Yes	Yes
Password aging and configurable warning period	Yes	No
Allow/refuse filter option for remote addresses	Yes	No
Option to change user passwords or reject passwords not meeting security requirements	Yes	No
Language configurable message catalogs	Yes	No

Currently, two upgrade options are available for Cisco Secure ACS for UNIX:

- **Upgrading from Cisco Secure ACS 1.x**—Users of the database included with Cisco Secure ACS 1.x can import their 1.x user database into the Cisco Secure ACS RDBMS.
- **Upgrading from Cisco Secure ACS 2.x**—Users of Cisco Secure ACS 2.x, don't have to do any imports because their database is supported in the current version of Cisco Secure ACS for UNIX upon installation.

Foundation Summary

The "Foundation Summary" section of each chapter lists the most important facts from the chapter. Although this section does not list every fact from the chapter that will be on your exam, a well-prepared candidate should at a minimum know all the details in each "Foundation Summary" section before going to take the exam.

Important points to remember about Cisco Secure ACS for Windows 2000/NT include the following:

- Helps centralize access control and accounting
- Can authenticate against many popular token servers
- Uses the TACACS+ and RADIUS protocols to provide AAA services that ensure a secure environment
- Provides AAA services to network devices that function as AAA clients, such as NASs, switches, PIX firewalls, VPN concentrators, and routers
- Enables network administrators to quickly administer accounts and globally change levels of service of service offerings for entire group of users
- Supports many popular user repository implementations, including Windows Active Directory

The major services that make up Cisco Secure ACS for Windows are as follows:

- **CSAdmin**—Provides the HTML interface for administration of Cisco Secure ACS
- **CSAuth**—Provides authentication services
- **CSDBSync**—Provides synchronization of the Cisco Secure user database with an external RDBMS application
- **CSLog**—Provides logging services, both for accounting and system activity
- **CSMon**—Provides monitoring, recording, and notification of Cisco Secure ACS performance, and includes automatic response to some scenarios
- **CSTacacs and CSRadius**—Provides communication between RADIUS or TACACS+ AAA clients and the CSAuth service

Q&A

As mentioned in the section, "How to Use This Book," in the Introduction to this book, you have two choices for review questions. The questions that follow next give you a bigger challenge than the exam itself by using an open-ended question format. By reviewing now with this more difficult question format, you can exercise your memory better and prove your conceptual and factual knowledge of this chapter. The answers to these questions are found in the appendix.

For more practice with exam-like question formats, including questions using a router simulator and multiple choice questions, use the exam engine on the CD-ROM.

1. Where does the Cisco Secure ACS write its accounting records?
2. Give one example of the user repository that Cisco Secure ACS supports?
3. Give one advantage of using Cisco Secure ACS?
4. Give two examples of the password protocols that are supported by Cisco Secure ACS?
5. Mike is a network administrator at an engineering firm. He would like to restrict access to consultants during the weekend. Can Cisco Secure ACS help Mike?
6. What are the core services of Cisco Secure ACS 3.0?
7. What is the function of CSAdmin?
8. What are some of the databases that Cisco Secure ACS for UNIX supports?
9. Which core service of the Cisco Secure ACS for Windows provides synchronization with external RDBMS applications?
10. Name two types of accounting logs generated by Cisco Secure ACS

This chapter covers the following subjects:

- Basic Deployment Factors for Cisco Secure ACS

- Installing Cisco Secure ACS for Windows

- Troubleshooting Cisco Secure ACS for Windows

CHAPTER 10

Administration of Cisco Secure Access Control Server

AAA was conceived originally to provide a centralized point of control for user access via dialup services. As user databases grew, more capability was required of the AAA server. Regional, and then global, requirements became common.

This chapter provides insight into the deployment process and presents a collection of factors that you should consider before deploying Cisco Secure Access Control Server (Cisco Secure ACS).

"Do I Know This Already?" Quiz

The purpose of the "Do I Know This Already?" quiz is to help you decide whether you really need to read the entire chapter. If you already intend to read the entire chapter, you do not necessarily need to answer these questions now.

The five-question quiz, derived from the major sections in "Foundation Topics" section of the chapter, helps you determine how to spend your limited study time.

Table 10-1 outlines the major topics discussed in this chapter and the "Do I Know This Already?" quiz questions that correspond to those topics.

Table 10-1 *"Do I Know This Already?" Foundation Topics Section-to-Question Mapping*

Foundation Topics Section	Questions Covered in This Section
Basic Deployment Factors for Cisco Secure ACS	1, 2, 5
Installing Cisco Secure ACS for Windows	3, 4

CAUTION The goal of self-assessment is to gauge your mastery of the topics in this chapter. If you do not know the answer to a question or are only partially sure of the answer, you should mark this question wrong for purposes of the self-assessment. Giving yourself credit for an answer you correctly guess skews your self-assessment results and might provide you with a false sense of security.

Chapter 10: Administration of Cisco Secure Access Control Server

1. Which of the following points do you have to consider before deploying Cisco Secure ACS?

    a. Dialup topology

    b. Number of users

    c. Remote access policy

    d. Number of Linux servers

2. Which of the following is the minimum CPU requirement for a Cisco Secure ACS server?

    a. At least a Pentium III 550 MHz

    b. At least Pentium II 330 MHZ

    c. Will work on any Pentium platform

    d. Both A and B

3. Which of the following are task buttons that are present on the web administrative interface of Cisco Secure ACS? How would network latency affect the deployment of Cisco Secure ACS?

    a. User Setup

    b. Group Setup

    c. Network Configuration

    d. System Configuration

4. Which of the following are checklist items that come up during the installation of Cisco Secure ACS?

    a. Windows server can successfully ping AAA clients.

    b. End users can successfully connect to AAA clients.

    c. Your version is at least Netscape version 6.02.

    d. You have a T1 connection.

5. What is the minimum browser version that is supported by Cisco ACS version 3.2?

    a. Netscape 6.02 and Microsoft Internet Explorer 6.0

    b. Mosaic 3.0 and Microsoft Internet Explorer 5.5

    c. Netscape 7.0 and Microsoft Internet Explorer 6.0

    d. Mosaic 3.0 and Netscape 7.02

The answers to the "Do I Know This Already?" quiz are found in the appendix. The suggested choices for your next step are as follows:

- **3 or less overall score**—Read the entire chapter. This includes the "Foundation Topics" and "Foundation Summary" sections and the "Q&A" section.

- **4 or 5 overall score**—If you want more review on these topics, skip to the "Foundation Summary" section and then go to the "Q&A" section. Otherwise, move on to the next chapter.

Foundation Topics

Basic Deployment Factors for Cisco Secure ACS

Generally, the ease in deploying Cisco Secure ACS is directly related to the complexity of the implementation planned and the degree to which you have defined your policies and requirements. Deployment factors include the following:

- Number of users
- Network topology
- Access policy
- Network latency and reliability
- Remote-access policy
- Administrative-access policy

The following factors are just a few things to consider when deploying Cisco Secure ACS. In addition, minimum hardware and operating system requirements apply when you are installing Cisco Secure ACS. The following sections detail these specifications.

Hardware Requirements

The computer running Cisco Secure ACS must meet the following minimum hardware requirements:

- Pentium III processor, 550 MHz or faster
- 256 MB of RAM
- At least 250 MB of free disk space if you are running an external database (if not, more disk space is required)
- Minimum graphics resolution of 256 colors at 800 by 600 lines

Operating System Requirements

The Cisco Secure ACS should be installed on a computer running an English language version of Windows 2000 Server with a minimum of Service Pack 3. Currently, Windows 2000 Advance Server and Windows 2000 Datacenter Server are not supported.

Browser Compatibility

Your Cisco Secure ACS server must have a compatible browser installed. Cisco Secure ACS 3.2 has been tested with English language versions of the following browsers on Microsoft Windows operating systems:

- Microsoft Internet Explorer Version 6.0
- Netscape Communicator Version 7.0

To use a web browser to access the Cisco Secure ACS HTML interface, you must enable both Java and JavaScript in the browser. Also, the web browser must not be configured to use a proxy server. If the browser used for an administrative session is configured to use a proxy server, Cisco Secure ACS sees the administrative session originating from the IP address of the proxy server rather than from the actual address of the computer.

Installing Cisco Secure ACS

After confirming your system requirements for Cisco Secure ACS for Windows, run the setup program to install the software. Figure 10-1 shows a checklist window that comes up during the first part of the installation process.

Figure 10-1 *Checklist Window That Appears During the Installation Process for Cisco ACS 3.2*

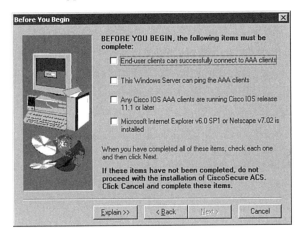

As shown in Figure 10-1, the installation process wants you to test and confirm a few things before moving forward with the installation process.

1. End users can successfully connect to the AAA client such as a network access server (NAS).
2. Verify connections between Windows NT/2000 server and other network devices. Make sure that the AAA devices on your network can reach (ping) your Windows NT/2000 server. This would make the installation smoother and helps reduce any troubleshooting issues later on when it's time to configure the Cisco Secure ACS and the devices that use it.
3. Check the Cisco IOS Software version on the AAA client and make sure that it is later than Release 11.1.
4. Make sure that your browser version complies with the required version for Microsoft Windows (Internet Explorer 6.0 and Netscape 7.0)

When the installation is complete, the HTML interface appears, in which you make administration and configuration changes to the Cisco Secure ACS.

The HTML interface provides a navigation bar at the left of the browser with task buttons on them. Figure 10-2 shows the HTML interface with the navigation bar containing the task buttons.

Figure 10-2 *The HTML Interface for Cisco Secure ACS*

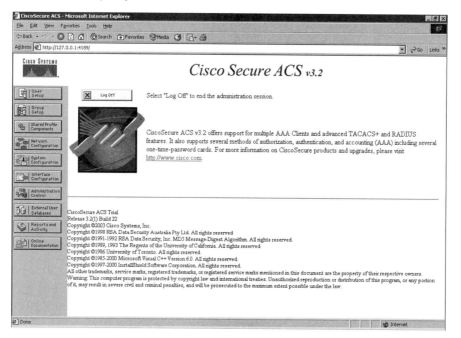

The task buttons are as follows:

- **User Setup**—Add and edit user profiles.
- **Group Setup**—Configure network services and protocols for groups of users.
- **Shared Profile Components**—Add and edit network access restriction and command authorization sets to be applied to users and groups.
- **Network Configuration**—Add and edit network access devices and configure distributed systems.
- **System Configuration**—Configure database information and accounting.
- **Interface Configuration**—Display or hide product features and options to be configured.
- **Administration Control**—Define and configure access policies.
- **External User Databases**—Configure external databases for authentication.
- **Reports and Activity**—Display accounting and logging information.
- **Online Documentation**—View the user guide.

Table 10-2 shows the ports that Cisco Secure ACS uses.

Table 10-2 *Cisco Secure ACS Ports Requirement*

Service Name	UDP	TCP
RADIUS authentication and authorization	1645, 1812	
RADIUS accounting	1646, 1813	
TACACS+ AAA		49
Replication and RDBMS synchronization		2000
ACS remote logging		2001
HTTP administrative access		2002

Suggested Deployment Sequence

Although there is no single process for all Cisco Secure ACS deployments, you should consider following the sequence keyed to the high-level functions represented in the navigation toolbar. Also bear in mind that many of these deployment activities are iterative in nature; you may find that you repeatedly return to such tasks as interface configuration as your deployment proceeds.

- **Configure administrators**—You should configure at least one administrator at the beginning of the deployment. This will provide remote administrative access.
- **Configure the Cisco Secure ACS HTML interface**—Select the features and controls that you intend to use through the HTML interface. This makes using Cisco Secure ACS easier than it would be if you had to contend with multiple parts of the HTML interface that you do not plan to use.

- **Configure system**—There are more than a dozen functions within the System Configuration section to be considered, from setting the format for the display of dates and password validation to configuring settings for database replication and RDBMS synchronization.

- **Configure network**—You control distributed and proxied AAA functions in the Network Configuration section of the HTML interface. From here, you establish the identity, location, and grouping of AAA clients and servers and determine which authentication protocols each is to use.

- **Configure external user database**—During this phase of deployment, you must decide whether and how you intend to implement an external database to establish and maintain user authentication accounts. Typically, this decision is made according to your existing network administration mechanisms.

- **Configure shared profile components**—With most aspects of network configuration already established and before configuring user groups, you should configure your shared profile components. When you set up and name the network access restrictions and command authorization sets you intend to use, you lay out an efficient basis for specifying user group and single-user access privileges.

- **Configure groups**—Having previously configured any external user databases you intend to use and before configuring your user groups, you should decide how to implement two other Cisco Secure ACS features related to external user databases: unknown user processing and database group mapping.

- **Configure users**—With groups established, you can establish user accounts. It is useful to remember that a particular user can belong to only one user group, and that settings made at the user level override settings made at the group level.

- **Configure reports**—Using the Reports and Activities section of the Cisco Secure ACS HTML interface, you can specify the nature and scope of logging that Cisco Secure ACS performs.

Troubleshooting Cisco Secure ACS for Windows

A good place to start troubleshooting Cisco Secure ACS-related AAA problems is the Failed Attempts Report under Reports and Activity. The report displays several types of failures. If no entry is found in the Failed Attempts Report, it could be that there is a misconfiguration between the Cisco Secure ACS and the router/client. In this case, do the following:

- Verify that the router can ping the server and that the server can ping the router.
- Verify that the TACACS+ host IP address is correctly configured on the router.
- Verify that the TACACS+ host key entered on both the router and the Cisco Secure ACS is the same.

Authentication Problems

If there are entries of authentication failure in the Failed Attempts Report and you are authenticating against a Windows 2000 user database, check the following items:

- Verify whether Cisco Secure ACS is configured to authenticate to the Windows 2000 user database.
- Verify whether the correct username and password is being used.
- Confirm the existence of the username.
- Check whether the user account has User Must Change Password at Next Login selected. If this option is selected, deselect it.
- Confirm that Cisco Secure ACS is configured to reference the Grant Dial-In Permission to User.
- Verify whether the retry interval is too brief. (The default is five seconds). Increase the retry interval (**tacacs-server timeout 20**) on the AAA client to 20 or greater "users."

Troubleshooting Authorization Problems

If the authentication is working but the authorization is failing, check the following items:

- Are the proper network services checked in the group settings?
- If IP is checked, how is the dial-in user obtaining an address?
- Is there an IP pool configured on the NAS?
- Has the radio button for the command been permitted?
- Has the radio button for the argument been permitted?

Administration Issues

Table 10-3 details how to approach some of the problems that may arise in a Cisco Secure ACS installation.

Table 10-3 *CS ACS Installation Troubleshooting*

Issue	Troubleshooting Tasks
Remote administrator cannot bring up the Cisco Secure ACS HTML interface in a browser or receives a warning that access is not permitted.	Ping Cisco Secure ACS to confirm connectivity. Verify that the remote administrator is using a valid administrator name and password that has already been added in Administration Control. Verify that Java functionality is enabled in the browser. Determine whether the remote administrator is trying to administer Cisco Secure ACS through a firewall, through a device performing network address translation or from a browser configured to use an HTTP proxy server.
Unauthorized users can log in.	Reject Listed IP Addresses is selected, but no start or stop IP addresses are listed. Go to Administrator Control: Access Policy and specify the Start IP Address and Stop IP Address.
No remote administrators can log in.	Allow Only Listed IP Addresses to Connect is selected, but no start or stop IP addresses are listed. Go to Administrator Control: Access Policy and specify the Start IP Address and Stop IP Address.

Other useful troubleshooting commands for NAS devices (IOS and CatOS) include the following:

- **debug tacacs+**
- **debug radius**
- **debug aaa authentication**
- **debug aaa authorization**

Foundation Summary

The "Foundation Summary" section of each chapter lists the most important facts from the chapter. Although this section does not list every fact from the chapter that will be on your exam, a well-prepared candidate should at a minimum know all the details in each "Foundation Summary" section before going to take the exam.

The following are the minimum hardware requirements for installing Cisco Secure ACS for Windows:

- Pentium III processor, 550 MHz or faster.
- 256 MB of RAM.
- At least 250 MB of free disk space. If you are running your database on the same machine, more disk space is required.
- Minimum graphics resolution of 256 colors at 800 by 600 lines.

Cisco Secure ACS deployment factors that you may need to consider include the following:

- Number of users
- Network topology
- Dialup topology
- Network latency and reliability
- Remote-access policy
- Administrative-access policy

A good place to start troubleshooting Cisco Secure ACS-related AAA problems is the Failed Attempts Report under Reports and Activity. The report displays several types of failures. Other useful troubleshooting commands include the following:

- **debug tacacs+**
- **debug radius**
- **debug aaa authentication**
- **debug aaa authorization**

Q&A

As mentioned in the section, "How to Use This Book," in the Introduction to this book, you have two choices for review questions. The questions that follow next give you a bigger challenge than the exam itself by using an open-ended question format. By reviewing now with this more difficult question format, you can exercise your memory better and prove your conceptual and factual knowledge of this chapter. The answers to these questions are found in the appendix.

For more practice with exam-like question formats, including questions using a router simulator and multiple choice questions, use the exam engine on the CD-ROM.

1. What factors should you consider when deploying Cisco Secure ACS?
2. What are the minimum hardware requirements to install Cisco Secure ACS?
3. How does Cisco Secure ACS provide control for remote-access policies?
4. Where would be a good place to start to troubleshoot Cisco Secure ACS-related AAA problems?
5. Does a browser using a proxy server have any effect in the administration of a Cisco Secure ACS remotely?

PART IV: The Cisco IOS Firewall Feature Set

Chapter 11   Securing the Network with a Cisco Router

Chapter 12   Access Lists

Chapter 13   The Cisco IOS Firewall

Chapter 14   Context-Based Access Control (CBAC)

Chapter 15   Authentication Proxy and the Cisco IOS Firewall

Chapter 16   Intrusion Detection and the Cisco IOS Firewall

This part of the book addresses the following exam objectives as posted at Cisco.com:

- Secure administrative access for Cisco routers
- Disable unused router services and interfaces
- Use access lists to mitigate common router security threats
- Define the Cisco IOS Firewall and CBAC
- Configure CBAC
- Describe how authentication proxy technology works
- Name the two types of signature implementations used by the Cisco IOS Firewall IDS
- Initialize a Cisco IOS Firewall IDS router

This chapter covers the following subject:

- Disable Unused Router Services and Interfaces

CHAPTER **11**

Securing the Network with a Cisco Router

Services or features on your router that are not in use on your network present potential vulnerabilities that could be easily be exploited by an intruder with limited skill. Disabling unnecessary services helps reduce the vulnerability of your network. Going forward, this chapter highlights some of the common services/features that you should consider disabling if they are not in use.

"Do I Know This Already?" Quiz

The purpose of the "Do I Know This Already?" quiz is to help you decide whether you really need to read the entire chapter. If you already intend to read the entire chapter, you do not necessarily need to answer these questions now.

The 10-question quiz, derived from the major sections in "Foundation Topics" section of the chapter, helps you determine how to spend your limited study time.

Table 11-1 outlines the major topics discussed in this chapter and the "Do I Know This Already?" quiz questions that correspond to those topics.

Table 11-1 *"Do I Know This Already?" Foundation Topics Section-to-Question Mapping*

Foundation Topics Section	Questions Covered in This Section
Disable Unused Router Services and Interfaces	1–10

CAUTION The goal of self-assessment is to gauge your mastery of the topics in this chapter. If you do not know the answer to a question or are only partially sure of the answer, you should mark this question wrong for purposes of the self-assessment. Giving yourself credit for an answer you correctly guess skews your self-assessment results and might provide you with a false sense of security.

Chapter 11: Securing the Network with a Cisco Router

1. Which of the following versions of SNMP does Cisco IOS Software support?
   a. SNMPv1
   b. SNMPv2
   c. SNMPv3
   d. SNMPv4

2. Which of the following is (are) true about SNMP version 1?
   a. Very secure
   b. Used very widely
   c. Uses a very weak authentication scheme based on "community string"
   d. All of the above

3. Why is it important to secure the SNMP management station? Select the best answer.
   a. The concentration of large information on the SNMP management station makes it a target.
   b. Because there could be only a single SNMP management station.
   c. SNMP management stations only operate older versions of the UNIX operating system.
   d. None of the above.

4. Which of the following is true about the HTTP server on the Cisco IOS Software?
   a. The HTTP server is on by default.
   b. The HTTP server uses MD5 for authentication by default.
   c. The HTTP server is off by default.
   d. The HTTP server requires authentication to provide access to the router.

5. To what type of attack does running **ip directed broadcast** expose the router?
   a. Smurf attack
   b. SMTP attack
   c. SPAM attack
   d. All of the above

6. Which of the following is the best answer in securing routing updates from routing protocols?
   a. Routing updates cannot be secure
   b. Increase physical security
   c. Disable the routing protocols
   d. Configure neighbor authentication

7. Which of the following are part of the small server services?

   a. Echo

   b. Chargen

   c. Discard

   d. CDP

8. Which of the following is true regarding the IP directed-broadcast service?

   a. The **no ip directed-broadcast** command is the default in Cisco IOS Software Release 12.0 and later.

   b. Reduces HTTP vulnerabilities.

   c. Increases security.

   d. Only A and C

9. What is the command to disable CDP on a particular interface?

   a. **no cdp neighbor**

   b. **no cdp running**

   c. **no cdp**

   d. **no cdp enable**

10. What is the command to enable the HTTPS server on the Cisco IOS router?

    a. **ip https server**

    b. **ip server https**

    c. **ip http secure-server**

    d. **ip secure-server**

The answers to the "Do I Know This Already?" quiz are found in the appendix. The suggested choices for your next step are as follows:

- **8 or less overall score**—Read the entire chapter. This includes the "Foundation Topics" and "Foundation Summary" sections and the "Q&A" section.

- **9 or 10 overall score**—If you want more review on these topics, skip to the "Foundation Summary" section and then go to the "Q&A" section. Otherwise, move on to the next chapter.

Foundation Topics

Unused but enabled services on routers could be a potential vulnerability for your network. Every network is unique in one way or another and therefore requires a different type of configuration on its routers. This chapter covers some of the Cisco IOS Software services that should be turned off in most network settings to prevent security breaches or network downtime. It also discusses some commonly configured management services and how to securely operate them.

Simple Network Management Protocol (SNMP)

SNMP is very widely used for router monitoring and frequently for router configuration changes as well. If not configured properly, SNMP could provide a wealth of information about the device to intruders running SNMP discovery tools.

Cisco IOS Software Release 12.1 supports the following versions of SNMP:

- **SNMPv1**—The Simple Network Management Protocol; a full Internet standard, defined in RFC 1157. Security is based on community strings.
- **SNMPv2c**—The community string-based administrative framework for SNMPv2. SNMPv2c (the "c" stands for "community") is an experimental Internet protocol defined in RFC 1901, RFC 1905, and RFC 1906.
- **SNMPv3**—Version 3 of the Simple Network Management Protocol. SNMPv3 is an interoperable standards-based protocol defined in RFCs 2273 through 2275. SNMPv3 provides secure access to devices by a combination of authenticating and encrypting packets over the network.

Unfortunately, version 1 of the SNMP protocol, which is the most commonly used, uses a very weak authentication scheme based on a community string, which amounts to a fixed password transmitted over the network without encryption. SNMPv1 is ill suited for use across the public Internet for the following reasons:

- It uses clear-text strings.
- Most SNMP implementations send those strings repeatedly as part of periodic polling.

You should carefully consider the implications before using it that way. If it is absolutely necessary that you use SNMP, it is recommended you use SNMPv3, which supports a Message Digest 5 (MD5)-based digest authentication scheme and allows for restricted access to various management data.

Another way to mitigate the potential threats posed when using SNMPv1 is to avoid using the same community strings for all network devices. Use a different string or strings for each device, or at least for each area of the network. Use strong community names. Do not make a read-only string the same as a read-write string. If possible, periodic SNMPv1 polling should be done with a read-only community string; read-write strings should be used only for actual write operations.

In most networks, legitimate SNMP messages come only from certain management stations. If this is true in your network, you should probably use the access list number option on the **snmp-server community** command to restrict SNMPv1 access to only the IP addresses of the management stations. Do not use the **snmp-server community** command for any purpose in a pure SNMPv2 environment; this command implicitly enables SNMPv1.

SNMPv3 uses a secure form of communication. The security features provided in SNMPv3 are as follows:

- **Message integrity**—Ensuring that a packet has not been tampered with in transit
- **Authentication**—Determining the message is from a valid source
- **Encryption**—Scrambling the contents of a packet to prevent it from being seen by an unauthorized source

SNMP management stations often have large databases of authentication information, such as community strings. This information may provide access to many routers and other network devices. This concentration of information makes the SNMP management station a natural target for attack, and it should be secured accordingly.

Controlling Interactive Access Through a Browser

Administrative access support via a browser is supported by Cisco IOS Software Release 11.0(6) and later. This feature is disabled by default but can be enabled by the **ip http server** command.

However, the use of HTTP to manage a router presents some inherent vulnerabilities. The Cisco IOS HTTP server provides authentication, but not encryption, for client connections. The data that the client and server transmit to each other is not encrypted. This leaves communication between clients and servers vulnerable to interception and attack. To reduce the risk posed by this vulnerability, it is possible to use the **ip http access-class** command to restrict the hosts that connect to the router via HTTP or use the Cisco secure HTTP server.

The Secure HTTP (HTTPS) feature provides the capability to connect to the Cisco IOS HTTPS server securely. It is enabled with the **ip http secure-server** command.

It uses Secure Sockets Layer (SSL) and Transport Layer Security (TLS) to provide device authentication and data encryption. HTTPS authenticates the client and the server with each other before establishing a connection. HTTPS supports the following standards:

- MD5
- Secure Hash Algorithm 1 (SHA1)
- Public key-based encryption:

    —RSA—Encryption/decryption/generation

    —DSA—Encryption/decryption/generation

    —Diffie-Hellman—Key exchange/key generation

    —X.509 digital certificates

Before you start configuring the HTTPS server, generate an RSA usage key pair with a length of 1024 bits or greater for the device using the **crypto key generate rsa usage 1024** command. If you do not generate an RSA usage key pair manually, an RSA usage key pair with a length of 768 bits is generated automatically when you connect to the HTTPS server for the first time. Unless you save these automatically generated keys manually to NVRAM, they will be lost when the device is rebooted. The following is an example of enabling HTTPS on a router:

```
FW1(config)#ip http secure-server
```

Disabling Directed Broadcasts

On IP networks, a packet can be directed to an individual machine or broadcast to an entire network. When a packet is sent to an IP broadcast address from a machine on the local network, that packet is delivered to all machines on that network. When a packet is sent to that IP broadcast address from a machine outside of the local network, it is broadcast to all machines on the target network.

IP broadcast addresses are usually network addresses with the host portion of the address having all 1 bits. For example, the IP broadcast address for the network 192.168.100.0 is 192.168.100.255. Network addresses with all 0s in the host portion, such as 192.168.100.0, can also produce a broadcast response. In the Smurf attack, attackers are using ICMP echo request packets directed to IP broadcast addresses from remote locations to generate DoS attacks. There are three parties in these attacks: the attacker, the intermediary, and the victim.

> **NOTE** These attacks have been referred to as Smurf attacks because the name of one of the exploit programs attackers use to execute this attack is called Smurf.

The intermediary receives an ICMP echo request packet directed to the IP broadcast address of their network. If the intermediary does not filter ICMP traffic directed to IP broadcast addresses, many of the machines on the network receive this ICMP echo request packet and send an ICMP echo reply packet back. When (potentially) all the machines on a network respond to this ICMP echo request, the result can be severe network congestion or outages.

When the attackers create these packets, they do not use the IP address of their own machine as the source address. Instead, they create forged packets that contain the spoofed source address of the attacker's intended victim. The result is that when all the machines at the intermediary's site respond to the ICMP echo requests, they send replies to the victim's machine. The victim is subjected to network congestion that could potentially make the network unusable.

Unless applications or other explicit requirements need the router interfaces to have IP directed broadcasts, it should be turned off, to suppress the effects of this attack. You can use the **no ip directed-broadcast** command to do so on the Cisco IOS Software.

The **no ip directed-broadcast** interface command is the default in Cisco IOS Software Release 12.0 and later. In earlier versions, the command should be applied to every LAN interface that isn't known to forward legitimate directed broadcasts.

Routing Protocol Authentication

One of the ways that routers update their routing tables is by route updates they receive from other routers by routing protocols. Routing protocols are vulnerable to spoofing of route updates. A mechanism for receiving reliable routing information from a trusted source router should be put in place to avoid getting bad updates by "rogue" or misconfigured routers. It is quite possible to have a rogue router provide bad routes to your router, which could cause the failure of your network. One way to combat this problem is to use authentication and encryption for the communication between routers that share routing updates.

When authentication is configured, neighbor authentication occurs whenever routing updates are exchanged between neighbor routers. This authentication ensures that a routing protocol receives reliable routing information from a trusted source.

The authentication process works by requiring a unique key to first verify the source (neighbor router) before a routing update is accepted by a routing protocol. This way "rogue" routers will not be able to participate in the route update process. The process of authentication occurs as follows (in summary):

1. A router sends a routing update with a key to the neighbor router.
2. The receiving (neighbor) router compares the received key against the key stored in its own memory.

3. If the two keys match, the receiving router accepts the routing update packet. If the two keys do not match, the routing update packet is rejected.

MD5 authentication works much like plain-text authentication, except that the key is never sent over the wire. Instead, the router uses the MD5 algorithm to produce a "message digest" of the key (also called a *hash*). The message digest is then sent rather than the key itself. This ensures that nobody can eavesdrop on the line and learn keys during transmission. Routing protocols such Open Shortest Path First (OSPF), Routing Information Protocol (RIP) version 2, Interior Gateway Routing Protocol (IGRP), and Border Gateway Protocol (BGP) use it.

Small Server Services

TCP and UDP small servers are services that run in the router and are useful for diagnostics. These include the following:

- **Echo (UDP, TCP)**—This simple port just echoes whatever is sent to it.
- **Chargen (UDP, TCP)**—Generates a stream of characters (TCP) or a packet containing characters (UDP).
- **Daytime (TCP)**—Responds with the current time of day. The protocol specification doesn't clearly define the format of the data returned, so every machine responds in a slightly different format. This can be used to fingerprint machines.
- **Discard (UDP, TCP)**—Throws traffic away.

These services, especially their UDP versions, are used for diagnostic purposes but can be used to launch DoS and other attacks that would otherwise be prevented by packet filtering. It is recommended that these services not be enabled unless doing so is absolutely necessary. These services could be exploited indirectly to gain information about the target system or directly as is the case with the Fraggle attack, which uses UDP echo.

> **NOTE** Fingerprinting is the technique of interpreting the responses of a system to figure out what it is. In particular, unexpected combinations of data are sometimes sent at the system to trigger these responses.

Exploitation of these services may result in symptoms such as the process table being full of error messages (%SYS-3 NOPROC) or very high CPU utilization. The small services are disabled by default in Cisco IOS Software 12.0 and later. In earlier software, you can disable them by using the commands **no service tcp-small-servers** and **no service udp-small-servers**.

Disabling Finger Services

Cisco routers provide an implementation of the finger service, which is used to find out which users are logged in to a network device. This service is equivalent to issuing a remote **show users** command. Although the information gained may seem harmless, it could be valuable to an attacker. You can disable the finger service with the command **no service finger**.

Disabling Network Time Protocol (NTP)

NTP isn't especially dangerous, but any unneeded service may represent a path for penetration. If NTP is actually used, it's important to explicitly configure a trusted time source and to use proper authentication, because corrupting the time base is a good way to subvert certain security protocols. If NTP isn't being used on a particular router interface, you can disable it with the interface command **no ntp enable**.

Disabling Cisco Discovery Protocol (CDP)

CDP is a Cisco proprietary Layer 2 protocol that is media and protocol independent and runs on all Cisco-manufactured equipment, including routers, access servers, and switches. CDP is primarily used to obtain protocol addresses of neighboring devices and discover the platform of those devices. CDP can also be used to show information about the interfaces your router uses.

The information provided by CDP can potentially be used by an attacker to compromise the neighboring device and consequently the network. If CDP is not used by your network, you should turn it off. CDP may be disabled with the global configuration command **no cdp running**. CDP may be disabled on a particular interface with **no cdp enable**.

Foundation Summary

The "Foundation Summary" section of each chapter lists the most important facts from the chapter. Although this section does not list every fact from the chapter that will be on your exam, a well-prepared candidate should at a minimum know all the details in each "Foundation Summary" section before going to take the exam.

Table 11-2 *Commands for Preventing Attacks Against the Cisco IOS Router*

Command	Description
no service tcp-small-servers **no service udp-small-servers**	Prevent abuse of the small services from DoS or other attacks.
no service finger	Avoid releasing user information to possible attackers.
no cdp running **no cdp enable**	Avoid releasing information about the router to directly connected devices.
no ntp enable	Prevent attacks against the NTP service.
no ip directed-broadcast	Prevent attackers from using the router as a Smurf amplifier.
snmp-server party... **authentication md5** *secret* ...	Configure MD5-based SNMPv2 authentication. Enable SNMP only if it's needed in your network.
ip http authentication *method*	Authenticate HTTP connection requests (if you've enabled HTTP on your router).
ip http access-class *list*	Further control HTTP access by restricting it to certain host addresses (if you've enabled HTTP on your router).

Q&A

As mentioned in the section, "How to Use This Book," in the Introduction to this book, you have two choices for review questions. The questions that follow next give you a bigger challenge than the exam itself by using an open-ended question format. By reviewing now with this more difficult question format, you can exercise your memory better and prove your conceptual and factual knowledge of this chapter. The answers to these questions are found in the appendix.

For more practice with exam-like question formats, including questions using a router simulator and multiple choice questions, use the exam engine on the CD-ROM.

1. Name the two types of routing protocol authentication (neighbor authentication)?
2. Name one weakness of SNMPv1.
3. How do you enable the HTTP service on the Cisco IOS router?
4. What are the security features that are provided by SNMPv3?
5. What is an IP directed broadcast?
6. What is the default password when accessing the router via the HTTP service?
7. What are the symptoms on the router when an attacker exploits the "small server services" that have been enabled on the router?

This chapter covers the following subject:

- What Are Access Lists

CHAPTER 12

Access Lists

Cisco provides basic traffic-filtering capabilities with access control lists (ACLs). ACLs can be configured for all routed network protocols, to filter those protocols' packets as the packets pass through a router.

You can configure ACLs at your router to control access to a network. ACLs can prevent certain traffic from entering or exiting a network.

"Do I Know This Already?" Quiz

The purpose of the "Do I Know This Already?" quiz is to help you decide whether you really need to read the entire chapter. If you already intend to read the entire chapter, you do not necessarily need to answer these questions now.

The 10-question quiz, derived from the major sections in "Foundation Topics" section of the chapter, helps you determine how to spend your limited study time.

Table 12-1 outlines the major topics discussed in this chapter and the "Do I Know This Already?" quiz questions that correspond to those topics.

Table 12-1 *"Do I Know This Already?" Foundation Topics Section-to-Question Mapping*

Foundation Topics Section	Questions Covered in This Section
Use Access Lists to Mitigate Common Router Security Threats	1–10

CAUTION The goal of self-assessment is to gauge your mastery of the topics in this chapter. If you do not know the answer to a question or are only partially sure of the answer, you should mark this question wrong for purposes of the self-assessment. Giving yourself credit for an answer you correctly guess skews your self-assessment results and might provide you with a false sense of security.

Chapter 12: Access Lists

1. What is an access control list (ACL)?

    a. An ACL is a method of only permitting IPX traffic.

    b. ACLs are rules that deny or permit packets coming in to or out of a router's interface.

    c. ACLs are used only on switches.

    d. ACLs are rules to prevent mail traffic from leaving a router interface only.

2. Which of the following steps are required to create an effective ACL?

    a. Define an ACL by specifying an ACL number or name and access condition.

    b. Administratively shut down the interface before applying the ACL.

    c. Reboot the router after creating the ACL.

    d. Apply the ACL to an interface or terminal line.

3. Which of the following ways can ACLs be used?

    a. To control virtual terminal line access

    b. To automatically shut down interfaces

    c. To restrict contents of routing updates

    d. To send alerts to the network administrator

4. Which of the following are ACL criteria?

    a. Source address of the traffic

    b. Length of the packet

    c. Destination address of the traffic

    d. Upper-layer protocol

5. What is the difference between a standard IP ACL and extended IP ACL?

    a. Standard ACLs use source and destination of the packets, whereas extended IP ACLs use both source and destination with an additional criteria of upper-layer protocol.

    b. Standard ACLs use IP ACL range 1 to 99, and extended IP ACLs use 100 to 199.

    c. Standard ACLs use IP ACL range 100 to 199, and extended IP ACLs use 1 to 99.

    d. Standard ACLs were introduced in the Cisco IOS Software 12.x.

6. What command enables you to apply an ACL to an interface?

   a. **ip access-group** *number* **in | out**

   b. **access-list in | out**

   c. **ip access-group in | out**

   d. **access-list** *number* **in | out**

7. Which of the range of numbers identify an extended IP ACL?

   a. 1–89

   b. 1–99

   c. 99–200

   d. 100–199

8. Which of the following is the correct syntax for a standard IP ACL?

   a. **access-list 50 192.168.1.87 deny 10.100.10.14**

   b. **access-list 101 deny ip host 192.168.1.87 10.100.10.14**

   c. **access-list 50 deny ip host 192.168.1.87**

   d. **access-list 101 host 192.168.1.87 deny 10.100.10.14**

9. Which is the correct syntax for blocking FTP access to host 192.168.10.1 from the FTP server 10.100.100.14 server?

   a. **access-list 11 deny ftp host 192.168.10.1 host 10.100.100.14**

   b. **access-list 101 deny tcp host 192.168.10.1 host 10.100.100.14 eq ftp**

   c. **access-list 11 tcp deny host 192.168.10.1 host 10.100.100.14 eq ftp**

   d. **access-list 101 deny host 192.168.10.1 eq ftp host 10.100.100.14**

10. Suppose you apply the command **access-list 6 permit 0.0.0.0 255.255.255.255**. What happens?

    a. Nothing is permitted.

    b. Everything is permitted.

    c. This an incorrect ACL.

    d. A and B.

The answers to the "Do I Know This Already?" quiz are found in the appendix. The suggested choices for your next step are as follows:

- **8 or less overall score**—Read the entire chapter. This includes the "Foundation Topics" and "Foundation Summary" sections and the "Q&A" section.

- **9 or 10 overall score**—If you want more review on these topics, skip to the "Foundation Summary" section and then go to the "Q&A" section. Otherwise, move on to the next chapter.

Foundation Topics

What Are Access Lists

ACLs are rules that deny or permit packets coming in or out of an interface. An ACL typically consists of multiple ACL entries (ACEs), organized internally by the router. When a packet is subjected to access control, the router searches this linked list in order from top to bottom to find a matching element. The matching element is then examined to determine whether the packet is allowed or denied. Figure 12-1 shows the behavior of a router that has an ACL configured on its interfaces.

Figure 12-1 *High-Level Overview of How an ACL Is Processed by a Router*

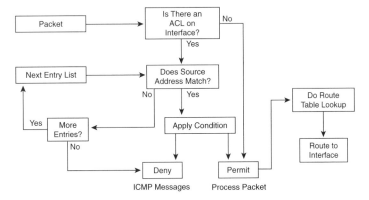

Some of the functions that ACLs are used for include the following:

- To control the transmission of packets coming in to or out from an interface
- To control virtual terminal line access
- To restrict contents of routing updates
- To define interesting traffic

Numbered ACEs are entered one line at a time, and the list is scanned for a match in that same order. If you must make a change, you have to re-enter the entire list.

ACL criteria can be the source address of the traffic, the destination address of the traffic, the upper-layer protocol, or other information.

There is an implied deny for traffic that is not permitted. A single-entry ACL with only one deny entry has the effect of denying all traffic. You must have at least one **permit** statement in an ACL; otherwise, all traffic will be blocked.

When to Configure Access Lists

To provide the security benefits of ACLs, you should at a minimum configure ACLs on border routers, which are routers situated at the edges of your networks. This provides a basic buffer from the outside network or from a less-controlled area of your own network into a more sensitive area of your network.

You can configure ACLs so that inbound traffic or outbound traffic or both are filtered on an interface. ACLs must be defined on a per-protocol basis. In other words, you should define ACLs for every protocol enabled on an interface if you want to control traffic flow for that protocol.

Types of IP ACLs

Cisco IOS Software supports the following types of ACLs for IP:

- **Standard IP ACLs**—Use source addresses for matching operations.
- **Extended IP ACLs**—Use source and destination addresses for matching operations and optional protocol type information for finer granularity of control.
- **Reflexive ACLs**—Allow IP packets to be filtered based on session information. Reflexive ACLs contain temporary entries and are nested within an extended, named IP ACLs.
- **Time-based ACLs**—Time-based ACLs, as the name intuitively indicates, are triggered by a time function.
- **Context-based access control (CBAC)**—CBAC was introduced in Cisco IOS Software Release 12.0.5.T and requires the Cisco IOS firewall feature set. CBAC inspects traffic that travels through the firewall to discover and manage state information for TCP and UDP sessions. This state information is used to create temporary openings in the firewall's ACLs. This is discussed in greater detail in Chapter 14, "Context-Based Access Control (CBAC)."

Each of these ACLs is discussed in detail in the following sections.

Standard IP ACLs

Standard IP ACLs are the oldest type of ACL, dating back as early as Cisco IOS Software Release 8.3. Standard IP ACLs control traffic by comparing the source address of the IP packets to the addresses configured in the ACL.

The following is the command syntax format of a standard IP ACL.

```
access-list access-list-number {permit | deny} {host | source source-wildcard | any}
   log
```

In all software releases, the *access-list-number* can be anything from 1 to 99. Table 12-2 shows the protocol and the corresponding number range for the ACL identification. In Cisco IOS Software Release 12.0.1, standard IP ACLs began using additional numbers (1300 to 1999). These additional numbers are referred to as *expanded IP ACLs*. In addition to using numbers to identify ACL, Cisco IOS Software Release 11.2 and later added the ability to use list *name* in standard IP ACLs.

You can monitor how many packets are being permitted or denied by a particular ACL, including the source address of each packet by the **log** option. The logging message includes the ACL number, whether the packet was permitted or denied, the source IP address of the packet, and the number of packets from that source permitted or denied in the prior five-minute interval.

Table 12-2 *Protocols and Their Corresponding Number Identification for an ACL*

Protocol	Range
Standard IP	1–99 and 1300–1999
Extended IP	100–199 and 2000–2699
Ethernet type code	200–299
Ethernet address	700–799
Transparent bridging (protocol type)	200–299
Transparent bridging (vendor code)	700–799
Extended transparent bridging	1100–1199
DECnet and extended DECnet	300–399
XNS	400–499
Extended XNS	500–599
AppleTalk	600–699
Source-route bridging (protocol type)	200–299
Source-route bridging (vendor code)	700–799
IPX	800–899
Extended IPX	900–999

continues

Table 12-2 *Protocols and Their Corresponding Number Identification for an ACL (Continued)*

Protocol	Range
IPX SAP	1000–1099
Standard VINES	1–100
Extended VINES	101–200
Simple VINES	201–300

Wildcard masks in conjunction with IP addresses are used to identify the source address in an ACL. Wildcard masks are also known as reverse netmasks. If your netmask normally is 255.255.255.0, for example, in binary that is

```
11111111 11111111 11111111 00000000
```

Swapping the bits, that yields the following:

```
00000000 00000000 00000000 11111111
```

or **0.0.0.255** (your wildcard mask)

Another way to calculate your wildcard mask is to take your network mask and subtract each octet from 255. If your network mask is 255.255.248.0, for example, you calculate your wildcard by subtracting 255 from each octet, yielding a 0.0.7.255 wildcard mask.

After defining an ACL, you must apply it to the interface (inbound or outbound).

```
interface interface
ip access-group number {in | out}
```

Example 12-1 shows the use of a standard IP ACL to block all traffic except that from source 192.168.100.x.

Example 12-1 *Sample ACL Configuration Permitting Network 192.168.100.0 and Implicitly Denying All Other IP Traffic*

```
Firewall(config)#access-list 1 permit 192.168.100.0  0.0.0.255
Firewall(config)#interface Ethernet0/0
Firewall(config-if)#ip address 192.168.100.1 255.255.255.0
Firewall(config-line)#ip access-group 1 in
```

The terms in, out, source, and destination are used as referenced by the router. Traffic on the router could be compared to traffic on the highway. If you were a law enforcement officer in the U.S. and wanted to stop a truck coming from Mexico into Canada, the truck's source would be Mexico and the truck's destination would be Canada. The roadblock could be applied at the U.S.-Canadian border ("out") or the U.S.-Mexican border ("in"). Refer to Figures 12-2 and 12-3.

Figure 12-2 *Border-Patrol Man (ACL) Stopping a Truck (Packet) from Entering the Country (U.S.) from Mexico*

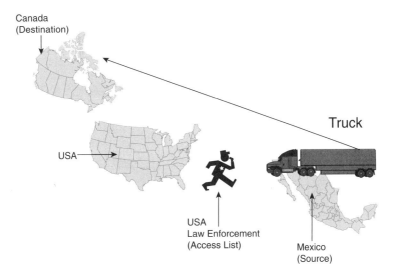

Figure 12-3 *Border-Patrol Man (ACL) Stopping a Truck from Mexico (Packet) Leaving the Country (U.S.)*

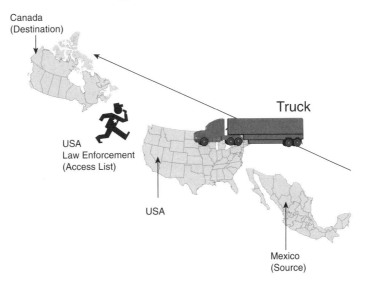

Chapter 12: Access Lists

When referring to a router, these terms have the following meanings.

- **Out**—Traffic that has already been through the router and is leaving the interface; the source is where it has been (on the other side of the router), and the destination is where it is going.
- **In**—Traffic that is arriving on the interface and which will go through the router; the source is where it has been, and the destination is where it is going (on the other side of the router).

The in ACL has a source on a segment of the interface to which it is applied and a destination off of any other interface. The out ACL has a source on a segment of any interface other than the interface to which it is applied and a destination off of the interface to which it is applied.

Extended IP ACLs

Extended IP ACLs were introduced in Cisco IOS Software Release 8.3. Extended IP ACLs control traffic by not only comparing the source and destination IP addresses but also comparing the source and destination port numbers of the IP packets to the configured in the ACL.

The following is the command syntax format of extended IP ACLs:

```
ip access-list access-list-number [dynamic dynamic-name [timeout minutes]]
    {deny | permit} protocol source source-wildcard destination destination-wildcard
    [precedence precedence] [tos tos] [log | log-input] [time-range time-range-name]
```

In all software releases, the *access-list-number* can be 101 to 199. In Cisco IOS Software Release 12.0.1, extended IP ACLs began using additional numbers (2000 to 2699). These additional numbers are referred to as *expanded IP ACLs*. Cisco IOS Software Release 11.2 added the ability to use list *name* in extended IP ACLs.

Example 12-2 shows an extended IP ACL used to permit traffic on the 192.168.100.x network (inside) and to receive ping responses from the outside while preventing unsolicited pings from people outside (permitting all other traffic).

Example 12-2 *Sample Configuration for an Extended IP ACL*

```
Firewall(config)#access-list 101 deny icmp any 192.168.100.0 0.0.0.255 echo
Firewall(config)#access-list 101 permit ip any 192.168.100.0 0.0.0.255
Firewall(config)#interface fastethernet0/1
Firewall(config-if)#ip address 172.16.8.1 255.255.255.0
Firewall(config-if)#ip access-group 101 in
```

Reflexive ACLs

Reflexive ACLs were introduced in Cisco IOS Software Release 11.3. Reflexive ACLs enable IP packets to be filtered based on upper-layer session information. They are generally used to allow outbound traffic and to limit inbound traffic in response to sessions originating inside the router.

Reflexive ACLs can be defined only with extended, named IP ACLs. They cannot be defined with numbered or standard, named IP ACLs or with other protocol ACLs. Reflexive ACLs can be used in conjunction with other standard and static extended IP ACLs.

Example 12-3 demonstrates the process of permitting ICMP outbound and inbound traffic. TCP traffic that had been initiated from inside is permitted in, whereas all other traffic is denied.

Example 12-3 *Sample Configuration for a Reflexive ACL*

```
Firewall(config)#ip access-list extended incoming
Firewall(config-ext-nacl)#permit icmp
  192.168.100.0 0.0.0.255 10.1.1.0 0.0.0.255
Firewall(config-ext-nacl)#evaluate traffic
Firewall(config-ext-nacl)# exit
Firewall(config)# ip access-list extended outgoing
Firewall(config-ext-nacl)# permit icmp
  10.10.10.0 0 0.0.0.255 192.168.1.0 0.0.0.255
Firewall(config-ext-nacl)#permit tcp
  10.10.10.0 0.0.0.255 192.168.1.0 0.0.0.255 reflect traffic
Firewall(config)#ip reflexive-list timeout 90
Firewall(config)#interface Ethernet0/0
Firewall(config-if)# ip address 192.168.100.1 255.255.255.0
Firewall(config-if)# ip access-group incoming in
Firewall(config-if)# ip access-group outgoing out
Firewall(config)#exit
```

Time-Based ACLs

Time-based ACLs were introduced in Cisco IOS Software Release 12.0.1.T. Although similar to extended IP ACLs in function, they allow for access control based on time. To implement time-based ACLs, a time range is created that defines specific times of the day and week. The time range is identified by a name and then referenced by a function. Therefore, the time restrictions are imposed on the function itself. The time range relies on the router's system clock. The router clock can be used, but the feature works best with Network Time Protocol (NTP) synchronization.

The following are the syntax for time-based ACL commands.

```
time-range time-range-name
periodic days-of-the-week hh:mm to [days-of-the-week] hh:mm
absolute [start time date] [end time date]
ip access-list name | number extended_definition time-range name_of_time-range
```

Example 12-4 shows a Telnet connection permitted from the inside to outside network on Monday, Tuesday, and Thursday during the hours of 7 a.m. until 6 p.m.

Example 12-4 *Sample Configuration for Time-Range ACL*

```
Firewall(config)#interface Ethernet0/0
Firewall(config-if)#ip address 192.168.100.253 255.255.255.0
Firewall(config-if)#ip access-group 111 in
Firewall(config)#access-list 111 permit tcp
  10.1.1.0 0.0.0.255 172.16.1.0 0.0.0.255
eq telnet time-range TelnetAccess
Firewall(config)#time-range TelnetAccess
Firewall(config-time-range)#periodic Monday Tuesday Thursday 7:00 to 18:00
```

Time ranges offer many possible benefits, including the following:

- The network administrator has more control over permitting or denying a user access to resources. These resources could be an application (identified by an IP address/mask pair and a port number), policy routing, or an on-demand link (identified as interesting traffic to the dialer).

- When provider access rates vary by time of day, it is possible to automatically reroute traffic cost-effectively.

- Service providers can dynamically change a committed access rate (CAR) configuration to support the quality of service (QoS) service level agreements (SLAs) that are negotiated for certain times of day.

- Network administrators can control logging messages. ACL entries can log traffic at certain times of the day but not constantly. Therefore, administrators can just deny access without needing to analyze many logs generated during peak hours.

- Policy-based routing and queuing functions are enhanced.

Configuring ACLs on a Router

When creating an ACL, you define criteria that is applied to each packet processed by the router; the router decides whether to forward or block each packet based on whether the packet matches the criteria.

Typical criteria you define in ACLs includes packet source addresses, packet destination addresses, or upper-layer protocol of the packet. However, each protocol has its own specific set of criteria that can be defined.

For a single ACL, you can define multiple criteria in multiple, separate ACL statements. Each of these statements should reference the same identifying name or number to tie the statements to the same ACL. You can have as many criteria statements as you want, limited only by the available memory. Of course, the more statements you have, the more difficult it will be to comprehend and manage your ACLs.

The two main tasks involved in using ACLs are as follows:

Step 1 Create an ACL by specifying an ACL number or name and access conditions.

Step 2 Apply the ACL to an interfaces or terminal lines.

Figure 12-4 *ACL webserver2 Being Applied to the Serial Interface of a Router*

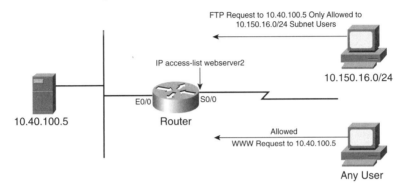

Example 12-5 shows an example of ACL configuration.

Example 12-5 *ACL Configuration Called webserver2 Permitting Web Access*

```
Firewall# configure terminal
Firewall(config)#ip access-list extended webserver2
Firewall(config-ext-nacl)#permit tcp any host 10.40.100.5 eq www
Firewall(config-ext-nacl)#permit tcp 10.150.16.0 0.0.0.255 host 10.40.100.5 eq ftp
```

In Example 12-5, an extended IP ACL called webserver2 is created. ACL webserver2 has ACL entries that permits TCP port 80 (WWW) from any source to 10.40.100.5 and FTP access to 10.40.100.5 192.168.100.0/24 only.

You can define ACLs without applying them. However, the ACLs will have no effect until they are applied to the router's interface. Example 12-6 applies the ACL server2 to the serial0 interface.

Example 12-6 *Applying the ACL server2 to the serial0 Interface*

```
Firewall(config)#interface serial0
Firewall(config-if)# ip access-group server2 in
```

Foundation Summary

The "Foundation Summary" section of each chapter lists the most important facts from the chapter. Although this section does not list every fact from the chapter that will be on your exam, a well-prepared candidate should at a minimum know all the details in each "Foundation Summary" section before going to take the exam.

ACLs filter network traffic by controlling whether routed packets are forwarded or blocked at the router's interfaces. Your router examines each packet to determine whether to forward or drop the packet, based on the criteria you specified within the ACLs.

The two main tasks involved in using ACLs are as follows:

- Create an ACL by specifying an ACL number or name and access conditions.
- Apply the ACL to interfaces or terminal lines.

Cisco IOS Software supports the following types of ACLs for IP:

- Standard IP ACLs
- Extended IP ACLs
- Reflexive ACLs
- Time-based ACLS
- Context-based access control

At the end of every ACL is an implied "deny all traffic" criteria statement. Therefore, if a packet does not match any of your criteria statements, the packet is blocked.

Q&A

As mentioned in the section, "How to Use This Book," in the Introduction to this book, you have two choices for review questions. The questions that follow next give you a bigger challenge than the exam itself by using an open-ended question format. By reviewing now with this more difficult question format, you can exercise your memory better and prove your conceptual and factual knowledge of this chapter. The answers to these questions are found in the appendix.

For more practice with exam-like question formats, including questions using a router simulator and multiple choice questions, use the exam engine on the CD-ROM.

1. What is the syntax to apply the IP ACL 107 for traffic leaving the interface?
2. Meron is a network administrator in a medium-size company. She wants to deny FTP access to the Marketing department on the 10.300.4.0 subnet on Friday, Saturday, and Sunday 7 a.m. until 10 p.m. Can she do this? If so, how?
3. What is the syntax to deny telnet access to source host 10.2.2.2 to telnet server 10.200.4.6?
4. Why do you use the words "in" or "out" when applying an ACL to an interface?
5. What is the command to apply ACL 101 for outgoing traffic from the internal network?
6. What range of numbers is used for extended IP ACLs?
7. Create an ACL to deny 192.168.10.0 255.255.255.0 network web access to web server 10.100.10.14.
8. At a minimum, on which routers should you configure ACLs?
9. What type of ACL would you use to prevent a particular host from accessing your FTP server?
10. Ryan configured the following ACL on his router: **access-list 113 deny tcp host 10.2.2.7 any** and **access-list 113 deny tcp host 10.2.2.8 any**. He then applied it to the serial interface of his router. No packets seem to passing through his router. Why?

This chapter covers the following subject:

- The Cisco IOS Firewall Feature Set

CHAPTER 13

The Cisco IOS Firewall

The IOS firewall is an optional add-on for Cisco IOS Software, offering an effective firewall and intrusion detection capability with features such as application-based filtering and encryption. Throughout this chapter the firewall feature of the Cisco IOS Software is referred to as the *Cisco IOS firewall feature set*.

"Do I Know This Already?" Quiz

The purpose of the "Do I Know This Already?" quiz is to help you decide whether you really need to read the entire chapter. If you already intend to read the entire chapter, you do not necessarily need to answer these questions now.

The five-question quiz, derived from the major sections in "Foundation Topics" section of the chapter, helps you determine how to spend your limited study time.

Table 13-1 outlines the major topics discussed in this chapter and the "Do I Know This Already?" quiz questions that correspond to those topics.

Table 13-1 *"Do I Know This Already?" Foundation Topics Section-to-Question Mapping*

Foundation Topics Section	Questions Covered in This Section
Define the Cisco IOS Firewall	1–5

CAUTION The goal of self-assessment is to gauge your mastery of the topics in this chapter. If you do not know the answer to a question or are only partially sure of the answer, you should mark this question wrong for purposes of the self-assessment. Giving yourself credit for an answer you correctly guess skews your self-assessment results and might provide you with a false sense of security.

1. The Cisco IOS firewall feature set is usually configured on a what?
   a. Firewall
   b. PIX
   c. Router
   d. Switch

2. Which of the following places would be the appropriate position to place your IOS firewall?
   a. Between subnetworks.
   b. Between the internal network and an external network such as the Internet.
   c. There is no appropriate place.
   d. Only on the DMZ network.

3. What are firewalls?
   a. Firewalls are devices that prevent access to your network.
   b. Firewalls are devices that permit access to your network for everyone.
   c. Firewalls are networking devices that control access to your organization's network assets.
   d. None of the above.

4. Which of the following is not part of the Cisco IOS feature set?
   a. Authentication proxy
   b. Intrusion detection
   c. Cisco PIX
   d. CBAC

5. Which of the following are the benefits of the Cisco IOS firewall feature set?
   a. Reduces spam e-mails
   b. Monitors traffic through network perimeters
   c. Increases DoS attacks
   d. Protects internal networks from unauthorized access

The answers to the "Do I Know This Already?" quiz are found in the appendix. The suggested choices for your next step are as follows:

- **4 or less overall score**—Read the entire chapter. This includes the "Foundation Topics" and "Foundation Summary" sections and the "Q&A" section.
- **5 overall score**—If you want more review on these topics, skip to the "Foundation Summary" section and then go to the "Q&A" section. Otherwise, move on to the next chapter.

Foundation Topics

Firewalls are networking devices that control access to your organization's network assets. Firewalls are usually positioned at the ingress/egress points into your network. If your network has multiple entrance points, you must position a firewall at each point to provide effective network access control.

The most basic function of a firewall is to monitor and filter traffic. In addition to placing firewalls on the perimeter of your network, you can also place firewalls within the network to control access to specific parts of your network. For example, you can position firewalls at all the entry points into a research and development network to prevent unauthorized access to proprietary information. Firewalls can be simple or elaborate, depending on your network requirements. Simple firewalls are usually easier to configure and manage.

The Cisco IOS Firewall Feature Set

The Cisco IOS firewall feature set combines existing Cisco IOS firewall technology and the context-based access control (CBAC), a feature discussed in detail in Chapter 14, "Context-Based Access Control (CBAC)." When you configure the Cisco IOS firewall feature set on your Cisco router, you turn your router into an effective firewall.

The Cisco IOS firewall feature set is designed to allow authorized users access to your network resources. This design prevents unauthorized, external individuals from gaining access to the internal network and blocks network attacks on your network.

At the core of the Cisco IOS firewall feature set is the Cisco advanced firewall engine. This engine tracks the state and context of network connections to secure traffic flow. It enhances security for TCP and UDP applications that use well-known ports, such as e-mail traffic (SMTP) and telnet traffic, by examining source and destination addresses.

The Cisco IOS firewall feature set provides the following benefits:

- Protects internal networks from intrusion
- Monitors traffic through network perimeters
- Enables network commerce via the World Wide Web

The following features are included in the Cisco IOS feature set. The most complex are discussed in more detail in the following sections.

- **Authentication proxy**—LAN-based, dynamic, per-user authentication and authorization via TACACS+ and RADIUS authentication servers for both inbound and outbound users.
- **Audit trail**—Details transactions. Records timestamp, source host, destination host, ports, duration, and total number of types transmitted for detailed reporting. Can be configured on a per-application, per-feature basis.
- **Basic and advanced traffic filtering**—Standard and extended IP access control lists (ACLs). Lock-and-key dynamic ACLs grant temporary access through firewalls upon user identification.
- **CBAC**—Provides internal users with secure, per-application access.
- **DoS detection and prevention**—Defends and protects router resources against common attacks.
- **Dynamic port mapping**—Allows CBAC-supported applications to run on nonstandard ports.
- **Event logging**—Enables administrators to track potential security breaches or other nonstandard activities in real time by logging system error message output to a console terminal or syslog server.
- **Firewall management**—A wizard-based network configuration tool that offers step-by-step guidance through network design, addressing, and Cisco firewall feature set implementation.
- **Java applet blocking**—Protects against unidentified, malicious Java applets.
- **Intrusion detection**—Intrusion detection capability in the critical packet path provides dynamic monitoring, interception, and reporting of well-known or common network attacks and misuse.
- **Network Address Translation (NAT)**—Hides the internal network from the outside for enhanced security.
- **Peer router authentication**—Ensures that routers receive reliable routing information from trusted sources.
- **Policy-based multi-interface support**—Provides the ability to control user access by IP address and interface as determined by the security policy.
- **Redundancy/failover**—Automatically routes traffic to a backup router if a failure occurs.

Authentication Proxy

When configuring authentication proxy, a direction at the interface is not assigned because it is always inbound. Authentication proxy intercepts the packet before it reaches the inbound ACL. Consequently, an inbound ACL can block all traffic, except for the special servers or devices that need to communicate with the Cisco IOS firewall.

Authentication proxy dynamically opens connections on the inbound ACL of the input interface where the proxy is enabled, as well as on the outbound ACL of the output interface where the packet exits. This enables the packet to leave and lets the firewall engine intercept and take control.

Authentication proxy is discussed in detail in Chapter 15, "Authentication Proxy and the Cisco IOS Firewall."

DoS Protection

Cisco IOS firewall provides protection from DoS attacks such as SYN flood denial, port scans, and packet injection.

Logging and Audit Trail

"Real-time alerts send syslog error messages to central management consoles upon the detection of suspicious activity. Enhanced audit trail features use syslog to track all transactions and to record timestamps, source host, destination host, ports used, session duration, and the total number of transmitted bytes for advanced, session-based reporting," which is from http://www.cisco.com/en/US/products/sw/secursw/ps1018/products_implementation_design_guide09186a00800fd670.html.

To enable logging and send messages to a syslog server, use the following commands:

```
Firewall(config)#logging on
Firewall(config)#logging 192.168.100.6
```

To enable an audit trail of firewall messages, use the following syntax:

```
Firewall(config)#ip inspect audit-trail
```

To control the amount of audit trail messages, you can enable or disable audit trail per protocol in the firewall rules.

Intrusion Detection

Intrusion detection technology is supported by the Cisco IOS firewall feature on most Cisco router models. It identifies 59 of the most common attacks using signatures to detect patterns of misuse in network traffic. The intrusion detection signatures included in the Cisco IOS firewall were chosen from a broad cross-section of intrusion detection signatures. The signatures represent severe breaches of security and the most common network attacks and information-gathering scans.

The Cisco IOS firewall IDS acts as an in-line intrusion detection sensor, monitoring packets and sessions as they flow through the router and scanning each to match any of the IDS signatures. When it detects suspicious activity, it responds before network security can be compromised and logs the event through Cisco IOS syslog or the Cisco Secure IDS Post Office Protocol. You can configure the

IDS system to choose the appropriate response to various threats. When packets in a session match a signature, the IDS system can be configured to take these actions:

- Send an alarm to a syslog server or a centralized management interface
- Drop the packet
- Reset the TCP connection

Individual signatures can be disabled in case of false positives. Although it is preferable to enable both the firewall and intrusion detection features of the CBAC security engine to support a network security policy, each of these features may be enabled independently and on different router interfaces. Cisco IOS Software-based intrusion detection is covered in greater detail in Chapter 16, "Intrusion Detection and the Cisco IOS Firewall."

Port-To-Application Mapping

Port-to-application mapping (PAM) enables you to customize TCP or UDP port numbers for network services or applications. PAM uses this information to support network environments that run services using ports that are different from the registered or well-known ports associated with an application.

PAM enables CBAC-supported applications to be run on nonstandard ports. Using PAM, network administrators can customize access control for specific applications and services to meet the distinct needs of their networks.

PAM also supports host- or subnet-specific port mapping, which enables you to apply PAM to a single host or subnet using standard ACLs. Host- or subnet-specific port mapping is done using standard IP ACLs. The PAM table provides three types of mapping information, each of which is discussed in more detail in the following sections.

- System-Defined Port Mapping
- User-Defined Port Mapping
- Host-Specific Port Mapping

System-Defined Port Mapping

By default a table of system-defined mapping entries using the well-known or registered port mapping is created. The system-defined entries comprise all the services supported by CBAC, which requires the system-defined mapping information to function properly. The system-defined mapping information cannot be deleted or changed; that is, you cannot map SMTP services to port 21 (FTP) or FTP services to port 80 (HTTP). Table 13-2 lists the default system-defined services and applications in the PAM table.

Table 13-2 *Default System-Defined Services and Applications in the PAM Table*

Application Name	Protocol Description	Port Number
cuseeme	CU-SeeMe Protocol	7648
Exec	Remote Process Execution	512
ftp	File Transfer Protocol (control port)	21
http	Hypertext Transfer Protocol	80
H323	H.323 Protocol (for example, Microsoft NetMeeting, Intel Video Phone)	1720
Login	Remote login	513
Mgcp	Media Gateway Control Protocol	2427
Msrpc	Microsoft Remote Procedure Call	135
netshow	Microsoft NetShow	1755
real-audio-video	RealAudio and RealVideo	7070
Rtsp	Real Time Streaming Protocol	8559
Shell	Remote command	514
Sip	Session Initiation Protocol	5060
Smtp	Simple Mail Transfer Protocol	25
Sqlnet	SQL-NET	1521
streamworks	StreamWorks Protocol	1558
Sunrpc	SUN Remote Procedure Call	111
telnet	Telnet	23
Tftp	Trivial File Transfer Protocol	69
vdolive	VDOLive Protocol	7000

(This table has been reproduced by Cisco Press with the permission of Cisco Systems Inc. Copyright © 2003 Cisco Systems, Inc. All Rights Reserved.)

User-Defined Port Mapping

Network services or applications that use nonstandard ports require user-defined entries in the PAM table. For example, your network might run telnet services on the nonstandard port 9000 rather than on the system-defined default port (port 23). In this case, you can use PAM to map port 9000 with telnet services. If telnet services run on other ports, use PAM to create additional port-mapping entries. After you define a port mapping, you can overwrite that entry at a later time by just mapping that specific port with a different application.

User-defined port mapping information can also specify a range of ports for an application by establishing a separate entry in the PAM table for each port number in the range.

Host-Specific Port Mapping

In some environments, it might be necessary to override the default port-mapping information for a specific host or subnet. With host-specific port mapping, you can use the same port number for different services on different hosts. This means that you can map port 8080 with HTTP services for one host, while mapping port 8080 with telnet services for another host.

Host-specific port mapping also enables you to apply PAM to a specific subnet when that subnet runs a service that uses a port number that differs from the port number defined in the default mapping information. For example, hosts on subnet 10.100.10.11 might run HTTP services on nonstandard port 8080, whereas other traffic through the firewall uses the default port for HTTP services, which is port 80.

Host-specific port mapping enables you to override a system-defined entry in the PAM table. If CBAC finds an entry in the PAM table that maps port 21 (the system-defined port for FTP) with SMTP for a specific host, for example, CBAC identifies port 21 as SMTP protocol traffic on that host.

To configure PAM, use the **ip port-map** command, as follows:

```
ip port-map appl_name port port_num [list acl_num]
```

Use the **list** option to associate this port mapping to the specific hosts in the ACL. (PAM uses standard IP ACLs only.) If an ACL is included, the hosts defined in that ACL have the application *appl_name* running on port *port_num*. The following example shows an HTTP mapped to port 8080 by an **ip port-map** command:

```
ip port-map http port 8080
```

Foundation Summary

The "Foundation Summary" section of each chapter lists the most important facts from the chapter. Although this section does not list every fact from the chapter that will be on your exam, a well-prepared candidate should at a minimum know all the details in each "Foundation Summary" section before going to take the exam.

The Cisco IOS firewall feature set provides the following benefits:

- Protects internal networks from intrusion
- Monitors traffic through network perimeters
- Enables network commerce via the World Wide Web

You can use the Cisco IOS firewall feature set to configure your Cisco IOS router as

- An Internet firewall or part of an Internet firewall.
- A firewall between groups in your internal network.
- A firewall providing secure connections to or from branch offices.
- A firewall between your company's network and your company's partners' networks.

Some of the IOS firewall features in Cisco IOS Software include the following:

- **Authentication proxy**—LAN-based, dynamic, per-user authentication and authorization via TACACS+ and RADIUS authentication servers enables setting individual security policies.
- **Logging and audit trail**—Configurable audit trail and alerts; Cisco IOS firewall alerts and audit trails are now configurable on a per-application basis. Java blocking is also configurable on a modular basis.
- **Dynamic port mapping**—Allows CBAC-supported applications to run on nonstandard ports
- **Intrusion detection**—Intrusion detection capability in the critical packet path provides dynamic monitoring, interception, and reporting of network attacks and misuse

Q&A

As mentioned in the section, "How to Use This Book," in the Introduction to this book, you have two choices for review questions. The questions that follow next give you a bigger challenge than the exam itself by using an open-ended question format. By reviewing now with this more difficult question format, you can exercise your memory better and prove your conceptual and factual knowledge of this chapter. The answers to these questions are found in the appendix.

For more practice with exam-like question formats, including questions using a router simulator and multiple choice questions, use the exam engine on the CD-ROM.

1. What does port-to-application mapping, otherwise known as PAM, do?

2. What is the command to configure PAM?

3. Name two benefits of the Cisco IOS firewall?

4. What are the different ways the IDS feature in the Cisco IOS firewall can be configured to respond to an attack or suspicious activity on the network?

5. What does the IDS feature use to detect and identify patterns of misuse in network traffic?

This chapter covers the following subjects:

- Define Cisco IOS Firewall and CBAC
- Configure CBAC

CHAPTER 14

Context-Based Access Control (CBAC)

The Cisco IOS firewall is a group of features that makes Cisco IOS Software more effective for perimeter security. The firewall features are based on inspection of data in IP packets, including data beyond the headers.

> **NOTE** The perimeter router running the Cisco IOS Software security feature is referred to as *IOS firewall* in this chapter.

"Do I Know This Already?" Quiz

The purpose of the "Do I Know This Already?" quiz is to help you decide whether you really need to read the entire chapter. If you already intend to read the entire chapter, you do not necessarily need to answer these questions now.

The 10-question quiz, derived from the major sections in the "Foundation Topics" portion of the chapter, helps you determine how to spend your limited study time.

Table 14-1 outlines the major topics discussed in this chapter and the "Do I Know This Already?" quiz questions that correspond to those topics.

Table 14-1 *"Do I Know This Already?" Foundation Topics Section-to-Question Mapping*

Foundation Topics Section	Questions Covered in This Section
Define Cisco IOS Firewall and CBAC	1–6
Configure CBAC	7–10

> **CAUTION** The goal of self-assessment is to gauge your mastery of the topics in this chapter. If you do not know the answer to a question or are only partially sure of the answer, you should mark this question wrong for purposes of the self-assessment. Giving yourself credit for an answer you correctly guess skews your self-assessment results and might provide you with a false sense of security.

1. Which of the following is *not* about a content-based access control?

   a. CBAC provides secure per-application access control across network perimeters.

   b. CBAC intelligently filters TCP and UDP packets based on application layer protocol session information.

   c. The CBAC feature is only available on Cisco switches.

   d. CBAC uses state information to create temporary openings in the firewall's ACL to allow return traffic.

2. What is the advantage of using CBAC versus ACLs?

   a. CBAC examines and inspects packets at the network, transport, and application layer level, whereas ACLs do not inspect all three levels.

   b. CBAC is less complicated to configure than ACLs.

   c. CBAC works on hubs.

   d. The CBAC memory requirement is less than ACL memory requirements.

3. How does CBAC handle UDP sessions?

   a. CBAC cannot build a state table for UDP sessions because UDP is a connectionless protocol.

   b. CBAC approximates UDP sessions by examining the information in the packet and determining whether the packet is similar to other UDP packets.

   c. CBAC does not inspect UDP packets.

   d. CBAC denies suspicious UDP packets randomly.

4. Approximately how much memory per connection does CBAC require?

   a. 2 KB

   b. 6 KB

   c. 200 bytes

   d. 600 bytes

5. Which of the following is true about ACLs created by CBAC?

   a. ACL entries are created and deleted dynamically.

   b. After they are created, they are saved to NVRAM.

   c. CBAC does not create or delete ACLs.

   d. CBAC creates ACL entries for temporary openings on the Cisco IOS firewall to permit only traffic that is part of the permissible session.

6. Which of the following protocols are supported by CBAC?

   a. FTP

   b. SMTP

   c. H.323

   d. OSPF

7. Which three types of **debug** command are used to debug CBAC?

   a. Network level debug commands

   b. Transport level debug command

   c. Application protocol debug command

   d. Generic debug commands

8. What is the command to define an inspection rule?

   a. **inspection rule** *name* **protocol**

   b. **ip inspect name** *inspection name* **protocol**

   c. **ip protocol inspect** *inspection name* **protocol**

   d. **ip protocol** *inspection name*

9. What is the command to inspect an application level protocol?

   a. **debug ip inspect** *protocol*

   b. **debug ip inspect tcp**

   c. **debug ip inspect udp**

   d. **debug up inspect app**

10. What command enables you to show existing sessions that are currently being tracked and inspected by CBAC?

    a. **show ip inspect session [detail]**

    b. **display current ip inspect**

    c. **show current ip inspect**

    d. **display ip inspect session [detail]**

The answers to the "Do I Know This Already?" quiz are found in the appendix. The suggested choices for your next step are as follows:

- **8 or less overall score**—Read the entire chapter. This includes the "Foundation Topics" and "Foundation Summary" sections and the "Q&A" section.
- **9 or 10 overall score**—If you want more review on these topics, skip to the "Foundation Summary" section and then go to the "Q&A" section. Otherwise, move on to the next chapter.

Foundation Topics

Content-Based Access Control

A context-based access control (CBAC) engine provides secure, per-application access control across network perimeters. CBAC lets the router maintain a persistent state, based on information from inspected packets, and use that information to decide which traffic should be forwarded. CBAC is the centerpiece of the firewall feature set, and the other features in the set build on CBAC. CBAC features include the following:

- DoS detection and prevention
- Generates real-time alerts and audit trails
- Secure per-application access control
- Filtering on generic TCP and UDP packets

CBAC can be used for intranets, extranets, and the Internet because if its inherent capability to distill packets (TCP and UDP) based on application protocol session information. For example, you can configure CBAC to permit specific TCP and UDP traffic through a Cisco IOS firewall only when the connection is initiated from within the network you want to protect. In other words, CBAC can inspect traffic for sessions that originate from the external network.

Unlike ACLs, which are limited to the examination of packets at the network level (at most transport layers), CBAC examines not only network layer and transport layer information but also examines the application layer protocol information (such as FTP connection information) to learn about the state of the TCP or UDP session. This allows support of protocols that involve multiple channels created as a result of negotiations in the control channel. Most of the multimedia protocols as well as some other protocols (such as FTP, RPC, and SQL*Net) involve multiple channels.

DoS Detection and Protection

CBAC inspects traffic that travels through the firewall to discover and manage state information for TCP and UDP sessions. This state information is used to create temporary openings in the firewall's ACLs to allow return traffic and additional data connections for permissible sessions.

Inspecting packets at the application layer, and maintaining TCP and UDP session information, provides CBAC with the capability to detect and prevent certain types of network attacks such as SYN flooding. TCP SYN messages are sent to servers from clients as a first step in a three-step process known as the TCP handshake to establish a TCP session. (See Figure 14-1.)

Figure 14-1 *The Three-Way TCP Handshake Process*

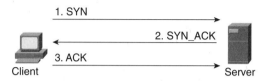

Client and server can now send service-specific data.

A SYN flood occurs when several hundred or thousand TCP SYN messages are sent to a server but never complete the TCP session. The resulting volume of half-open connections can overwhelm the server, causing it to deny service to valid requests. Network attacks that deny access to a network device are called DoS attacks.

CBAC helps to protect against DoS attacks in other ways. CBAC inspects packet sequence numbers in TCP connections to see whether they are within expected ranges. You can also configure CBAC to drop half-open connections. Additionally, CBAC can detect unusually high rates of new connections and issue alert messages.

Alerts and Audit Trails

CBAC also generates real-time alerts and audit trails. Enhanced audit trail features use syslog to track all network transactions—recording timestamps, source host, destination host, ports used, and the total number of transmitted bytes for advanced, session-based reporting. Real-time alerts send syslog error messages to central management consoles upon detecting suspicious activity. Using CBAC inspection rules, you can configure alerts and audit trail information on a per-application protocol basis. If you want to generate audit trail information for HTTP traffic, for example, you can specify that in the CBAC rule covering HTTP inspection.

CBAC is available only for IP protocol traffic. Only TCP and UDP packets are inspected. Other IP traffic, such as ICMP, cannot be filtered with CBAC and should be filtered with extended IP ACLs instead.

> **NOTE** CBAC does not protect against attacks originating from within the protected network. CBAC only detects and protects against attacks that travel through the Cisco IOS firewall.

How CBAC Works

A CBAC inspection rule is created to specify which protocols you want to be inspected. You then apply the rule to the desired interface and specify the direction (in or out). Only specified protocols are inspected by CBAC. Packets entering the Cisco IOS firewall are inspected by CBAC only if they first pass the inbound ACL at the interface. If a packet is denied by the ACL, the packet is just dropped and not inspected by CBAC.

CBAC creates temporary openings in ACLs at Cisco IOS firewall interfaces. These openings are created when specified traffic exits your internal network through the Cisco IOS firewall. The openings allow returning traffic that would normally be blocked. The traffic is allowed back through the Cisco IOS firewall only if it is part of the same session as the original traffic that triggered CBAC when exiting through the Cisco IOS firewall. Figure 14-2 shows a telnet user trying to access a server with CBAC enabled on the router.

Figure 14-2 *A Telnet User Trying to Access a Server with CBAC Enabled on the Router*

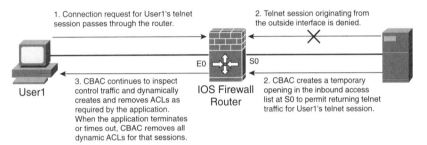

In Figure 14-2, the inbound ACL at S1 is configured to block telnet traffic, and there is no outbound ACL configured at E1. When the connection request for User1's telnet session passes through the Cisco IOS firewall, CBAC creates a temporary opening in the inbound ACL at S1 to permit returning telnet traffic for User1's telnet session.

CBAC inspects and monitors only the control channels of connections, not the data channels. For example, during FTP sessions both the control and data channels, which are created when a data file is transferred, are monitored for state changes. However, only the control channel is inspected.

CBAC inspection recognizes application-specific commands in the control channel, and detects and prevents certain application level attacks.

Whenever a packet is inspected, a state table is updated to include information about the state of the packet's connection. The traffic permitted back through the Cisco IOS firewall is comprised of packets that have a permissible session from the state table.

UDP Sessions

Unlike TCP sessions, UDP sessions are a connectionless service. This characteristic of UDP sessions makes it harder to identify packets that belong to the same session. CBAC in these cases uses source/destination addresses and port numbers and whether the packet was detected soon after another similar UDP packet to determine if the packet belongs to that particular session. "Soon" means within the configurable UDP idle timeout period.

ACL Entries

The state table information helps CBAC create and delete ACL entries dynamically at the firewall interface. These ACL entries are applied to the interfaces to examine traffic flowing back into the internal network. These entries create temporary openings in the Cisco IOS firewall to permit only traffic that is part of a permissible session.

The temporary ACL entries are never saved to NVRAM.

CBAC Restrictions

CBAC has the following restrictions:

- Packets with the firewall as the source or destination address are not inspected by CBAC.
- If you reconfigure your ACLs when you configure CBAC, be aware that if your ACLs block TFTP traffic into an interface, you will not be able to netboot over that interface. (This is not a CBAC-specific limitation but is part of existing ACL functionality.)
- CBAC is available only for IP protocol traffic. Only TCP and UDP packets are inspected. Other IP traffic, such as ICMP, cannot be inspected with CBAC and should be filtered with extended ACLs instead.
- H.323 v2 and RTSP protocol inspection supports only the following multimedia client/server applications: Cisco IP/TV, RealNetworks RealAudio G2 Player, Apple QuickTime 4.

Supported Protocols

CBAC can be configured to inspect all TCP and UDP sessions. You can also configure CBAC to specifically inspect certain application layer protocols. The following application layer protocols can all be configured for CBAC:

- FTP
- SMTP
- SQL*Net
- TFTP
- UNIX R commands (such as **rlogin**, **rexec**, and **rsh**)
- RPC (Sun RPC, not DCE RPC or Microsoft RPC)
- HTTP (Java blocking)

- Java
- Microsoft Netshow
- RealAudio
- StreamWorks
- VDOLive
- CU-SeeMe (only the White Pine version)
- H.323 (such as NetMeeting, ProShare)

When a protocol is configured for CBAC, the protocol's traffic will be inspected, state information will be maintained, and in general, packets will be allowed back through the Cisco IOS firewall only if they belong to a permissible session. When CBAC inspects FTP traffic, it only allows data channels with the destination port in the range of 1024 to 65,535. It will not open a data channel if the FTP client-server authentication fails.

Memory and Performance Impact

Even though CBAC uses slightly less than 600 bytes of memory per connection, it can still impact the efficiency of your router. Because of this memory usage, you should use CBAC only when you need to. There is also a slight amount of additional processing that occurs whenever packets are inspected.

Configuring CBAC

To configure CBAC, follow these steps:

1. Select an interface.
2. Configure IP ACLs at the interface.
3. Configure global timeouts and thresholds.
4. Define an inspection rule.
5. Apply the inspection rule to an interface.

Select an Interface

This step is the planning stage, from which the rest of the configuration for CBAC will work. You first must determine on what (an internal or external interface) you want to configure CBAC. It is also possible to configure CBAC on both internal and external interfaces. Configure CBAC in two directions when the networks on both sides of the firewall require protection, such as with extranet or intranet configurations, and for protection against DoS attacks.

Configure IP ACLs at the Interface

Configuring your ACL correctly is critical for CBAC to work properly. Follow these two general rules when evaluating your IP ACLs at the Cisco IOS firewall:

- Permit CBAC traffic leaving the network through the Cisco IOS firewall.
- Use extended ACLs to deny traffic entering the network (from the external interface) through the Cisco IOS firewall.

All ACLs that evaluate traffic leaving the protected network should permit traffic that will be inspected by CBAC. If telnet will be inspected by CBAC, for example, telnet traffic should be permitted on all ACLs that apply to traffic leaving the network.

Configure Global Timeouts and Thresholds

Global timeouts and thresholds help CBAC determine how long to manage state information for a session and when to drop sessions that do not become fully established. All the available CBAC timeouts and thresholds are listed in Table 14-2 along with the corresponding command and default value.

Table 14-2 *Default Timeout and Threshold Values for CBAC Inspections*

Timeout or Threshold Value to Change	Command	Default
The length of time the software waits for a TCP session to reach the established state before dropping the session	**ip inspect tcp synwait-time** *seconds*	30 seconds
The length of time a TCP session will still be managed after the firewall detects a FIN exchange.	**ip inspect tcp finwait-time** *seconds*	5 seconds
The length of time a TCP session will still be managed after no activity (the TCP idle timeout)	**ip inspect tcp idle-time** *seconds*	3600 seconds (1 hour)
The length of time a UDP session will still be managed after no activity (the UDP idle timeout)	**ip inspect udp idle-time** *seconds*	30 seconds
The length of time a DNS name lookup session will still be managed after no activity	**ip inspect dns-timeout** *seconds*	5 seconds
The number of existing half-open sessions that will cause the software to start deleting half-open sessions	**ip inspect max-incomplete high** *number*	500 existing half-open sessions

Table 14-2 *Default Timeout and Threshold Values for CBAC Inspections (Continued)*

Timeout or Threshold Value to Change	Command	Default
The number of existing half-open sessions that will cause the software to stop deleting half-open sessions	**ip inspect max-incomplete low** *number*	400 existing half-open sessions
The rate of new unestablished sessions that will cause the software to start deleting half-open sessions	**ip inspect one-minute high** *number*	500 half-open sessions per minute
The rate of new unestablished sessions that will cause the software to stop deleting half-open sessions	**ip inspect one-minute low** *number*	400 half-open sessions per minute
The number of existing half-open TCP sessions with the same destination host address that will cause the software to start dropping half-open sessions to the same destination host address	**ip inspect tcp max-incomplete host** *number* **block-time** *minutes*	50 existing half-open TCP sessions; 0 minute

Source: Cisco.com: Context-Based Access Control.

(This table has been reproduced by Cisco Press with the permission of Cisco Systems Inc. Copyright © 2003 Cisco Systems, Inc. All Rights Reserved.)

Define an Inspection Rule

The inspection rule defines the IP traffic monitored by CBAC. The **ip inspect name** command enables you to define a set of inspection rules. Table 14-3 shows the **ip inspect** command parameters.

```
ip inspect name inspection-name protocol [alert {on | off}]
  [audit-trail {on | off}] [timeout seconds]
  no ip inspect name [inspection-name protocol]
```

Table 14-3 *The **ip inspect name** Command Parameters*

Parameter	Description
inspection-name	Names the set of inspection rules. If you want to add a protocol to an existing set of rules, use the same *inspection-name* as the existing set of rules.
protocol	A protocol keyword listed in (FTP, Java, SMTP, and so on).

continues

Table 14-3 *The* **ip inspect name** *Command Parameters (Continued)*

Parameter	Description
**alert {on	off}**	(Optional) For each inspected protocol, the generation of alert messages can be set be on or off. If **no** option is selected, alerts are generated based on the setting of the **ip inspect alert-off** command.
**audit-trail {on	off}**	(Optional) For each inspected protocol, audit trail can be set on or off. If **no** option is selected, audit trail messages are generated based on the setting of the **ip inspect audit-trail** command.
http	(Optional) Specifies the HTTP protocol for Java applet blocking.
timeout *seconds*	(Optional) To override the global TCP or UDP idle timeouts for the specified protocol, specify the number of seconds for a different idle timeout. This timeout overrides the global TCP and UPD timeouts but does not override the global Domain Name System timeout.
java-list *access-list*	(Optional) Specifies the ACL (name or number) to use to determine "friendly" sites. This keyword is available only for the HTTP protocol for Java applet blocking. Java blocking only works with standard ACLs.
rpc program-number *number*	Specifies the program number to permit. This keyword is available only for the remote-procedure call protocol.
wait-time *minutes*	(Optional) Specifies the number of minutes to keep a small hole in the firewall to allow subsequent connections from the same source address and to the same destination address and port. The default wait-time is zero minutes. This keyword is available only for the RPC protocol.
fragment	Specifies fragment inspection for the named rule.
max *number*	(Optional) Specifies the maximum number of unassembled packets for which state information (structures) is allocated by Cisco IOS Software. Unassembled packets are packets that arrive at the Cisco IOS firewall interface before the initial packet for a session. The acceptable range is 50 through 10,000. The default is 256 state entries. Memory is allocated for the state structures, and setting this value to a larger number may cause memory resources to be exhausted.
timeout *seconds* (fragmentation)	(Optional) Configures the number of seconds that a packet state structure remains active. When the timeout value expires, the Cisco IOS firewall drops the unassembled packet, freeing that structure for use by another packet. The default timeout value is one second. If this number is set to a value greater that one second, it is automatically adjusted by the Cisco IOS Software when the number of free state structures goes below certain thresholds: When the number of free states is less than 32, the timeout is divided by 2; when the number of free states is less than 16, the timeout is set to 1.

Usually one inspection rule is defined per interface. Sometimes, however, you may want to configure an inspection rule in both directions on a single firewall interface. In these situations, you should configure two rules, one for each direction. The inspection rule includes a series of statements each listing a protocol and specifying the same inspection rule name.

Configure Generic TCP and UDP Inspection

To configure CBAC inspection for TCP or UDP packets, use one or both of the following global configuration commands:

- **ip inspect name** *inspection-name* **tcp** [**timeout** *seconds*]
- **ip inspect name** *inspection-name* **udp** [**timeout** *seconds*]

With TCP and UDP inspection, packets entering the network must match the corresponding packet that previously exited the network. The entering packets must have the same source/destination addresses and source/destination port numbers as the exiting packet (but reversed); otherwise, the entering packets are blocked at the interface.

With UDP inspection configured, replies are only permitted back in through the firewall if they are received within a configurable time after the last request was sent out. (This time is configured with the **ip inspect udp idle-time** command.)

Configure Java Inspection

To reduce the threats from malicious Java applets, you can configure CBAC to filter Java applets at the firewall. This will allow users to download only applets residing within the firewall and permitted applets from outside the firewall.

```
ip inspect name inspection-name http [java-list access-list] [alert {on | off}]
  [audit-trail {on | off}] [timeout seconds]
```

Example 14-1 shows an inspection named test1 for blocking Java applets.

Example 14-1 *Sample* **ip inspect** *Command Used for Java Inspection*

```
ip inspect name test1 http java-list 3 audit-trail on
```

> **NOTE** CBAC does not detect or block encapsulated Java applets. Java applets contained in .zip or .jar format are not blocked at the firewall. CBAC also does not detect or block applets loaded from FTP, gopher, and HTTP on a nonstandard port.

Apply the Inspection Rule to an Interface

To apply an inspection rule to an interface, use the **ip inspect** *inspection-name* {**in** | **out**} command in interface configuration mode. In the following example, inspection test1 is applied to the Ethernet interface in an inward direction:

```
Router(config)#interface Ethernet0
Router(config-int)# ip inspect test1 in
```

Verifying and Debugging CBAC

You can check your CBAC configuration by using the **show** commands listed in Table 14-4. In addition to the **show** commands, the **debug** commands are very useful in monitoring and troubleshooting your CBAC configuration.

Table 14-4 *Some of the Commands Used to Check Your CBAC Configuration*

Command	Purpose
show ip inspect name *inspection-name*	Show a particular configured inspection rule.
show ip inspect config	Show the complete CBAC inspection configuration.
show ip inspect interfaces	Show interface configuration with regard to applied inspection rules and access lists.
show ip inspect session [detail]	Show existing sessions that are currently being tracked and inspected by CBAC.
show ip inspect all	Show all CBAC configurations and all existing sessions that are currently being tracked and inspected by CBAC.

Debugging Context-Based Access Control

The following three types of debug commands are available for debugging CBAC:

- Generic **debug** commands
- Transport level **debug** commands
- Application protocol **debug** commands

To assist CBAC debugging, you can turn on audit trail messages that will be displayed on the console after each CBAC session closes. To turn on audit trail messages, use the following global configuration command:

```
ip inspect audit trail
```

Generic debug Commands

You can use the following generic **debug** commands listed in Table 14-5.

Table 14-5 *Generic **debug** Commands*

Command	Purpose
debug ip inspect function-trace	Display messages about software functions called by CBAC.
debug ip inspect object-creation	Display messages about software objects being created by CBAC. Object creation corresponds to the beginning of CBAC-inspected sessions.
debug ip inspect object-deletion	Display messages about software objects being deleted by CBAC. Object deletion corresponds to the closing of CBAC-inspected sessions.
debug ip inspect events	Display messages about CBAC software events, including information about CBAC packet processing.
debug ip inspect timers	Display messages about CBAC timer events such as when a CBAC idle timeout is reached.
debug ip inspect detailed	Enable the detailed option, which can be used in combination with other options to get additional information.

Transport Level debug Commands

To monitor and troubleshoot CBAC TCP and UDP inspection configuration, use the transport level **debug** commands:

- **debug ip inspect tcp**—Display messages about CBAC-inspected TCP events, including details about TCP packets.

- **debug ip inspect udp**—Display messages about CBAC-inspected UDP events, including details about UDP packets.

CBAC Configuration Example

For this example, CBAC is being configured to inspect inbound. As shown in Figure 14-3, interface Ethernet0 is the protected network and interface Serial1 is the unprotected network. The security policy for the protected site uses ACLs to restrict inbound traffic on the unprotected interface to specific ICMP protocol traffic, denying inbound access for TCP and UDP protocol traffic. Inbound access for specific protocol traffic is provided through dynamic ACLs, which are generated according to CBAC inspection rules.

Figure 14-3 *A Sample Application of CBAC*

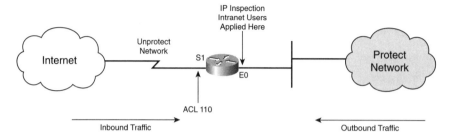

ACL 110 denies TCP and UDP traffic from any source or destination while permitting specific ICMP protocol traffic. The final **deny** statement is not required but is included. The final entry in any ACL is an implicit denial of all IP protocol traffic.

```
Firewall(config)# access-list 110 deny tcp any any
Firewall(config)# access-list 110 deny udp any any
Firewall(config)# access-list 110 permit icmp any any echo-reply
Firewall(config)# access-list 110 permit icmp any any time-exceeded
Firewall(config)# access-list 110 permit icmp any any traceroute
Firewall(config)# access-list 110 permit icmp any any unreachable
Firewall(config)# access-list 110 deny ip any any
```

ACL 110 is applied inbound at interface Serial1 to block all access from the unprotected network to the protected network.

```
Firewall(config)# interface serial1
Firewall(config-if)# ip access-group 110 in
```

An inspection rule is created for Intranetusers.

```
Firewall(config)# ip inspect name intranetusers ftp
Firewall(config)# ip inspect name intranetusers http
Firewall(config)# ip inspect name intranetusers rcmd
Firewall(config)# ip inspect name intranetusers realaudio
Firewall(config)# ip inspect name intranetusers smtp timeout 3600
Firewall(config)# ip inspect name intranetusers tftp timeout 30
Firewall(config)# ip inspect name intranetusers udp timeout 15
Firewall(config)# ip inspect name intranetusers tcp timeout 3600
```

The inspection rule is applied inbound at interface Ethernet0 to inspect traffic from users on the protected network.

```
Firewall(config)# interface Ethernet0
Firewall(config-if)# ip inspect intranetusers in
```

Foundation Summary

The "Foundation Summary" section of each chapter lists the most important facts from the chapter. Although this section does not list every fact from the chapter that will be on your SECUR exam, a well-prepared candidate should at a minimum know all the details in each "Foundation Summary" before going to take the exam.

- CBAC is one of the key features in Cisco IOS firewall.
- The CBAC engine provides secure, per-application access control across network perimeters.
- CBAC intelligently filters TCP and UDP packets based on application layer protocol session information and can be used for intranets, extranets, and the Internet.
- Even though CBAC uses slightly less than 600 bytes of memory per connection, it can still impact the efficiency of your router. Because of this memory usage, you should use CBAC only when you need to.
- ACLs are created and deleted by CBAC dynamically at the Cisco IOS firewall interfaces, according to the information maintained in the state tables.
- The three types of debugging command for CBAC are generic, transport level, and application level **debug** commands.
- To assist with debugging, you can enable audit trail messages that will display on the console after each CBAC session closes.
- CBAC is available only for IP protocol traffic. Only TCP and UDP packets are inspected. Other IP traffic, such as ICMP, cannot be inspected with CBAC and should be filtered with basic ACLs instead.

Q&A

As mentioned in the section, "How to Use This Book," in the Introduction to this book, you have two choices for review questions. The questions that follow next give you a bigger challenge than the exam itself by using an open-ended question format. By reviewing now with this more difficult question format, you can exercise your memory better and prove your conceptual and factual knowledge of this chapter. The answers to these questions are found in the appendix.

For more practice with exam-like question formats, including questions using a router simulator and multiple choice questions, use the exam engine on the CD-ROM.

1. What are the steps in the CBAC configuration process?
2. Are inspection rules a requirement for CBAC configuration?
3. What are the three categories of **debug** commands that are commonly used to debug CBAC configuration?
4. Can CBAC be configured to inspect all TCP, UDP, and ICMP packets?
5. What command enables you to show a complete CBAC inspection configured on the Cisco IOS firewall?
6. What command do you use to turn on audit trail messages?
7. What are indicators in half-open sessions that CBAC measures before it takes steps to prevent a DoS attack?
8. Does CBAC block malicious Java applets that are on .jar format?
9. Name two features of the CBAC.
10. Name one restriction with using CBAC.

This chapter covers the following subjects:

- Understanding Authentication Proxy

- Authentication Proxy and the IOS Firewall

- Configuring Authentication Proxy on the IOS Firewall

- Using Authentication Proxy with TACACS+

- Using Authentication Proxy with RADIUS

- Limitations of Authentication Proxy

CHAPTER 15

Authentication Proxy and the Cisco IOS Firewall

Authentication proxy is a function that enables users to authenticate via the firewall when accessing specific resources. The Cisco IOS firewall is designed to interface with AAA servers using standard authentication protocols to perform this function. This functionality enables administrators to create a very granular and dynamic per-user security policy. This chapter discusses authentication proxy and how it is used to authenticate both inbound and outbound connections. The Cisco IOS firewall supports TACACS+ and RADIUS AAA servers. The configuration steps for authentication proxy using TACACS+ or RADIUS are covered in this chapter along with the introduction to the Cisco Secure Access Control Server (CSACS), which can perform both TACACS+ and RADIUS functions. Because no solution can support the needs of every implementation, it is important to understand the limitations of authentication proxy.

"Do I Know This Already?" Quiz

The purpose of the "Do I Know This Already?" quiz is to help you decide whether you really need to read the entire chapter. If you already intend to read the entire chapter, you do not necessarily need to answer these questions now.

The nine-question quiz, derived from the major sections in the "Foundation Topics" portion of the chapter, helps you determine how to spend your limited study time.

Table 15-1 outlines the major topics discussed in this chapter and the "Do I Know This Already?" quiz questions that correspond to those topics.

Table 15-1 *"Do I Know This Already?" Foundation Topics Section-to-Question Mapping*

Foundation Topics Section	Questions Covered in This Section
Understanding Authentication Proxy	1–3
Configuring Authentication Proxy on the IOS Firewall	4–7
Using Authentication Proxy with TACACS+	8–9

> **CAUTION** The goal of self-assessment is to gauge your mastery of the topics in this chapter. If you do not know the answer to a question or are only partially sure of the answer, you should mark this question wrong for purposes of the self-assessment. Giving yourself credit for an answer you correctly guess skews your self-assessment results and might provide you with a false sense of security.

1. Authentication proxy enables administrators to restrict access to resources _____.

   a. by IP address of the source.

   b. by the IP address of the destination.

   c. on a per-user basis.

   d. by limiting groups to a specific resource.

   e. on a cache-limit basis.

2. Authentication proxy is not a transparent service because _____.

   a. it only works with HTTP.

   b. it requires the user to input a username and password.

   c. it can block access to the requested resource.

   d. it can only be configured to allow outbound access.

   e. it only works with JavaScript.

3. How is authentication proxy triggered?

   a. By an HTTP request to the firewall

   b. By an FTP request to the destination

   c. By an HTTP request to the AAA server

   d. By an HTTP request to the destination

   e. By a telnet request to the firewall

4. Authentication proxy first became available with what version of the Cisco IOS Software?

   a. 11.3

   b. 12.0.2.J

   c. 12.0.5.T

   d. 12.1(2)

   e. 12.2

5. What configuration mode should you be in on the Cisco IOS firewall to configure AAA?

   a. EXEC mode
   b. Interface configuration mode
   c. AAA configuration mode
   d. Global configuration mode
   e. Remote configuration mode

6. What command enables AAA on the Cisco IOS firewall?

   a. **aaa new-model**
   b. **aaa-server**
   c. **auth-proxy**
   d. **aaa authentication**
   e. **config aaa**

7. What command shows the Cisco IOS firewall host name on the login page?

   a. **aaa banner**
   b. **ip auth-proxy auth-proxy-banner**
   c. **show hostname**
   d. **ip auth-proxy login banner**
   e. **None of the above**

8. What are the two authentication protocols supported by the CSACS and used for authentication proxy? (Choose two.)

   a. TACACS
   b. TACACS+
   c. CHAP
   d. PAP
   e. RADIUS

9. Where do you add the authentication proxy as a new service on the CSACS? (Choose two.)

   a. Network configuration window
   b. Administration Control window
   c. Protocol configuration window
   d. Interface configuration window
   e. TACACS Services window

The answers to the "Do I Know This Already?" quiz are found in the appendix. The suggested choices for your next step are as follows:

- **7 or less overall score**—Read the entire chapter. This includes the "Foundation Topics" and "Foundation Summary" sections and the "Q&A" section.

- **8 or 9 overall score**—If you want more review on these topics, skip to the "Foundation Summary" section and then go to the "Q&A" section. Otherwise, move on to the next chapter.

Foundation Topics

Understanding Authentication Proxy

Authentication proxy is one of the core components of the Cisco IOS firewall feature set. Prior to the implementation of authentication proxy, access to a resource was normally restricted by the IP address of the requesting source and a single policy was applied to that source or network. There was no way to ensure that only authorized users had physical access to the workstation or that unauthorized users were not attempting to access a resource outside of their privilege level.

Authentication proxy enables administrators to restrict access to resources on a per-user basis and tailor the privileges of each individual instead of applying a generic policy to all users.

It is difficult to determine how authentication proxy will be addressed on the SECUR exam. At the time this writing, Cisco emphasized the importance of understanding "how" authentication proxy works. This does not mean that you shouldn't be familiar with the commands used to configure authentication proxy, but you should certainly be very familiar with the mechanics of how authentication proxy functions and the steps required to implement it.

How Authentication Proxy Works

Unlike many Cisco IOS firewall functions, authentication proxy is not a service that is transparent to the user. On the contrary, it requires user interaction. The authentication proxy is triggered when the user initiates an HTTP session through the Cisco IOS firewall. The firewall checks to see whether the user has already been authenticated. If the user has previously authenticated, it allows the connection. If the user has not previously authenticated, the firewall prompts the user for a username and password and verifies the user input with a TACACS+ or RADIUS server.

There are three steps in the authentication proxy process when a source initiates a connection to the destination on the other side of the Cisco IOS firewall. "On the other side" in this context refers to internal sources initiating outbound connections and external hosts initiating inbound connections. Figure 15-1 depicts the steps required for an internal host to complete an outbound connection to an external destination.

Figure 15-1 *Internal Host Connection to External Destination*

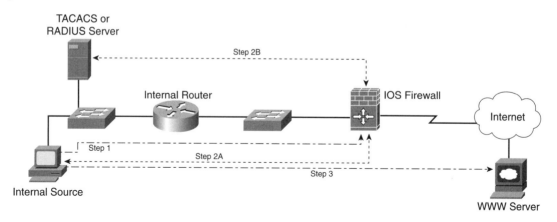

As Figure 15-1 illustrates, three steps are required to complete the connection from the source to the destination.

Step 1   The source host initiates an HTTP connection that is intended to pass through the Cisco IOS firewall to reach its destination.

Step 2   The Cisco IOS firewall checks to see whether the source has already been authenticated.

   a. If the source has not previously authenticated, the firewall sends a login prompt to the user.

   b. The user completes the username and password and the Cisco IOS firewall verifies the user account information with the AAA server.

Step 3   If the user provides the correct account information and is authenticated by the AAA server, the firewall allows the connection to complete.

Figure 15-2 shows that the same steps are required for communication in the opposite direction. It depicts a user on the internal network attempting to access a website on the Internet.

What Authentication Proxy Looks Like

When the user initiates the HTTP connection, the Cisco IOS firewall checks to see whether the user has already been authenticated. If the user has not been previously authenticated, the firewall responds with a HTTP login page.

Figure 15-3 depicts the authentication proxy login page. The user must fill in the correct username and password to successfully authenticate and connect to the desired resource.

Figure 15-2 *External Host Connection to Internal Destination*

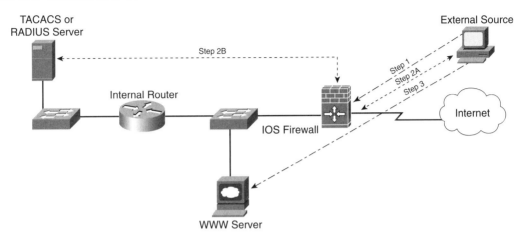

Figure 15-3 *Authentication Proxy Login Page*

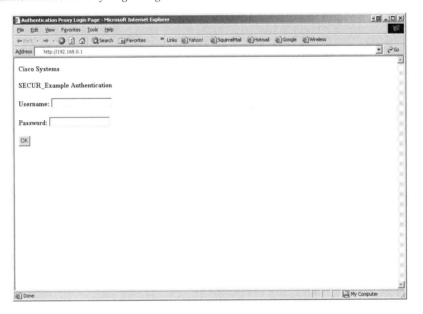

After successfully authenticating, the user sees a login success page similar to Figure 15-4.

Figure 15-4 *Successful Login Screen*

Authentication Proxy and the Cisco IOS Firewall

Authentication proxy is a feature that became available with Cisco IOS Software Release 12.0.5.T. Authentication proxy is compatible with the following Cisco IOS Software security features:

- **Context-based access control (CBAC)**—CBAC was discussed in great detail in Chapter 14, "Context-Based Access Control (CBAC)." If you configure authentication proxy to work with CBAC, you can create dynamic access control entries. If you do not configure authentication proxy with CBAC, you need to reference static access lists on the Cisco IOS firewall.

- **Network Address Translation (NAT)**—NAT enables you to translate internal addresses to external (normally public) addresses. If you are using authentication proxy on a firewall that is also performing NAT, you must also use CBAC to ensure that session translations do not conflict.

- **IPSec encryption**—Authentication proxy works transparently with IPSec encryption.

- **VPN client software**—Authentication proxy can be used for user authentication when creating a VPN connection. This feature provides an additional level of security for administrators by authenticating the user before the encrypted connection is created.

- **Cisco IDS firewall intrusion detection system (IDS)**—Authentication proxy works transparently with IOS firewall IDS.

Configuring Authentication Proxy on the Cisco IOS Firewall

Authentication proxy enables users to connect through the firewall to a resource only after their credentials have been verified by a AAA server. After the authentication is complete, the Cisco IOS firewall receives authorization information from the AAA server in the form of a dynamic access list. It is always a good idea to ensure that all traffic is properly flowing through the Cisco IOS firewall prior to implementing authentication proxy. Access lists applied to the Cisco IOS firewall determine the level of security (for example, what traffic requires authentication proxy). It is possible to require authentication proxy for all traffic or to limit the requirement only to specific sources or destinations. There are many different ways to configure authentication proxy, and each one is slightly different depending on the Cisco IOS firewall services used and the direction the traffic is traveling in relation to the Cisco IOS firewall. Cisco publishes specific configuration guides with examples for each type of configuration at http://www.cisco.com/en/US/products/sw/secursw/ps1018/prod_configuration_examples_list.html.

The authentication proxy configurations published by Cisco include the following:

- Authentication proxy inbound (no CBAC or NAT)
- Authentication proxy outbound (no CBAC or NAT)
- Authentication proxy inbound (with CBAC, but no NAT)
- Authentication proxy outbound (with CBAC, but no NAT)
- Authentication proxy inbound (with CBAC and NAT)
- Authentication proxy outbound (with CBAC and NAT)
- Authentication proxy inbound with IPSec and VPN client (no CBAC or NAT)
- Authentication proxy outbound with IPSec and VPN client (no CBAC or NAT)
- Authentication proxy inbound with IPSec and VPN client (with CBAC and NAT)
- Authentication proxy outbound with IPSec and VPN client (with CBAC and NAT)

This chapter focuses on configuring the Cisco IOS firewall for inbound and outbound traffic without using CBAC, NAT, IPSec, or the VPN client.

Authentication Proxy Configuration Steps

A number of steps are required to configure authentication proxy on the Cisco IOS firewall. Authentication proxy requires the firewall to communicate with many different systems, and each of these systems must be put into the firewall configuration. This section describes the configuration steps and individual commands used to configure the authentication proxy. There are examples of these configuration commands in the section titled "Authentication Proxy Configuration Examples." It is important to understand the different steps, the commands within each step, and how they relate to each other. As with any other component configuration, you must understand how the commands relate to troubleshoot problems with the authentication proxy. For the purpose of the SECUR examination, it will most likely be critical to recognize which commands are missing or in the wrong syntax. Try to remember the four individual steps and consider how each step references the other. This will enable you to troubleshoot the configuration and determine what portion is not correctly configured. The configuration steps for the Cisco IOS firewall are as follows:

1. Configure AAA.
2. Configure the HTTP server.
3. Configure authentication proxy.
4. Verify the authentication proxy configuration.

Step 1: Configure AAA

You must first configure the Cisco IOS firewall to perform authentication, authorization, and accounting (AAA) functions. Doing so consists of seven individual Cisco IOS Software commands, listed in Table 15-2. Each of these commands must be entered when in the global configuration mode.

Table 15-2 *IOS Commands Required to Configure AAA*

Command	Description
aaa new-model	This command enables the AAA functionality on the Cisco IOS firewall.
**aaa authentication login default [tacacs+	radius]**	This command defines the authentication method to be utilized at login.
aaa authorization auth-proxy default [*method1*] [*method2*...]]	The **auth-proxy** keyword in this command enables authentication proxy for that method of AAA authentication (for example, TACACS+ or RADIUS) and allows the router to download dynamic access control lists from the AAA server.
aaa accounting auth-proxy default start-stop group tacacs+	The **auth-proxy** keyword in this command activates authentication proxy accounting functions.
tacacs-server host *hostname* or **radius-server host** *hostname*	This command identifies the AAA server by host name or IP address.
tacacs-server key *key* or **radius-server key** *key*	This command configures the authentication and encryption key to ensure secure communication between the Cisco IOS firewall and the AAA server.

Table 15-2 *IOS Commands Required to Configure AAA (Continued)*

Command	Description
access-list [*access-list-number*] **permit tcp host** *source* **eq tacacs	radius host** *destination*	This command creates the access list to allow traffic from the AAA server to return to the Cisco IOS firewall. The *source* address is the address of the AAA server, and the *destination* address is the address of the interface on the Cisco IOS firewall that connects to the AAA server.

Step 2: Configure the HTTP Server

In Step 2, you configure the Cisco IOS firewall to function as an HTTP server and set up the authentication method. Table 15-3 lists and describes the three commands required to configure the HTTP server. You must enter each of these commands when in the global configuration mode.

Table 15-3 *HTTP Server Configuration Commands*

Command	Description
ip http server	This command enables the HTTP server on the Cisco IOS firewall. The HTTP server is used by the Cisco IOS firewall to send the login page to the client.
ip http authentication aaa	This command sets the HTTP server authentication method to AAA.
access-list *access-list-number* **deny any**	A standard access list must be created to deny any host.
ip http access-class *access-list-number*	This command specifies the access list to be used by the HTTP server. The *access-list-number* that was created in the previous row is used to prevent any host from connecting directly to the HTTP server.

Step 3: Configure the Authentication Proxy

In Step 3, you configure authentication proxy on the Cisco IOS firewall. Table 15-4 lists and describes commands and options used to configure authentication proxy on the Cisco IOS firewall. You must enter each of these commands when in the global configuration mode.

Table 15-4 *Authentication Proxy Configuration Commands*

Command	Description
ip auth-proxy auth-cache-time *min*	This command sets the global authentication proxy idle timeout. All authentication entries and dynamic access lists are removed from the Cisco IOS firewall when the idle timeout is exceeded. This value is in minutes, and the default value is 60 (minutes).
ip auth-proxy auth-proxy-banner	(Optional) This command enables you to display the firewall name on the authentication proxy login page. This feature is disabled by default.
ip auth-proxy name *auth-proxy-name* **http** [**auth-cache-time** *min*] [**list** {**acl** | *acl-name*}]	This command configures the individual authentication proxy rules. The [**auth-cache-time** *min*] portion of the command is optional and is used to specify the **auth-cache-time** for that specific rule instead of using the global configuration. The [**list** {**acl** | *acl-name*}] portion of the command is also optional and is used to specific access lists to the rule.
interface *type*	This command specifies the interface type on which the authentication proxy is applied. This command also puts the Cisco IOS firewall in the interface configuration mode.
ip auth-proxy *auth-proxy-name*	This command is run in interface configuration mode. It applies the authentication proxy rule (by the rule name) to the interface. It is important to ensure that you apply the authentication proxy rule to the correct interface. The rule must be applied to the first interface in the Cisco IOS firewall that the request will hit. For example, the rule should be applied to the internal interface of the Cisco IOS firewall for outbound traffic or the external interface for inbound traffic.

Step 4: Verify the Authentication Proxy Configuration

After configuring authentication proxy, it is important that you verify the configuration. This can greatly reduce troubleshooting in the event the users are unable to connect due to an error in the configuration of the Cisco IOS firewall. Use the **show ip auth-proxy configuration** command to display and verify the authentication proxy configuration.

Authentication Proxy Configuration Examples

The steps required to configure authentication proxy were listed and defined in the preceding section. In this section, authentication proxy is configured for both inbound and outbound connections through the Cisco IOS firewall.

Figure 15-5 depicts the environment used for the configuration of authentication proxy on the 3640 Cisco IOS firewall.

Figure 15-5 *Network Diagram of Authentication Proxy Source and Destination (External Host)*

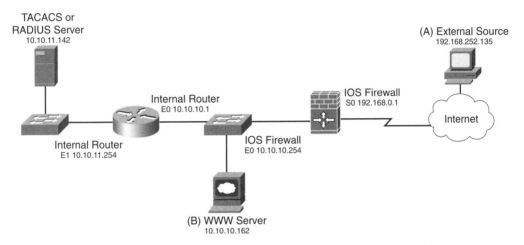

As Figure 15-5 illustrates, the source (A) is using the IP address 192.168.252.135, and the destination is the World Wide Web server (B), located on the internal network at 10.10.10.162. For the purpose of this exercise, NAT is not used for any address space. The Cisco IOS firewall will require any external host attempting to access 10.10.10.162 to authenticate before allowing access.

NOTE Remember that you are only using the 192.168.0.0/16 addresses to represent public Internet addresses. That address space is normally reserved per RFC 1918.

Example 15-1 depicts the configuration of the Cisco IOS firewall to allow authentication proxy for sources requesting access to a resource on the internal network. Authentication proxy is not a bidirectional function; you must configure it for each direction that the user traffic should flow.

Example 15-1 *Configuring Inbound Authentication Proxy on the Cisco IOS Firewall*

```
Router1#configure terminal
! - - - Enable authentication on the Cisco IOS firewall
Router1(config)#aaa new-model
! - - - Define TACACS+ as the authentication method used for login
Router1(config)#aaa authentication login default group tacacs+
! - - - The auth-proxy keyword is used to enable authentication proxy for TACACS+
Router1(config)#aaa authorization auth-proxy default group tacacs+
! - - - Activate authentication proxy accounting
Router1(config)#aaa accounting auth-proxy default start-stop group tacacs+
! - - - Define the AAA server
Router1(config)#tacacs-server host 10.10.11.142
! - - -  Define the key for encryption between the AAA server and the Cisco IOS firewall
Router1(config)#tacacs-server key abc123
! - - - Create an access list to allow traffic from the AAA server back to the router
Router1(config)#access-list 103 permit tcp host 10.10.11.142 eq tacacs host 10.10.10.254
! - - - Enable the HTTP server on the Cisco IOS firewall
Router1(config)#ip http server
! - - - Set the authentication to AAA
Router1(config)#ip http authentication aaa
! - - - Create a standard access list denying all traffic
Router1(config)#access-list 22 deny any
! - - - Define standard access list 22 for the HTTP server
Router1(config)#ip http access-class 22
! - - - Define the global authentication timeout to 30 minutes
Router1(config)#ip auth-proxy auth-cache-time 30
! - - - Display the firewall name on the login page
Router1(config)#ip auth-proxy auth-proxy-banner
! - - - Create the auth-proxy rules with the name allowed-inbound
Router1(config)#ip auth-proxy name allowed-inbound http
! - - - Enter the interface configuration mode
Router1(config)#interface s0
! - - - Configure the IP address of the interface
Router1(config-if)#ip address 192.168.0.1 255.255.255.0
! - - -  Apply the named auth-proxy rule to the interface
Router1(config-if)#ip auth-proxy allowed-inbound
! - - - Exit the interface configuration mode
Router1(config)#CTL-Z
Router1(config)#
```

Next you will configure the Cisco IOS firewall for an internal source and an external destination. Figure 15-6 depicts the network with an internal source and external destination.

Figure 15-6 *Network Diagram of Authentication Proxy Source and Destination (Internal Host)*

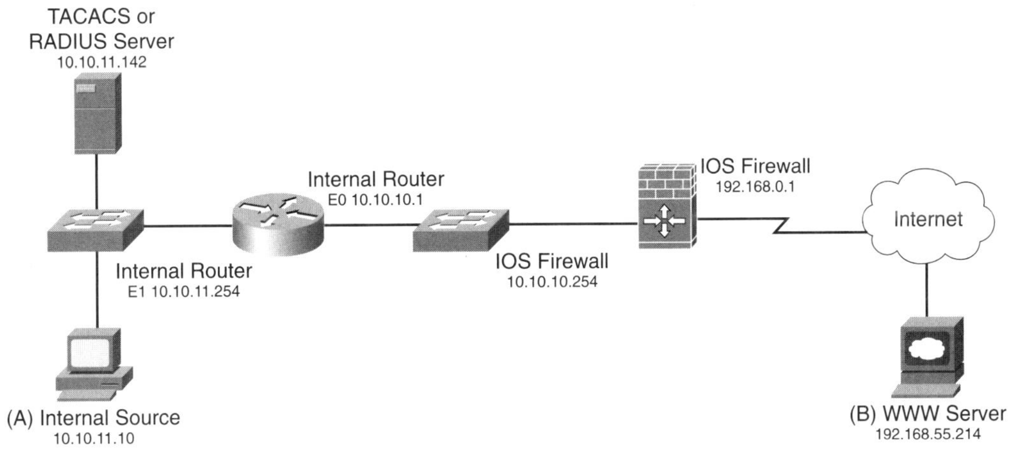

As Figure 15-6 illustrates, the source (A) is located on the internal network using the IP address 10.10.11.10, and the destination is a World Wide Web server (B), located on the Internet at 192.168.55.214. Again, this exercise does not use NAT for any address space. The Cisco IOS firewall requires, any internal host attempting to access the Internet to authenticate before allowing access.

> **NOTE** Remember that you are using only the 192.168.0.0/16 addresses to represent public Internet addresses. That address space is normally reserved per RFC 1918.

Example 15-2 depicts the configuration of the perimeter router to perform authentication proxy for sources on the internal network attempting to access resources on the Internet. Again, authentication proxy is not a bidirectional function; it must be configured for each direction that the user traffic should flow.

Example 15-2 *Configuring Outbound Authentication Proxy on the Perimeter Router*

```
Router1#configure terminal
! - - - Enable authentication on the Cisco IOS firewall
Router1(config)#aaa new-model
! - - - Define TACACS+ as the authentication method used for login
Router1(config)#aaa authentication login default group tacacs+
```
continues

Example 15-2 *Configuring Outbound Authentication Proxy on the Perimeter Router (Continued)*

```
! - - - The auth-proxy keyword is used to enable authentication proxy for TACACS+
Router1(config)#aaa authorization auth-proxy default group tacacs+
! - - - Activate authentication proxy accounting
Router1(config)#aaa accounting auth-proxy default start-stop group tacacs+
! - - - Define the AAA server
Router1(config)#tacacs-server host 10.10.11.142
! - - - Define the key for encryption between the AAA server and the Cisco IOS firewall
Router1(config)#tacacs-server key abc123
! - - - Create an access list to allow traffic from the AAA server back to the router
Router1(config)#access-list 103 permit tcp host 10.10.11.142 eq tacacs host 10.10.10.254
! - - - Enable the HTTP server on the Cisco IOS firewall
Router1(config)#ip http server
! - - - Set the authentication to AAA
Router1(config)#ip http authentication aaa
! - - - Create a standard access list denying all traffic
Router1(config)# access-list 22 deny any
! - - - Define standard access list 22 for the HTTP server
Router1(config)#ip http access-class 22
- - - Define the global authentication timeout to 30 minutes
Router1(config)#ip auth-proxy auth-cache-time 30
! - - - Display the firewall name on the login page
Router1(config)#ip auth-proxy auth-proxy-banner
! - - - Create the auth-proxy rules with the name allowed-outbound
Router1(config)#ip auth-proxy name allowed-outbound http
! - - - Enter the interface configuration mode
Router1(config)#interface e0
! - - - Configure the IP address of the interface
Router1(config-if)#ip address 10.10.10.254 255.255.255.0
! - - - Apply the named auth-proxy rule to the interface
Router1(config-if)#ip auth-proxy allowed-outbound
! - - - Exit the interface configuration mode
Router1(config)#CTL-Z
Router1(config)#
```

Notice from Example 15-2 that the major difference in the configuration is where the access list is applied to the Cisco IOS firewall. The access list must be applied on the interface that is facing the source in order to facilitate the communication between the source and the Cisco IOS firewall.

Using Authentication Proxy with TACACS+

CSACS provides both TACACS+ and RADIUS functionality. CSACS was discussed in detail in Chapter 9, "Cisco Secure Access Control Server." This section discusses configuring TACACS+

using the CSACS. If the CASACS is already configured, you only need to make a few configuration changes to run TACACS+. You must complete three steps for this configuration:

Step 1   Complete the network configuration.

Step 2   Complete the interface configuration.

Step 3   Complete the group setup.

Step 1: Complete the Network Configuration

To complete the network configuration, connect to the CSACS using your browser and click the Network Configuration icon on the left border. Figure 15-7 depicts the Network Configuration page of the CSACS.

Figure 15-7   *CSACS Network Configuration Page*

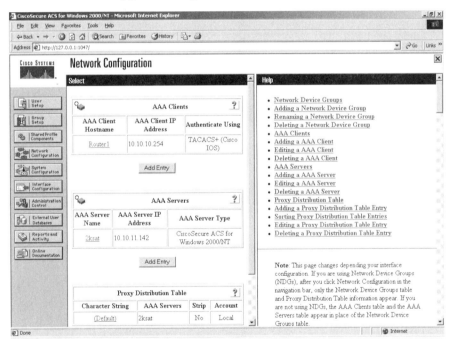

Ensure that the Cisco IOS firewall is listed as a AAA client. The IP address should be the address of the interface that faces the AAA server, and the Authenticate Using field should match the authentication protocol being used—in this case, TACACS+ (Cisco IOS). To change any parameters for the AAA client, just click the client (link) and the Edit window will appear. Figure 15-8 depicts the Edit window for the AAA client.

Figure 15-8 *AAA Client Edit Window*

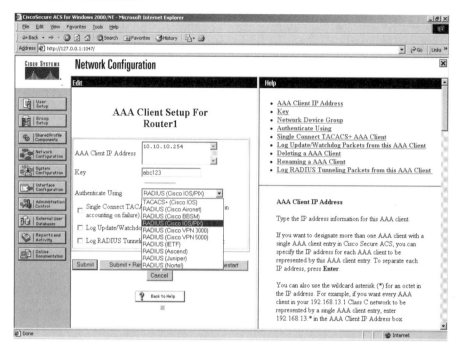

In Figure 15-8 you can see that it is possible to change the AAA client IP address and key. The authentication protocols are selected from a drop-down list.

NOTE Ensure that you click Submit + Restart after making any changes to the AAA client configuration.

Step 2: Complete the Interface Configuration

The next step is to complete the interface configuration. Select the Interface Configuration icon on the left border and scroll down in the Edit window until you get to the TACACS+ Services configuration box. Figure 15-9 depicts this area.

In Figure 15-9, you can see that TACACS+ services can be assigned to either users or groups. In the New Services block, check the Group box and list the service as **auth-proxy**.

Figure 15-9 *Interface Configuration Window*

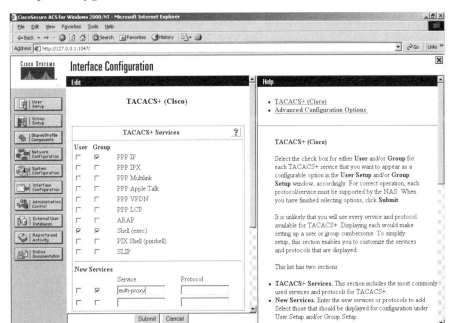

Step 3: Complete the Group Setup

The next step is to configure the parameters of the dynamic access control lists (ACLs). This is completed in the Group Setup window, which you access by clicking the Group Setup icon on the left border and scrolling down to the auth-proxy window. Figure 15-10 depicts the attributes configuration window.

Figure 15-10 *Group Setup Configuration Window*

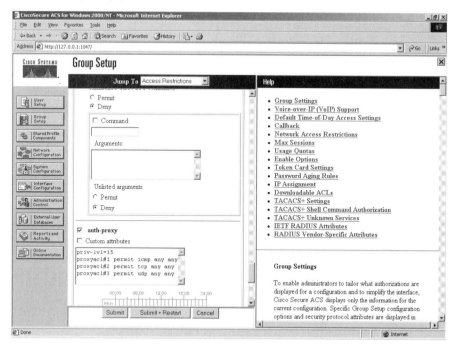

In Figure 15-10, four lines are added to the auth-proxy attributes. This is a very open policy and allows anyone who successfully authenticates to have open access to internal resources. Obviously, you want to use a more restrictive policy when configuring your authentication proxy in a production environment.

```
priv-lvl=15
proxyacl#1=permit icmp any any
proxyacl#2=permit tcp any any
proxyacl#3=permit udp any any
```

Using Authentication Proxy with RADIUS

Configuring the CSACS for RADIUS requires the same steps as TACACS+, although they need a slightly different configuration. Figure 15-11 depicts the Network Configuration window. This time you need to ensure that the AAA client is using the RADIUS authentication protocol.

In Figure 15-11, the Authenticate Using box now says RADIUS (Cisco IOS/PIX). The next step is to configure the RADIUS properties in the Interface Configuration window. Figure 15-12 depicts the Interface Configuration window.

In Figure 15-12, the boxes are checked for the different RADIUS configurations. In this case, you are only using the first item listed (cisco-av-pair). The final step is to configure the attributes for cisco-av-pair. This is completed in the Group Setup window. Figure 15-13 depicts the Group Setup window.

Figure 15-11 *Network Configuration Window*

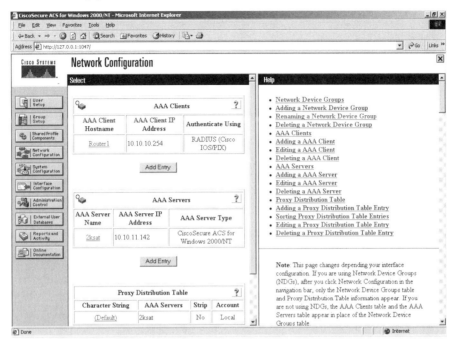

Figure 15-12 *Interface Configuration Window*

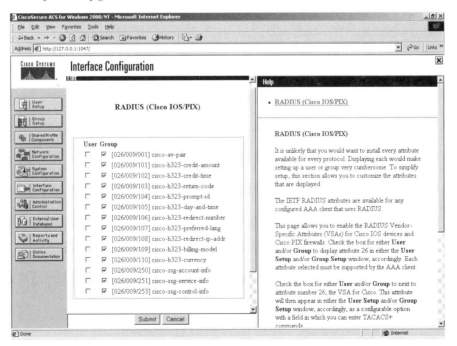

Figure 15-13 *Group Setup Configuration Window*

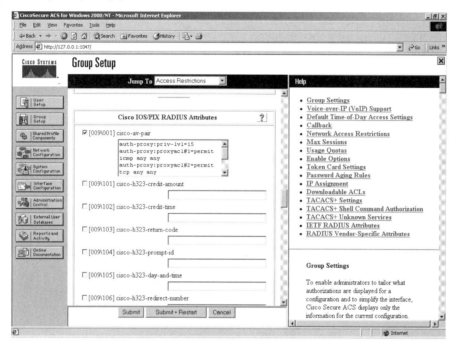

In Figure 15-13, it is only possible to see the first three of four configuration entries added to the Cisco IOS/PIX RADIUS Attributes box because of the limited size of the window. As with the TACACS+ configuration, this is a very liberal configuration that allows access to all resources after the user successfully authenticates. Four lines are added to the auth-proxy attributes. The four lines that are included in the cisco-av-pair window are

```
auth-proxy:priv-lvl=15
auth-proxy:proxyacl#1=permit icmp any any
auth-proxy:proxyacl#2=permit tcp any any
auth-proxy:proxyacl#3=permit udp any any
```

Limitations of Authentication Proxy

To properly design a solution using authentication proxy, it is important to understand the limitations. It is always best to design a solution that can completely fulfill the business requirement. The following are limitations to authentication proxy:

- The authentication proxy triggers only on HTTP connections.
- HTTP services must be running on the standard (well-known) port, which is port 80 for HTTP.
- Client browsers must enable JavaScript for secure authentication.

- The authentication proxy access lists apply to traffic passing through the router. Traffic destined to the router is authenticated by the existing Cisco IOS Software authentication methods.
- The authentication proxy does not support concurrent usage; that is, if two users try to log in from the same host at the same time, authentication and authorization applies only to the user who first submits a valid username and password.
- Load balancing using multiple or different AAA servers is not supported.

Foundation Summary

The "Foundation Summary" section of each chapter lists the most important facts from the chapter. Although this section does not list every fact from the chapter that will be on your SECUR exam, a well-prepared SECUR candidate should at a minimum know all the details in each "Foundation Summary" before going to take the exam.

Authentication proxy facilitates communication between the Cisco IOS firewall and a AAA server. This enables administrators to restrict access to resources down to the individual "authenticated" user level. Authentication proxy requires you to configure both the Cisco IOS firewall and the AAA server. Configuring the Cisco IOS firewall requires four tasks:

1. Configure AAA.
2. Configure the HTTP server.
3. Configure authentication proxy.
4. Verify the authentication proxy configuration.

The following three primary tasks are required to configure the CSACS as a TACACS+ or RADIUS server:

- Network configuration
- Interface configuration
- Authentication proxy configuration

Authentication proxy is not a bidirectional service. You must configure authentication proxy to respond to requests from internal or external sources. If you need to configure authentication proxy to function in both directions, you must create an inbound configuration and an outbound configuration.

It is important to understand the limitations of authentication proxy to ensure that the correct solution is designed to fulfill the business requirement. Some of the limitations of authentication proxy include the following:

- Authentication proxy is triggered only by HTTP connections.
- Authentication proxy only supports HTTP on port 80.
- Authentication proxy requires that the client browser be configured to support JavaScript to perform secure authentication.

- Authentication proxy does not support access directly to the Cisco IOS firewall.
- Only a single user account can be logged on at a time. Authentication proxy does not support concurrent usage.
- Authentication proxy can only be configured to a single AAA server or server type.

Q&A

As mentioned in the section, "How to Use This Book," in the Introduction to this book, you have two choices for review questions. The questions that follow next give you a bigger challenge than the exam itself by using an open-ended question format. By reviewing now with this more difficult question format, you can exercise your memory better and prove your conceptual and factual knowledge of this chapter. The answers to these questions are found in the appendix.

For more practice with exam-like question formats, including questions using a router simulator and multiple choice questions, use the exam engine on the CD-ROM.

1. What happens if the user has previously authenticated and that authentication has not timed out?
2. If you are using NAT with authentication proxy, what other feature must you also use?
3. What are the three steps for configuring authentication proxy on the Cisco IOS firewall?
4. True or False: The host name is required on the HTTP login page to ensure that users log in to the correct firewall?
5. What are the three steps for configuring TACACS+ on the CSACS?
6. Where is the Cisco IOS firewall configured on the CSACS?
7. Where are dynamic ACLs configured on the CSACS for RADIUS?
8. What must be running on the client browser to ensure secure login?
9. What happens if you attempt authentication proxy using SSL?
10. How many AAA servers can you match with a single Cisco IOS firewall for authentication proxy?

This chapter covers the following subjects:

- Cisco IOS Firewall IDS Features
- Compatibility with the Cisco Secure IDS
- Cisco IOS Firewall IDS Configuration
- Verifying the IOS Firewall IDS Configuration
- Cisco IOS Firewall IDS Deployment Strategies

CHAPTER 16

Intrusion Detection and the Cisco IOS Firewall

Intrusion detection is a key component of any network security design. An intrusion detection sensor (IDS) provides security administrators with the ability to detect and react to potentially malicious activity on the network. The key difference between firewall and IDS activity is that firewalls just apply rules to network traffic, whereas IDSs normally scan the traffic and can react to content within the packet. Additionally, a firewall may drop the traffic and add an entry in the firewall logs, whereas an IDS normally generates an alarm and can react in other ways to malicious traffic. It is most common on enterprise networks to use a combination of firewalls and IDSs. Cisco produces the Cisco Secure Intrusion Detection Sensor (CSIDS), the IDS Switch Module (IDSM-2), the IDS Network Module (for IOS routers), and the Cisco PIX Firewall. The Cisco IOS firewall feature set is a component that enables you to perform both firewall and IDS functions using a Cisco router as a Cisco IOS firewall. This chapter discusses the Cisco IOS firewall IDS.

"Do I Know This Already?" Quiz

The purpose of the "Do I Know This Already?" quiz is to help you decide whether you really need to read the entire chapter. If you already intend to read the entire chapter, you do not necessarily need to answer these questions now.

The 10-question quiz, derived from the major sections in the "Foundation Topics" portion of the chapter, helps you determine how to spend your limited study time.

Table 16-1 outlines the major topics discussed in this chapter and the "Do I Know This Already?" quiz questions that correspond to those topics.

Chapter 16: Intrusion Detection and the Cisco IOS Firewall

Table 16-1 *"Do I Know This Already?" Foundation Topics Section-to-Question Mapping*

Foundation Topics Section	Questions Covered in This Section
IOS Firewall IDS Features	1–4
Compatibility with the Cisco Secure IDS	
IOS Firewall IDS Configuration	5–9
Verifying the IOS Firewall IDS Configuration	10
IOS Firewall IDS Deployment Strategies	

> **CAUTION** The goal of self-assessment is to gauge your mastery of the topics in this chapter. If you do not know the answer to a question or are only partially sure of the answer, you should mark this question wrong for purposes of the self-assessment. Giving yourself credit for an answer you correctly guess skews your self-assessment results and might provide you with a false sense of security.

1. What advantages does the Cisco IOS firewall IDS provide security administrators? (Choose two.)

   a. Detect malicious activity

   b. Combine features of routing and switching

   c. Work well with syslog servers

   d. Can respond to potential threats

   e. None of the above

2. The Cisco IOS firewall IDS is a(n) _____.

   a. integrated appliance.

   b. package that runs on Windows 2000.

   c. software-based feature set for 500 series routers.

   d. system that runs on the PIX firewall.

   e. software-based feature set developed for mid-range to high-end routers.

3. How does the Cisco IOS firewall IDS identify potential attacks?

   a. It scans the network.
   b. It matches packets against signatures.
   c. It matches audit rules.
   d. It scans packet headers.
   e. It scans for potential viruses.

4. How does the Cisco IOS firewall IDS operate with CBAC?

   a. It doesn't.
   b. They can run in concert or be applied to different interfaces.
   c. It must be applied to different interfaces.
   d. They must be applied to the same interface.
   e. None of the above.

5. What configuration mode must you be in to configure "notification types"?

   a. Notification configuration mode
   b. Privilege EXEC mode
   c. Interface configuration mode
   d. Global configuration mode
   e. IOS configuration mode

6. What are you configuring with the **ip audit notify** command?

   a. E-mail address for attack notification
   b. Where to send alerts if the router fails
   c. What server to log to
   d. IDS routing protocols
   e. Defines the alert format if a signature match occurs

282 Chapter 16: Intrusion Detection and the Cisco IOS Firewall

7. What is the default port for the POP?

   a. TCP 4500

   b. UDP 45000

   c. TCP 45000

   d. UDP 4500

   e. TCP 3021

8. Why should you define a "protected network"?

   a. So you know who is attacking your network.

   b. To protect yourself from disgruntled employees.

   c. The signatures only apply to the protected network.

   d. It is a requirement to make the IDS function work.

   e. None of the above.

9. What is the difference between an atomic signature and a compound signature?

   a. Atomic signatures are really bad.

   b. Compound signatures require more memory.

   c. Atomic signatures only see oversized packets.

   d. Atomic signatures can overload your router.

   e. None of the above.

10. What command is used to reset statistics?

    a. **reset ip audit statistics**

    b. **clear ip audit statistics**

    c. **delete ip audit statistics**

    d. **no statistics**

    e. **disable ip audit statistics**

The answers to the "Do I Know This Already?" quiz are found in the appendix. The suggested choices for your next step are as follows:

- **8 or less overall score**—Read the entire chapter. This includes the "Foundation Topics" and "Foundation Summary" sections and the "Q&A" section.

- **9 or 10 overall score**—If you want more review on these topics, skip to the "Foundation Summary" section and then go to the "Q&A" section. Otherwise, move on to the next chapter.

Foundation Topics

This chapter discusses the Cisco IOS firewall IDS. It is important to understand the interaction between firewall functions and IDS functions. When properly configured, the two combined provide an excellent level of security to the network. There are six major topics pertaining to the Cisco IOS firewall IDS covered in this chapter:

- Cisco IOS firewall IDS features
- Compatibility with the CSIDS
- Cisco IOS firewall IDS configuration
- Working with Cisco IOS firewall IDS signatures and audit rules
- Verifying the Cisco IOS firewall IDS configuration
- Cisco IOS firewall IDS deployment strategies

Cisco IOS Firewall IDS Features

Cisco IOS Software-based intrusion detection was developed as part of the Cisco IOS firewall feature set for mid-range and high-end routers and has since been adapted to the smaller small office/home office (SOHO) and remote office/home office (ROHO) models. It allows the firewall to act as an in-line IDS. The Cisco IOS firewall IDS scans packets that flow through the firewall looking for any traffic that matches specific signatures that indicate malicious traffic. If the IDS finds traffic that matches a signature, it can react quickly and eliminate the threat before it adversely affects the network. The Cisco IOS firewall IDS can be configured to react to suspected malicious traffic in any combination of three ways:

- **Send an alarm**—The Cisco IOS firewall IDS can be configured to send an alarm to a syslog server or a centralized management system such as the Cisco Secure IDS Director, the IDS Management Console (IDS MC), the Cisco IDS Event Viewer, or the Cisco Secure Policy Manager (CSPM).
- **Drop the packet**—The Cisco IOS firewall can dynamically create an access list that allows the system to drop the incoming packet.
- **Reset the TCP connection**—The Cisco IOS firewall can forward packets to both source and destination with the RESET flag set.

NOTE For the latest list of routers that support the Cisco IOS firewall IDS, consult the products section at Cisco.com.

284 Chapter 16: Intrusion Detection and the Cisco IOS Firewall

Figure 16-1 shows how the Cisco IOS firewall IDS functions when it discovers traffic that matches an attack signature and is considered to be malicious.

Figure 16-1 *Cisco IOS Firewall IDS Attack Response*

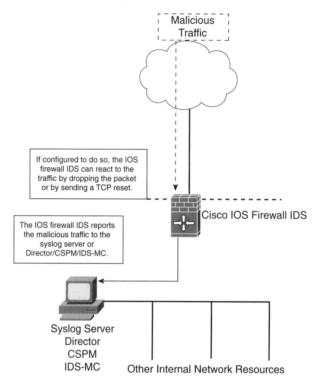

Figure 16-1 illustrates how the Cisco IOS firewall IDS responds to an attack. The Cisco IOS firewall IDS can function in concert with CBAC but can also function independently. It is possible to enable and disable signatures as necessary to reduce the number of false positive alerts by the IDS. The Cisco IOS firewall IDS is ideal for implementation on the network perimeter and at critical points on the network where administrators need the ability to automatically react to internal and external threats.

Compatibility with the CSIDS

The Cisco IOS firewall IDS is completely compatible with the CSIDS. The CSIDS is designed to detect and react to unauthorized activity in real time on enterprise networks. The CSIDS is a group of products that are centrally managed and provide host-based or network-based protection. The network-based portion of the CSIDS monitors and analyzes the content of the network traffic and matches it against signatures looking for patterns that indicate suspicious or malicious traffic.

Host-based IDS resides on a individual host and responds to requests or changes to that host. The CSIDS consists of three components:

- **Sensor**—This includes the Cisco IDS appliance, the IDSM-2, the IOS Firewall IDS, and the Cisco HIDS software.
- **Central management**—This includes the IDS MC, the Cisco IDS Event Viewer, the Cisco IDS Director, or the CSPM. The centralized management system is used as a consolidation point for all sensor logs and a platform for managing individual sensors. Management tasks include sensor configuration and signature distribution/installation. Both the Cisco IDS Director and the CSPM are discontinued products and are no longer supported.
- **POP**—This is a proprietary protocol that allows sensors to communicate with each other and with the management system. POP is a connection-oriented protocol that can route as necessary to maintain a point-to-point connection between the nodes. When using POP, you must configure each device with a host ID and an organizational ID. Each device must be configured for the same organizational ID as its manager for them to communicate. Each device must also have a different host ID to prevent communication conflicts.

NOTE The Cisco IOS firewall IDS signatures differ from the Cisco IDS (appliance) signatures.

Cisco IOS Firewall IDS Configuration

Specific tasks are required to configure the Cisco IOS firewall IDS. These steps should be completed in the following order to ensure that the IDS is implemented correctly:

1. Initialize the Cisco IOS firewall IDS on the router.
2. Configure information and attack signatures.
3. Create and apply audit rules.
4. Add the Cisco IOS firewall IDS to the centralized management.

These addresses for the Cisco IOS firewall IDS and the CSPM are used in the configuration examples for this section:

```
CSPM
10.10.10.200
Host ID = 11
ORG ID = 100
Host Name = [Host Name]
ORG Name = [ORG Name]
```

The IP address of our CSPM is 10.10.10.200 with a host ID of 11 and an organizational ID of 100. The ethernet0 interface of the Cisco IOS firewall is 10.10.10.254, and the serial interface is

192.168.0.1 with a host ID of 10 and an organizational ID of 100. Remember that the organizational ID of the IDS and the Director must match in order for the devices to communicate. These IP addresses and host/organizational IDs are used in the following configuration examples.

Initialize the Cisco IOS Firewall IDS on the Router

Initializing the Cisco IOS firewall IDS includes four subtasks needed to configure the Cisco IOS firewall IDS to respond to malicious traffic. The initialization tasks include configuring the notification type, configuring the Cisco IOS firewall IDS and central management post office parameters, defining the protected network, and configuring the router maximum queue for alarms. Each is discussed in more detail in the following sections.

Configuring the Notification Type

Use the **ip audit notify** to configure the Cisco IOS firewall IDS to forward alerts to the Cisco Director, the CSPM, IDS MC, Event Viewer, or a syslog server. You must be in the global configuration mode to do so. Table 16-2 lists the notification commands with a brief description.

Table 16-2 *Setting Notification Commands*

Command	Description
ip audit notify nr-director	Send the alarms in post office format to the central manager (Director, SCPM, router MC, Event Viewer, or other IDS sensors).
ip audit notify log	Send messages in syslog format to the syslog server or router console.

Example 16-1 shows the commands used to set the notification type.

Example 16-1 *Configuring the Notification Type*

```
Router1#configure terminal
Router1(config)#ip audit notify nr-director
   <<< OR >>>
Router1(config)# ip audit notify log
```

Configure the IOS Firewall IDS and Central Management Post Office Parameters

Configuring the Cisco IOS firewall IDS and central management post office parameters facilitates communication between the Cisco IOS firewall and its central manager. The post office parameters identify the IDS by host ID and organizational ID. For the IDS to communicate with its central manager, both devices must have the same organizational ID. This command is completed in the global configuration mode. The post office parameters must be configured on both the Cisco IOS firewall and the Director, CSPM, IDS MC, or Event Viewer.

The command required to configure the post office parameters on the Cisco IOS firewall IDS is as follows:

```
ip audit po local hostid host-id orgid org-id
```

The *host-id* must be a unique number between 1 and 65,535, and the *org-id* must also be a unique number between 1 and 65,535.

Example 16-2 shows the command used to set the POP on the router.

Example 16-2 *Configuring the Post Office Protocol*

```
Router1#configure terminal
Router1(config)#ip audit po local hostid 10 orgid  100
```

The commands required to configure the Director's post office parameters have slightly more options. Keep in mind that these parameters are also configured on the Cisco IOS firewall IDS. Table 16-3 lists the command options available when configuring the Director's post office parameters on the Cisco IOS firewall IDS.

Table 16-3 *Configuration Options for the Director's Post Office Parameters*

Command	Description
hostid *host-id*	The host ID must be a unique number between 1 and 65,535.
orgid *org-id*	The organizational ID must also be a unique number between 1 and 65,535.
rmtaddress *ip-addr*	Specifies the interface address of the Director.
localaddress *ip-addr*	Specifies the interface address of the Cisco IOS firewall IDS.
port *port-num*	Specifies the port number that the Director listens on. The default is UDP port 45,000.
preference *preference-number*	The preference number is an integer that represents the priority of a Director.
timeout *seconds*	Specifies the timeout value for heartbeat communications between the IDS and Director. The default is five seconds.
application director|**logger**	Defines the application that the IDS is sending post office data to. The keyword **logger** indicates the data that is being sent to a CSIDS.

Example 16-3 shows the command used to set the Director's POP on the router.

Example 16-3 *Configuring the Director's POP*

```
Router1#configure terminal
Router1(config)#ip audit po remote hostid 11 orgid  100 rmtaddress 10.10.10.200
   localaddress 10.10.10.254 port 45000 preference 50 timeout 10 application logger
```

Define the Protected Network

To effectively identify an attack, the Cisco IOS firewall IDS must be able to determine the IP address range of the protected network. This function does not affect the operation of the IDS but is used to log traffic as inbound or outbound. The following command specifies the beginning and end of the address range for the protected network:

> **ip audit protected** *ip-addr* **to** *ip-addr*

Example 16-4 shows the command used to configure the protected network.

Example 16-4 *Configuring a Protected Network*

```
Router1#configure terminal
Router1(config)#ip audit protected 10.10.10.1 to 10.10.10.254
```

Configure the Router Maximum Queue for Alarms

Keeping in mind that the Cisco IOS firewall IDS functionality can consume memory and potentially reduce the performance capability of the router, it is very important to limit the amount of memory reserved for alerts/alarms. The following command sets the notification queue size:

> **ip audit po max-events** *num-of-events*

The *num-of-events* is an integer between 1 and 65,535 that designates the maximum number of events that can remain in the queue. The default value for **max-events** is 100.

Example 16-5 shows the command used to set the maximum queue size.

Example 16-5 *Configuring the Maximum Queue Size*

```
Router1#configure terminal
Router1(config)#ip audit po max-events 200
```

Configure Info and Attack Signatures

The Cisco IOS firewall compares network traffic to specific signatures to determine malicious traffic. There are two different categories of signatures and two types of signatures in each category. The signature categories are separated by activity:

- **Info**—This category includes activity that is normally associated with network reconnaissance. This includes network scans or port scans.
- **Attack**—Attack signatures detect attacks against the network or specific host on the network.

The two signature types can apply to either category:

- **Atomic**—Atomic signatures are signatures that trigger the IDS with a single packet. Because the IDS is not required to gather large amounts of data, the atomic signatures tend to be less memory intensive to the Cisco IOS firewall.
- **Compound**—Compound signatures require the IDS to gather and compare greater amounts of data to trigger an event. Compound signatures require a greater memory allocation from the router.

It is important to define *normal traffic* on the network and configure your signatures accordingly. This will ensure that your IDS reacts to traffic that is truly malicious. If the IDS reacts to normal network traffic, the alert is referred to as a *false positive*. A *false negative* occurs when the IDS incorrectly interprets malicious traffic as normal for the network. To further reduce the number of false positive alerts, it is important to correctly configure the signature thresholds (in other words, spam threshold) and disable or exclude specific signatures. Disabling a signature turns the signature off completely. When you exclude a signature, it designates specific hosts of networks that are not inspected for a signature. All IDS signatures are identified by a signature number. You can find the signature numbers and explanations at Cisco.com.

To disable a signature, just list the signature by its number and apply the **disable** command. This command is completed in the global configuration mode. Example 16-6 shows the **signature disable** command.

Example 16-6 *Disabling Signatures*

```
Router1#configure terminal
Router1(config)#ip audit signature 1004 disable
Router1(config)#ip audit signature 1102 disable
Router1(config)#ip audit signature 2151 disable
```

It is also possible to exclude signatures by either a host or network. To exclude a signature, you must first create an access list and then apply the signature to that access list. Example 16-7 shows the access list and how it is applied to exclude the host 192.168.103.42.

Example 16-7 *Excluding Signatures*

```
Router1#configure terminal
Router1(config)#access-list 74 deny host 192.168.103.42
Router1(config)#access-list 74 permit any
Router1(config)#ip audit signature 2154 list 74
Router1(config)#ip audit signature 3104 list 74
Router1(config)#ip audit signature 3152 list 74
```

It is also possible to create the access list defining a network range 192.168.103.0 0.0.0.255 or using a wildcard (**any**) address such as 0.0.0.0. Example 16-8 shows the access list and how it is applied to exclude the network 192.168.103.0/24.

Example 16-8 *Excluding Signatures*

```
Router1#configure terminal
Router1(config)#access-list 74 deny 192.168.103.0 0.0.0.255
Router1(config)#access-list 74 permit any
Router1(config)#ip audit signature 2154 list 74
Router1(config)#ip audit signature 3104 list 74
Router1(config)#ip audit signature 3152 list 74
```

Create and Apply Audit Rules

The next task requires you to create the audit rules and apply them to the correct interface of the Cisco IOS firewall. It is possible to create an audit rule that excludes specific hosts or networks and apply that rule to the interface. Creating and applying the audit rules is a four-step process.

Configure the Default Actions

You must configure the IDS to respond to information and attack signatures. The response can be one or more of the of three actions:

- **alarm**—This command sends an alarm to the syslog server or the centralized manager.
- **drop**—This command configures the router to drop the packets.
- **reset**—The router will send the RESET flag to both parties on the connection.

The default actions are configured using the **ip audit info** or **ip audit attack** commands. The term *default* refers to the action that the system will take for all signatures that are not configured with a specific action. It is possible to configure specific actions for signatures that are a greater threat to your network and use the default actions for all others. Example 16-9 shows the configuration of the actions for the info and attack signatures. The default setting for both info and attack is **alert**.

Example 16-9 *Configuring Actions*

```
Router1#configure terminal
Router1(config)#ip audit info action alarm drop
Router1(config)#ip audit attack action alarm reset
```

Create the IDS Audit Rule

The **ip audit name** command creates the audit rule. Both the info and attack signature types should share the same audit name. You can exclude specific hosts or subnets from the audit rule by applying an access list. This is another method used to reduce the number of false positives. Example 16-10 lists the syntax for creating the audit rule router1 on the Cisco IOS firewall. Because we do not expect any attacks from our internal network (10.10.10.0/24), we will also apply access list 75. This access list does not deny any traffic from the internal network but filters it from the audit process. The line **permit any** forces all other traffic through the audit process.

Example 16-10 *Creating the Audit Rule*

```
Router1#configure terminal
Router1(config)#ip audit name router1 info
Router1(config)#ip audit name router1 attack list 75
Router1(config)#access-list 75 deny 10.10.10.0 0.0.0.255
Router1(config)#access-list 75 permit any
```

Create the IDS Audit Exclusions

Signatures can be disabled with the **ip audit signature** *signature-id* **disable** command or can be modified by creating an access list that is applied to the signature using the **ip audit signature** *signature-id* **list** *access-list*. The exclusions are defined by the access list and applied to the audit rule using **ip audit name**. Example 16-11 configures the Cisco IOS firewall IDS to disable signature 3106 (spam) when large amounts of mail are received from 192.168.21.25. You use this if you have multiple users who all receive messages from a specific list server and the expected mail count exceeds 250 messages (the default setting for this signature).

Example 16-11 *Creating an Audit Exclusion*

```
Router1#configure terminal
Router1(config)#ip audit signature 3106 list 76
Router1(config)#access-list 76 deny host 192.168.21.25
Router1(config)#access-list 76 permit any
```

Apply the IDS Audit Rule

The **ip audit** command applies the rule to the interface on the router. This command must be applied when in the interface configuration mode and is directional **in** | **out** relative to the flow of traffic to the Cisco IOS firewall. Example 16-12 applies the IDS rule router1 to the outside interface of the Cisco IOS firewall to affect traffic that is inbound to the network.

Example 16-12 *Applying the Audit Rules*

```
Router1#configure terminal
Router1(config)#interface s0
Router1(config-if)#ip audit router1 in
```

Add the Cisco IOS Firewall IDS to the Centralized Management

This step requires you to add the Cisco IOS firewall IDS to the Cisco Director, CSPM, IDS MC, or Event Viewer. As stated earlier in this chapter, the Cisco Director has reached product end-of-life. The IDS Management Console is a CiscoWorks component, and the CSPM and Event Viewer are both applications written to run on a Wintel platform. The individual commands for each centralized manager are different, but each of these systems uses a GUI interface and is relatively simple to navigate. The information required for all management platforms is the same. To configure your centralized manager to communicate with your Cisco IOS firewall IDS, you must configure the following items:

- Sensor IP address
- Organization name
- Organizational ID
- Host name
- Host ID
- Post office port (the default port is 45,000)

You also can configure an optional heartbeat interval. (The default interval is five minutes.) After you have configured your centralized manager, it automatically creates a connection with the Cisco IOS firewall IDS. You must reload the router after completing any post office configuration changes for those changes to take effect.

Verifying the Cisco IOS Firewall IDS Configuration

It is important to ensure that your system is properly configured. You can use three commands to verify the configuration of the Cisco IOS firewall IDS:

- **show**—The **show** command is entered in the privileged EXEC mode and is used to see the current Cisco IOS firewall IDS configuration. Table 16-4 lists the **show** commands with a brief description of each.

Verifying the Cisco IOS Firewall IDS Configuration

Table 16-4 show *Commands*

Command	Description
show ip audit statistics	This command displays the number of packets audited and the number of alarms sent. These numbers can be reset using the **clear ip audit statistics** command.
show ip audit configuration	This command displays the complete audit configuration to include any default commands that are not displayed as part of the **show run** command.
show ip audit interface	This command displays the audit configuration for all interfaces.

Example 16-13 displays the output from the **show ip audit statistics** command.

Example 16-13 show ip audit statistics *Output*

```
Router1#show ip audit statistics
Event notification through syslog is enabled
Event notification through Net Director is disabled
Default action(s) for info signature is drop
Default action(s) for attack signature is reset
Default threshold of recipients for spam is 250
PostOffice:HostID:10 OrgID:100 Msg dropped 0
      Curr Event Buf Size:100 Configured:100
HID:14 OID:100 S:1 A:2 H:02 HA:49 DA:0 R:0 Q:0
 ID:1 Dest:10.10.10.200:45000 Loc: 10.10.10.254:45000 T:5 s:ESTAB *


Audit Rule Configuration
 Audit name router1
```

Example 16-14 displays the output from the **show ip audit interface** command.

Example 16-14 show ip audit interface *Output*

```
Router1#show ip audit interface
Interface Serial0
Inbound IDS audit rule is router1
Info actions alarm drop
Attack actions alarm reset
Outgoing IDS rule is not set
Interface Ethernet0
Inbound IDS rule not set
Outgoing IDS rule not set
```

- **clear**—The **clear** command enables you to clear statistics and configurations. Table 16-5 lists the available **clear** commands.

Table 16-5 clear *Commands*

Command	Description
clear ip audit statistics	This command enables you to reset the statistics counters. It proves very useful when you are trying to gather new information about network activity.
clear ip audit configuration	This command removes all IDS configurations from the router. It disables the IDS functionality and releases all dynamic resources.

- **debug**—The **debug** command displays the current situation. It enables you to see how the router is functioning as traffic is processed. Table 16-6 lists the available **debug** commands.

Table 16-6 debug *Commands*

Command	Description
debug ip audit timers	This command displays the active audit timers.
debug ip audit object-creation	This command displays which audit objects are created.
debug ip audit object-deletion	This command displays which audit objects are deleted.
debug ip audit function- trace	This command displays which audit functions are currently running.
debug ip audit detailed	This command displays a full detail of the audit processes.
debug ip audit ftp-cmd	This command displays the detail of any FTP command sessions.
debug ip audit ftp-token	This command displays the detail of any FTP token sessions.
debug ip audit icmp	This command displays the detail of any ICMP sessions.
debug ip audit ip	This command displays the detail of any IP sessions.
debug ip audit rpc	This command displays the detail of any remote-procedure call sessions.
debug ip audit smtp	This command displays the detail of any SMTP sessions.
debug ip audit tcp	This command displays the detail of any TCP sessions.
debug ip audit tftp	This command displays the detail of any TFTP sessions.
debug ip audit udp	This command displays the detail of any UDP sessions.

Cisco IOS Firewall IDS Deployment Strategies

As discussed earlier in this chapter, the primary advantage with the Cisco IOS firewall IDS is that it provides an additional level of security to administrators by enabling them to automatically respond to specific threats on internal and external networks. The Cisco IOS firewall IDS features can be deployed with other Cisco IOS firewall features and tailored as necessary for the network environment. The Cisco IOS firewall IDS is the perfect solution for network segments that do not require, or may not support, the use of a CSIDS. There are several strategies that are best supported by the deployment of the Cisco IOS firewall IDS:

- Branch offices, intranet, and extranet perimeters that act as an extension of the enterprise and require an extra level of protection
- Small and medium-size networks that require a cost-effective router with integrated firewall and IDS
- Managed service providers that want to employ a cost-effective combination of security solutions integrated into a single router

Foundation Summary

The "Foundation Summary" section of each chapter lists the most important facts from the chapter. Although this section does not list every fact from the chapter that will be on your SECUR exam, a well-prepared SECUR candidate should at a minimum know all the details in each "Foundation Summary" before going to take the exam.

The Cisco IOS firewall IDS is designed to complement the security infrastructure by integrating IDS and firewall functionality into a single Cisco IOS router. This integration of technologies makes the Cisco IOS router a very cost-effective and functional tool. You must remember a few simple concepts about the Cisco IOS firewall IDS:

- The Cisco IOS firewall can communicate with the CSIDS, Cisco Director, IDS MC, Event Viewer, and CSPM.
- The devices communicate with each other using POP. You configure the communication by configuring the post office parameters, which consist primarily of the IP address, host ID, and organizational ID.
- The two categories of signatures include info and attack. Info signatures indicate some type of network reconnaissance, whereas attack signatures indicate an actual network attack.
- The two signature types are atomic and compound. Atomic signatures react to a single packet, whereas compound signatures require more data.
- Four actions are required to configure the IDS:

1. Initialize the Cisco IOS firewall IDS on the router.

   — Configure the notification type.

   — Configure the post office parameters.

   — Define the protected network.

   — Configure the maximum queue for alarms.

2. Configure info and attack signatures.

   — Define "normal" traffic.

   — Disable specific signatures.

3. Create and apply audit rules.

    — Define the default actions.

    — Create the IDS audit rule.

    — Apply the IDS audit rule to the correct interface.

4. Add the Cisco IOS firewall IDS to the centralized management.

- The key advantage to the Cisco IOS firewall IDS is that it enables administrators to detect and respond to malicious activity on the network.

Q&A

As mentioned in the section, "How to Use This Book," in the Introduction to this book, you have two choices for review questions. The questions that follow next give you a bigger challenge than the exam itself by using an open-ended question format. By reviewing now with this more difficult question format, you can exercise your memory better and prove your conceptual and factual knowledge of this chapter. The answers to these questions are found in the appendix.

For more practice with exam-like question formats, including questions using a router simulator and multiple choice questions, use the exam engine on the CD-ROM.

1. How are signatures listed in the Cisco IOS firewall?
2. How does the Cisco IOS firewall IDS operate?
3. What are the three actions that are performed by the IOS firewall IDS when malicious traffic is discovered?
4. Why would you want to disable some signatures?
5. What is POP?
6. What are the four steps to configuring the firewall IDS?
7. What must match for POP to work?
8. In the command **ip audit po remote . . . timeout**, what timeout are you configuring?
9. When you configure **ip audit po protected**, are you configuring a subnet or address range?
10. Why should you configure a maximum queue for alarms?
11. Which signatures create a greater load on the router performance?
12. How do you exclude a signature?
13. What is the first step to creating an audit rule?

PART V: Virtual Private Networks

Chapter 17 Building a VPN Using IPSec

Chapter 18 Scaling a VPN Using IPSec with a Certificate Authority

Chapter 19 Configuring Remote Access Using Easy VPN

Chapter 20 Scaling Management of an Enterprise VPN Environment

This part of the book addresses the following exam objectives as posted at Cisco.com:

- Configure a Cisco router for IPSec using preshared keys
- Verify the IKE and IPSec configuration
- Explain the issues regarding configuring IPSec manually and using RSA encrypted nonces
- Advanced IPSec VPNs using Cisco Routers and CAs
- Describe the Easy VPN Server
- Managing Enterprise VPN Routers

This chapter covers the following subjects:

- Configuring a Cisco Router for IPSec Using Preshared Keys

- Configuring Manual IPSec

- Configuring IPSec Using RSA Encrypted Nonces

- Configure the RSA Keys

CHAPTER 17

Building a VPN Using IPSec

Prior to the creation of VPN technology, the only way to secure communications between two locations was to purchase a "dedicated circuit." To secure communications across an enterprise would be tremendously expensive, and securing communications with remote users was just cost prohibitive. VPN technology provides the ability to secure communications that travel across the Internet. VPN technology allows organizations to interconnect their different locations without having to purchase dedicated lines, greatly reducing the cost of the network infrastructure.

"Do I Know This Already?" Quiz

The purpose of the "Do I Know This Already?" quiz is to help you decide whether you really need to read the entire chapter. If you already intend to read the entire chapter, you do not necessarily need to answer these questions now.

The 10-question quiz, derived from the major sections in "Foundation Topics" section of the chapter helps you determine how to spend your limited study time.

Table 17-1 outlines the major topics discussed in this chapter and the "Do I Know This Already?" quiz questions that correspond to those topics.

Table 17-1 *"Do I Know This Already?" Foundation Topics Section-to-Question Mapping*

Foundation Topics Section	Questions Covered in This Section
Configure a Cisco Router for IPSec Using Preshared Keys	1, 3, 5, 6–9
Verify the IKE and IPSec Configuration	2, 4
Explain the Issues Regarding Configuring IPSec Manually and Using RSA-Encrypted Nonces	10

> **CAUTION** The goal of self-assessment is to gauge your mastery of the topics in this chapter. If you do not know the answer to a question or are only partially sure of the answer, you should mark this question wrong for purposes of the self-assessment. Giving yourself credit for an answer you correctly guess skews your self-assessment results and might provide you with a false sense of security.

1. What is the purpose of the intranet VPN?

   a. For dialup users to access the intranet

   b. For business partners to trade data

   c. To securely interconnect business locations

   d. To allow access to the intranet server

   e. None of the above

2. What should you be most aware of when using the **debug crypto isakmp** command?

   a. The command generates traffic that could bring the VPN down.

   b. The command generates a tremendous amount of output.

   c. The command should only be used in high-traffic environments.

   d. The command resets your IKE SAs.

   e. This is not a valid command.

3. What are two methods of peer authentication used with IKE? (Choose two.)

   a. RSA digitized signatures

   b. RSA-encrypted nonces

   c. TACACS+

   d. Diffie-Hellman signatures

   e. Preshared keys

4. What command tells you the state of your connection to your IKE SA peer?

   a. **show crypto sa**

   b. **show sa peer ipsec**

   c. **show ipsec peer sa**

   d. **show crypto isakmp sa**

   e. **show crypto ipsec sa**

5. Diffie-Hellman Key Exchange is a public key cryptography protocol. Group 1 consists of _____-bit encryption.

   a. 168
   b. 1024
   c. 768
   d. 128
   e. 1536

6. What UDP port cannot be blocked on the perimeter router for IKE to function?

   a. 443
   b. 500
   c. 505
   d. 1521
   e. None of the above

7. What steps are required to configure IKE on the router?

   a. Enable IKE, configure preshared key, create the IKE policy, and verify the IKE configuration.
   b. Verify connectivity, enable IKE, create the ACLs, and verify the IKE configuration.
   c. Verify the IKE configuration, enable IKE, configure preshared key, and reboot the router.
   d. Enter the global config mode, enter the interface config mode, enable IKE, test connectivity, and configure IKE.

8. What happens if you configure multiple transform sets on the router?

   a. The peers do not connect.
   b. The peers look for a match.
   c. The router does not send clear-text data.
   d. Authentication works but not encryption.
   e. Only bidirectional traffic is possible.

Chapter 17: Building a VPN Using IPSec

9. What is the correct command syntax for configuring the IPSec SA lifetime?

   a. **crypto ipsec sa lifetime**

   b. **ipsec sa** *time*

   c. **crypto sa timeout**

   d. **crypto ipsec security-association lifetime**

   e. None of the above

10. What information does the **show crypto key pubkey-chain rsa** give you?

    a. It tells you whether the information was manually configured or extracted from a certificate.

    b. It gives you the host name of the peer.

    c. It provides the IP address of the peer.

    d. All of the above.

    e. None of the above.

The answers to the "Do I Know This Already?" quiz are found in the appendix. The suggested choices for your next step are as follows:

- **8 or less overall score**—Read the entire chapter. This includes the "Foundation Topics" and "Foundation Summary" sections and the "Q&A" section.

- **9 or 10 overall score**—If you want more review on these topics, skip to the "Foundation Summary" section and then go to the "Q&A" section. Otherwise, move on to the next chapter.

Foundation Topics

Before beginning to configure the Cisco router as an endpoint for a VPN tunnel, it is important to understand the different types of VPNs and what part the Cisco router plays in each of these connections. Site to site and access are the two types of VPNs:

- **Site-to-site VPN**—A site-to-site VPN usually consists of two or more endpoints configured as a VPN peer with the other end. The term *endpoint* refers to the point where the VPN terminates. In other words, this is where the encrypted connection begins and ends. Designated traffic that travels from one end to the other is encrypted as it passes through the first endpoint and decrypted as it passes through the other endpoint. The encryption is manually configured on both ends or negotiated by each VPN peer. The endpoints for site-to-site VPNs are normally routers, VPN-enabled firewalls, or VPN hardware appliances. For the purpose of this chapter, the focus is on creating VPN connections using Cisco routers. Figure 17-1 depicts a site-to-site VPN connection between New York and Boston.

Figure 17-1 *Site-to-Site VPN Between New York and Boston*

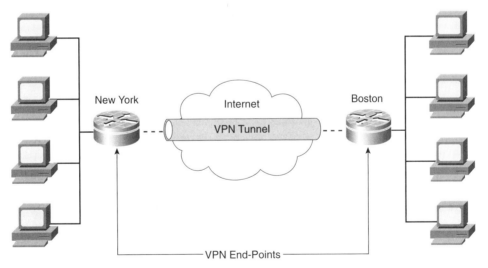

As Figure 17-1 illustrates, all traffic between the New York and Boston locations travels across the Internet but through an encrypted VPN tunnel to maintain data confidentiality and integrity. Not all data is required to travel through the VPN tunnel. It is possible to configure the endpoints to encrypt only specific traffic. It is also important to note that traffic on the internal network is not encrypted. This traffic is only encrypted as it enters the router on its way to its destination. Site-to-site VPNs are broken into two categories:

— **Intranet VPNs**—Intranet VPNs are used to securely interconnect the different locations of an organization. Intranet VPNs allow an organization that may be spread across multiple locations globally to function as a single secure enterprise network.

— **Extranet VPNs**—Extranet VPNs provide a secure channel for communications between an organization and its business partners (for example, suppliers, customers, and so on.)

- **Access VPNs**—Access VPNs, also known as *remote access VPNs*, normally incorporate a VPN client software package installed on the remote user's computer. The remote user can connect to the Internet via dialup, cable modem, DSL, or even from a different organization's LAN connection. When a connection is made to the user's network, the VPN client software creates an encrypted connection from that workstation to the VPN endpoint. The VPN endpoints for remote access VPNs are routers, VPN-enabled firewalls, or VPN concentrators. This chapter focuses on VPN routers because they are commonly used to create both types of VPNs and will most likely be emphasized on the exam. Figure 17-2 depicts remote access VPN connections to the office in New York and illustrates that all traffic from the remote users to New York is encrypted at the user's computer and remains encrypted until it reaches the router in New York.

Figure 17-2 *Remote Access VPNs to the New York Office*

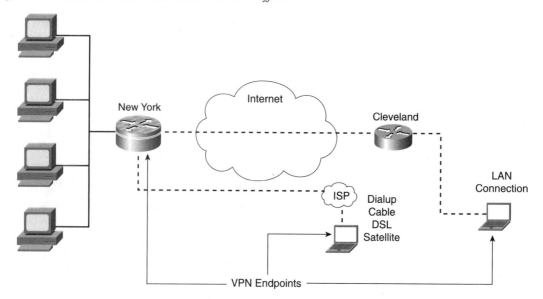

The method used to access the Internet does not normally affect the use of VPN client software so long as it is not blocked by an access list or firewall rule. The standard design for a large enterprise network is to install the VPN endpoint inside of the perimeter router or firewall.

Configuring a Cisco Router for IPSec Using Preshared Keys

IPSec is not a protocol but a framework of open-standard protocol suites that provide origin authentication, data integrity, and data confidentiality, and antireplay protection. IPSec runs over IP and uses Internet Key Exchange (IKE) to negotiate the security association (SA) between the peers. Parameters must be configured for both IKE and IPSec SAs.

How IPSec Works

Five specific steps are required to create and terminate an IPSec VPN tunnel. The endpoints perform different functions to establish the encrypted connection at each step. Figure 17-3 provides a description of the steps required to create and terminate the IPSec tunnel.

Figure 17-3 *Creating a IPSec VPN Tunnel*

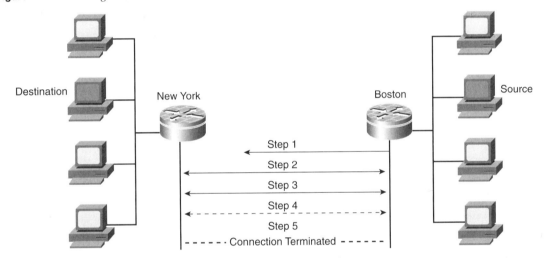

Step 1 The user at the source computer in Boston initiates a connection to the destination system in New York. The router in Boston recognizes the traffic as "interesting traffic" and initiates the IKE process with the router in New York.

Step 2 The endpoint routers use IKE to authenticate each other as IKE peers and negotiate the IKE SA. At this time, a secure channel is established allowing for negotiation of the IPSec SA. This is referred to as *IKE phase 1*.

Step 3 IKE is again used to negotiate the IPSec SA between the peers. When the negotiation is completed, the IPSec peers have an established SA and are prepared to transfer data. This is referred to as *IKE phase 2*.

Step 4 The tunnel is established and the IPSec SA information is stored in the SA database on both SA peers. Further key negotiations take place per the parameters negotiated during phase 2.

Step 5 The connection terminates when it times out or is deleted from either peer.

This section deals configuring VPN routers with preshared keys for site-to-site with VPNs.

> **NOTE** Internet Key Exchange (IKE) is a protocol based on ISAKMP/Oakley, which stands for *Internet Security Association and Key Management Protocol* (with Oakley distribution), and supports IPSec by providing a private, authenticated key management channel through which the peers can communicate and negotiate session keys for AH and ESP and to negotiate encryption, authentication, and compression algorithms for the session. IKE is used to perform authentication for IPSec peers, negotiation of IKE and IPSec SAs, and establishment of keys for the encryption algorithms used by IPSec. The terms *IKE* and *ISAKMP* are used interchangeably throughout this chapter.

To configure IPSec encryption on the Cisco router, you must complete four steps. Each task includes specific subtasks:

Step 1 Select the IKE and IPSec parameters.

Step 2 Configure IKE.

Step 3 Configure IPSec.

Step 4 Test and verify the IPSec configuration.

Step 1: Select the IKE and IPSec Parameters

The process for configuring a router for an IPSec VPN is not a difficult one. It is, however, a very complex process with multiple tasks and subtasks and requires significant attention to detail. The first task involves selecting the initial configuration parameters for the VPN connection and determining which configuration is most appropriate. If all of the configuration decisions are taken prior to configuring either device, the risk of a configuration error on either peer can be greatly reduced. This task is divided into five subtasks:

Step 1 Define the IKE (phase 1) policy.

Step 2 Define the IPSec policies.

Step 3 Verify the current router configuration.

Step 4 Verify connectivity.

Step 5 Ensure compatible access lists.

Define the IKE (Phase 1) Policy

The importance of IKE phase 1 is that it provides the negotiation to create a secure channel through which the phase 2 negotiation can take place. You must consider several items when determining the IKE phase 1 policies. Following is a list of each item with its specific purpose:

- **Select a key distribution method**—This item is usually determined by the expected size of the network. For networks that only require a few VPN peers, it is possible to manually distribute the keys (configure each peer manually). For large networks, it is recommended to use a certificate authority (CA) server. This method allows for significant growth because a trusted CA identifies each IPSec peer. If you are not manually distributing the keys, you will need to implement the ISAKMP to support the method of key distribution you have selected.

- **Select an authentication method**—There are several ways to configure the routers to authenticate themselves during phase 1 of the IKE negotiation when establishing the SA. The configuration to be used is usually determined by the number of VPNs that are connected to the router and how dynamic the network environment will be. Three different configuration types are used:

    — **Preshared keys**—If your organization only requires VPN connectivity with very few locations, you may want to use a static configuration on the router. This static configuration is referred to as *preshared keys* because the keys are manually configured on both peers. Preshared keys are alphanumeric keys (similar to passwords) that are configured on each router and must match exactly for the routers to negotiate the connection. Management of multiple VPN connections using preshared keys can become cumbersome as the number of connections grows.

    — **RSA signatures**—RSA is a public key cryptography system using digital certificates authenticated by RSA signatures.

    — **RSA-encrypted nonces**—An RSA nonce is a random value generated by the peer that is encrypted using RSA encryption. This method requires you to configure the RSA public key and designate the peer. This method is more secure because a different nonce is created with every negotiation.

- **Identify the ISAKMP peer**—The ISAKMP peer is the router at the other end of the VPN connection that is functioning as the termination point. It is the device that you negotiate with to create the VPN tunnel. The IPSec peer is identified either by IP address or host name.

- **Select the ISAKMP policies for the connection**—It is very important that the ISAKMP policies for both peers match. If the configurations differ on each peer, they will be unable to negotiate the VPN connection. It is possible to configure multiple policies on each router, however, because each router will search for a matching policy. The following items must be determined when selecting the ISAKMP policies:

  — **Message encryption algorithm**—Cisco IOS VPN routers support two encryption algorithms:

    Data Encryption Standard (DES)—DES is a 56-bit symmetric encryption algorithm. It uses a 64-bit block of plain text and converts it into cipher text of the same size, encrypting it with a secret key. The key length is also 64 bits, but 8 bits are used for parity, leaving the effective key length at 56 bits. Although still widely used, DES is a somewhat outdated algorithm and should not be used if your data is highly sensitive. It is commonly used for VPN connections to locations outside the U.S. that cannot purchase higher levels of encryption due to U.S. technology export policies.

    Triple Data Encryption Standard (3DES)—3DES is a 168-bit symmetric encryption algorithm. 3DES just applies three different phases of DES, effectively tripling the key length to 168 bits.

  — **Message integrity (hash) algorithm**—The hash algorithm converts message input into a fixed-length output called the *message digest*. The message digest is then put into a digital signature algorithm and the output becomes a digital signature for the message. Because the message digest is usually much smaller than the actual message, it is more efficient to sign the digest rather than the message itself. Keyed-Hashing for Message Authentication (HMAC) is a variant that provides an additional layer of security by performing additional cryptographic keying and a secret key for calculation and verification of the message authentication values. HMAC is a variant that can be added to the supported hash algorithms. Cisco IOS VPN routers support two hash algorithms:

    Secure Hash Algorithm 1 (SHA-1)—The output of SHA-1 is 160 bit. Because the output is larger than MD5, SHA-1 is considered to be more secure; however, it requires more CPU cycles to process.

    Message Digest 5 (MD5)—The output of MD5 is 128 bit. MD5 is slightly faster to process because of its smaller message digest.

  — **Peer authentication method**—This is the method that each peer uses to authenticate itself to the other peer. The three methods are explained in the previous section (preshared keys, RSA signatures, and RSA-encrypted nonces).

  — **Diffie-Hellman key exchange**— Diffie-Hellman is a public key cryptography protocol that is used between two IPSec peers to derive a shared secret over an unsecured channel without transmitting it to each other. There are seven Diffie-Hellman groups with varying key lengths. This chapter focuses on the first two Diffie-Hellman groups because they are currently the most commonly used on VPN enabled routers: group 1 is 768 bit, and group 2 is 1024 bit.

— **IKE SA lifetime**—The SA lifetime is the time that each system waits before initiating another key exchange. This allows the systems to constantly renegotiate the connection, greatly reducing any chance of an unauthorized listener being able to decrypt the connection.

Table 17-2 lists the IKE policy parameters that can be used when determining the IKE phase 1 policies.

Table 17-2 *IKE Policy Parameters (Phase 1)*

Parameter	Strong	Stronger
Encryption algorithm	DES	3DES
Hash algorithm	MD5	SHA-1
Authentication method	Preshare	RSA signature RSA-encrypted nonce
Diffie-Hellman key exchange	Group 1	Group 2
SA lifetime	86,400 seconds	< 86,400 seconds

The peers will not be able to negotiate the connection if the policies on both peers do not match. Figure 17-4 depicts the peer configurations for the VPN connection between New York and Boston.

As Figure 17-4 illustrates, the IKE configuration parameters on both routers must match for the negotiation to complete successfully.

Define the IPSec Policies

IPSec uses two different modes for VPNs. Each of these modes has a specific purpose, and it is important to select the correct mode when configuring your VPN. The two VPN modes are as follows:

- **Tunnel mode**—The tunnel mode is commonly used for both site-to-site VPNs and access VPNs where the destination is not the VPN endpoint. Both the source and destination (in the original IP header) information are encrypted when using the tunnel mode and are not decrypted until they reach the destination endpoint.

- **Transport mode**—The transport mode is most commonly used when the destination is the VPN endpoint. The original IP header is not encrypted when using the transport mode.

Figure 17-4 *Peer Configurations (New York and Boston)*

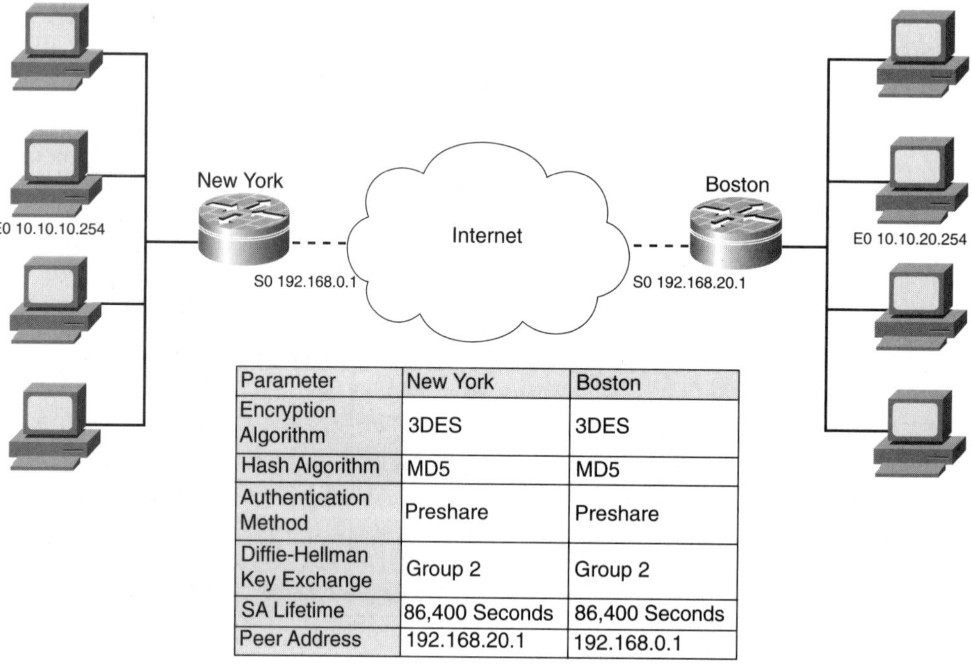

Parameter	New York	Boston
Encryption Algorithm	3DES	3DES
Hash Algorithm	MD5	MD5
Authentication Method	Preshare	Preshare
Diffie-Hellman Key Exchange	Group 2	Group 2
SA Lifetime	86,400 Seconds	86,400 Seconds
Peer Address	192.168.20.1	192.168.0.1

The IPSec policies are often referred to as the *IKE phase 2* policies because they occur during phase 2 of the IKE negotiation. IKE phase 1 establishes a bidirectional secure tunnel known as the *IKE SA*, which is used to complete the negotiation of the IPSec SA. The routers must negotiate two separate unidirectional IPSec SAs to facilitate bidirectional traffic between the peers.

Many configuration options are available when configuring IPSec. It is important to select the best possible configuration for the VPN connection. Follow these steps when defining the IPSec parameters:

1. **Identify the IPSec protocol necessary for the type of traffic.** There are two different IPSec protocols that perform specific functions:

    — **Encapsulating Security Payload (ESP)**—ESP provides data authentication, encryption, and antireplay services. ESP is protocol number 50 assigned by the Internet Assigned Numbers Authority (IANA). ESP is primarily responsible for getting the data from the source to the destination in a secure manner, verifying that the data has not been altered, and ensuring that the session cannot be hijacked. ESP provides origin authentication, data integrity, and antireplay protection. ESP can also be used to authenticate the sender either by itself or in conjunction with AH. ESP can be configured to encrypt the entire data packet or only the payload of the packet. Figure 17-4 shows how ESP encapsulates the normal IPv4 packet in the transport mode and in the tunnel mode.

Figure 17-5 illustrates the normal IPv4 packet before and after encapsulation by ESP.

Figure 17-5 *ESP and the IPv4 Packet*

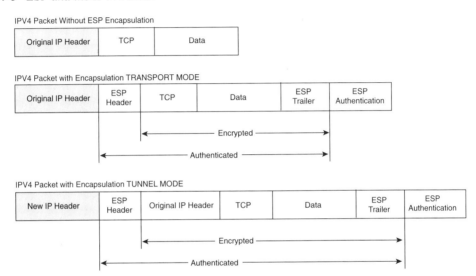

— **Authentication Header (AH)**—AH provides data authentication and antireplay services. AH is protocol number 51 assigned by the IANA. The primary function of AH is origin authentication. AH does not provide any data encryption; it provides only origin authentication or verification that the data is from the sender. This functionality also prevents session hijacking. It is important to note that ESP only authenticates the payload, whereas AH authenticates the IP header. AH is not compatible with NAT or PAT because they change the source IP address, making it different from the source address in the authentication header. The traffic is then rejected by the IPSec peer because the source address in the IP header and the authentication header do not match. Figure 17-6 shows how AH effects the normal IPv4 packet in both the transport and tunnel modes.

Figure 17-6 *AH and the IPv4 packet*

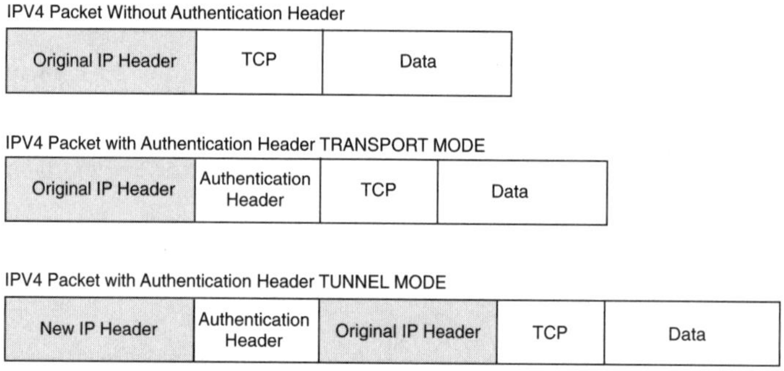

IPV4 Packet Without Authentication Header

| Original IP Header | TCP | Data |

IPV4 Packet with Authentication Header TRANSPORT MODE

| Original IP Header | Authentication Header | TCP | Data |

IPV4 Packet with Authentication Header TUNNEL MODE

| New IP Header | Authentication Header | Original IP Header | TCP | Data |

2. **Select the appropriate IPSec transforms.** Transforms and transform sets are the defined combination of IPSec algorithm and encryption algorithm. The combination you select can focus more on authentication, encryption, or combine to cover both. The following protocols, algorithms, and so on are combined to create your transforms:

   — **IPSec protocol**—AH and ESP

   — **Encryption algorithm**—DES and 3DES

   — **Hash algorithm**—SHA-1 and MD5 (with or without HMAC)

   Table 17-3 lists the possible combinations for transforms. Once combined, the transforms make a *transform set*.

Table 17-3 *IPSec Transforms*

AH Transform	Description
AH-MD5-HMAC	AH, MD5 hash, HMAC variant (authentication)
AH-SHA-HMAC	AH, SHA-1 hash, HMAC variant (authentication)
ESP Transform	**Description**
ESP-DES	ESP, DES (encryption)
ESP-3DES	ESP, 3DES (encryption)
ESP-MD5-HMAC	ESP, MD5, HMAC variant (This transform would be combined with ESP-DES, ESP-3DES, or ESP-NULL.)
ESP-SHA-HMAC	ESP, SHA-1, HMAC variant (This transform would be combined with ESP-DES, ESP-3DES, or ESP-NULL.)

3. **Define the IPSec Peer.** You must define the router at the other end of the VPN connection by either host name or IP address.

4. **Define the local hosts or networks.** Identify which local hosts or networks are allowed to send traffic through the VPN connection.

5. **Select the type of SA initiation**. Determine whether the IPSec SA should be negotiated by IKE or by using manual IPSec.

Verify the Current Router Configuration

You must verify that the current configuration of the router will not conflict with the new items that you want to add. You can use three commands to display the current router configuration:

- **show running-configuration**—The **show running-configuration** command displays the current configuration that is running on the router. The **show configuration** command shows the last configuration that was saved to memory but does not display any changes that took place but were not saved. This command is the same as the **show startup configuration** because it displays the configuration the router will have when it starts—any unsaved configuration changes will be lost during a reboot.

- **show crypto isakmp policy**—This command displays the current ISAKMP policy that is configured on the router. You can then verify that your planned configuration will not conflict with the current configuration.

- **show crypto map**—This command can include the interface or the map name and displays any crypto map entries configured on the router. The crypto map includes the name, interface and local address of the router, peer address, crypto access list, SA lifetime, and transform set name. The **show crypto map** command also tells you whether Perfect Forward Secrecy has been enabled for that connection. *Perfect Forward Secrecy* is a key establishment protocol that generates a new public/private key pair with each session. The result is a very dynamic key exchange that prevents an eavesdropper from decrypting messages using keys derived from previously captured data.

Verify Connectivity

Remember that encryption adds complexity to any network connection. You should always ensure connectivity between the SA peers before attempting to create a VPN connection. The best way to verify your connectivity is to attempt the type of connection that you intend to use after the encrypted connection is established. This ensures that you do not have any filters preventing the connection. If there is no connectivity between the peers, it will be impossible for them to negotiate the IKE SA and build the encrypted tunnel.

Ensure Compatible Access Lists

You must ensure that the access lists on the perimeter routers allow IPSec traffic. IKE runs over UDP port 500. If your perimeter routers are blocking UPD 500, you won't be able to negotiate the IKE SA. In addition, ESP and AH are protocol numbers 50 and 51 respectively. It is important that you verify that your current access lists do not block these protocols.

Step 2: Configure IKE

Now that you understand the importance of planning the configuration beforehand, refer to Figure 17-7 for the configuration settings for task 2.

Figure 17-7 *IKE Configuration Settings*

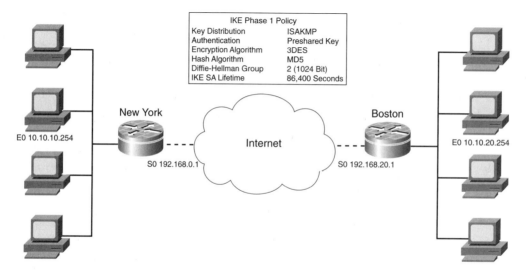

Figure 17-7 shows all the information needed to configure IKE on both peers. This section shows the configuration of the router in New York for the VPN between New York and Boston. Configuration steps and commands are very common for the Cisco certification exams. This exercise is designed to familiarize you with the different commands for configuring IKE, the purpose for each command, and how the commands interact. To configure IKE on the router, follow these four steps:

- **Step 1**   Enable IKE.
- **Step 2**   Create the IKE policy.
- **Step 3**   Configure the preshared key.
- **Step 4**   Verify the IKE configuration.

Each of these steps is discussed in detail in the following sections.

Enable IKE

IKE is enabled by default. You should verify that it is enabled when you check the current configuration. IKE is enabled globally (on all interfaces) and must be enabled before you can use it on the router. Example 17-1 shows the command for enabling IKE on the router.

Example 17-1 *Enabling IKE*

```
NewYork#configure terminal
NewYork (config)#crypto isakmp enable
```

Create the IKE Policy

It is possible to configure multiple IKE policies on a single router. The router runs through each policy in order based on the **policy priority**. The policy priority is a number between 1 and 10,000 that is assigned when the policy is created: the lower the number, the higher the priority. Because the router checks each policy in order, it is a good idea to give the most secure policy the lower number. The **crypto isakmp policy** command is input from the global configuration mode and will put you in the config-isakmp mode. Example 17-2 shows the command for creating the IKE policy.

Example 17-2 *Creating IKE Policy*

```
NewYork#configure terminal
NewYork (config)#crypto isakmp policy 100
NewYork (config-isakmp)#authentication pre-share
NewYork (config-isakmp)#encryption 3des
NewYork (config-isakmp)#hash md5
NewYork (config-isakmp)#group 2
NewYork (config-isakmp)#lifetime 86400
```

Configure Preshared Key

Preshared keys (also know as *preshared secrets*) are alphanumeric keys manually configured on each peer. You must identify the peer and the key when performing the configuration. The peer is identified either by host name or IP address. The command for configuring the preshared key is as follows:

crypto isakmp key *keystring* **address** *peer-address* [*mask*]

or

crypto isakmp key *keystring* **hostname** *peer-hostname*

Example 17-3 shows the command for defining the preshared key and the peer.

Example 17-3 *Defining the Preshared Key and Peer*

```
NewYork#configure terminal
NewYork (config)#crypto isakmp policy 100
NewYork (config-isakmp)#authentication pre-share
NewYork (config-isakmp)#encryption 3des
NewYork (config-isakmp)#hash md5
NewYork (config-isakmp)#group 2
NewYork (config-isakmp)#lifetime 3600
NewYork (config)#crypto isakmp key abc123 address 192.168.20.1 255.255.255.255
```

Verify the IKE Configuration

Before moving on to the next task, it is a good idea to verify the changes you have just completed. It is much easier to correctly configure each step rather than troubleshoot the configuration if the VPN does not work. The command used to view the current configuration is **show crypto isakmp policy**, and the output should match the combined examples listed above. Example 17-4 shows the output from **show crypto isakmp policy**.

Example 17-4 *Verifying the IKE Policy*

```
NewYork#configure terminal
NewYork (config)#crypto isakmp key abc123 address 192.168.20.1 255.255.255.255
NewYork (config)#crypto isakmp policy 100
NewYork (config-isakmp)#authentication pre-share
NewYork (config-isakmp)#encryption 3des
NewYork (config-isakmp)#hash md5
NewYork (config-isakmp)#group 2
NewYork (config-isakmp)#lifetime 86400
NewYork (config-isakmp)#exit
NewYork#show crypto isakmp policy
Protection suite priority 100
encryption algorithm: 3DES - 3 Data Encryption Standard (168 bit keys).
hash algorithm: Message Digest 5
authentication method:Pre-Shared Key
Diffie-Hellman group: #2 (1024 bit)
lifetime: 86400 seconds, no volume list
Default protection suite
encryption algorithm: DES - Data Encryption Standard (56 bit keys).
hash algorithm: Secure Hash Standard
authentication method:Rivest-Shamir-Adleman Signature
Diffie-Hellman group:#1 (768 bit)
lifetime: 86400 seconds, no volume list
```

Step 3: Configure IPSec

Just like the IKE configuration, it is important that the IPSec configuration matches on both peers for them to negotiate the IPSec SA. Refer to Figure 17-8 for the configuration settings for task 3.

Figure 17-8 *IPSec Configuration Settings*

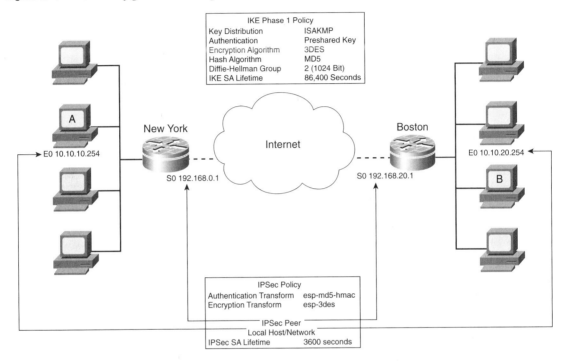

Figure 17-8 shows all the information needed to configure IPSec on both peers. This exercise configures only the router in New York. To configure IPSec on the router, follow these five steps:

- **Step 1** Create the IPSec transform set.
- **Step 2** Configure IPSec SA lifetimes.
- **Step 3** Create the crypto access lists.
- **Step 4** Create the crypto map.
- **Step 5** Apply the crypto map.

Each of these steps is discussed in detail in the following sections.

Create the IPSec Transform Set

The IPSec transform set defines the parameters that each peer uses when negotiating the VPN connection. It is possible to configure multiple transform sets on the router. When negotiating the connection, each router compares transform sets until finding a match. (This negotiation takes place during IKE phase 2.) This is not to say that the routers negotiate the transform sets; they just compare the transform sets until they find a match. If the routers do not find transform sets that match, they cannot create the VPN tunnel. Figure 17-8 depicts how the routers compare the transform sets when negotiating the VPN connection.

Figure 17-9 shows the routers Comparing transform sets until they find a match at **esp-3des**, **esp-md5-hmac**.

Figure 17-9 *Transform Set Comparison*

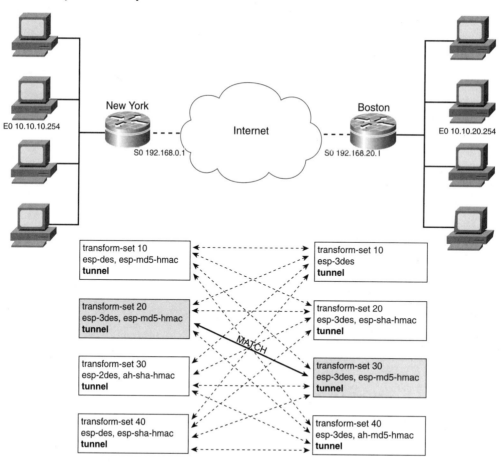

The command syntax for creating the IPSec transform set is as follows:

```
crypto ipsec transform-set transform set name [transform1][transform2][transform3]
```

Example 17-5 shows the command for creating the IPSec transform set.

Example 17-5 *Creating the IPSec Transform Set*

```
NewYork#configure terminal
NewYork (config)#crypto ipsec transform-set 20 esp-3des esp-md5-hmac
```

Configure IPSec SA Lifetimes

The IPSec SA lifetime determines at what interval the routers renegotiate the connection. A constantly changing connection is extremely difficult to decrypt because the data sample continues to change, leaving no consistent data available for a cryptographer to decrypt. If a cryptographer were able to discover the keys for a connection, it would take more than the hour that those keys are valid. The global IPSec SA lifetime is configured in either seconds or kilobytes (amount of data that pass through the tunnel). The command syntax for defining the global IPSec SA lifetime is as follows:

```
crypto ipsec security-association lifetime { seconds #### | kilobytes ####}
```

The default value is 3600 seconds (1 hour) or 4,608,000 kilobytes. The global IPSec SA lifetime is overridden by the SA lifetime that is added to the crypto map, and Cisco recommends that you use the default values. Example 17-6 shows the command for configuring the global IPSec SA lifetime to 30 minutes, or 4,400,000 kilobytes.

Example 17-6 *Configuring the Global IPSec SA Lifetime*

```
NewYork#configure terminal
NewYork (config)#crypto ipsec security-association lifetime seconds 1800
or
NewYork (config)#crypto ipsec security-association lifetime kilobytes 4400000
```

Create the Crypto ACLs

The crypto ACL defines interesting traffic for the router. *Interesting traffic* is the traffic that is protected by the VPN connection. Crypto ACLs determine which outbound traffic is encrypted and which goes out as clear text. Inbound traffic is compared to the crypto ACL also. If traffic comes in as clear text and should be encrypted, the router drops the traffic. When creating the crypto ACL, the terms *permit* and *deny* refer to *encrypt* and *do not encrypt,* respectively. The syntax of the command is as follows:

```
access-list ACL-number permit | deny protocol
source-ip source wildcard destination-ip destination wildcard
```

Example 17-7 shows the command for configuring the crypto ACL for the connection from New York to Boston to encrypt all TCP traffic between those networks.

Example 17-7 *Crypto ACL on the New York Router*

```
NewYork#configure terminal
NewYork (config)#access-list 105 permit ip 10.10.10.0 0.0.0.255 10.10.20.0 0.0.0.255
```

With the preceding configuration, the router encrypts all traffic from the internal network at New York (10.10.10.0/24) destined for the Boston network (10.10.20.0/24) and expects that all traffic from Boston be encrypted. It is important that the crypto ACLs match at both ends of the connection to ensure that the traffic is able to flow.

> **NOTE** Because the IPSec SA is a unidirectional connection, it is possible to configure the peers to only allow encrypted traffic to travel in one direction.

Create the Crypto Map

The crypto map is the component that consolidates all the IPSec configuration pieces. The following items are defined in the crypto map:

- Which traffic is to be encrypted (reference to the access list)
- How granular the protected data flow should be
- Where the encrypted data should be sent (the SA peer)
- The local address used for encrypted data (local router interface address)
- What security should be applied to the traffic (reference to transform sets)
- How the IPSec SA should be established (manual or IKE)
- Any other parameters for the IPSec SA

This command requires multiple lines. Each line of the command addresses a different portion of the configuration. The syntax of the **crypto map** command is as follows:

```
crypto map map-name seq-number connection
```

The command **crypto map** is entered from the global configuration mode and identifies the crypto map by name and sequence number. It also configures how the IPSec SA should be established. Table 17-4 lists the possible commands for configuring the IPSec SA.

Table 17-4 *Crypto Map IPSec SA Commands*

AH Transform	Description
cisco	This is the default value and indicates that IPSec will not be used but will be replaced with CET. This transform is being phased out.
ipsec-manual	This value indicates that IKE will not be used to establish the IPSec SA.
ipsec-isakmp	This value indicates that IKE will be used to establish the IPSec SA.
dynamic	This optional command specifies that a preexisting static crypto map be referenced for the correct configuration. This option is only available after the **ipsec-isakmp** parameter.

Example 17-8 shows the command for configuring the crypto map for the connection from New York to Boston.

Example 17-8 *Crypto Map on the New York Router*

```
NewYork#configure terminal
NewYork(config)#crypto map boston 120 ipsec-isakmp
NewYork(config-crypto-map)#match address 105
NewYork(config-crypto-map)#set peer 192.168.20.1
NewYork(config-crypto-map)#set pfs group2
NewYork(config-crypto-map)#set transform-set 20
NewYork(config-crypto-map)#set security-association lifetime seconds 1800
```

If you want to create the same type of VPN connection to another IPSec peer, it is possible to add another **set peer** line to the crypto map as long as the traffic matches that same access list.

Apply the Crypto Map to the Correct Interface

For the crypto map to take effect, it must be applied to the interface facing the peer. You must enter the interface configuration mode to apply the crypto map. Example 17-9 shows the command applying the crypto map to the Serial 0 interface on the router in New York.

Example 17-9 *Applying the Crypto Map to Interface S0*

```
NewYork#configure terminal
NewYork(config)#interface S0
NewYork(config-if)#crypto map boston
```

Step 4: Test and Verify the IPSec Configuration

Once again, it is best to verify your configuration beforehand instead of having to troubleshoot the connection if it is not working. A variety of **show** and **debug** commands enable you to check the current configuration, including the following:

- **show crypto isakmp policy**—This command displays the configured IKE policies.
- **show crypto ipsec transform-set**—This command displays the configured transform sets.
- **show crypto ipsec sa**—This command displays the current state of your IPSec SAs.
- **show crypto map**—This command displays your current crypto maps.
- **show crypto dynamic-map**—This command displays your dynamic crypto map set.
- **debug crypto isakmp**—This command enables debugging of IKE events. This generates a tremendous amount of output and should be used only when traffic is low.
- **debug crypto ipsec**—This command enables debugging of IPSec events. This generates a tremendous amount of output and should be used only when traffic is low.

Remembering that the configurations must match on both peers, it is best to compare the configuration from each router if possible. Figure 17-10 shows the configuration settings for this task.

Figure 17-10 *Configuration Settings New York-Boston*

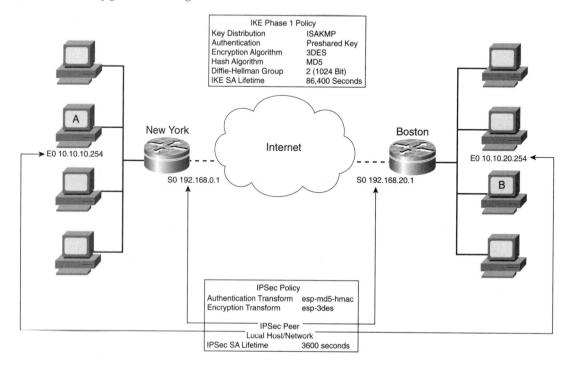

Table 17-5 shows the output from each command. You must verify that the configurations are sufficient for the VPN to function between New York and Boston.

Table 17-5 show *Command Output from Peers*

New York	**Boston**
NewYork#**show crypto isakmp policy** Protection suite priority 100 encryption algorithm: 3DES - 3 Data Encryption Standard (168 bit keys). hash algorithm: Message Digest 5 authentication method: Pre-Shared Key Diffie-Hellman group: #2 (1024 bit) lifetime: 86400 seconds, no volume list Default protection suite encryption algorithm: DES - Data Encryption Standard (56 bit keys). hash algorithm: Secure Hash Standard authentication method: Rivest-Shamir-Adleman Signature Diffie-Hellman group: #1 (768 bit) lifetime: 86400 seconds, no volume list	Boston#**show crypto isakmp policy** Protection suite priority 105 encryption algorithm: 3DES - 3 Data Encryption Standard (168 bit keys). hash algorithm: Message Digest 5 authentication method: Pre-Shared Key Diffie-Hellman group: #2 (1024 bit) lifetime: 86400 seconds, no volume list Default protection suite encryption algorithm: DES - Data Encryption Standard (56 bit keys). hash algorithm: Secure Hash Standard authentication method: Rivest-Shamir-Adleman Signature Diffie-Hellman group: #1 (768 bit) lifetime: 86400 seconds, no volume list

NewYork#**show crypto ipsec transform-set**
Transform set 10: (esp-des esp-md5-hmac)
    will negotiate = (Tunnel,),
 	
Transform set 20: (esp-3des esp-md5-hmac)
    will negotiate = (Tunnel,),
 	
Transform set 30: (esp-3des ah-sha-hmac)
    Will negotiate = (Tunnel,),
 	
Transform set 40 (esp-des esp-sha-hmac)
    Will negotiate = (Tunnel,),
	Boston#**show crypto ipsec transform-set**
	Transform set 10: (esp-3des)
	    will negotiate = (Tunnel,),
	
	Transform set 20: (esp-3des esp-sha-hmac)
	    will negotiate = (Tunnel,),
	
	Transform set 30: (esp-3des esp-md5-hmac)
	    Will negotiate = (Tunnel,),
	
	Transform set 40 (esp-3des ha-md5-hmac)
	    Will negotiate = (Tunnel,),

NewYork#**show crypto ipsec sa**
Interface: serial0/0
    Crypto map tag: newyork, local addr. 192.168.0.1
Local ident (addr/mask/prot/port): (192.168.0.1/255.255.255.255/0/0)
Remote ident (addr/mask/prot/port): (192.168.20.1/255.255.255.255/0/0)
Current peer: 192.168.20.1
      PERMIT, flags= {origin_is_acl,}
#pkts encaps: 10, #pkts encrypt: 10, #pkts digest 10
#pkts decaps: 10, #pkts decrypt: 10, #pkts verify 10
#send errors 0, #recv errors 0
  local crypto endpt.: 192.168.0.1, remote crypto endpt.: 192.168.20.1
  path mtu 1500, media mtu 1500
          current outbound spi: 41830A51	

continues

Table 17-5 show *Command Output from Peers (Continued)*

New York	Boston

NewYork#`show crypto map`
Crypto map "boston" 120 ipsec-isakmp
    Peer = 192.168.20.1
    Extended IP access list 105
access-list 105 permit tcp 10.10.10.0
0.0.0.255 10.10.20.0 0.0.0.255
 	
    Current peer: 192.168.20.1
    Security Association lifetime: 3600 seconds
    PFS (Y/N): N
    Transform sets=(20,)
	Boston#`show crypto map`
	Crypto map "newyork" 150 ipsec-isakmp
	    Peer = 192.168. 0.1
	    Extended IP access list 100
	access-list 100 permit tcp 10.10.20.0
	0.0.0.255 10.10.10.0 0.0.0.255
	
	    Current peer: 192.168.0.1
	    Security Association lifetime: 3600 seconds
	    PFS (Y/N): N
	    Transform sets=(20,)

Configuring Manual IPSec

It is possible to manually configure your IPSec connection from the crypto-map configuration mode. When you manually configure the IPSec parameters, you manually input all the keys necessary to create the connection. This configuration removes the functionality that allows the peers to renegotiate and constantly change the connection parameters and greatly reduces the security of the connection. The commands for configuring manual IPSec are

```
set session-key inbound | outbound ah/esp spi hex-key-string
set session-key inbound | outbound ah/esp spi authentication cipher hex-key-string
```

NOTE Cisco recommends against the use of manual IPSec because it is difficult to manage and relatively insecure as compared to configurations using IKE.

Configuring IPSec Using RSA Encrypted Nonces

As discussed earlier in this chapter, an RSA nonce is a random value generated by the peer that is encrypted using RSA encryption. It provides a very strong method of authentication using Diffie-Hellman key exchange. RSA nonces require that peers possess each other's public key without the use of a CA. It is important that the encrypted nonces are initially exchanged via a secure source. There are two drawbacks to using RSA encrypted nonces:

- **Initial key exchange**—If you are using RSA-encrypted nonces, you must either manually configure and exchange RSA keys or use RSA signatures from a previously successful ISAKMP negotiation with the peer.

- **Management**—RSA-encrypted nonces can be difficult (and complex) to configure and exchange and are therefore more difficult to manage for enterprise networks.

Configuring IPSec Using RSA Encrypted Nonces

The tasks required to configure IPSec using RSA-encrypted nonces are very similar to the normal IPSec configuration with the exception of the second task (configuring RSA keys):

1. Select the IKE and IPSec parameters.
2. Configure the RSA keys.
3. Configure IKE.
4. Configure IPSec.
5. Test and verify the IPSec configuration.

This section focuses on the second task because all the other tasks have been discussed earlier in this chapter.

Configure the RSA Keys

As with any VPN configuration, management of RSA keys is not a difficult task, but it can be a complex undertaking. It is important to completely plan your implementation before you begin to configure the peers. To configure and generate your public keys and enter the public keys of your peer, follow these six steps:

Step 1 Plan the implementation using RSA keys.

Step 2 Configure the router host name and domain name.

Step 3 Generate the RSA keys.

Step 4 Enter your peer RSA public keys.

Step 5 Verify the key configuration.

Step 6 Manage the RSA keys.

Each of these steps is discussed in detail in the following sections.

Plan the Implementation Using RSA Keys

Planning a VPN implementation using RSA keys follows the same process as other IPSec configurations; however, you should ensure that you have carefully planned the key generation and exchange. As with any VPN configuration, little margin for error exists when configuring a VPN using RSA keys. It is best to have every portion of the configuration defined before you begin the implementation.

Configure the Router Host Name and Domain Name

An important part of authentication is that the system must be able to correctly identify itself. For this reason, you must configure the host name and domain name of the router. By configuring the host name and domain name on the router prior to generating the RSA keys, you can be sure that the router keys properly identify the router. To configure the host name of the router, use the hostname command while in the global configuration mode. To configure the domain name of the router, use the **ip domain-name** command with the correct domain name for the router. Example 17-10 shows the commands required to configure the host name and domain name for the router in New York.

Example 17-10 *Configuring the Host Name and Domain Name*

```
NewYork#configure terminal
NewYork(config)#hostname NewYork
NewYork(config)#ip domain-name NewYork.com
```

Generate the RSA Keys

By default, RSA key pairs do not exist on the Cisco router. You need to add the optional command **usage-keys** to the command to generate an encryption key pair and an authentication key pair. The command for generating RSA key pairs is **crypto key generate rsa usage-keys**. This command generates a key pair (one public and one private key). When generating RSA keys, you must select a "modulus length." RSA keys can be generated in four lengths: 360 bit, 512 bit, 1024 bit, and 2048 bit. The longer the modulus length, the more secure the key, and the more time required to generate the key. Cisco recommends a minimum modulus length of 1024 bits. The generation of RSA keys is discussed in greater detail in Chapter 18, "Scaling a VPN Using IPSec with Certificate Authority."

Enter Your Peer RSA Public Keys

After receiving the public key from your peer (in a secure manner), you need to enter the public key into the router. Several commands are required to complete this process:

```
crypto key pubkey-chain
crypto key pubkey-chain rsa
addressed-key key-address
named-key key-name
key-string
```

Example 17-11 shows the commands required to install the public key from Boston into the peer router in New York.

Configuring IPSec Using RSA Encrypted Nonces

Example 17-11 *Installing the Public Key in the New York Router*

```
NewYork(config)# crypto key pubkey-chain rsa
NewYork (config-pubkey-chain)# addressed-key 192.168.20.1
NewYork (config-pubkey-key)# key-string
NewYork (config-pubkey)# 00302017 4A7D385B 1234EF29 335FC973
NewYork (config-pubkey)# 2DD50A37 C4F4B0FD 9DADE748 429618D5
NewYork (config-pubkey)# 18242BA3 2EDFBDD3 4296142A DDF7D3D8
NewYork (config-pubkey)# 08407685 2F2190A0 0B43F1BD 9A8A26DB
NewYork (config-pubkey)# 07953829 791FCDE9 A98420F0 6A82045B
NewYork (config-pubkey)# 90288A26 DBC64468 7789F76E EE21
NewYork (config-pubkey)# quit
NewYork (config-pubkey-key)# exit
```

Verify the Key Configuration

Two commands are used to show the current key configurations on the router. The first command (**show crypto key mypubkey rsa**) displays the public keys that are installed on the router, and the second (**show crypto key pubkey-chain rsa**) displays all peer keys installed. Example 17-12 shows the output from the **show crypto key pubkey rsa** command.

Example 17-12 *Viewing RSA Public Keys on the New York Router*

```
NewYork# show crypto key mypubkey rsa

% Key pair was generated at: 18:13:49 UTC Mar 23 2003
Key name: NewYork.newyork.com
Usage: Signature Key
Key Data:
005C300D 06092A86 4886F70D 01010105 00034B00 30480241 00C5E23B 55D6AB22
04AEF1BA A54028A6 9ACC01C5 129D99E4 64CAB820 847EDAD9 DF0B4E4C 73A05DD2
BD62A8A9 FA603DD2 E2A8A6F8 98F76E28 D58AD221 B583D7A4 71020301 0001
% Key pair was generated at: 18:13:49 UTC Mar 23 2003
Key name: NewYork.newyork.com
Usage: Encryption Key
Key Data:
00302017 4A7D385B 1234EF29 335FC973 2DD50A37 C4F4B0FD 9DADE748 429618D5
18242BA3 2EDFBDD3 4296142A DDF7D3D8 08407685 2F2190A0 0B43F1BD 9A8A26DB
07953829 791FCDE9 A98420F0 6A82045B 90288A26 DBC64468 7789F76E EE21
```

Example 17-13 shows the output from the **show crypto key pubkey-chain rsa** command.

Example 17-13 *Viewing RSA Public Keys on the New York Router*

```
NewYork# show crypto key pubkey-chain rsa
Codes: M - Manually Configured, C - Extracted from certificate
Code   Usage       IP-address      Name
M      Signature   192.168.20.1    Boston.boston.com
M      Encryption  192.168.20.1    Boston.boston.com
```

Manage the RSA Keys

Once generated and installed, the only management of RSA keys that is required is to remove old unused keys. The **crypto key zeroize rsa** command enables you to remove old keys.

Foundation Summary

The "Foundation Summary" section of each chapter lists the most important facts from the chapter. Although this section does not list every fact from the chapter that will be on your SECUR exam, a well-prepared candidate should at a minimum know all the details in each "Foundation Summary" section before going to take the exam.

Configure a Cisco Router for IPSec Using Preshared Keys

Several tasks and subtasks are required to configure the router for an IPSec VPN using preshared keys:

1. Select the IKE and IPSec parameters.

    a. Define the IKE (phase 1) policy.

    - Define the key distribution method.
        - Manual key distribution
        - ISAKMP
    - Define the authentication method.
        - Preshared secret
        - RSA signatures
        - RSA nonces
    - Identify the IKE SA peer by IP address or host name.
    - Define the IKE phase 1 policy.
        - Encryption algorithm (DES, 3DES)
        - Hash algorithm (SHA-1, MD5)
        - IKE SA lifetime

    b. Define the IPSec policies.

    - Select the IPSec protocol (AH, ESP).
    - Configure transforms and transform sets.
    - Define the IPSec peer by host name or IP address.
    - Define local hosts/networks.
    - Select SA initiation type (manual, IKE).

c. Verify the current router configuration (**show running-configuration**).
   d. Verify connectivity.
      - Ping through to the peer.
   e. Ensure compatible access lists.
      - Verify you are not blocking protocol 50/51 or UDP 500.
2. Configure IKE.
   - Enable IKE.
   - Create policies (per plan listed previously).
   - Validate the configuration.
3. Configure IPSec.
   - Define transforms.
   - Create the crypto ACLs.
   - Create the crypto maps.
   - Apply the crypto maps.

Verifying the IKE and IPSec Configuration

The best way to verify your VPN configuration is to attempt to connect to a destination at the other end of the VPN. If you're unable to successfully connect, the following commands enable you to verify your VPN configuration:

- **show** commands:
  - **show crypto isakmp policy** displays the current IKE policies.
  - **show crypto ipsec transform-set** displays the current transform sets.
  - **show crypto ipsec sa** displays the current state of your IPSec SAs.
  - **show crypto map** displays your current crypto maps.
  - **show crypto dynamic-map** displays your dynamic crypto map set.
- **debug** commands:
  - **debug crypto isakmp** enables debugging of IKE events.
  - **debug crypto ipsec** enables debugging of IPSec events.
  - Both **debug** commands generate a tremendous amount of output and should be used only when traffic is low.

Explain the Issues Regarding Configuring IPSec Manually and Using RSA Encrypted Nonces

The only additional process required for implementing IPSec using RSA nonces is the key generation and exchange process. The following steps are required to generate and exchange RSA keys:

Step 1 Plan the implementation using RSA keys.

Step 2 Configure the router host name and domain name.

Step 3 Generate the RSA keys.

Step 4 Enter your peer RSA public keys.

Step 5 Verify the key configuration.

Step 6 Manage the RSA keys.

Q&A

As mentioned in the section, "How to Use This Book," in the Introduction to this book, you have two choices for review questions. The questions that follow next give you a bigger challenge than the exam itself by using an open-ended question format. By reviewing now with this more difficult question format, you can exercise your memory better and prove your conceptual and factual knowledge of this chapter. The answers to these questions are found in the appendix.

For more practice with exam-like question formats, including questions using a router simulator and multiple choice questions, use the exam engine on the CD-ROM.

1. What is the preferred key distribution method for configuring VPN peers?
2. What is DES?
3. Of the two hash algorithms, which is more secure?
4. What are the protocol numbers for ESP and AH?
5. Why is it a good idea to verify connectivity before attempting to configure a VPN connection?
6. What is a policy priority?
7. What is the first command you should input when creating an IKE policy?
8. What policy priority number has greater precedence?
9. What is the default timeout for the global IPSec SA lifetime?
10. True or False: Crypto access lists are bidirectional?
11. What must you do to activate a crypto map?
12. What does Cisco recommend about manual IPSec?
13. How could you find out the router host name and domain name of your peer?
14. What is the command for generating RSA key pairs?

This chapter covers the following subjects:

- Advanced IPSec VPNs Using Cisco Routers and CAs

CHAPTER 18

Scaling a VPN Using IPSec with a Certificate Authority

Cisco IOS devices are designed with a feature called *CA interoperability support* that allows them to interact with certificate authorities (CAs) when deploying IPSec. This functionality allows for a scalable and manageable enterprise VPN solution.

"Do I Know This Already?" Quiz

The purpose of the "Do I Know This Already?" quiz is to help you decide whether you really need to read the entire chapter. If you already intend to read the entire chapter, you do not necessarily need to answer these questions now.

The 10-question quiz, derived from the major sections in "Foundation Topics" section of the chapter helps you determine how to spend your limited study time.

Table 18-1 outlines the major topics discussed in this chapter and the "Do I Know This Already?" quiz questions that correspond to those topics.

Table 18-1 *"Do I Know This Already?" Foundation Topics Section-to-Question Mapping*

Foundation Topics Section	Questions Covered in This Section
Advanced IPSec VPNs Using Cisco Routers and CAs	1–3 5–10
Explain the Issues Regarding Configuring IPSec Manually and Using RSA Encrypted Nonces	4

> **CAUTION** The goal of self-assessment is to gauge your mastery of the topics in this chapter. If you do not know the answer to a question or are only partially sure of the answer, you should mark this question wrong for purposes of the self-assessment. Giving yourself credit for an answer you correctly guess skews your self-assessment results and might provide you with a false sense of security.

1. What is the primary advantage of creating IPSec VPNs using CA support?

    a. They are easy to configure.
    b. They are easy to manage.
    c. They cannot be interrupted.
    d. Microsoft makes a CA product.
    e. None of the above.

2. Which is not a supported X.509 CA product?

    a. VeriSign OnSite 7.5
    b. Entrust Technologies
    c. Windows 2000 Certificate Server 5.0
    d. Baltimore Technologies
    e. None of the above

3. What details are not required to configure a CA server?

    a. CA server type
    b. CA server OS
    c. CA sdministrator contact info
    d. CA server URL
    e. CA server host name

4. What is the correct command for generating RSA key pairs for use with RSA-encrypted nonces?

    a. **config rsa keys**
    b. **crypto key generate rsa usage keys**
    c. **crypto key rsa generate usage keys**
    d. **crypto key generate rsa nonces**
    e. None of the above

5. What feature does the router use to connect to the CA server?

   a. It resolves the DNS on the Internet.

   b. It resolves the DNS at the root server.

   c. It resolves an entry in the host table on the router.

   d. It connects by IP address.

   e. The router performs a DNS reverse lookup.

6. Which is not a modulus length for generating RSA keys?

   a. 2048

   b. 512

   c. 256

   d. 360

   e. 1024

7. What configuration mode are you in when you enter the **crypto ca trustpoint** command?

   a. Crypto CA mode

   b. Config-crypto mode

   c. EXEC mode

   d. Global configuration mode

   e. Privileged EXEC mode

8. What does the command **crypto ca enroll** do?

   a. Requests certificates from the CA for all router RSA key pairs

   b. Enrolls the router in the CA public key list

   c. Requests the CA validate all certificates that are currently on the router

   d. Requests the CA validate only peer certificates

   e. Answers C and D

9. Why is it extremely important to save your password when enrolling with the CA server?

   a. Because the password is not saved on the router

   b. Because the password is incorporated into the certificate

   c. Because the CA will ask you for the password again at the end of the enrollment process

   d. Because you will need to provide it to the CA administrator to revoke the certificate

   e. Because you might forget it and be locked out of the CA server

10. What does the "M" code mean when shown in the output from **show crypto key pubkey-chain** command?

   a. The CA server is a Microsoft server.

   b. The certificate is configured manually.

   c. The certificate is only good for main mode exchanges.

   d. The key is only valid for manual IPSec.

   e. None of the above.

The answers to the "Do I Know This Already?" quiz are found in the appendix. The suggested choices for your next step are as follows:

- **8 or less overall score**—Read the entire chapter. This includes the "Foundation Topics" and "Foundation Summary" sections and the "Q&A" section.

- **9 or 10 overall score**—If you want more review on these topics, skip to the "Foundation Summary" section and then go to the "Q&A" section. Otherwise, move on to the next chapter.

Foundation Topics

Building VPNs using IPSec was discussed at length in Chapter 17, "Building a VPN Using IPSec." This chapter builds on the information from the preceding chapter and includes what is needed to build more scalable enterprise VPNs using CAs.

Advanced IPSec VPNs Using Cisco Routers and CAs

This section is dedicated to configuring the Cisco router for advanced scalable IPSec VPNs using CAs. It contains an overview of the CA support and configuration steps required to deploy IPSec VPNs using CA support.

Overview of Cisco Router CA Support

The advantage of using CA support is that peers no longer have to manually exchange preshared keys or nonces. When two peers begin the IKE negotiation, they just exchange public keys, which are then authenticated by the CA. This process greatly improves manageability because there is no requirement to track keys. As a result, this solution is very easy to scale. Cisco IOS Software supports the following CA standards:

- **RSA keys**—RSA is an asymmetric public key cryptography system. RSA keys come in key pairs (one public and one private). When generating RSA keys, it is also possible to generate an authentication pair and an encryption pair.
- **IKE**—Internet Key Exchange is a combination of ISAKMP and the Oakley key exchange protocols. Also referred to as *ISAKMP/Oakley*, it provides a method of authentication and negotiation to create a secure environment for the IPSec negotiation.
- **CA interoperability**—CA interoperability is the component that provides communication functionality between Cisco devices and CA servers. A main component of CA interoperability is the Simple Certificate Enrollment Protocol (SCEP).
    — SCEP is a lightweight transaction-oriented protocol that uses Public Key Cryptography Standard #7 (PKCS#7) and PKCS#10. SCEP requires either manual authentication or a preshared key during enrollment.

- **X.509v3 certificates**—X.509 is a digital certificate standard that was created using the X.500 standard as its foundation. It allows peers to exchange digital certificates to authenticate their identity. This solution removes the requirement for manually exchanging public keys between peers. The following CA services use X.509v3 certificates and also support SCEP:
    - VeriSign OnSite 4.5
    - Entrust Technologies
    - Baltimore Technologies
    - Windows 2000 Certificate Server 5.0
- **PKCS#7**—A standard from RSA used to encrypt, sign, and package certificate enrollment messages.
- **PKCS#10**—A standard from RSA that defines the syntax for certificate requests.

Several things take place when sending traffic from the source to the destination via a VPN connection. Figure 18-1 shows how traffic gets from the source system on the New York network to the destination system on the Boston network and how the peers communicate with each other and the CA server for peer authentication. Source A generates traffic that is destined for destination B, and the traffic is passed to the router. The router (New York) compares the traffic to its current security policy and determines that the traffic must be encrypted and forwarded to the VPN endpoint router (Boston). The New York network checks for an existing IPSec SA with the Boston router and if no IPSec security association (SA) exists, the router initiates the negotiation of an IKE SA. As part of the IKE SA negotiation, both routers exchange digital certificates that have been signed by a CA that is trusted by both peers. Upon receiving the certificate from the peer, each router downloads a certificate revocation list (CRL) from either the CA or a CRL distribution point and verifies that the certificate from the peer has not been revoked. After verifying the certificates, the peers complete the negotiation of the IKE SA, followed by the negotiation of the IPSec SA. The data is transferred between the source and destination as soon as the VPN tunnel is created.

As Figure 18-1 illustrates, the CA server is accessible to both peers. The peers exchange digital certificates, and the CA server validates the certificate. The CA maintains a list of certificates that are no longer valid called a *certificate revocation list* (CRL). The peers ensure that a certificate is valid by checking it against the CRL.

Figure 18-1 *Peer Authentication Using a CA*

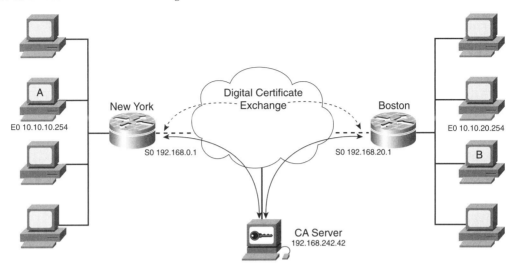

Configuring the Cisco Router for IPSec VPNs Using CA Support

To configure the router for IPSec VPNs using CA support, you must complete five tasks. Each task contains several subtasks. As always, the most important component is thorough planning and meticulous implementation. Because of the complexity of this process, any error can prevent the VPN from functioning properly. The five tasks are as follows:

1. Select the IKE and IPSec parameters.
2. Configure the router CA support.
3. Configure IKE using RSA signatures.
4. Configure IPSec using RSA signatures.
5. Test and verify the configuration.

Step 1: Select the IKE and IPSec Parameters

Selecting the IKE and IPSec parameters is just the process of predetermining which settings will be used on both peers to ensure successful negotiation of the connection. Many of these items were covered in Chapter 17. This task is divided into six subtasks, as follows:

1. Plan for CA support.

    Get the details of the CA server to include the server type, IP address, host name, URL, and server administrator contact information. Coordinate with the CA server administrator to ensure that your certificates are properly validated.

2. Define the IKE (phase 1) policy.

   See Chapter 17.

3. Define the IPSec policies.

   See Chapter 17.

4. Verify the current router configuration.

5. Verify connectivity.

   See Chapter 17.

6. Ensure compatible access lists.

   See Chapter 17.

Step 2: Configure the Router CA Support

To configure a router for CA support and verify that configuration, you must complete 11 different steps. These steps include configuring the router, generating keys, and communicating with the CA server.

Step 1 **Configure the router host name and domain name.** The host name and domain name are written to the key pairs. It is important that you have the correct identity information configured on the router before you generate the key pair. The syntax for these global configuration commands is as follows:

- **hostname** *name* sets the host name for the router.

- **ip domain-name** *name* sets the default domain name on the router, which is used to convert unqualified host names to fully qualified domain names (FQDN).

Example 18-1 shows the correct syntax for configuring the host name and domain name on the router in New York.

Example 18-1 *Configuring the Host Name and Domain Name*

```
router#configure terminal
router(config)#hostname NewYork
router(config)#ip domain-name newyork.com
```

Step 2 **Set the router date, time, and time zone.** The time on the router must be accurate to enroll with the CA server. The **clock set** command is entered with the router in privileged EXEC mode, and the **clock timezone** command is entered in global configuration mode. The syntax for these commands is as follows:

- **clock timezone** sets the correct time zone on the router.

- **clock set** configures the date and time on the router.

Example 18-2 shows the correct syntax for entering the date, time, and time zone on the router in New York.

Example 18-2 *Configuring the Date, Time, and Time Zone*

```
NewYork#configure terminal
NewYork(config)#clock timezone est -5
NewYork(config)#exit
NewYork#clock set 19:00:00 30 march 2003
```

The most accurate way to ensure the correct time on the router is to configure it to synchronize time with a network time server using the Network Time Protocol (NTP). Cisco products support both NTP and the Simple Network Time Protocol (SNTP). NTP maintains communication between the router and the NTP server via UDP port 123, and the router can then relay time to other systems on the network. SNTP is a protocol used mainly by low-end routers and acts as a client-only mode. SNTP maintains communication between the client and server using UDP port 580. To activate NTP, you must enable NTP while in the interface configuration mode. You should limit NTP to a specific interface and only allow the router to access time updates from specific NTP peers. The command for configuring NTP on the Cisco router is **ntp access-group [query-only | serve-only | server | peer]** *access-list number*. Table 18-2 lists the configuration options for the **ntp access-group** command.

Table 18-2 **ntp access-group** *Command Options*

Term	Definition
query-only	Allows NTP control queries only.
serve-only	Allows and serves NTP time requests only.
serve	Allows NTP time requests, but does not synchronize with the remote system.
peer	Allows NTP control queries and time requests. Also allows the router to synchronize time with the remote system.

Step 3 **Add the CA server to the router host table.** By adding the CA server IP address to the router host table, you define a static host name-to-IP address mapping and remove the requirement for using DNS. Removing the requirement for DNS increases the performance of the router because it is no longer affected by any delay of the DNS server.

- **ip host** *name address1* [*address2*]

Example 18-3 shows the correct syntax for adding the CA server to the host table on the router in New York.

Example 18-3 *Adding the CA Server to the Host Table*

```
NewYork#configure terminal
NewYork(config)#ip host CA-Server 192.168.242.42
```

Step 4 **Generate the RSA key pair.** The RSA keys are used to authenticate the router to its SA peer. The command syntax for key generation is **crypto key generate rsa usage keys**. The option **usage keys** enables you to generate two special-purpose key pairs (authentication pair and encryption pair for RSA-encrypted nonces). If you do not use the optional command, you will generate a single "general-purpose" public/private key pair. It is also possible to select the modulus length when generating keys. General-purpose keys are sufficient for standard authentication using RSA signatures. The available modulus lengths are 360, 512, 1024, and 2048 bits. The longer the modulus length, the longer it will take the router to generate the keys.

Step 5 **Declare the CA.** Configure the trusted CA on the router in the global configuration mode with the **crypto ca identity** *name* command. This identifies the trusted CA for the router and puts you in the ca-identity configuration mode.

A variety of commands are available in the ca-identity configuration mode:

- **enrollment url**—Specifies the URL for the CA.

- **enrollment mode ra**—Specifies the URL of your CA server that provides registration authority (RA). This command is only necessary if your CA also provides an RA.

- **query url**—If your CA server supports RA with LDAP, this command specifies the URL of the LDAP server. This command is only used if your CA provides RA and supports LDAP.

- **enrollment retry period** *minutes*—This optional command specifies the wait period between enrollment retries. The default retry period is 1 minute and the available range is from 1 to 60 minutes.

- **enrollment retry count**—This optional command specifies the number of enrollment attempts the router should make. The default setting is 0, which allows the router an unlimited number of retries. The available range is 1 to 100 retry attempts.

- **crl optional**—The CRL is a list of certificates that are no longer valid and have been revoked by the CA. If the peer certificate is found on the CRL, the router will not accept that certificate and cannot authenticate the router. The **crl optional** command is optional and allows the routers to accept peers' certificates if the CRL is not accessible.

Example 18-4 shows the correct syntax declaring the CA server as the CA on the router in New York.

Example 18-4 *Declaring the CA*

```
NewYork#configure terminal
NewYork(config)#crypto ca identity CA-Server
NewYork(cfg-ca-id)#enrollment url http://CS-Server/certserv/mscep/mscep.dll
NewYork(cfg-ca-id)#enrollment mode ra
```

Cisco IOS Software version 12.3 introduces a new command that replaced crypto ca identity. This command is crypto ca trustpoint. Using this command places you into the ca-trustpoint configuration mode. Example 18-5 shows the syntax for declaring a CA using Cisco IOS Software version 12.3

Example 18-5 *Declaring the CA with Cisco IOS Software Version 12.3*

```
NewYork(config)#crypto ca trustpoint CA_Server
NewYork(ca-trustpoint)#enrollment url http:// CS-Server/certserv/mscep/mscep.dll
NewYork(ca-trustpoint)#enrollment mode ra
```

Step 6 **Authenticate the CA.** The router authenticates the CA by retrieving the CA self-signed certificate and the CA's public key. The command for this action is **crypto ca authenticate**. This command initiates the authentication process with the CA by sending the CA/RA request to the CA. The CA generates the CA/RA certificate and returns it to the router. The router authenticates the CA/RA certificate using the CA/RA fingerprint. Example 18-6 shows the correct syntax for authenticating the CA on the router in New York.

Example 18-6 *Authenticating the CA*

```
NewYork#configure terminal
NewYork(config)#crypto ca authenticate CA-Server
```

Step 7 **Request your certificate.** The router must request a certificate from the CA server with the **crypto ca enroll** command. This command requests certificates from the CA for all the router RSA key pairs. The router sends the key pairs to the CA server, which generates and signs the identity certificates.

Finally, the CA server sends the identity certificates back to the router and posts a copy in its public repository. Example 18-7 shows the correct syntax for requesting a certificate from the CA.

Example 18-7 *Requesting a Certificate from the CA*

```
NewYork#configure terminal
NewYork(config)#crypto ca enroll CA-Server
% Start certificate enrollment…
% Create a challenge password. You need to verbally provide this
password to the CA administrator to revoke your certificate.
For security reasons, your password will not be saved in the configuration.
Please make a note of it.

Password: <password>
Re-enter password: <password>

% The subject name in the certificate will be: NewYork.newyork.com
% Include the router serial number in the subject name? (yes/no): no
% Include the IP address in the subject name? (yes/no): no
Request certificate from CA? (yes/no) yes
% Certificate request sent to certificate authority
% The certificate request fingerprint will be displayed.
% The show crypto ca certificate command will also show the fingerprint.

NewYork(config)#
        Signing Certificate Request Fingerprint:
        1D017C1F 9AE457BD 501BA5DF CF472D21

        Encryption Certificate Request Fingerprint:
        2FF054AB 01DC2A22 AB147620 05C5AB5F
```

Step 8 **Save the configuration to the router.** Ensure that the current configuration is saved. Write the configuration to memory using the **COPY running-config startup-config** command.

NOTE It is also a good idea to save the configuration to prevent certificate loss in the event of a system reboot and to back up the configuration in case of hardware failure.

Figure 18-2 depicts the communications between the router and the CA server that are required to complete the authentication, enrollment, and certificate-generation process.

Figure 18-2 *Communication Between the Router and CA*

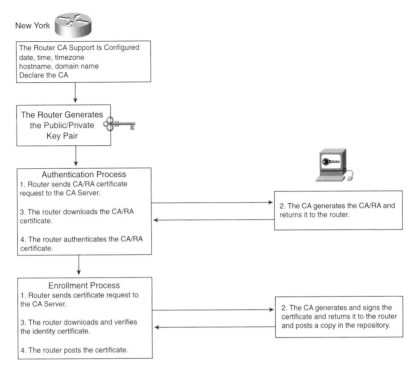

Many of the steps shown in Figure 18-2 are completed automatically by SCEP.

Step 9 **Manage key storage in NVRAM.** Memory management is an option available to prevent the number of stored certificates and CRLs from occupying memory space.

Step 10 **Manage the keys on the router.** Key management is an option that enables you to delete keys and certificates from the router and to request a CRL from the CA.

Step 11 **Verify the CA configuration.** Three commands enable you to view the status of certificates and keys on the router, as follows:

- **show crypto ca certificates** displays certificates currently on the router. Example 18-8 shows the output from the **show crypto ca certificates** command.

Example 18-8 show crypto ca certificates *Output*

```
NewYork# show crypto ca certificates
Certificate
Subject Name
Name: NewYork.newyork.com
IP Address: 192.168.0.1
Status: Available
Certificate Serial Number: 428125BDA34196003F6C78316CD8FA95
Key Usage: Signature
Certificate
Subject Name
Name: NewYork.newyork.com
IP Address: 192.168.0.1
Status: Available
Certificate Serial Number: AB352356AFCD0395E333CCFD7CD33897
Key Usage: Encryption
CA Certificate
Status: Available
Certificate Serial Number: 3051DF7123BEE31B8341DFE4B3A338E5F
Key Usage: Not Set
```

- **show crypto key mypubkey rsa** displays public keys for the router. Example 18-9 shows the output from the **show crypto key mypubkey rsa** command.

Example 18-9 show crypto key mypubkey rsa *Output*

```
NewYork# show crypto key mypubkey rsa
% Key pair was generated at: 19:07:49 UTC Mar 30 2003
Key name: NewYork.newyork.com
Usage: Signature Key
Key Data:
005C300D 06092A86 4886F70D 01010105 00034B00 30480241 00C5E23B 55D6AB22
04AEF1BA A54028A6 9ACC01C5 129D99E4 64CAB820 847EDAD9 DF0B4E4C 73A05DD2
BD62A8A9 FA603DD2 E2A8A6F8 98F76E28 D58AD221 B583D7A4 71020301 0001
% Key pair was generated at: 19:07:50 UTC Mar 30 2003
Key name: NewYork.newyork.com
Usage: Encryption Key
Key Data:
00302017 4A7D385B 1234EF29 335FC973 2DD50A37 C4F4B0FD 9DADE748 429618D5
18242BA3 2EDFBDD3 4296142A DDF7D3D8 08407685 2F2190A0 0B43F1BD 9A8A26DB
07953829 791FCDE9 A98420F0 6A82045B 90288A26 DBC64468 7789F76E EE21
```

- **show crypto key pubkey-chain rsa** displays the peer public keys on the router. Example 18-10 shows the output from the **show crypto key pubkey-chain rsa** command.

Example 18-10 show crypto key pubkey-chain rsa *Output*

```
NewYork# show crypto key pubkey-chain rsa
Codes: M - Manually Configured, C - Extracted from certificate
Code   Usage        IP-address      Name
C      Signature    192.168.20.1    Boston.boston.com
C      Encryption   192.168.20.1    Boston.boston.com
M      Signature    172.16.0.1      LA.losangeles.com
M      Encryption   172.16.0.1      LA.losangeles.com
C      General      192.168.10.3    atlanta.georgia.com
```

Step 3: Configure IKE Using RSA Signatures

Chapter 17 covered these configuration steps in great detail. For the purpose of this exercise, Figure 18-3 provides the configuration parameters for the VPN connection between New York and Boston.

Figure 18-3 *IKE Configuration Parameters*

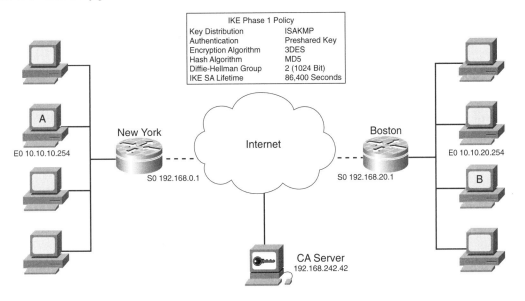

Example 18-11 shows the commands used to configure IKE using RSA signatures on the router in New York.

Example 18-11 *Configuring IKE Using RSA Signatures*

```
NewYork# configure terminal
NewYork (config)# crypto isakmp policy 120
NewYork (config-isakmp)# authentication rsa-sig
NewYork (config-isakmp)# encryption 3des
NewYork (config-isakmp)# hash md5
NewYork (config-isakmp)# group 2
NewYork (config-isakmp)# lifetime 86400
```

Step 4: Configure IPSec

Chapter 17 also covered these configuration steps in great detail. For the purpose of this exercise, Figure 18-4 provides the configuration parameters for the VPN connection between New York and Boston.

Figure 18-4 *IPSec Configuration Parameters*

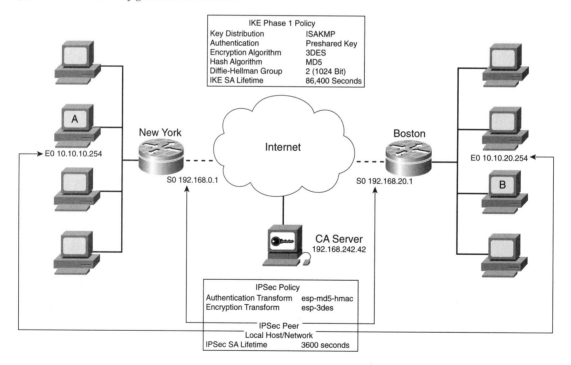

Example 18-12 shows the commands used to configure the following IPSec parameters on the New York router:

1. Create the IPSec transform set.
2. Configure IPSec SA lifetimes.
3. Create the crypto access lists (ACLs).
4. Create the crypto map.
5. Apply the crypto maps.

Example 18-12 *Configuring IPSec Parameters*

```
NewYork# configure terminal
NewYork (config)#crypto ipsec transform-set 20 esp-3des esp-md5-hmac
NewYork (cfg-crypto-trans)#exit

NewYork (config)#crypto ipsec security-association lifetime seconds 3600
NewYork (config)#access-list 105 permit ip 10.10.10.0 0.0.0.255 10.10.20.0 0.0.0.255

NewYork(config)#crypto map boston 120 ipsec-isakmp
NewYork(config-crypto-map)#match address 105
NewYork(config-crypto-map)#set peer 192.168.20.1
NewYork(config-crypto-map)#set pfs group2
NewYork(config-crypto-map)#set transform-set 20
NewYork(config-crypto-map)# set security-association lifetime seconds 86400
NewYork(config-crypto-map)#interface S0

NewYork(config-if)#crypto map boston
```

Step 5: Test and Verify the Configuration

The following three commands enable you to verify your configuration when working with CAs:

- **crypto ca identity**—This command displays the CA that your router is configured to use.
- **debug crypto pki** {*callbacks, messages, transactions*}—This command enables you to display the callbacks, transactions, or messages that occur between the router and the CA.
- **show crypto ca certificates**—This command displays information about the certificate of your CA and any RAs.

Foundation Summary

The "Foundation Summary" section of each chapter lists the most important facts from the chapter. Although this section does not list every fact from the chapter that will be on your SECUR exam, a well-prepared candidate should at a minimum know all the details in each "Foundation Summary" section before going to take the exam.

Advanced IPSec VPNs Using Cisco Routers and CAs

Although configuring the connection to a CA server is complex, once correctly configured the functionality is very scalable and easy to manage. The main focus of this chapter has been the configuration and enrollment process. Cisco IOS Software supports the following CA products using CA interoperability:

- VeriSign OnSite 4.5
- Entrust Technologies
- Baltimore Technologies
- Windows 2000 Certificate Server 5.0

Multiple tasks are required to configure the router for CA support:

- Configure the router host name and domain name.
- Set the router date, time, time zone, and/or configure for NTP.
- Add the CA server to the router host table.
- Generate the RSA key pair.
- Declare the CA.
- Authenticate the CA.
- Request your certificate.
- Save the configuration to the router.
- Manage key storage in NVRAM.
- Manage the keys on the router.
- Verify the CA configuration.

Q&A

As mentioned in the section, "How to Use This Book," in the Introduction to this book, you have two choices for review questions. The questions that follow next give you a bigger challenge than the exam itself by using an open-ended question format. By reviewing now with this more difficult question format, you can exercise your memory better and prove your conceptual and factual knowledge of this chapter. The answers to these questions are found in the appendix.

For more practice with exam-like question formats, including questions using a router simulator and multiple choice questions, use the exam engine on the CD-ROM.

1. What protocols are used by SCEP?
2. Why is it important to configure the router host name and domain name before requesting a certificate?
3. What is the best alternative to configuring the date, time, and time zone on your router?
4. What does the option **usage keys** do when generating RSA key pairs?
5. How do you configure the router to accept peer certificates if the CRL is not accessible?
6. How does the router authenticate the CA?
7. What command sends out a CA/RA request?
8. Why should you save the configuration after enrolling with the CA?
9. What does the command **show crypto key pubkey-chain rsa** display?

This chapter covers the following subject:

- Describe the Easy VPN Server

CHAPTER 19

Configuring Remote Access Using Easy VPN

Cisco Easy VPN is a client/server application that allows for VPN security parameters to be "pushed out" to the remote locations that connect using Cisco SOHO/ROHO products. The server portion is a component of Cisco IOS Software Release 12.2(8)T, and the client portion is available for the 800 to 1700 series routers, PIX 501 Firewall, 3002 VPN hardware client, and Easy Remote VPN software client 3.x.

> **NOTE** For a complete listing of products that support Cisco Easy VPN, check the products listing at Cisco.com.

"Do I Know This Already?" Quiz

The purpose of the "Do I Know This Already?" quiz is to help you decide whether you really need to read the entire chapter. If you already intend to read the entire chapter, you do not necessarily need to answer these questions now.

The eight-question quiz, derived from the major sections in the "Foundation Topics" portion of the chapter, helps you determine how to spend your limited study time.

Table 19-1 outlines the major topics discussed in this chapter and the "Do I Know This Already?" quiz questions that correspond to those topics.

Table 19-1 *"Do I Know This Already?" Foundation Topics Section-to-Question Mapping*

Foundation Topics Section	Questions Covered in This Section
Describe the Easy VPN Server	1–8

> **CAUTION** The goal of self-assessment is to gauge your mastery of the topics in this chapter. If you do not know the answer to a question or are only partially sure of the answer, you should mark this question wrong for purposes of the self-assessment. Giving yourself credit for an answer you correctly guess skews your self-assessment results and might provide you with a false sense of security.

1. What version of Cisco IOS Software supports Easy VPN Server?

   a. 12.1(13)

   b. 12.2(8)T

   c. 12.5

   d. 12.0(8)J

   e. None of the above

2. What device does not support Easy VPN client?

   a. Cisco 800 Series router

   b. Cisco 3002 hardware VPN client

   c. Cisco PIX 535 Firewall

   d. Cisco PIX 501 Firewall

   e. Cisco 1700 Series router

3. What is "group-based policy control"?

   a. Group-based policy control enables you to apply policies on a per-user or per-group basis.

   b. Group-based policy control enables you to apply policies if you are a member of the administrators group.

   c. Group-based policy control enables you to apply policies to users only.

   d. Group-based policy control enables you to apply policies to groups only.

   e. None of the above.

4. What Diffie-Hellman groups are supported by Easy VPN Server?

   a. 1, 2, 3, 4, and 5

   b. 1 and 2 only

   c. 2 and 4 only

   d. 1 and 4 only

   e. 2 and 5 only

5. What configuration mode must you be in to configure the IP address pool?

   a. Pool-configuration mode

   b. Global configuration mode

   c. Privileged EXEC mode

   d. Interface configuration mode

   e. Enable mode

6. What do you not configure when creating the ISAKMP policy for the remote VPN clients?

   a. Peer authentication method

   b. Policy priority

   c. Encryption algorithm

   d. Hash algorithm

   e. Diffie-Hellman group

7. What configuration mode must you be in to configure RRI?

   a. Crypto-map configuration mode

   b. Global configuration mode

   c. Privileged EXEC mode

   d. Interface configuration mode

   e. Enable mode

8. What is the time range (in seconds) for DPD keepalive "retries"?

   a. 10 to 3600

   b. 60 to 3600

   c. 2 to 3600

   d. 2 to 60

   e. 2 to 1800

The answers to the "Do I Know This Already?" quiz are found in the appendix. The suggested choices for your next step are as follows:

- **6 or less overall score**—Read the entire chapter. This includes the "Foundation Topics" and "Foundation Summary" sections and the "Q&A" section.

- **7 of 8 overall score**—If you want more review on these topics, skip to the "Foundation Summary" section and then go to the "Q&A" section. Otherwise, move on to the next chapter.

Foundation Topics

Describe the Easy VPN Server

As mentioned in the beginning of this chapter, Easy VPN is a client/server product that allows for simplified VPN connectivity with branch offices, remote offices, and remote users. The server portion of this product is called Cisco Easy VPN Server and is a component of Cisco IOS Software Release 12.2(8)T. The client component installs on Cisco routers designed for remote office/home office (ROHO) use, Cisco PIX 501 Firewall, the 3002 hardware VPN client, and the Cisco VPN client software (version 3.x). The functionality that makes Easy VPN "easy" is that it allows the client to connect with the server and download its VPN configuration. This precludes the requirement of configuring each client endpoint for the VPN. Figure 19-1 depicts how Easy VPN would be used by the New York headquarters to provide secure connectivity to their branch offices, remote offices, and remote users.

Figure 19-1 *Easy VPN Deployment for New York*

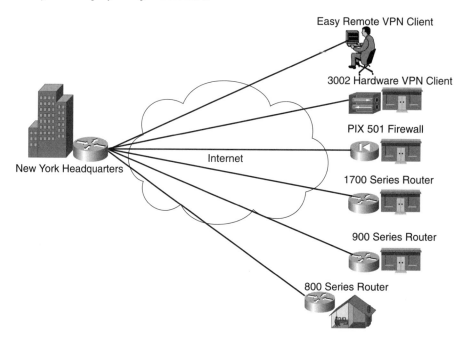

As Figure 19-1 illustrates, the VPN connection for each remote location terminates at the Cisco IOS router in the New York headquarters.

Easy VPN Server Functionality

Easy VPN Server came about with Cisco IOS Software Release 12.2(8)T. It is the first Cisco IOS Software version to provide server support for Cisco VPN client 3.x and the Cisco VPN 3002 hardware clients. The Easy VPN Server manages all IPSec policies centrally and pushes the policy out to the client. This design minimizes the configuration required on the client end.

The following functionality is integrated into the Cisco IOS Software 12.2(8)T with Easy VPN Server:

- **Split tunneling control**—Split tunneling occurs when the remote user is able to connect to their intranet using the VPN and still maintain a connection to the Internet outside of the VPN. Many security experts consider split tunneling to be a significant security risk because it allows somewhat of a backdoor connection to the intranet via the remote user system. Split tunneling control allows the VPN administrator to force all traffic from the client to go through the VPN tunnel to include traffic destined for the Internet. Split tunneling is often mitigated by using a firewall at the remote end. The type of firewall deployed at the remote end depends on the connection at that end and could range from a firewall appliance (such as the Cisco PIX firewall) on the LAN to a personal firewall that is installed on the workstation that is using the Easy Remote VPN client.

- **IKE dead peer detection (DPD)**—DPD incorporates a series of keepalive messages between the IPSec peers when there is no other traffic passing through the VPN tunnel. DPD is automatically configured on the client end and must be configured on the server to determine the health of the client connection. In the event that either end determines the connection is lost, it notifies the user and redistributes resources that were used by that connection.

- **Initial contact**—If a client is inadvertently disconnected, their connection is not removed from the IKE and IPSec SA tables until they exceed the timeout values. If the user attempts to reconnect, the connection is refused because the server thinks there is currently a valid connection running. The initial contact feature integrates an initial contact flag into the message that tells the peer to remove any previous IKE and IPSec information for that SA from the connection tables. This feature resolves connection problems associated with invalid SPI messages resulting from SA synchronization problems.

- **Extended authentication (xauth) version 6 support**—IKE xauth enables you to configure an authentication list using the crypto map command. Additional features have been integrated into xauth version 6.

- **Mode configuration version 6 support**—Mode configuration is the method by which a VPN client receives the configuration settings necessary to successfully create the VPN tunnel.

- **Group-based policy control**—The Easy VPN Server can configure policy parameters on a per-group or per-user basis.

Table 19-2 lists the IPSec attributes supported by Cisco IOS Software 12.2(8)T and Cisco Easy VPN Server.

Table 19-2 *Supported IPSec Attributes*

Option	Supported Attribute
Authentication type	Preshared keys
	RSA signatures
Hash algorithm	MD5-HMAC
	SHA1-HMAC
Diffie-Hellman group	Group 2 (768 bit)
	Group 5 (1536 bit)
IKE encryption algorithm	DES (56 bit)
	3DES (168 bit)
IPSec encryption algorithm	DES (56 bit)
	3DES (168 bit)
	Null
IPSec protocols	ESP
	IPCOMP-LZS
IPSec mode	Tunnel mode

Configuring the Easy VPN Server

Remember the Easy VPN Server configuration is the most important because it is the central location where the other VPN client connections terminate. To configure Easy VPN Server on your Cisco IOS 12.2(8)T or later router, follow these steps:

Step 1 Prepare the router for Easy VPN Server.

Step 2 Configure the group policy lookup.

Step 3 Create the ISAKMP policy for the remote VPN clients.

Step 4 Define a group policy for a mode configuration push.

Step 5 Create the transform set.

Step 6   Create the dynamic crypto maps with Reverse Route Injection (RRI).

Step 7   Apply the mode configuration to the dynamic crypto map.

Step 8   Apply the dynamic crypto map to the interface.

Step 9   Enable IKE DPD.

Step 10 Configure xauth.

For the purpose of this exercise, reference Figure 19-2. This figure depicts the address space used between the headquarters and the remote office. The remote office is located in the resort town of Windham, New York, and is connected to the Internet via a 1700 series router.

Figure 19-2 *VPN Connection Between New York HQ and Remote Office*

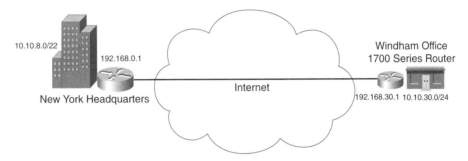

Prepare the Router for Easy VPN Server

When preparing for the Easy VPN Server, the first configuration task is to enable AAA on the router. The command is entered in the global configuration mode. The next step is to configure a local address pool that will be used for assigning addresses to remote users. Use the following commands:

```
aaa new-model
ip local pool pool-name low-address high-address
```

Example 19-1 shows what the configuration would look like on the router at the New York headquarters.

Example 19-1 *Preparing the Router for Easy VPN Server*

```
NewYork#configure terminal
NewYork(config)#aaa new-model
NewYork(config)#ip local pool windham-office 10.10.8.1 10.10.8.50
```

Configure the Group Policy Lookup

The group policy lookup is the method used to authenticate the remote users attempting to gain access. It is possible to use a RADIUS server as well as the local group. The servers will be tried in the order listed. The command for this configuration is as follows:

```
aaa authorization network group-name local [radius]
```

Example 19-2 shows the command for configuring the group policy lookup for the local group.

Example 19-2 *Configuring the Policy Lookup*

```
NewYork#configure terminal
NewYork(config)#aaa authorization network windham-vpn-users local group radius
```

Create the ISAKMP Policy for the Remote VPN Clients

Configuring the ISAKMP policy for the VPN users is no different from the configuration required for any other VPN connection. ISAKMP is enabled by default on the Cisco router; however, you will need to select the following IKE parameters:

- Peer authentication method
- Encryption algorithm
- Diffie-Hellman group

Refer to Table 19-2 for a list of supported options for each category. Example 19-3 lists the commands used to configure the ISAKMP policy.

Example 19-3 *Configuring the ISAKMP Policy*

```
crypto isakmp enable
crypto isakmp policy priority_number
authentication peer_authentication_method
encryption  encryption_algorithm
group diffie-hellman_group
exit
```

Example 19-4 shows the configuration of ISAKMP policy for the remote users on the New York headquarters router.

Example 19-4 *Defining the ISAKMP Policy*

```
NewYork#configure terminal
NewYork(config)#crypto isakmp enable
NewYork(config)#crypto isakmp policy 10
NewYork(config-isakmp)#authentication pre-share
```

Example 19-4 *Defining the ISAKMP Policy (Continued)*

```
NewYork(config-isakmp)# encryption 3des
NewYork(config-isakmp)# group 2
NewYork(config-isakmp)#exit
```

Define a Group Policy for a Mode Configuration Push

The *mode configuration push* is the policy configuration that is pushed out to the remote users when they connect to the Easy VPN Server. To configure this group policy, follow these steps:

Step 1 Create the group that is being defined.

Step 2 Configure the preshared key. This is the password that the user enters when using the VPN client software.

Step 3 Specify the DNS servers—that is, designate the DNS servers to be used via the VPN connection.

Step 4 Specify the DNS domain. By doing so, you identify the FQDN for the network the Easy VPN Server is protecting.

Step 5 Specify WINS servers—that is, designate the WINS servers to be used via the VPN connection.

Step 6 Specify the local IP address pool. By doing so, you identify the IP address scope to be assigned to remote VPN users that connect via the Easy VPN Server.

The commands required for each step of this configuration are as follows:

```
crypto isakmp client configuration group {group-name | default}
```

NOTE If you use the **default** group name, the policy will apply to all remote access users.

```
key pre-shared_key
dns primary_server secondary_server
domain domain_name
wins primary_server secondary_server
pool name
```

Example 19-5 displays the group policy for the configuration push to the Windham remote office.

Example 19-5 *Defining the Group Policy Configuration Mode*

```
NewYork#configure terminal
NewYork(config)#crypto isakmp client configuration group windham-vpn-users
NewYork(config-isakmp-group)#key abc123
```

continues

Example 19-5 *Defining the Group Policy Configuration Mode (Continued)*

```
NewYork(config-isakmp-group)#dns 10.10.8.252 10.10.10.252
NewYork(config-isakmp-group)#domain newyork.com
NewYork(config-isakmp-group)#wins 10.10.8.251 10.10.10.251
NewYork(config-isakmp-group)#pool windham-office
NewYork(config-isakmp-group)#exit
```

Create the Transform Set

This transform set is used by the remote clients that attempt to establish the IPSec tunnel to this endpoint. The steps required are the same as for any other transform set. If you refer back to Table 19-2, you will notice that AH is not a supported IPSec protocol. The command for this configuration is as follows:

```
crypto ipsec transform-set name [transform1] [transform2] [transform 3]
```

Example 19-6 shows the transform set configured for 3DES and MD5-HMAC.

Example 19-6 *Creating the Transform Set*

```
NewYork#configure terminal
NewYork(config)#crypto ipsec transform-set windhamtransform esp-3des esp-md5-hmac
NewYork(cfg-crypto-trans)#exit
```

Create the Dynamic Crypto Maps with Reverse Route Injection (RRI)

This three-step process creates and assigns the crypto maps that the remote client connections will use. RRI is enabled to ensure that returning data that is destined for a specific tunnel can find that tunnel. The commands used for this configuration step are as follows:

```
crypto dynamic-map dynamic_map_name sequence_number
set transform-set transform-set_name
reverse route
```

It is possible to configure multiple transform sets.

Example 19-7 depicts the configuration of the Easy VPN Server for the connection to the Windham office.

Example 19-7 *Configuring Crypto Maps with RRI*

```
NewYork#configure terminal
NewYork(config)#crypto dynamic-map windham-map 1
NewYork(config-crypto-map)#set transform-set windhamtransform
NewYork(config-crypto-map)#reverse-route
NewYork(config-crypto=map)#exit
```

Apply the Mode Configuration to the Dynamic Crypto Map

This three-step process configures the Easy VPN Server to respond to mode configuration requests and begin sending the information required to create the VPN connection with the remote client. The following three steps are required for this task:

Step 1   Configure the router to respond to requests.

Step 2   Enable IKE queries for group policy lookup.

Step 3   Apply the changes to the dynamic crypto map.

The commands for these configuration steps are as follows:

```
crypto map map_name client configuration address respond
crypto map map_name isakmp authorization list list_name
crypto map map_name sequence_number ipsec-isakmp dynamic dynamic_map_name
```

Example 19-8 shows this configuration being completed on the Easy VPN Server for the connection to the Windham office.

Example 19-8 *Applying Mode Configuration*

```
NewYork#configure terminal
NewYork(config)# crypto map windham-map client configuration address respond
NewYork(config)# crypto map windham-map isakmp authorization list windham-vpn-users
NewYork(config)# crypto map windham-map 10 ipsec-isakmp dynamic windham-map
NewYork(config)#exit
```

Apply the Dynamic Crypto Map to the Interface

This command applies the dynamic crypto map to the interface. It is the same process as applying any other function to an interface:

```
interface interface_name
crypto map map_name
```

Example 19-9 shows the crypto map being applied to the router at the New York headquarters.

Example 19-9 *Applying Dynamic Crypto Maps to the Interface*

```
NewYork#configure terminal
NewYork(config)#interface serial 0/0
NewYork(config-if)#crypto map windham-map
NewYork(config-if)#exit
```

Enable IKE DPD

As discussed earlier in this chapter, IKE DPD monitors the status of the connection by sending keepalives when there is no traffic passing over the connection. This allows the system to ensure the connection is functioning and removes any resources that are not required when the connection drops. When configuring IKE DPD, you just need to tell the router how often to send the keepalive message and how long to wait between retries if it does not get a response. The range for the keepalive messages is between 10 and 3600 seconds, and the range for the retries is between 2 and 60 seconds. The command for enabling IKE DPD is as follows:

```
crypto isakmp keepalive seconds retries
```

Example 19-10 depicts this configuration on the router, enabling a keepalive packet every 60 seconds and specifying to retry every 20 seconds if it does not get a response.

Example 19-10 *Enabling IKE DPD*

```
NewYork#configure terminal
NewYork (config)#crypto isakmp keepalive 60 20
```

Configure xauth

Xauth is a process for using AAA authentication for VPN connections. The following three steps are required to configure xauth on the Easy VPN Server:

Step 1 Enable AAA login authentication.

Step 2 Configure the xauth timeout value. (This is the time that the user will have to input the user ID and password.)

Step 3 Configure the xauth dynamic crypto map.

The commands for configuring xauth are as follows:

```
aaa authentication login list_name method1 [method 2]
crypto isakmp xauth timeout seconds
crypto map map_name client authentication list list_name
```

Example 19-11 shows how xauth is configured on the Easy VPN Server for the connection to the Windham remote office.

Example 19-11 *Configuring Xauth*

```
NewYork#configure terminal
NewYork(config)#aaa authentication login windham-vpn-users pre-share
NewYork(config)#crypto isakmp xauth timeout 30
NewYork(config-if)#crypto map windham-map client authentication list windham-vpn-users local
```

Easy VPN Modes of Operation

The Easy VPN can use two different remote phase II modes for VPN connectivity, which mainly affect how the remote user is addressed when connected to the destination network. Both configurations support split tunneling. The two modes are as follows:

- **Client mode**—This mode allows whatever changes necessary to connect the client to the destination network via the VPN connection. In the client mode, the client is automatically configured with NAT/PAT and the access lists needed to create the VPN connection.
- **Network extension mode**—This mode treats the VPN client systems as components of the original network. The client systems must have fully routable IP addresses and cannot use NAT or PAT.

> **NOTE** The term *fully routable* only refers to address space that does not conflict on either end of the connection. This is not a reference to the use of RFC 1918 addressing.

Foundation Summary

The "Foundation Summary" section of each chapter lists the most important facts from the chapter. Although this section does not list every fact from the chapter that will be on your SECUR exam, a well-prepared SECUR candidate should at a minimum know all the details in each "Foundation Summary" before going to take the exam.

Describe the Easy VPN Server

The Easy VPN Server is a product of Cisco IOS Software 12.2(8)T and enables administrators to consolidate IPSec and user policies at a single manageable location that is the endpoint for multiple VPN connections. Each client that connects to this endpoint will download its policy during the VPN negotiation.

Easy VPN Server Functionality

The Easy VPN Server provides the following functionality:

- Split tunneling control
- IKE dead peer detection (DPD)
- Initial contact
- Xauth version 6 support
- Mode configuration version 6 support
- Group-based policy control

Configuring the Easy VPN Server

To configure Easy VPN Server on your Cisco IOS router, you must complete the following tasks:

1. Prepare the router for Easy VPN Server.

   Enable AAA on the router.

   - Command: **aaa new-model**

   Define an address pool.

   - Command: **ip local pool** *pool-name low-address high-address*

2. Configure the group policy lookup.

   Command: **aaa authorization network** *group-name* **local** [local][radius]

3. Create the ISAKMP policy for the remote VPN clients.

   Enable ISAKMP.

   - Command: **crypto isakmp enable**

   Define the IKE priority.

   - Command: **crypto isakmp policy** *priority_number*

   Define the Peer authentication method

   - Command: **authen** *peer_authentication_method*

   Define the Encryption algorithm

   - Command: **encryption** *encryption_algorithm*

   Diffie-Hellman group

   - Command: **group diffie-hellman_group**

4. Define a group policy for a mode configuration push.

   Create the group that is being defined.

   - Command: **crypto isakmp client configuration group** *group-name*

   Configure the preshared key. This is the password that the user enters when using the VPN client software.

   - Command: **key** *preshared_key*

   Specify the DNS servers. By doing so, you designate the DNS servers to be used via the VPN connection.

   - Command: **dns** *primary_server secondary_server*

   Specify the DNS domain. By doing so, you identify the FQDN for the network the Easy VPN Server is protecting.

   - Command: **domain** *domain_name*

   Specify WINS servers. By doing so, you designate the WINS servers to be used via the VPN connection.

   - Command: **wins** *primary_server secondary_server*

   Specify the local IP address pool. By doing so, you identify the IP address scope to be assigned to remote VPN users that connect via the Easy VPN Server.

   - Command: **pool** *name*

5. Create the transform set.

   Command: **crypto ipsec transform-set** *name* [*transform1*] [*transform2*] [*transform 3*]

6. Create the dynamic crypto maps with RRI.

Create the dynamic crypto map.

- Command: **crypto dynamic-map** *dynamic_map_name sequence_number*

Define the transform set.

- Command: **set transform-set** *transform-set_name*

Enable RRI.

- Command: **reverse-route**

7. Apply the mode configuration to the dynamic crypto map.

Configure the router to respond to requests.

- Command: **crypto map** *map_name* **client configuration address respond**

Enable IKE queries for group policy lookup.

- Command: **crypto map** *map_name* **isakmp authorization list** *list_name*

Apply the changes to the dynamic crypto map.

- Command: **crypto map** *map_name sequence_number* **ipsec-isakmp dynamic** *dynamic_map_name*

8. Apply the dynamic crypto map to the interface.

Enter the interface configuration mode.

- Command: **interface** *interface_name*

Apply the crypto map.

- Command: **crypto map** *map_name*

9. Enable IKE DPD.

- Command: **crypto isakmp keepalive** *seconds retries*

10. Configure xauth.

Enable AAA login authentication.

- Command: **aaa authentication login** *list_name method1* [*method 2*]

Configure the xauth timeout value.

- Command: **crypto isakmp xauth timeout** *seconds*

Configure the xauth dynamic crypto map.

- Command: **crypto map** *map_name* **client authentication list** *list_name*

Easy VPN Modes of Operation

- **Client mode**—Supports and requires NAT/PAT
- **Network extension mode**—Does not support NAT/PAT

Q&A

As mentioned in the section, "How to Use This Book," in the Introduction to this book, you have two choices for review questions. The questions that follow next give you a bigger challenge than the exam itself by using an open-ended question format. By reviewing now with this more difficult question format, you can exercise your memory better and prove your conceptual and factual knowledge of this chapter. The answers to these questions are found in the appendix.

For more practice with exam-like question formats, including questions using a router simulator and multiple choice questions, use the exam engine on the CD-ROM.

1. How does the Easy VPN Server control VPN policies for remote clients?
2. What is dead peer detection (DPD)?
3. How does the command **aaa new model** prepare the router for Easy VPN Server?
4. What must you do before selecting your IKE parameters for remote VPN clients?
5. What servers should you designate when defining the group policy for mode configuration push?
6. What must you do to make a dynamic crypto map function?
7. What is the difference between **crypto isakmp keepalive seconds** and **retries**?
8. What is xauth?
9. How many different remote phase II modes does Easy VPN Server support?
10. Which remote phase II mode does not support NAT or PAT?

This chapter covers the following subject:

- Managing Enterprise VPN Routers

CHAPTER 20

Scaling Management of an Enterprise VPN Environment

Administration of any enterprise network can be a very difficult objective. The sheer size of a network and diverse range of components used on that network can make centralized administration an extremely challenging task. Cisco has developed tools that enable administrators to organize, configure, and effectively monitor Cisco virtual private network (VPN) routers deployed throughout the enterprise.

"Do I Know This Already?" Quiz

The purpose of the "Do I Know This Already?" quiz is to help you decide whether you really need to read the entire chapter. If you already intend to read the entire chapter, you do not necessarily need to answer these questions now.

The 10-question quiz, derived from the major sections in "Foundation Topics" section of the chapter, helps you determine how to spend your limited study time.

Table 20-1 outlines the major topics discussed in this chapter and the "Do I Know This Already?" quiz questions that correspond to those topics.

Table 20-1 *"Do I Know This Already?" Foundation Topics Section-to-Question Mapping*

Foundation Topics Section	Questions Covered in This Section
Managing Enterprise VPN Routers	1–10

CAUTION The goal of self-assessment is to gauge your mastery of the topics in this chapter. If you do not know the answer to a question or are only partially sure of the answer, you should mark this question wrong for purposes of the self-assessment. Giving yourself credit for an answer you correctly guess skews your self-assessment results and might provide you with a false sense of security.

1. Which of the following is not supported by CiscoWorks 2000?

    a. Management and monitoring of PIX firewalls

    b. Management and monitoring of the CSIDS

    c. Management and monitoring of Cisco HIDS

    d. Management and monitoring of syslog servers

    e. Web-based interface for the configuration, management, and troubleshooting of VPNs

2. Which of the following operating systems support the installation of CiscoWorks 2000? (Choose all that apply)

    a. Red Hat Linux

    b. Windows 2000 Server

    c. Sun Solaris 9

    d. Windows 2000 Professional

    e. Open BSD

3. Which server platform is required for the installation of the Router MC? (Choose all that apply)

    a. Windows 2000 Advanced Server

    b. CiscoWorks 2000

    c. Sun Solaris 2.6

    d. VPN/Security Management Solution

    e. Windows 2000 Server

4. Where is the "hub" normally located when creating a "hub-and-spoke" network?

    a. In the geographic center of the network, to ensure a relatively equal distance between spoke sites

    b. In a central location that is primarily determined by the throughput available for each spoke site

    c. At the site with the best Internet connection

    d. At a location that is logically central to the organization, such as the corporate headquarters

    e. At the site with the least complex network

5. In a "hub-and-spoke" network design, how do the spoke locations communicate?

   a. The spokes do not communicate with each other.

   b. All traffic is routed through the "hub."

   c. All spoke sites are configured for a full-mesh VPN.

   d. The hub proxies all connections back out to the spokes.

   e. None of the above.

6. When configuring the hub settings in the context of the VPN and firewall policies, exactly which items are configured?

   a. How many VPN connections can be accepted by the hub router

   b. The type of router that is used at the hub location

   c. The internal interfaces and networks on the "hub side"

   d. The central site router that has priority for the connection

   e. All of the above

7. How long will an activity be available for editing by any user?

   a. Until it has been "deployed"

   b. Until it has been "submitted"

   c. Until it has been "approved"

   d. Until it has been "deleted"

   e. Until it has been "rejected"

8. When configuring the firewall settings of the VPN and firewall policies, what component are you configuring?

   a. CBAC

   b. The PIX firewall

   c. Access control lists

   d. Cisco Secure ACS

   e. All of the above

   f. None of the above

9. What doe the term "inheritance" mean when talking about the Router MC?

   a. Any changes made to the "hub" will affect the "spokes."

   b. Any policies applied to a device will affect the group that the device is assigned to.

   c. Any policies applied to a device level group will affect the global group.

   d. Policy changes will not affect a device if it is in the "locked group."

   e. None of the above.

10. Which components can be used multiple times when configuring the Router MC?

   a. Device names

   b. Organizational IDs

   c. VPN policies

   d. Building blocks

   e. None of the above

The answers to the "Do I Know This Already?" quiz are found in the appendix. The suggested choices for your next step are as follows:

- **8 or less overall score**—Read the entire chapter. This includes the "Foundation Topics" and "Foundation Summary" sections and the "Q&A" section.

- **9 or 10 overall score**—If you want more review on these topics, skip to the "Foundation Summary" section and then go to the "Q&A" section. Otherwise, move on to the next chapter.

Foundation Topics

This chapter discusses the following three specific network management tools available from Cisco:

- CiscoWorks 2000
- VPN/Security Management Solution (VMS)
- Management Center for VPN (Router MC)

These tools were developed by Cisco and work together to assist in the administration of enterprise network components. This chapter focuses on the administration of VPN routers through the enterprise.

Managing Enterprise VPN Routers

Obviously, the management of any enterprise network is a very complex task. The management of VPN routers on the enterprise can add an additional level of complexity due to the strict configuration requirements for each device to maintain VPN connectivity. It is imperative that the configurations of both VPN endpoints include enough matching components to allow the VPN to come up. If the configuration is changed on either end and no longer matches its peer, the systems cannot create the VPN and the connection is effectively down. The Cisco management tools enable you to organize your enterprise in a manner that is understandable and simple to manage. To run the Router MC, you need to have either CiscoWorks 2000 or VMS version 2.1. Both are discussed in the following sections.

CiscoWorks 2000

CiscoWorks 2000 is a family of bundled advanced network management tools that can run on either a Windows platform or Sun Solaris. CiscoWorks is a client/server-based product that allows for easy access and management of Cisco AVVID architecture components. CiscoWorks 2000 provides the following network administration and management functionality:

- Management and monitoring of Cisco PIX firewalls
- Management and monitoring of CSIDSs
- Management and monitoring of Cisco HIDS
- A web-based interface for configuration, monitoring, and troubleshooting of VPNs

Table 20-2 lists the hardware and operating system requirements for the installation of CiscoWorks2000 on a Microsoft Windows platform.

Table 20-2 *System Requirements for CiscoWorks 2000 (Windows Platform)*

Server Hardware	IBM-compatible PC with 600-MHz processor
	VGA monitor capable of 256 colors
	CD-ROM drive
	10-Mbps network connection
System Memory (RAM)	1 GB minimum
Disk Drive Space	9 GB minimum
	2-GB virtual memory
	(Note: The hard drive should be partitioned as an NTFS partition.)
Windows 2000 Software	Windows 2000 Professional/Server/Advanced Server
	Service Pack 2
	ODBC Driver Manager 3.510
Windows NT Software	Windows NT Workstation/Server
	Service Pack 6a

Table 20-3 lists the hardware and operating system requirements for the installation of CiscoWorks2000 on a Sun Solaris platform.

Table 20-3 *System Requirements for CiscoWorks 2000 (Sun Platform)*

Server Hardware	Ultra 60 or later with 440-Mhz processor
	VGA monitor capable of 256 colors
	CD-ROM drive
	10-Mbps network connection
System Memory (RAM)	1 GB minimum
Disk Drive Space	9 GB minimum
	2-GB swap space
Operating System	Solaris 2.6
	Solaris 2.7
	All recommended patches

VPN/Security Management Solution (VMS)

VMS was developed by Cisco and released in late 2001 as a snap-in for CiscoWorks for Windows (the predecessor to CiscoWorks 2000). The VMS "common services" are required to facilitate communication between the CiscoWorks server and the VPN routers. The hardware and operating system requirements for VMS are essentially the same as those required for CiscoWorks 2000.

Management Center for VPN Routers (Router MC)

Router MC is a web-based application designed for management of enterprise VPN and firewall configurations on Cisco IOS routers. Router MC allows for remote management and monitoring of both firewall and VPN features on the Cisco router. The Router MC is installed on either a CiscoWorks 2000 or CiscoWorks VMS server and can be accessed from client machines using a web browser and a Secure Sockets Layer (SSL) connection. The Router MC allows for a centralized configuration of Internet Key Exchange (IKE) and tunnel policies for multiple VPN devices and is scalable to allow administration of a large number of VPN routers. Figure 20-1 depicts how the client connects to the CiscoWorks server and how it communicates with the routers deployed across a fictitious enterprise in North America.

NOTE Figure 20-1 only represents the communication between the Router MC and individual locations. This diagram does not represent the hub-and-spoke method, which is standard for router deployments.

Figure 20-1 *Router MC Communication*

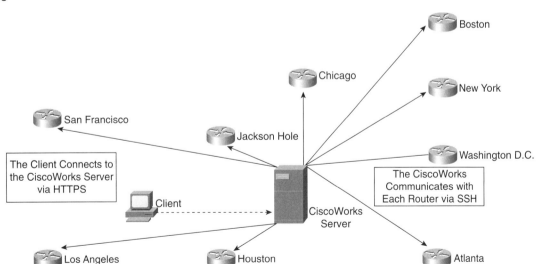

To connect with the Router MC, you need a client system that meets the specifications defined in Table 20-4.

Table 20-4 *System Requirements for a Router MC Client*

Hardware	IBM-compatible PC with 300-MHz CPU
	10-Mbps network connection
	Sun SPARCstation or Sun Ultra 10 with 333-MHz processor
System Memory (RAM)	256 MB minimum
Disk Drive Space	400-MB virtual memory (Windows)
	512-MB swap space (Solaris)
Operating System	Windows 98/NT/2000 SP2
	Solaris 2.6 or 2.7
Browser	Internet Explorer 5.5 (SP2) or 6.0

Concepts of the Router MC

To understand the Router MC, you must first understand the basic concepts used in its development and operation. The basic concepts are listed here with a brief explanation. For further information on these concepts, see "Using Management Center for VPN Routers." You can find this document through a search at Cisco.com.

- **Hub-and-spoke topology**—The hub-and-spoke topology is commonly used when connecting branch offices to the main office. A central Cisco IOS router located at the main office acts as the hub and maintains a separate secure tunnel with each "spoke" router located at the branch offices. The networks at the spoke locations tend to be less complex, containing only a few subnets. Spoke locations do not communicate directly with each other. All communication between the spokes must go through the hub. Figure 20-2 depicts the typical hub-and-spoke topology.

- **VPN and firewall policies**—VPN and firewall policies are configured on the Router MC and translated into command-line interface (CLI) commands as they are deployed to the router. The VPN settings determine the configuration of the VPN connectivity across the network. VPN settings are broken into the following four categories:

    — **General VPN settings**—General VPN settings determine the routing, IPSec failover, and fragmentation parameters of the network. The hub is commonly a high-availability pair configured for IPSec failover. This provides redundancy in the event of a failure of the primary hub router. Failover can be performed using either IKE keepalives, IPSec, or Generic Routing Encapsulation (GRE). It is possible to define multiple routing and failover policies within the object hierarchy, yet only one policy will apply per device. It is important to ensure that the spoke has a routing and failover policy that matches that of the hub.

Figure 20-2 *Forward Acknowledgement*

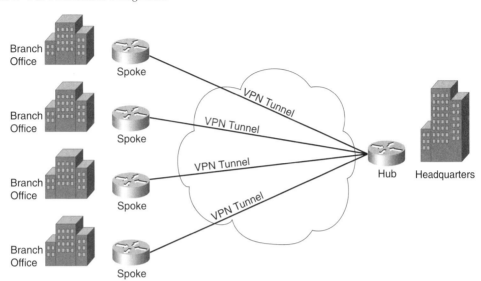

- **Hub settings**—Hub settings determine the configuration of the "central site" or hub of the network. The internal interfaces and networks of the hub side are configured in the hub settings.

- **Spoke settings**—The spoke settings are used to configure the internal interfaces and networks on the spoke side of the VPN connection.

- **Firewall settings**—Firewall settings are used to configure the parameters for implementation of CBAC, defining access rules, embryonic connections, fragmentation timeouts, and logging.

■ **Device hierarchy and inheritance**—The Router MC maintains all devices in a multilevel hierarchy. All devices are contained in a "global" group. Devices are grouped together to facilitate efficient management of large numbers of VPN connections. These groups are referred to as *objects*. Policies that are defined at the *global* level are inherited by devices at the device group level. Policies defined at the device group level are only inherited by devices in that specific device group. Policies defined to individual devices only apply to that specific device. It is important to carefully plan your device grouping to ensure efficient management of your VPN connections.

■ **Activities**—An activity is a temporary context within which you make configuration changes to global, device group, or individual objects. These configuration changes do not take effect until and unless the activity has been approved. An activity can only be opened by a single user at a time; however, multiple users can make changes to an activity after it has been opened. All devices within the specific object that is affected by the activity are locked while the activity is open and cannot accept any configuration changes. Upon completion, activities are either approved (pushed out to the devices) or deleted.

- **Jobs**—Jobs are configuration changes that are translated into CLI commands and prepared for deployment to the specified devices within the object. It is possible to deploy the jobs to a file or directly to the network device after the job has been previewed and approved. To deploy the job to the device, you must ensure that SSH is enabled on the device router.

- **Building blocks**—Building blocks are global components that can be named and reused within multiple policies. Because building blocks can be used multiple times, they aid in ensuring uniform application of policies. It is important to understand that any changes to a building block will effect all policies that use that building block. A good example of a building block is a *transform set*.

- **Device import**—To import a device is to bring information about that device into the Router MC. This is completed by either reading the device information directly from that device or from a device file. Devices are imported either individually or in groups.

- **Upload of existing policies on devices into Router MC**—Policies that exist on devices can be uploaded to the Router MC. This enables you to bring up a new Router MC and pull the current device configuration instead of having to manually build the policies for each existing device.

- **Predefined device groups and policies**—The Router MC is configured with predefined device groups, IKE policies, and transform sets.

Supported Tunneling Technologies

The Router MC supports three tunneling technologies:

- **IPSec**—IPSec is the framework of open standards that provide security services at the IP layer. Data integrity, data confidentiality, and data origin authentication are maintained over public networks by using IKE to negotiate IPSec peers, keys, and security associations. The Router MC supports authentication using preshared keys, RSA signatures, and digital certificates. IPSec tunnels are kept operational through the use of IKE keepalive packets that detect any loss of connectivity.

- **IPSec with Generic Routing Encapsulation (GRE)**—GRE is used to encapsulate many protocol packet types within IP tunnels to create a virtual point-to-point tunnel. IPSec is used over GRE to perform encryption of the entire GRE packet (including the GRE header). All authentication and encryption is completed as negotiated within the IKE parameters. IPSec over GRE can be used to encrypt routing protocols because GRE supports multiple protocols.

This allows for resiliency because the routing protocols can detect an interruption of service and reroute the traffic via a backup GRE tunnel. The advantage of GRE is that it enables you to tunnel non-IP, multicast, and broadcast traffic across IPSec tunnels.

- **IPSec with GRE over Frame Relay**—IPSec with GRE over a Frame Relay uses the relay as the hub for each VPN connection. Each spoke acts as both the VPN endpoint and the Frame Relay endpoint.

Router MC Integration with CiscoWorks Common Services

CiscoWorks common services provide the core server-side components required to facilitate communication with the Router MC. Although many of the core administrative functions are not performed within the Router MC, many are performed within CiscoWorks. The tasks performed by CiscoWorks common services include the following:

- Data backup and restoration
- Integration with other CiscoWorks packages such as Cisco Secure Access Control Server
- Database administration and service control
- Logging of administration tasks
- License tracking

Installation and Login to Router MC

The Router MC is installed on the CiscoWorks 2000 server from the Router MC CD-ROM. If you are installing the Router MC on a Windows server, you can use the Installation Wizard and follow the default settings. The Router MC defaults to the CiscoWorks common services folder (C:\Program Files\CSCOpx\) and automatically creates its database as part of the installation process. The Installation Wizard will show an Installation Complete window upon successful installation, prompting you to click **Finish** and restart the system.

After you have installed the Router MC and restarted your server, verify connectivity with the Router MC from the client. On the client system, open the browser and select http://CiscoWorksServer:1741. You must use either the correct DNS name for the server or the correct IP address. If you are unable to connect to the server and have local access to the system, attempt to connect to the server using the loopback address http://127.0.0.1:1741.

Figure 20-3 shows the logon screen for CiscoWorks 2000. The default username is admin and the default password is admin after the initial installation is complete.

Figure 20-3 *CiscoWorks 2000 Logon Screen*

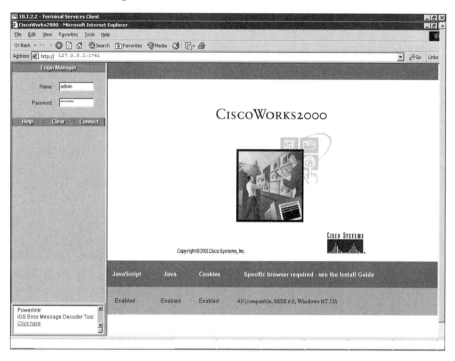

After you have successfully completed the login, the first action you should take is to add a CiscoWorks user. This task is completed by selecting the following drop-down boxes in the left frame of CiscoWorks 2000:

- Server Configuration
- Setup
- Security
- Add Users

After the Add User box opens, you need to complete the following entries:

- **User Name**—This is the name you have selected for the user.
- **Local Password**—The password assigned to the user.
- **Confirm Password**—Password confirmation.

- **E-Mail**—E-mail address for the user. (This is an optional field unless you have selected "approve" as an authorization field.)
- **CCO Login Name**—If the user has a CCO login ID, you would want to list it here. (This is an optional field.)
- **CCO Password**—The password that accompanies the CCO login ID. (This is an optional field.)
- **Proxy Login**—If you must connect to a proxy server on the network, enter the username for that connection here. (This is an optional field.)
- **Proxy Password**—This field is for the password associated with the proxy server connection. (This is an optional field.)
- **Confirm Password**—Password confirmation.

  You must then select authorization privileges for the user. The following authorization options are available:

  — **Help Desk**—This is a read-only account for viewing devices, device groups, and the entire scope of a VPN.

  — **Approver**—This account can review policy changes and accept or reject any changes or deployment jobs.

  — **Network Operator**—The network operator can create and submit jobs but cannot make inventory changes. All network operator deployment jobs must be approved by an approver.

  — **System Administrator**—The system administrator can perform administrative tasks on the CiscoWorks server and Router MC. This includes making changes to the device hierarchy and any administrative changes.

  — **Network Administrator**—The network administrator can perform all tasks on the CiscoWorks server and Router MC.

NOTE It is possible to assign more than one authorization role to a single user

- **Select Add**—After configuring all the user parameters, you must click the Add button to save that user account to the database.

NOTE It is also possible to control user permissions with the Cisco Secure Access Control Server. For further information see the document "Using Management Center for VPN" available from Cisco.com.

Connecting to the Router MC

The Router MC is accessed by selecting the following items as they drop down in the left frame of the CiscoWorks 2000 window:

- VPN Security Management Solution
- Management Center
- VPN Routers

This will bring up a Security Alert window. At this point, accept the security certificate. The Router MC will open in a separate window. You may want to minimize the CiscoWorks window to avoid confusion.

Router MC Workflow

After connecting to the Router MC, you will want to begin your VPN router configurations. The workflow for this task is as follows:

1. **Create the activity.** As discussed earlier in this chapter, the activity is defined as the virtual context, in which tasks are performed. You must create the activity to create the devices, groups, and tasks that you want to perform. At this point, the activity is in "editable" status and can be changed by any other user who has the correct permissions. If an activity has been created, any user may open or close that activity.

2. **Create device groups.** Defining device groups is the step that requires the greatest amount of planning. All devices are grouped logically to facilitate efficient administration. It is very important that your devices be grouped in a logical manner to minimize confusion.

3. **Import devices.** If you already have devices deployed, it is possible to import the device information to reduce the manual data entry required to configure the Router MC for each device.

4. **Define the VPN or firewall settings.** VPN settings include the definition of internal interfaces and networks for the hub-and-spoke segments. Spoke segments must define the VPN interface and must be assigned to a specific hub. Failover, routing, and fragmentation are also defined within the VPN settings.

5. **Configure access rules.** Access rules are used to define the router security policy. You can define a rule as either a mandatory or default rule. And you must define the standard parameters for any ACL to include the following:

    —Source

    —Destination

    —Services

    —Action

—Enable/disable rule

6. **Define the IKE policy.** The IKE policy defines the parameters used for the IKE negotiation and authentication of SA peers. These parameters include the encryption algorithm, hash algorithm, authentication method, Diffie-Hellman group, and key lifetime for each connection.

7. **Define the tunnel policy.** The tunnel policies define the authentication and encryption algorithms used for the VPN connection. Tunnel policies are defined from the spoke to the hub.

8. **Define translation rules.** NAT and address pools (if applicable) can be defined for each connection.

9. **Approve the activity.** After the preceding tasks are completed, double-check your work and approve the activity. Remember that you cannot create a deployment job until the activity has been approved. An activity can be "submitted" for approval. This places the activity in "submitted" status to ensure that the activity cannot be edited and will not be changed until it has been approved, rejected, or deleted.

10. **Create and deploy the job.** After the activity has been approved, you must select the devices or device groups that you want to configure and create the deployment job. At this point, you must select whether to deploy directly to the devices or to write the deployment job to a file. When the deployment job is created, the activity is translated into CLI commands and sent to either the device or the file. The following functions can be performed:

    —**Create a job**—Creating the job requires you to define the specific device or device group to be configured.

    —**Open a job**—A job that has been created but not deployed can be opened. You need to open a job to view the actual CLI commands that will be deployed to the target device(s).

    —**Approve or reject a job**—Some organizations require that a job be approved before it can be deployed. This is done to further ensure that device configurations are thoroughly checked prior to the configuration change taking effect.

    —**Deploy the job**—Deploying the job involves transferring the CLI commands out to the device or a configuration file on the network.

    —**Redeploy a job**—In the unlikely event that a deployment failed, it is possible to redeploy the job.

    —**Rollback**—It is possible to rollback to a previous configuration in the event that the deployment did not produce the desired result. It is possible to complete a rollback of a device with either deployed or redeployed status.

NOTE A rollback is not completed on live devices. The previous configuration is copied to a specific directory.

Table 20-5 lists the job statuses that can occur when performing the deployment or rollback functions listed previously.

Table 20-5 *Router MC Concepts*

Generating	The job is generating the CLI commands to be pushed out to the target devices(s) or files.
Generated	The CLI commands have been completed and are ready for deployment.
Rejected	The job and its configuration have been rejected. No actions can be performed on a rejected job and the device(s) become available for inclusion in other jobs. It is possible to determine why the job was rejected by viewing the completed CLI configuration.
Deploying	This is the status when the CLI commands are being pushed out to the target device(s) or files.
Deployed	This is the status after successful completion of the job deployment.
Rollback in progress	The previous configuration is being restored to a specific directory.
Rollback complete	The previous device configurations have been restored.
Failed	Deployment to one or more devices in the job have failed. You can determine the cause by viewing the Job Deployment Status page.

Foundation Summary

The "Foundation Summary" section of each chapter lists the most important facts from the chapter. Although this section does not list every fact from the chapter that will be on your exam, a well-prepared candidate should at a minimum know all the details in each "Foundation Summary" section before going to take the exam.

Managing Enterprise VPN Routers

Three tools work together to facilitate the centralized management of Cisco VPN routers, PIX firewalls, Cisco IDSs, and Cisco HIDSs:

- CiscoWorks 2000
- VPN/Security Management Solution (VMS)
- Management Center for VPN (Router MC)

CiscoWorks 2000 or VMS is the required server application to support the Router MC. These applications can run on either Microsoft Windows or Sun Solaris platforms with the appropriate hardware. These applications function as the server in a client/server environment. The client connects to the Router MC via an HTTPS (Secure Sockets Layer) connection and the Router MC communicates with the controlled devices via Secure Shell Protocol (SSH). The Router MC performs four specific functions to assist in simplifying the administration of VPN routers.

1. Deploy VPN configurations to individual devices or device groups.
2. Import router VPN settings directly from the device or from a network configuration file.
3. Support a large enterprise implementation of VPN routers with centralized administration, management, and monitoring.
4. Centralize the configuration of IKE negotiations and VPN tunnel policies for multiple devices that are logically organized.

Table 20-6 outlines the various concepts used by the Router MC.

Table 20-6 *Router MC Concepts*

Term	Definition
Hub-and-spoke topology	The hub router is located at a central location (normally the headquarters), and the spoke routers are located at branch offices.
VPN and firewall policies	Configuration changes are made within the Router MC, translated into CLI commands, and deployed to the target devices or files.
Device hierarchy and inheritance	Devices are grouped for logical administration. Properties from the upper (global) groups are inherited by devices in lower groups. Any changes made to a specific group affect all devices in that group.
Activities	A temporary context within which configuration changes are created and submitted for approval.
Jobs	The preparation and deployment of configuration changes that are initiated within "activities."
Building blocks	Components that are created and can be reused within multiple configurations.
Device import	The ability to pull information from existing devices and import it into a new Router MC.
Upload of existing policies on devices into Router MC	Similar to device import function, this is the ability to import the configuration from an existing device and import it into a new Router MC.
Predefined device groups and policies	Specific objects, groups, and configuration settings are predefined to simplify the configuration of new devices.

The Router MC supports three tunneling technologies:

- IPSec
- IPSec with GRE
- IPSec with GRE over Frame Relay

After accessing CiscoWorks 2000 using a browser and the host DNS name or IP address, you will want to change the default username and password. It is also important to create new user accounts as necessary for each new user who use the CiscoWorks 2000 server and the Router MC.

Table 20-7 defines the five different types of user accounts and their assigned account permissions.

Table 20-7 *User Accounts and Permissions*

Term	Definition
Help Desk	This is a read-only account.
Approver	This account can review policy changes and accept or reject any changes or deployment jobs.
Network Operator	The network operator can create and submit jobs but cannot make inventory changes. All network operator deployment jobs must be approved by an approver.
System Administrator	The system administrator can perform administrative tasks on the CiscoWorks server and Router MC. This includes making changes to the device hierarchy and any administrative changes.
Network Administrator	The network administrator can perform all tasks on the CiscoWorks server and Router MC.

After establishing the SSL connection with the Router MC and properly authenticating, you perform the following functions when configuring your VPN routers:

- Create the activity.
- Create device groups.
- Import devices.
- Define VPN settings.
- Define IKE policies.
- Define tunnel policies.
- Define translation rules.
- Approve the activity.
- Create and deploy the job.

Q&A

As mentioned in the section, "How to Use This Book," in the Introduction to this book, you have two choices for review questions. The questions that follow next give you a bigger challenge than the exam itself by using an open-ended question format. By reviewing now with this more difficult question format, you can exercise your memory better and prove your conceptual and factual knowledge of this chapter. The answers to these questions are found in the appendix.

For more practice with exam-like question formats, including questions using a router simulator and multiple choice questions, use the exam engine on the CD-ROM.

1. If you install CiscoWorks 2000 on any Windows platform, which additional packages are required?
2. What is the significance of configuring the "hub" of the "hub-and-spoke" network to be located at the corporate headquarters?
3. What are some of the general settings when configuring the VPN and firewall policies on the Router MC?
4. What is meant by "device hierarchy and inheritance"?
5. I have just completed deploying a job and it appears that the VPN is having connectivity issues. What steps can I take to repair the damage?
6. What is the method used to capture data about existing devices and send it to the Router MC?
7. What items are predefined in the Router MC?
8. What is the definition of IPSec?
9. What additional functionality do you get by tunneling IPSec with GRE?
10. What is defined within the "tunnel policies"?
11. How long can a job remain open?
12. What should you do if a job deployment doesn't "stick"?
13. What CiscoWorks 2000 account has read-only permissions?

PART VI: Scenarios

Chapter 21   Final Scenarios

This chapter tests your abilities on all of the concepts that you have learned throughout the book so that you will be better prepared for the hands-on questions that you will encounter on the SECUR exam.

CHAPTER 21

Final Scenarios

Your team of consultants has been hired by the MCNS Financial Group. This organization has a medium-sized network with headquarters in New York City and branch offices in Atlanta and Los Angeles. They also have approximately 20 sales personnel who need remote connectivity.

The organization contracted your services after their network was breached and they narrowly averted a public relations nightmare. They currently have all locations connected to the Internet via T1 connections purchased from local Internet service providers. The sales personnel currently dial in directly to the headquarters network.

The organization wants to leverage their existing infrastructure to secure the network. After reviewing the current configuration, you have determined that the following tasks must be completed:

Task 1. Secure the routers at all locations.

   a. Secure administrative access to each router.

   b. Implement AAA for vty access to each router.

   c. Implement SSH (disable telnet access) and restrict access to each router by configuring ACLs.

   d. Disable all unnecessary services on each router.

   e. Implement ACLs for antispoofing purposes.

Task 2. Secure site-to-site connectivity.

   a. Define VPN configuration parameters.

   b. Configure the IKE parameters.

   c. Configure the IPSec parameters.

   d. Create ACLs.

   e. Create and apply crypto maps.

Task 3. Configure CA support.

    a. Configure host name and domain name.

    b. Configure NTP.

    c. Enroll with the CA.

Task 4. Secure remote access.

    a. Implement AAA.

    b. ACLs.

    c. VPN client.

    d. Implement VPNs using CA.

MCNS is negotiating to acquire another organization that consists of five locations and they want to merge the networks and implement a scalable VPN solution. The CIO wants to manage network traffic to secure each location and to ensure employees adhere to the organization's acceptable use policy.

Task 5. Secure the enterprise network.

    a. Implement the Cisco IOS firewall IDS.

    b. Implement authentication proxy.

    c. Implement CBAC.

Task 1: Secure the Routers at All Locations

The first task is to secure the routers for all MCNS locations. This task consists of the following four subtasks:

a. Secure administrative access to each router.

b. Implement AAA for vty access to each router.

c. Implement SSH (disable telnet access) and restrict access to each router by configuring access lists.

d. Disable all unnecessary services on each router.

> **NOTE** All passwords used in this chapter have been selected to correlate with the router location and command function. The passwords are not intended to be the secure passwords discussed in Chapter 2, "Attack Threats Defined and Detailed," but are simplified so that they are more recognizable within the router configuration.

Change All Administrative Access on All the Routers

The first task is to secure all the routers at each location. As part of this task, you replace the weak administrative access passwords on all the site routers with passwords that are relatively strong.

Step 1 Reconfigure the console port user-level password.

- Console password access to New York

```
NewYork(config)#line console 0
NewYork(config-line)#password NY@conaccess
```

- Console password access to Atlanta

```
Atlanta(config)#line console 0
Atlanta(config-line)#password ATL@conaccess
```

- Console password access to Los Angeles

```
LosAngeles(config)#)#line  console 0
LosAngeles(config-line)#)#password LA@conaccess
```

Step 2 Reconfigure all enable secret passwords at all three sites.

- Enable secret password of nYenable on the New York router.

```
NewYork(config)#enable secret nYenable
```

- Enable secret password of ATLenable on the Atlanta router.

```
Atlanta(config)#enable secret ATLenable
```

- Enable secret password of LAenable on the Los Angeles router.

```
LosAngeles(config)#enable secret LAenable
```

Step 3 Reconfigure the vty user-level password at all three sites.

- The vty password access to New York

```
NewYork(config)#line vty 0 4
NewYork(config-line)#password NY$vtyaccess
```

- The vty password access to Atlanta

```
Atlanta(config)#line vty 0 4
Atlanta(config-line)#password ATL$vtyaccess
```

- The vty password access to Los Angeles

```
LosAngeles(config)#)#line vty 0 4
LosAngeles(config-line)#)#password LA$vtyaccess
```

After you change all the administrative access passwords to the routers, encrypt all clear-text passwords using the **service password-encryption** command:

```
NY(config)#service password-encryption
```

Do the same for the Los Angeles and Atlanta routers.

Configure Local Database Authentication Using AAA

By requiring two tokens, a username and a password, rather than just a password, you can make the routers more secure. To do so, configure a local username and password on the router and configure AAA authentication.

Step 1   Configure AAA authentication for console access.

```
NewYork(config)# aaa new-model
NewYork(config)# aaa authentication login con-access local
NewYork(config)# username nyadmin password conxss4NY
NewYork(config)# line con 0
NewYork(Config-line)# login authentication con-access

Atlanta(config)# aaa new-model
Atlanta(config)# aaa authentication login con-access local
Atlanta(config)# username atladmin password conxss4ATL
Atlanta(config)# line con 0
Atlanta(Config-line)# login authentication con-access

LosAngeles(config)#)# aaa new-model
LosAngeles(config)#)# aaa authentication login con-access local
LosAngeles(config)#)# username laadmin password conxss4LA
LosAngeles(config)#)# line con 0
LosAngeles(config)#-line)# login authentication con-access
```

Step 2   Configure AAA authentication for vty access.

```
NewYork(config)# aaa authentication login vty-access local
NewYork(config)# username nyRmtadmin password vtyxss4NY
NewYork(config)# line vty 0 4
NewYork(config-line)# login authentication vty-access

Atlanta(config)# aaa authentication login vty-access local
Atlanta(config)# username atlRmtadmin password vtyxss4ATL
Atlanta(config)# line vty 0
Atlanta(config-line)# login authentication vty-access

LosAngeles(config)#)# aaa authentication login vty-access local
LosAngeles(config)#)# username laRmtadmin password vtyxss4LA
LosAngeles(config)#)# line vty 0 4
LosAngeles(config)#-line)# login authentication vty-access
```

Configure a Secure Method for Remote Access of the Routers

The current use of telnet to remotely access the routers is not a secure method of access. Configure SSH and disable telnet. To enable SSH support on the routers, follow these four steps:

1. Verify that you have a host name
2. Configure the router DNS domain.
3. Generate the SSH key to be used.
4. Enable SSH transport support for the vtys.

Each individual step is discussed below.

Step 1 Verify the router host name.

You can verify that the router has a host name configured by looking at the command prompt in any configuration mode. In this case, each router is named after its respective location.

```
NewYork#
Atlanta#
LosAngeles#
```

Step 2 Configure the router DNS domain.

```
NewYork(config)#ip domain-name example-secur.com
Atlanta(config)#ip domain-name example-secur.com
LosAngeles(config)#)#ip domain-name example-secur.com
```

Step 3 Generate the SSH key.

```
NewYork(config)#crypto key generate rsa
NewYork(config)#ip ssh time-out 60
NewYork(config)#ip ssh authentication-retries 3

Atlanta(config)#crypto key generate rsa
Atlanta(config)#ip ssh time-out 60
Atlanta(config)#ip ssh authentication-retries 3

LosAngeles(config)#)#crypto key generate rsa
LosAngeles(config)#)#ip ssh time-out 60
LosAngeles(config)#)#ip ssh authentication-retries 3
```

Step 4 Enable SSH transport support for the vtys.

```
NewYork(config)#line vty 0 4
NewYork(config-line)#transport input SSH

Atlanta(config)#line vty 0 4
Atlanta(config-line)#transport input SSH

LosAngeles(config)#)#line vty 0 4
LosAngeles(config)#transport input SSH
```

Disable Unnecessary Services

Ensuring that all services that are not required on the network are disabled reduces the vulnerability of the routers to security breaches. Disabling the HTTP service greatly reduces exposure of the router to threats on a commonly used port (TCP port 80). Disabling small servers for UDP and TCP protects against Smurf attacks and IP spoofing. The following services on all three routers are turned off:

- Disable the IP HTTP server.
- Disable Cisco Discovery Protocol on all externally facing interfaces.
- Disable the finger service.
- Disable UDP and TCP minor services (small servers).

- Disable directed broadcasts.
- Disable proxy ARP.
- Disable small servers service.

The following configuration for each router shows the selected services disabled.

- New York router

```
NewYork(config)#no ip http server
NewYork(config-if)#no ip directed-broadcast
NewYork(config)#no service tcp-small-servers
NewYork(config)#no service udp-small-servers
NewYork(config)#no cdp run
NewYork(config-if)#no proxy-arp
```

- Atlanta router

```
Atlanta(config)#no ip http server
Atlanta(config-if)#no ip directed-broadcast
Atlanta(config)#no service tcp-small-servers
Atlanta(config)#no service udp-small-servers
Atlanta(config)#no cdp run
Atlanta(config-if)#no proxy-arp
```

- Los Angeles router

```
LosAngeles(config)#no ip http server
LosAngeles(config-if)#no ip directed-broadcast
LosAngeles(config)#no service tcp-small-servers
LosAngeles(config)#no service udp-small-servers
LosAngeles(config)#no cdp run
LosAngeles(config-if)#no proxy-arp
```

Implement ACLs for Antispoofing Purposes

Add antispoofing protection by denying traffic with a source address matching a host on the Ethernet interface for each site (RFC 2827, RFC 3330).

> **NOTE** You would need to configure RFC 1918 in a production network. This scenario uses the 10.x.x.x and 192.168.x.x, and therefore RFC 1918 has not been implemented

- New York router

```
NewYork(config)# access-list 107 permit ip 10.10.30.0 0.0.0.255 any
NewYork(config)# access-list 107 permit ip 10.10.20.0 0.0.0.255 any
NewYork(config)# access-list 107 deny ip 10.10.10.0 0.0.0.255 any
NewYork(config)# access-list 107 deny ip 172.16.0.0 0.15.255.255 any
NewYork(config)# access-list 107 deny ip 127.0.0.0 0.255.255.255 any
NewYork(config)# access-list 107 deny ip 224.0.0.0 31.255.255.255 any
NewYork(config)# access-list 107 deny ip host 255.255.255.255 any
NewYork(config)# access-list 107 deny ip any any log
NewYork(config)# interface serial 0
NewYork(config-if)# ip access-group 107 in
```

- Atlanta router

```
Atlanta(config)#access-list 107 permit ip 10.10.10.0 0.0.0.255 any
Atlanta(config)#access-list 107 permit ip 10.10.20.0 0.0.0.255 any
Atlanta(config)#access-list 107 deny ip 10.10.30.0 0.0.0.255 any
Atlanta(config)#access-list 107 deny ip 172.16.0.0 0.15.255.255 any
Atlanta(config)#access-list 107 deny ip 127.0.0.0 0.255.255.255 any
Atlanta(config)#access-list 107 deny ip 224.0.0.0 31.255.255.255 any
Atlanta(config)#access-list 107 deny ip host 255.255.255.255 any
Atlanta(config)#access-list 107 deny ip any any log
Atlanta(config)#interface serial  0
Atlanta(config-if)#ip access-group 107 in
```

- Los Angeles router

```
LosAngeles(config)# access-list 107 permit ip 10.10.10.0 0.0.0.255 any
LosAngeles(config)# access-list 107 permit ip 10.10.20.0 0.0.0.255 any
LosAngeles(config)# access-list 107 deny ip 10.10.20.0 0.0.0.255 any
LosAngeles(config)# access-list 107 deny ip 172.16.0.0 0.15.255.255 any
LosAngeles(config)# access-list 107 deny ip 127.0.0.0 0.255.255.255 any
LosAngeles(config)# access-list 107 deny ip 224.0.0.0 31.255.255.255 any
LosAngeles(config)# access-list 107 deny ip host 255.255.255.255 any
LosAngeles(config)# access-list 107 deny ip any any log
LosAngeles(config)# interface serial  0
LosAngeles(config-if)# ip access-group 107 in
```

Task 2: Secure Site-to-Site Connectivity

The CIO wants to ensure that all corporate communication among the three locations is secured. Because the locations are interconnected via the Internet, you determine that the best possible solution is to configure a full-mesh VPN connection interconnecting all the sites. This task consists of the following five subtasks:

a. Define VPN configuration parameters.

b. Configure the IKE parameters.

c. Configure the IPSec parameters.

d. Create ACLs.

e. Create and apply crypto maps.

Define VPN Configuration Parameters

Now that you have selected the method for securing communications among the three corporate locations, the next step is to define the VPN parameters. Before you can configure the VPN, you must first determine which parameters are to be used for each connection. Remember that Chapter 17, "Building a VPN Using IPSec," emphasized the importance of completely planning your VPN connectivity before you begin the implementation (because of the complexity of the configuration and zero margin for error). Figure 21-1 depicts the current addressing structure for each location of the organization.

Figure 21-1 *MCNS Financial Group Site Addresses*

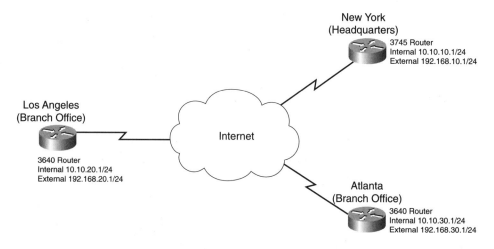

For this series of connections, you have selected the following configuration options:

- **IKE parameters**

    This information is used to configure your IKE phase 1 negotiation and establish the security association:

    —**Key distribution method**—ISAKMP

    —**Peer authentication**—Preshared key (abc123)

    > **NOTE** It is not recommended that you use the same preshared key for multiple locations, although it must be used on both sides of the connection. The key abc123 is used on all locations to simplify the router configurations and make the key recognizable in the configuration for this exercise only.

    —**Identify the ISAKMP peer**—New York, Los Angeles, and Atlanta (full-mesh VPN)

    —**Encryption algorithm**—3DES

    —**Hash algorithm**—MD5

    —**Diffie-Hellman group**—2

    —**SA lifetime**—2400 seconds

- **IPSec parameters**

   This information is used to configure your transform sets, SA lifetime, and to create crypto ACLs and crypto maps:

   — **The protocols and algorithms used in the address transform** — ESP with 3DES and ESP with MD5 (hmac variant)

   — **The IPSec SA lifetime** — 1800 seconds

   — **The protocols permitted through the VPN tunnel (interesting traffic, crypto ACL)** — All traffic destined for any other corporate entity should be encrypted. Traffic from any location to any noncorporate entity should not be encrypted.

   — **The external IP address of the IPSec peer**

   — **New York** — 192.168.30.1 (Atlanta) 192.168.20.1 (Los Angeles)

   — **Atlanta** — 192.168.10.1 (New York) 192.168.20.1 (Los Angeles)

   — **Los Angeles** — 192.168.10.1 (New York) 192.168.30.1 (Atlanta)

   — **Key exchange method** — ISAKMP

Configure the IKE Parameters

Now that the configuration options for each location have been selected, it's time to begin configuring each router. The first step is to verify connectivity between each location. The simplest way to confirm connectivity is to ping the peer router. You must also verify that any "upstream" devices are not filtering the traffic that is required to build the VPN. Having verified connectivity, you now begin to configure the routers at each location. You should begin by configuring IKE on each router. There are several steps required to configure IKE.

Step 1   Verify the IKE is enabled on the router.

By default, IKE is enabled on the router but the time it takes to run the enable command can be much less than the time required to troubleshoot the connection just to discover that IKE had been disabled before you began configuring the router for this VPN connection. If this is the first VPN configuration for this router, you may want to ensure the IKE is enabled by using the **crypto isakmp enable** command.

```
NewYork(config)#crypto isakmp enable
Atlanta(config)#crypto isakmp enable
LosAngeles(config)#crypto isakmp enable
```

Step 2 Configure IKE on the router.

A series of commands defines the IKE parameters on the router:

The command **crypto isakmp policy 100** configures ISAKMP as your key distribution method, establishes a policy "priority" of 100, and puts you in the config-isakmp mode.

The command **authentication pre-share** defines your peer authentication method as preshared key. (The key and peer are configured later.)

The **encryption** command identifies the encryption algorithm to be used for phase 1 of the IKE negotiation. Encryption ensures the confidentiality of the data.

The command **hash** identifies the hash algorithm. The hash ensures the integrity of the data.

The command **group** defines your Diffie-Hellman key exchange group

The **lifetime** command defines the security association lifetime (the time between key exchanges). This line is not required if you intend to use a lifetime of 86400 because it is the default setting. It is, however, a good habit to add all the configuration parameters just to ensure that they are correct.

- Configure IKE on the New York router.

```
NewYork(config)#crypto isakmp policy 100
NewYork(config-isakmp)#authentication pre-share
NewYork(config-isakmp)#encryption 3des
NewYork(config-isakmp)#hash md5
NewYork(config-isakmp)#group 2
NewYork(config-isakmp)#lifetime 2400
```

- Configure IKE on the Atlanta router.

```
Atlanta(config)#crypto isakmp policy 100
Atlanta(config-isakmp)#authentication pre-share
Atlanta(config-isakmp)#encryption 3des
Atlanta(config-isakmp)#hash md5
Atlanta(config-isakmp)#group 2
Atlanta(config-isakmp)#lifetime 2400
```

- Configure IKE on the Los Angeles router.

```
LosAngeles(config)#crypto isakmp policy 100
LosAngeles(config-isakmp)#authentication pre-share
LosAngeles(config-isakmp)#encryption 3des
LosAngeles(config-isakmp)#hash md5
LosAngeles(config-isakmp)#group 2
LosAngeles(config-isakmp)#lifetime 2400
```

Step 3 Configure the preshared key and SA peer on the router.

Having defined the preceding IKE parameters, it is now time to configure the preshared key and SA peer. The command for configuring the preshared key is **crypto isakmp key** *key-string* **address** *peer-address-and-mask*.

- Configure the shared key and SA peer on the New York router.

  ```
  NewYork(config)#crypto isakmp key abc123 address 192.168.20.1
  NewYork(config)#crypto isakmp key abc123 address 192.168.30.1
  ```

- Configure the shared key and SA peer on the Atlanta router.

  ```
  Atlanta(config)#crypto isakmp key abc123 address 192.168.10.1
  Atlanta(config)#crypto isakmp key abc123 address 192.168.30.1
  ```

- Configure the shared key and SA peer on the Los Angeles router.

  ```
  LosAngeles(config)#crypto isakmp key abc123 address 192.168.10.1
  LosAngeles(config)#crypto isakmp key abc123 address 192.168.20.1
  ```

Configure the IPSec Parameters

Remember that IKE establishes the secure connection used to negotiate the IPSec SA. You must correctly configure the IPSec parameters for the VPN to work. For IPSec, you must configure multiple parameters. This section deals with the configuration of the IPSec transform sets and IPSec SA lifetimes. The **crypto ipsec transform-set** command is used to create the transform sets, and the **crypto ipsec security-association lifetime** command is used to define the IPSec SA lifetime. Because there are three corporate locations, you must configure each router to establish a connection with the other two locations.

- Configure the IPSec transform sets on the New York router.

  ```
  NewYork(config)#crypto ipsec transform-set NY-to-ATL esp-3des esp-md5-hmac
  NewYork(config)#crypto ipsec transform-set NY-to-LA esp-3des esp-md5-hmac
  ```

- Configure the IPSec transform sets on the Atlanta router.

  ```
  Atlanta(config)#crypto ipsec transform-set ATL-to-NY esp-3des esp-md5-hmac
  Atlanta(config)#crypto ipsec transform-set ATL-to-LA esp-3des esp-md5-hmac
  ```

- Configure the IPSec transform sets on the Los Angeles router.

  ```
  LosAngeles(config)#crypto ipsec transform-set LA-to-NY esp-3des esp-md5-hmac
  LosAngeles(config)#crypto ipsec transform-set LA-to-ATL esp-3des esp-md5-hmac
  ```

- Configure the IPSec SA lifetime on the New York router.

  ```
  NewYork(config)#crypto ipsec security-association lifetime seconds 1800
  ```

- Configure the IPSec SA lifetime on the Atlanta router.

  ```
  Atlanta(config)#crypto ipsec security-association lifetime seconds 1800
  ```

- Configure the IPSec SA lifetime on the Los Angeles router.

  ```
  Los Angeles(config)#crypto ipsec security-association lifetime seconds 1800
  ```

Configure ACLs

Crypto ACLs are used to identify interesting traffic to the router. *Interesting traffic* is traffic that must be encrypted when leaving the router or traffic that must be encrypted when it arrives at the router (from the peer). Obviously the router encrypts the outbound interesting traffic en route to the peer. If the router receives traffic from the peer that should be encrypted but is not, the traffic is dropped. The configuration for this enterprise network is referred to as a *full-mesh VPN* because all traffic among the three locations is encrypted. Each router must be configured to encrypt traffic destined for the other two peers. The **access-list** command enables you to create the necessary ACLs for these connections.

> **NOTE** The ACLs do not require the same ACL number, although it simplifies troubleshooting of VPN connections if both peers have very similar configuration settings.

- Configure the crypto ACLs on the New York router.

    ```
    NewYork(config)#access-list 110 permit ip 10.10.10.0 0.0.0.255 10.10.20.0 0.0.0.255
    NewYork(config)#access-list 120 permit ip 10.10.10.0 0.0.0.255 10.10.30.0 0.0.0.255
    ```

- Configure the crypto ACLs on the Atlanta router.

    ```
    Atlanta(config)#access-list 120 permit ip 10.10.30.0 0.0.0.255 10.10.10.0 0.0.0.255
    Atlanta(config)#access-list 130 permit ip 10.10.30.0 0.0.0.255 10.10.20.0 0.0.0.255
    ```

- Configure the crypto ACLs on the Los Angeles router.

    ```
    LosAngeles(config)#access-list 110 permit ip 10.10.20.0 0.0.0.255 10.10.10.0
       0.0.0.255
    LosAngeles(config)#access-list 130 permit ip 10.10.20.0 0.0.0.255 10.10.30.0
       0.0.0.255
    ```

Create and Apply Crypto Maps

The crypto map is used to apply the ACLs, define the addresses for the local and remote peers, and define how the IPSec SA is established and maintained. Each crypto map is given a sequence number and a name. For this exercise, the name crypto-map is used after the peer location.

- Configure the crypto maps on the New York router.

    ```
    NewYork(config)#crypto map MCNS 10 ipsec-isakmp
    NewYork(config)#match address 110
    NewYork(config)#set peer 192.168.20.1
    NewYork(config)#set pfs group2
    NewYork(config)#set transform-set NY-to-LA
    NewYork(config)#set security-association lifetime seconds 1800
    NewYork(config)#crypto map MCNS 20 ipsec-isakmp
    ```

```
NewYork(config)#match address 120
NewYork(config)#set peer 192.168.30.1
NewYork(config)#set pfs group2
NewYork(config)#set transform-set NY-to-ATL
NewYork(config)#set security-association lifetime seconds 1800
NewYork(config)#interface serial0
NewYork(config-if)#crypto-map MCNS
```

- Configure the crypto maps on the Atlanta router.

```
Atlanta(config)#crypto map MCNS 10 ipsec-isakmp
Atlanta(config)#match address 120
Atlanta(config)#set peer 192.168.10.1
Atlanta(config)#set pfs group2
Atlanta(config)#set transform-set ATL-to-NY
Atlanta(config)#set security-association lifetime seconds 1800
Atlanta(config)#crypto map MCNS 20 ipsec-isakmp
Atlanta(config)#match address 130
Atlanta(config)#set peer 192.168.20.1
Atlanta(config)#set pfs group2
Atlanta(config)#set transform-set ATL-to-LA
Atlanta(config)#set security-association lifetime seconds 1800
Atlanta(config)#interface serial0
Atlanta(config-if)#crypto-map MCNS
```

- Configure the crypto maps on the Los Angeles router.

```
LosAngeles(config)#crypto map MCNS 10 ipsec-isakmp
LosAngeles(config)#match address 110
LosAngeles(config)#set peer 192.168.10.1
LosAngeles(config)#set pfs group2
LosAngeles(config)#set transform-set LA-to-NY
LosAngeles(config)#set security-association lifetime seconds 1800
LosAngeles(config)#crypto map MCNS 20 ipsec-isakmp
LosAngeles(config)#match address 130
LosAngeles(config)#set peer 192.168.30.1
LosAngeles(config)#set pfs group2
LosAngeles(config)#set transform-set LA-to-ATL
LosAngeles(config)#set security-association lifetime seconds 1800
LosAngeles(config)#interface serial0
LosAngeles(config)#crypto-map MCNS
```

MCNS is currently negotiating to acquire another organization that consists of 15 locations. The CIO wants to implement a certificate server to ensure that their VPN solution is able to scale with company growth. The CA is an Entrust CA server and is hosted on the Internet at 192.168.242.42. The same organization that hosts the CA server is also hosting an NTP server at 192.168.242.47. All MCNS border routers are configured to pull time from this NTP server. Figure 21-2 shows the current addressing structure for each location of the organization along with the location of the CA server. For the moment you are just to enroll all locations with the CA. You will complete the migration of the VPNs if and when MCNS completes the acquisition of the new organization.

Figure 21-2 *MCNS and CA Server*

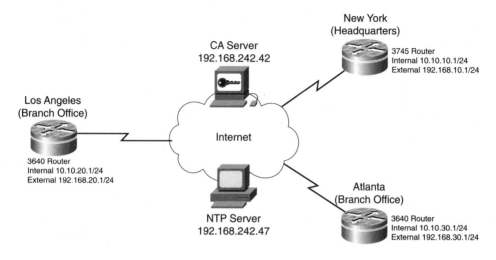

Task 3: Configure CA Support

Only a few steps are required to configure the router for CA support. Configure the host name and domain name for the router and configure time (or NTP). NTP is the better alternative because it ensures that all routers maintain the correct, synchronized time. This task consists of the following subtasks:

a. Configure host name and domain name.

b. Configure NTP.

c. Enroll with the CA.

Configure Host Name and Domain Name

Configure each of the routers to connect with the CA. You must first configure the domain name on the router, define the CA, and generate the RSA keys.

- Configure CA support on the New York router.

```
NewYork(config)#ip domain-name example-secur.com
NewYork(config)#ip host CA-Server 192.168.242.42
NewYork(config)#crypto key generate rsa 1024
NewYork(config)#crypto ca identity CA_Server
NewYork(cfg-ca-id)#enrollment mode ra
NewYork(cfg-ca-id)#enrollment url http://CA-Server/certsrv/mscep/mscep.dll
NewYork(cfg-ca-id)#crl optional
NewYork(cfg-ca-id)#Ctrl Z
```

```
NewYork#write memory
NewYork#configure terminal
NewYork(config)#crypto ca authenticate CA-Server
```

You receive the following response:

```
Certificate has the following attributes:
Fingerprint: 8547FECA ABAC4C7C 77E5A11 6A6A9951
% Do you accept this certificate? [yes/no]: y
```

- Configure CA support on the Atlanta router.

```
Atlanta(config)# ip domain-name example-secur.com
Atlanta(config)# ip host CA-Server 192.168.242.42
Atlanta(config)# crypto key generate rsa 1024
Atlanta(config)#crypto ca identity CA_Server
Atlanta(cfg-ca-id)#enrollment mode ra
Atlanta(cfg-ca-id)#enrollment url http://CA-Server/certsrv/mscep/mscep.dll
Atlanta(cfg-ca-id)#crl optional
Atlanta(cfg-ca-id)#Ctrl Z
Atlanta#write memory
Atlanta#configure terminal
Atlanta(config)#crypto ca authenticate CA-Server
```

You receive the following response:

```
Certificate has the following attributes:
Fingerprint: 145DD254 AAB54ABA 7A85D54A1 D2DB22D54
% Do you accept this certificate? [yes/no]: y
```

- Configure CA support lists on the Los Angeles router.

```
LosAngeles(config)# ip domain-name example-secur.com
LosAngeles(config)# ip host CA-Server 192.168.242.42
LosAngeles(config)# crypto key generate rsa 1024
LosAngeles(config)#crypto ca identity CA_Server
LosAngeles(cfg-ca-id)#enrollment mode ra
LosAngeles(cfg-ca-id)#enrollment url http://CA-Server/certsrv/mscep/mscep.dll
LosAngeles(cfg-ca-id)#crl optional
LosAngeles(cfg-ca-id)#Ctrl Z
LosAngeles#write memory
LosAngeles#configure terminal
LosAngeles(config)#crypto ca authenticate CA-Server
```

You receive the following response:

```
Certificate has the following attributes:
Fingerprint: BC20A268 E41F584C FFF589A6 AB15A47E
% Do you accept this certificate? [yes/no]: y
```

Configure NTP

Configuring NTP on the routers ensures that all routers maintain time from the same source. This can greatly assist you with troubleshooting because activities that occur at different locations have the same time in both system log files. In addition, the correct time is necessary to ensure that there is no time difference between the routers and the CA server. In this exercise, you to use a single NTP source; however, you should also use a backup NTP source.

- Configure NTP on the New York router.

    ```
    NewYork(config)#clock timezone EST -5
    NewYork(config)# ntp server 192.168.242.47
    NewYork(config)# ntp broadcast client
    ```

- Configure NTP on the Atlanta router.

    ```
    Atlanta(config)# clock timezone EST -5
    Atlanta(config)# ntp server 192.168.242.47
    Atlanta(config)# ntp broadcast client
    ```

- Configure NTP lists on the Los Angeles router.

    ```
    LosAngeles(config)# clock timezone PST -8
    LosAngeles(config)# ntp server 192.168.242.47
    LosAngeles(config)# ntp broadcast client
    ```

Enroll with the CA

For the moment the perimeter routers only need to enroll with the CA. The VPN connections may be converted over to the CA solution after the company merger is completed and the networks converge.

- Enroll the New York router.

    ```
    NewYork(config)#crypto ca enroll CA_Server
    %Start certificate enrollment . .
    %Create a challenge password. You will need to verbally provide
      this password to the CA Administrator in order to revoke your certificate.
      For security reasons your password will not be saved on the configuration.
      Please make a note of it.
    Password: New-York
    Re-enter password: New-York

    %The subject name in the certificate will be: NewYork.secur-example.com
    %Include the router serial number in the subject name? [yes/no}: n
    %Include an IP address in the subject name? [yes/no]: n
    Request certificate from CA? [yes/no]: y
    %Certificate request sent to Certificate Authority
    %The certificate request fingerprint will be displayed.
    %The 'show crypto ca certificate' command will also show the fingerprint.

    NewYork(config)#exit
    NewYork# write memory
    ```

- Enroll the Atlanta router.

    ```
    Atlanta(config)#crypto ca enroll CA_Server
    %Start certificate enrollment . .
    %Create a challenge password. You will need to verbally provide
      this password to the CA Administrator in order to revoke your certificate.
      For security reasons your password will not be saved on the configuration.
      Please make a note of it.
    Password: Atlanta
    Re-enter password: Atlanta

    %The subject name in the certificate will be: Atlanta.secur-example.com
    %Include the router serial number in the subject name? [yes/no}: n
    %Include an IP address in the subject name? [yes/no]: n
    ```

```
                    Request certificate from CA? [yes/no]: y
                    %Certificate request sent to Certificate Authority
                    %The certificate request fingerprint will be displayed.
                    %The 'show crypto ca certificate' command will also show the fingerprint.

                    Atlanta(config)#exit
                    Atlanta# write memory
```

- Enroll the Los Angeles router.

```
                    LosAngeles(config)#crypto ca enroll CA_Server
                    %Start certificate enrollment . .
                    %Create a challenge password. You will need to verbally provide
                      this password to the CA Administrator in order to revoke your certificate.
                      For security reasons your password will not be saved on the configuration.
                      Please make a note of it.
                    Password: Los-Angeles
                    Re-enter password: Los-Angeles

                    %The subject name in the certificate will be: LosAngeles.secur-example.com
                    %Include the router serial number in the subject name? [yes/no}: n
                    %Include an IP address in the subject name? [yes/no]: n
                    Request certificate from CA? [yes/no]: y
                    %Certificate request sent to Certificate Authority
                    %The certificate request fingerprint will be displayed.
                    %The 'show crypto ca certificate' command will also show the fingerprint.

                    LosAngeles(config)#exit
                    LosAngeles# write memory
```

Task 4: Secure Remote Access

The corporate office, New York, will serve as the central point where remote salespeople will connect. The following configuration will be added to the New York router. The network segment 192.168.100.0 255.255.255.224 will be used. Dynamic crypto maps are used when you are not completely sure of the configuration of the remote peer. This allows the router to negotiate a connection with the remote access users. This task consists of four subtasks:

a. Implement AAA.

b. Configure ACLs.

c. Install the VPN client on the remote user system.

d. Implement VPNs using CA.

```
                    NewYork(config)#crypto isakmp policy 200
                    NewYork(config-iskamp)#hash md5
                    NewYork(config-iskamp)#authentication pre-share
                    NewYork(config)#crypto isakmp key userkey address 192.168.100.0 0.0.0.31
                    NewYork(config-iskamp)#crypto ipsec transform-set remotepolicy esp-des esp-md5-hmac
                    NewYork(config)#crypto dynamic-map dyna 40
                    NewYork(config-dynamic)#set transform-set remotepolicy
                    NewYork(config)#crypto map remoteusers 40 ipsec-isakmp dynamic dyna
                    NewYork(config)#interface serial 0
                    NewYork(config)#crypto map remoteusers
```

Task 5: Secure the Enterprise Network

The final task is to secure the enterprise network. There are three subtasks:

a. Implement the Cisco IOS firewall IDS.

b. Implement authentication proxy.

c. Implement CBAC.

Implement the Cisco IOS Firewall IDS

Configuring the Cisco IOS firewall IDS as the border router for each location enables you to determine what type of traffic is attempting to access the network. Much of this information can be derived from the Cisco IOS firewall logs; however, the Cisco IOS firewall IDS generates specific alerts and can perform other actions to drop or reset the connection. It is important to establish a network baseline so that you can identify normal traffic and reduce the number of false positive alerts. For this exercise, the Cisco IOS firewall IDS at each location is configured to merely send an alert, and the specific concern in this exercise is traffic coming from 192.168.103.0/24. Before configuring the Cisco IOS firewall IDS, you must first define the configuration parameters:

- **Sensor IP address**—Internal interface IP address for each location
- **Organization name**—MCNS
- **Organization ID**—100
- **Host name**—The router name for each location
- **Host ID**—This is the third octet for each internal interface IP
- **Post office port**—45000

Figure 21-3 depicts the current network configuration for the implementation of the Cisco IOS firewall IDS.

Step 1 Configure the notification type.

Each router must be configured to send alerts to a syslog server.

- Configure notification type on the New York router.
  ```
  NewYork(config)# ip audit notify log
  ```

- Configure notification type on the Atlanta router.
  ```
  Atlanta(config)# ip audit notify log
  ```

- Configure notification type on the Los Angeles router.
  ```
  LosAngeles(config)# ip audit notify log
  ```

Task 5: Secure the Enterprise Network   421

Figure 21-3 *MCNS Network Configuration of IDS*

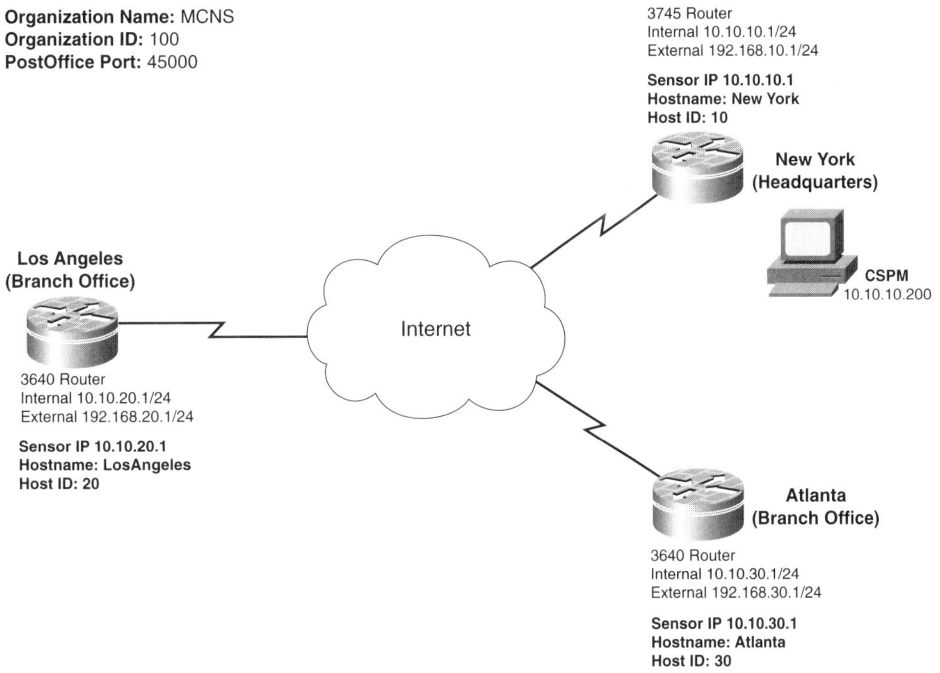

Organization Name: MCNS
Organization ID: 100
PostOffice Port: 45000

3745 Router
Internal 10.10.10.1/24
External 192.168.10.1/24

Sensor IP 10.10.10.1
Hostname: New York
Host ID: 10

New York
(Headquarters)

CSPM
10.10.10.200

Los Angeles
(Branch Office)

3640 Router
Internal 10.10.20.1/24
External 192.168.20.1/24

Sensor IP 10.10.20.1
Hostname: LosAngeles
Host ID: 20

Internet

Atlanta
(Branch Office)

3640 Router
Internal 10.10.30.1/24
External 192.168.30.1/24

Sensor IP 10.10.30.1
Hostname: Atlanta
Host ID: 30

Step 2   Configure the post office parameters.

Each router must be configured to communicate with centralized management.

- Configure post office parameters on the New York router.

    ```
    NewYork(config)# ip audit po remote hostid 10 orgid 100
       rmtaddress 10.10.10.200 localaddress 10.10.10.1 port 45000 preferences
       50 timeout 10 application logger
    ```

- Configure post office parameters on the Atlanta router.

    ```
    Atlanta(config)# ip audit po remote hostid 30 orgid 100 rmtaddress
       10.10.10.200 localaddress 10.10.30.1 port 45000 preferences
       50 timeout 10 application logger
    ```

- Configure post office parameters on the Los Angeles router.

    ```
    LosAngeles(config)# ip audit po remote hostid 20 orgid 100 rmtaddress
       10.10.10.200 localaddress 10.10.20.1 port 45000 preferences
       50 timeout 10 application logger
    ```

Step 3   Define the protected network.

- Define the protected network on the New York router.

  ```
  NewYork(config)# ip audit protected 10.10.10.1 to 10.10.10.254
  ```

- Define the protected network on the Atlanta router.

  ```
  Atlanta(config)# ip audit protected 10.10.30.1 to 10.10.30.254
  ```

- Define the protected network on the Los Angeles router.

  ```
  LosAngeles(config)# ip audit protected 10.10.20.1 to 10.10.20.254
  ```

Step 4   Define the info and attack actions.

- Define the info and attack actions on the New York router.

  ```
  NewYork(config)# ip audit info action alarm
  NewYork(config)# ip audit attack action alarm
  ```

- Define the info and attack actions on the Atlanta router.

  ```
  Atlanta(config)# ip audit info action alarm
  Atlanta(config)# ip audit attack action alarm
  ```

- Define the info and attack actions on the Los Angeles router.

  ```
  LosAngeles(config)# ip audit info action alarm
  LosAngeles(config)# ip audit attack action alarm
  ```

Step 5   Exclude specific signatures.

- Exclude signatures on the New York router.

  ```
  NewYork(config)#access-list 74 deny 192.168.103.0 0.0.0.255
  NewYork(config)#access-list 74 permit any
  NewYork(config)#ip audit signature 2154 list 74
  NewYork(config)#ip audit signature 3104 list 74
  NewYork(config)#ip audit signature 3152 list 74
  ```

- Exclude signatures on the Atlanta router.

  ```
  Atlanta(config)#access-list 74 deny 192.168.103.0 0.0.0.255
  Atlanta(config)#access-list 74 permit any
  Atlanta(config)#ip audit signature 2154 list 74
  Atlanta(config)#ip audit signature 3104 list 74
  Atlanta(config)#ip audit signature 3152 list 74
  ```

- Exclude signatures on the Los Angeles router.

  ```
  LosAngeles(config)# access-list 74 deny 192.168.103.0 0.0.0.255
  LosAngeles(config)#access-list 74 permit any
  LosAngeles(config)#ip audit signature 2154 list 74
  LosAngeles(config)#ip audit signature 3104 list 74
  LosAngeles (config)#ip audit signature 3152 list 74
  ```

Step 6 Create the audit rule.

- Create the audit rules on the New York router.

  ```
  NewYork(config)#ip audit name NewYork info
  NewYork(config)#ip audit name NewYork attack list 75
  NewYork(config)#access-list 75 deny 10.10.10.0 0.0.0.255
  NewYork(config)#access-list 75 permit any
  ```

- Create the audit rules on the Atlanta router.

  ```
  Atlanta(config)#ip audit name Atlanta info
  Atlanta(config)#ip audit name Atlanta attack list 75
  Atlanta(config)#access-list 75 deny 10.10.30.0 0.0.0.255
  Atlanta(config)#access-list 75 permit any
  ```

- Create the audit rules on the Los Angeles router.

  ```
  LosAngeles(config)#ip audit name LosAngeles info
  LosAngeles(config)#ip audit name LosAngeles attack list 75
  LosAngeles(config)#access-list 75 deny 10.10.20.0 0.0.0.255
  LosAngeles(config)#access-list 75 permit any
  ```

Step 7 Apply the IDS audit rule.

- Apply the IDS audit rule on the New York router.

  ```
  NewYork(config)#interface s0
  NewYork(config-if)#ip audit NewYork in
  ```

- Apply the IDS audit rule on the Atlanta router.

  ```
  Atlanta(config)#interface s0
  Atlanta(config-if)#ip audit Atlanta in
  ```

- Apply the IDS audit rule on the Los Angeles router.

  ```
  LosAngeles(config)#interface s0
  LosAngeles(config-if)#ip audit LosAngeles in
  ```

Implement Authentication Proxy

MCNS maintains a DMZ segment in New York and hosts an application that needs to be available to their business partners. This example configures the Cisco IOS firewall to perform authentication proxy inbound without CBAC or NAT for any source attempting to access this application by the destination address 172.16.10.101. Configuration of the authentication proxy requires the following three steps:

1. Configure AAA.
2. Configure the HTTP server.
3. Configure the authentication proxy.

Figure 21-4 show the location of the AAA server and partner application in New York.

Figure 21-4 *New York Partner Application*

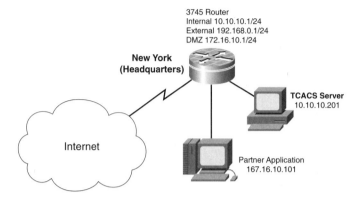

Step 1 Configure AAA.

The Cisco IOS firewall first needs to be configured to communicate with the TACACS+ server.

```
NewYork(config)#aaa new-model
NewYork(config)#aaa group server tacacs+ Partner
NewYork(config)#aaa authentication login default group tacacs+
NewYork(config)#aaa authorization auth-proxy default group Partner
NewYork(config)#tacacs-server host 10.10.10.201
NewYork(config)#tacacs-server key abc123
NewYork(config)#access-list 103 permit tcp host 10.10.10.201 eq
  tacacs host 10.10.10.1
```

Step 2 Configure the HTTP server.

```
NewYork(config)#ip http server
NewYork(config)#ip http authentication aaa
```

Step 3 Configure the authentication proxy.

```
NewYork(config)#access-list 25 deny any
NewYork(config)#ip http access-class 25
NewYork(config)#ip auth-proxy name Partner http
NewYork(config)#interface S0
NewYork(config-if)#ip auth-proxy Partner
```

Implement CBAC

Configure an inspection rule called examineNY, examineATL, and examineLA for the New York, Atlanta, and Los Angeles routers, respectively. Apply the rule on the Ethernet interface so that inbound traffic (which is exiting the network) is inspected; return traffic is only permitted back through the firewall if part of a session, which begins from within the network.

Task 5: Secure the Enterprise Network

- New York router CBAC configuration

    Define the CBAC rule.

    ```
    NewYork(config)#ip inspect name examineNY ftp timeout 3600
    NewYork(config)#ip inspect name examineNY rcmd timeout 3600
    NewYork(config)#ip inspect name examineNY realaudio timeout 3600
    NewYork(config)#ip inspect name examineNY http timeout 3600
    NewYork(config)#ip inspect name examineNY smtp timeout 3600
    NewYork(config)#ip inspect name examineNY tftp timeout 30
    NewYork(config)#ip inspect name examineNY udp timeout 15
    NewYork(config)#ip inspect name examineNY tcp timeout 3600
    NewYork(config)#interface fastethernet0/0
    NewYork(config-if)#ip inspect examineNY in
    ```

- Atlanta router CBAC configuration

    Define the CBAC rule.

    ```
    Atlanta(config)#ip inspect name examineATL ftp timeout 3600
    Atlanta(config)#ip inspect name examineATL rcmd timeout 3600
    Atlanta(config)#ip inspect name examineATL http timeout 3600
    Atlanta(config)#ip inspect name examineATL realaudio timeout 3600
    Atlanta(config)#ip inspect name examineATL smtp timeout 3600
    Atlanta(config)#ip inspect name examineATL tftp timeout 30
    Atlanta(config)#ip inspect name examineATL udp timeout 15
    Atlanta(config)#ip inspect name examineATL tcp timeout 3600
    Atlanta(config)#interface fastethernet0/0
    Atlanta(config-if)#ip inspect examineATL in
    ```

- Los Angeles router CBAC configuration

    Define the CBAC rule.

    ```
    LosAngeles(config)##ip inspect name examineLA ftp timeout 3600
    LosAngeles(config)##ip inspect name examineLA rcmd timeout 3600
    LosAngeles(config)#ip inspect name examineLA http timeout 3600
    LosAngeles(config)#ip inspect name examineLA realaudio timeout 3600
    LosAngeles(config)#ip inspect name examineLA smtp timeout 3600
    LosAngeles(config)#ip inspect name examineLA tftp timeout 30
    LosAngeles(config)#ip inspect name examineLA udp timeout 15
    LosAngeles(config)#ip inspect name examineLA tcp timeout 3600
    LosAngeles(config)#)#interface fastethernet0/0
    LosAngeles(config-if)#ip inspect examineLA in
    ```

APPENDIX

Answers to the "Do I Know This Already?" Quizzes and Q&A Sections

Chapter 1

"Do I Know This Already?" Quiz

1. *a, c, d, e*
2. *e*
3. *a, d*
4. *b, d, e*
5. *a, d*
6. *a, b, e*
7. *True*
8. *b, c, e, f, g, i*
9. *e*
10. *b*
11. *False*

Q&A

1. *Why is consistency important in a network policy?*

   Answer: Consistency is important for two main reasons. First, it may be nearly impossible to enforce something that is not consistently applied. Second, a consistent policy is less open to interpretation. Therefore, there is a greater chance that the goals of the policy are fulfilled.

2. *Why is it so important that management accept the policy?*

Answer: Because management's task is to make the company run, they are ultimately in charge of what initiatives take precedence over other initiatives. Also, because management is tasked with ensuring that employees obey policies, no policy can succeed unless management agrees with that policy.

3. *How often should testing occur?*

Answer: There is no specific time between testing cycles. Because the security wheel is a never-ending process, testing needs to occur after any significant change to the network. In very large organizations, testing can and should be a continuous process. In a very small organization, testing may occur only once per year.

4. *When should monitoring occur?*

Answer: Monitoring should be continuous, with new monitoring added when changes to the network occur.

5. *Why is it necessary to even have a written security policy?*

Answer: Without a written policy, there can be no formalized way of ensuring that the goals for network security are fulfilled. The written plan, among other benefits, enables management and the technical team to gain feedback on their efforts.

6. *Why is it important to specify sanctions for failing to abide by the security policy?*

Answer: To effectively enforce the policy, there must be sanctions for failing to abide by that policy. In the same way that almost all human resources departments have sanctions for unacceptable behavior, the security policy must have sanctions.

7. *Why is it not a security risk to publish the security policy on a public website?*

Answer: The security policy is not a technical document. No IP addresses, specific equipment, or specific techniques should be stated within the document. If the policy is written correctly, distributing the policy is not a security concern. The implementation plan for a section of the policy is where specifics, such as the equipment used or the specific configurations, are stated.

8. *Why is the security policy shown in the center of the security wheel?*

Answer: The security policy is the driving force that causes all four of the steps of the security wheel to occur. It is the policy that dictates the need to secure, test, monitor, and improve.

9. *Why should a policy be implemented globally? Why not just implement it at one site?*

    Answer: Many companies with electronic communications between sites fail to properly secure between these sites. In these cases, a breach at any one site exposes the whole of the corporate network to attacks. Although it is possible to implement specific equipment and configurations at individual sites, only a comprehensive approach to security ensures that the entire corporate network is as secure as possible.

10. *Why is flexibility important in a security policy?*

    Answer: The security policy should be specific enough to define all requirements, but not so inflexible that it does not account for growth within the organization or changes in infrastructure. Keep in mind that the security policy is a living document and should constantly be reviewed and modified as necessary to ensure its relevance for the organization.

11. *What organization published the* Site Security Handbook*?*

    Answer: Internet Engineering Task Force (IETF)

Chapter 2

"Do I Know This Already?" Quiz

1. a, d
2. a
3. a
4. c
5. e
6. d
7. d
8. b
9. c
10. False

Q&A

1. *An application that is supposed to monitor your network and alert you in the event of an outage is being considered by your manager. You begin testing the product and discover that it requires a management connection to every network component (each requiring a password) but maintains these nonencrypted (clear-text) connections. This would require that the system send clear-text passwords to every network component that you want to manage. Would you consider this product for you network and why?*

   Answer: Any product that requires you to send passwords in clear text poses a significant risk. The passwords could be intercepted and used for a variety of different attacks.

2. *How many TCP ports can an can a system communicate over if no ports are blocked and a service is listening on every available port?*

   Answer: It is possible to remotely connect to a computer on any of 65,535 ports.

3. *What are three "self-imposed vulnerabilities"?*

   Answer: There are three main reasons that security attacks can become effective and damage networks: lack of effective policy (policy weakness), configuration weakness, and technology weakness.

4. *Can a system misconfiguration be a security vulnerability.*

   Answer: Yes. A simple misconfiguration can cause severe security issues.

5. *Why would you not want to install security devices using the default settings?*

   Answer: The default settings are the same on most network components when they ship from the factory. If you implement a component and do not change the password, that system could be accessed by anyone who knows the default password for that product. A very common type of attack includes using every default password combination to access a device.

6. *How does NFS make network connections and why can it be difficult to secure?*

   Answer: Because NFS uses a random selection of ports, it can be difficult for an administrator to limit access.

7. *Why is it difficult to determine whether IP traffic is spoofed?*

    Answer: The header and footer on an IP packet can be intercepted and modified without leaving evidence of the change.

8. *What is a structured threat?*

    Answer: A structured thread is an organized effort to breach a specific target.

9. *Which type of threat is more common: structured or unstructured?*

    Answer: Unstructured threats are by far the most common.

10. *Why should your security administrator be well trained and very familiar with the product that she is using?*

    Answer: A poorly trained administrator of a firewall can mistakenly allow too many services to traverse the firewall and allow access to services that expose vulnerabilities and increase the potential success of an attack on the network.

11. *What is the goal of a reconnaissance attack?*

    Answer: The goal of this reconnaissance is to determine the makeup of the targeted computer or network and to search for and map any vulnerabilities.

12. *What is a "vertical scan"?*

    Answer: Scanning the service ports of a single host and requesting different services at each port.

13. *What is a "worm"?*

    Answer: A worm attaches itself to other files or programs and exploits vulnerabilities on networked systems to replicate itself.

14. *What is a DDoS attack?*

    Answer: A DDoS attack is an attack launched from multiple systems against a single target and is intended to interrupt that system or network by overwhelming it with traffic.

Chapter 3

"Do I Know This Already?" Quiz

1. d
2. a, b
3. e
4. e
5. a
6. b
7. a, b
8. b, c

Q&A

1. *Define the term* internetworking.

   Answer: The task of connecting networks so that they can share resources.

2. *How does the use of RFC 1918 addressing on internal networks help prevent attacks that originate from the Internet?*

   Answer: RFC 1918 address space is not routable across the Internet.

3. *What is a major limitation of a statically configured firewall?*

   Answer: It can only protect against "known attacks."

4. *What type of IDS uses a system baseline for acceptable behavior?*

   Answer: Anomaly-based IDS.

5. *What processes enable you to look at events on the network from different views?*

   Answer: Correlation and trending.

6. *What is the goal of the security process?*

   Answer: Constant improvement of the network.

Chapter 4

"Do I Know This Already?" Quiz

1. c
2. b
3. e
4. d
5. a
6. e
7. b
8. b
9. e
10. f

Q&A

1. *You have just started work at a new facility and need to configure an old unused router. Unfortunately you cannot find the current password for the router. What router configuration mode would you need to enter to change the password?*

    Answer: You need to be in the ROM monitor mode to change the password.

2. c, a, b, e, d

3. *What is the best way to ensure that your configuration changes are not lost if the router is rebooted?*

    Answer: Copy the running configuration to the startup configuration.

4. *If it has not been changed using the **prompt** command, what will the prompt for RouterA look like in the global configuration mode?*

    Answer: RouterA(config)#

5. *What is the difference between the* **end** *and the* **exit** *commands?*

Answer: The **end** command returns you to the privileged EXEC mode, and the **exit** command returns you to the global configuration mode.

6. *What command enables you to see the available commands in your current configuration mode?*

Answer: ?

7. *How do you configure CBAC to implement reflexive access lists?*

Answer: Reflexive ACLs cannot be used with CBAC.

8. *What type of cable is required to complete a telnet connection to the router via Ethernet 0/0 interface.*

Answer: The connection is completed via the router's Ethernet interface. This requires that the router be connected to the network using an Ethernet cable (RJ-45).

9. *What type of router management is considered to be the most secure, yet the most difficult to use for enterprise networks? (Explain your answer.)*

Answer: The console connection is considered the most secure because it requires physical access to the router. It can also be the most difficult to maintain in a large enterprise network because the routers may be installed all over the world.

10. *What command generates the key used for SSH on the IOS router?*

Answer: **crypto key generate rsa** [*key-length*]

11. *What Cisco IOS firewall feature enables administrators to configure access to services on nonstandard ports?*

Answer: Port-to-application mapping

12. *What AAA server types can interact with the IOS firewall?*

Answer: TACACS+, RADIUS, Kerberos

13. *How does the Cisco IOS firewall ensure that routing updates are valid?*

Answer: It validated the source by using peer authentication.

Chapter 5

"Do I Know This Already?" Quiz

1. *a, c, d*
2. *c*
3. *c*
4. *b*
5. *a*
6. *a, c, d*
7. *b*
8. *a*
9. *a, b*
10. *c*

Q&A

1. *How many levels of command access does the CLI have?*

    Answer: Cisco IOS Software has two levels of access to commands by default: user EXEC mode (level 1) and privileged EXEC mode (level 15).

2. *What are some of the characteristics of the enable password?*

    Answer: It must contain from 1 to 25 uppercase and lowercase alphanumeric characters. It must not have a number as the first character. It can have leading spaces, but they are ignored. However, intermediate and trailing spaces are recognized. And it can contain the question mark (?) character.

3. *What are the commands associated with privileged level 0?*

    Answer: There are five commands associated with privilege level 0: **disable**, **enable**, **exit**, **help**, and **logout**.

4. *What is the* **banner login** *command used for?*

Answer: The **banner login** command is used for informational messages displayed when the users log in to a router or switch. The banner could inform the users that if they are unauthorized users accessing the device, they could be disconnected immediately or could face legal actions by the owners of the device.

5. *Give one example of telnet vulnerability?*

Answer: Passwords sent over a telnet session are in clear text. This makes it an insecure method for remote access, especially over public networks.

6. *Give two advantages of using SSH for connecting to your device?*

Answer: By using SSH one can mitigate against spoofing, man-in-the-middle attacks, and session hijacking.

7. *What is maximum number of MAC addresses allowed on a port?*

Answer: The total number of MAC addresses on any port cannot exceed 1025

8. *What does the* **service password-encryption** *command do?*

Answer: The **service password-encryption** command stores passwords in an encrypted manner in the router configuration.

9. *What is the advantage of using the* **enable secret** *command over* **enable password** *command?*

Answer: The **enable secret** command provides better security by storing the enable secret password using a nonreversible cryptographic function.

10. *What are the steps required to configure SSH on a Cisco IOS router?*

Answer: The four steps required to enable SSH support on a Cisco IOS router are as follows:

1. Configure the **hostname** command.

2. Configure the DNS domain.

3. Generate the SSH key to be used.

4. Enable SSH transport for vty lines.

Chapter 6

"Do I Know This Already?" Quiz

1. a, c
2. a, b
3. d
4. a
5. c
6. a
7. d
8. a

Q&A

1. *Which port is reserved TACACS+ use?*

   Answer: TCP 49

2. *Why is PAP considered insecure compared to other authentication protocols such CHAP and MS-CHAP?*

   Answer: It sends username and password in clear text.

3. *What type of encryption algorithm does CHAP uses during the three-way handshake?*

   Answer: MD5

4. *Who developed and designed the Kerberos authentication protocol?*

   Answer: Massachusetts Institute of Technology

5. *Give one difference between CHAP and MS-CHAP?*

   Answer: CHAP defines a set of "reason-for failure" codes returned in the failure packet Message field.

6. *Which versions of the TACACS protocol in Cisco IOS Software have officially reached end-of-maintenance?*

    Answer: The TACACS and XTACACS protocols in Cisco IOS Software are officially considered end-of-maintenance and are no longer maintained by Cisco for bug fixes or enhancement

7. *What command is used to disable the console password for a network access server?*

    Answer: The command **no login** is used in the global configuration mode.

8. *Which two popular authentication methods does PPP support?*

    Answer: PAP and CHAP are the two authentication methods that PPP supports.

9. *In the RADIUS security architecture, what is the network access server?*

    Answer: The network access server is the client in the RADIUS security architecture.

Chapter 7

"Do I Know This Already?" Quiz

1. c
2. d
3. b
4. c
5. d
6. b
7. b
8. e
9. b
10. c

Q&A

1. *What command enables AAA on a router/NAS?*

    Answer: **aaa new-model**

2. *Which of the AAA services can be used for billing and auditing?*

   Answer: Accounting

3. *What are the seven types of AAA authorization that are supported on the Cisco IOS Software?*

   Answer: The seven types of AAA authorization are auth-proxy, commands, EXEC, network, reverse access, configuration, and IP mobile

4. *What AAA command would you use to configure authentication for login to an access server?*

   Answer: **aaa authentication login**

5. *Name* two *authorization methods supported by AAA?*

   Answer: TACACS, local, if-authenticated, and RADIUS are all supported by AAA as authorization methods.

6. *What command enables you to troubleshoot a AAA authorization problem?*

   Answer: **debug aaa authorization**

7. *How many authentication methods can you specify in AAA configuration?*

   You can specify up to four authentication methods. The additional methods of authentication are used only if the preceding method returns an error, not if it fails. To specify that the authentication should succeed even if all methods return an error, specify **none** as the final method in the command line.

8. *What is the difference between a FAIL response and an ERROR response in a AAA configuration?*

   Answer: A FAIL response occurs when a user submits an incorrect username and password combination. An ERROR response occurs when the security server fails to respond to an authentication request.

9. *How would you display all the accounting records for actively accounted functions?*

   Answer: **show accounting**

10. *What command disables AAA functionality on your access server?*

    Answer: **no aaa new-model**. This command is done in the global configuration mode.

Chapter 8

"Do I Know This Already?" Quiz

1. a
2. b
3. b
4. a
5. a
6. a, c, d
7. c
8. b

Q&A

1. *What is the command that specifies a TACACS server?*

   Answer: **tacacs-server host**

2. *Give two commands to test and verify your RADIUS configuration?*

   Answer: **debug radius, debug aaa authentication**

3. *What is the purpose of the **tacacs-server key** command?*

   Answer: The **tacacs-server key** command specifies the encryption key that will be used.

4. *What is the purpose of the keyword **local** in the following configuration line?*

   aaa authentication ppp test1 tacacs local

   Answer: Keyword **local** indicates that authentication is attempted using the local database on the router if the TACACS server returns an error.

5. *Is it possible to change the default port used by RADIUS authentication?*

   Answer: Yes. The command **radius-server host** {*hostname|ip address*} {**auth-port** *port-number*} can change the default port 1645.

6. *What is the command to delete the RADIUS server configuration?*

   Answer: **no radius-server host**

7. *What is the command to enable network-level authorization to use a TACACS+ server?*

   Answer: **aaa authorization network tacacs**

8. *Which testing and verifying command used for TACACS+ produces a substantial amount of output?*

   Answer: **debug tacacs events**

9. *What is the default port that is reserved for TACACS?*

   Answer: The default port reserved for TACACS is TCP 49.

10. *Is it possible to have both RADIUS and TACACS configuration on a single router/NAS?*

    Answer: A single router can have both RADIUS and TACACS server configured.

Chapter 9

"Do I Know This Already?" Quiz

1. a
2. a
3. a, b, c
4. d
5. a
6. a, c, d
7. d
8. c
9. c
10. a, b, c

Q&A

1. *Where does the Cisco Secure ACS write its accounting records?*

   Answer: Cisco Secure ACS writes accounting records to a comma-separated value (CSV) log file or ODBC database.

2. *Give one example of the user repository that Cisco Secure ACS supports?*

   Answer: Windows Active Directory, Generic LDAP, Novell NetWare Directory Services, CRYPTOCard token server, SafeWord token server, PassGo token server, RSA SecureID token server, AXENT, LEAP proxy agent, Safeword, ActivCard token server, Vasco token server.

3. *Give one advantage of using Cisco Secure ACS?*

   Answer: Centralized access control and accounting

4. *Give two examples of the password protocols that are supported by Cisco Secure ACS?*

   Answer: Cisco Secure ACS supports many common password protocols including EAP-CHAP, EAP-TLS, LEAP, ARAP, ASCII/PAP, CHAP, and MS-CHAP

5. *Mike is a network administrator at an engineering firm. He would like to restrict access to consultants during the weekend. Can Cisco Secure ACS help Mike?*

   Answer: The Cisco Secure ACS access-restrictions feature enables Mike to deny logins based on day of week.

6. *What are the core services of Cisco Secure ACS 3.0?*

   Answer: CSAdmin, CSAuth, CSDBSync, CSLog, CSMon

7. *What is the function of CSAdmin?*

   Answer: CSAdmin is the service that provides the HTML interface for Cisco Secure ACS.

8. *What are some of the databases that Cisco Secure ACS for UNIX supports?*

   Answer: Cisco Secure ACS for UNIX supports Sybase and Oracle relational database.

9. *Which core service of the Cisco Secure ACS for Windows provides synchronization with external RDBMS applications?*

   Answer: The CSDBSync service provides synchronization of the Cisco Secure user database with an external RDBMS application.

10. *Name two types of accounting logs generated by Cisco Secure ACS*

    Answer: Administrative accounting, RADIUS accounting

Chapter 10

"Do I Know This Already?" Quiz

1. a, b, c
2. a
3. a, b, c, d
4. a, b
5. c

Q&A

1. *What factors should you consider when deploying Cisco Secure ACS?*

   Answer: The factors that should be considered during Cisco Secure ACS deployment include the following:

   - Number of users
   - Network topology
   - Access policy
   - Network latency and reliability
   - Remote-access policy
   - Administrative-access policy

2. *What are the minimum hardware requirements to install Cisco Secure ACS?*

   Answer: The minimum hardware requirements are as follows:

   - Pentium III processor, 550 MHz or faster
   - 256 MB of RAM
   - At least 250 MB of free disk space if you are running an external database (if not, more disk space required)
   - Minimum graphics resolution of 256 colors at 800 by 600 lines

3. *How does Cisco Secure ACS provide control for remote-access policies?*

   Answer: Cisco Secure ACS provides control by using a central authentication and authorization of remote user.

4. *Where would be a good place to start to troubleshoot Cisco Secure ACS-related AAA problems?*

   Answer: A good place to start troubleshooting Cisco Secure ACS-related AAA problems is checking the Failed Attempts Report under Reports and Activity.

5. *Does a browser using a proxy server have any effect in the administration of a Cisco Secure ACS remotely?*

   Answer: Yes, it does. If the browser used for an administrative session is configured to use a proxy server, Cisco Secure ACS sees the administrative session originating from the IP address of the proxy server rather than from the actual address of the computer and will not work.

Chapter 11

"Do I Know This Already?" Quiz

1. a, b, c
2. b, c
3. a
4. c
5. a
6. d
7. a, b, c
8. a
9. d
10. c

Q&A

1. *Name the two types of routing protocol authentication (neighbor authentication)?*

   Answer: The two types of neighbor authentication are plain text and MD5.

2. *Name one weakness of SNMPv1.*

   Answer: SNMPv1 sends in clear text community strings that can easily be captured over a network. SNMPv1 also uses a very weak authentication scheme based on a community string.

3. *How do you enable the HTTP service on the Cisco IOS router?*

   Answer: The HTTP service is enabled with **ip http server** command on the Cisco IOS router.

4. *What are the security features that are provided by SNMPv3?*

   Answer: SNMPv3 provides the following security features:

   - Message integrity
   - Authentication
   - Encryption

5. *What is an IP directed broadcast?*

   Answer: An IP directed broadcast is a datagram sent to the broadcast address of a subnet to which the sending machine is not directly attached. The directed broadcast is routed through the network as a unicast packet until it arrives at the target subnet, where it is converted into a link-layer broadcast.

6. *What is the default password when accessing the router via the HTTP service?*

   Answer: The default password for accessing the HTTP service is the same as the enable password.

7. *What are the symptoms on the router when an attacker exploits the "small server services" that have been enabled on the router?*

   Answer: The external manifestation of the problem may be a process table full error message (%SYS-3 NOPROC) or a very high CPU utilization. The EXEC command **show process** shows a lot of processes with the same name, such as "UDP Echo."

Chapter 12

"Do I Know This Already?" Quiz

1. b
2. a, d
3. a, c
4. a, c, d
5. b
6. a
7. d
8. c
9. b
10. b

Q&A

1. What is the syntax to apply the IP ACL 107 for traffic leaving the interface?

   Answer: **ip access-group 107 out**

2. Meron is a network administrator in a medium-size company. She wants to deny FTP access to the Marketing department on the 10.300.4.0 subnet on Friday, Saturday, and Sunday 7 a.m. until 10 p.m. Can she do this? If so, how?

   Answer: Yes. Meron can use time-based ACL to fulfill her requirements. A sample configuration for Meron might look like the following:

   ```
   Firewall(config-if)#ip access-group 110 in
   Firewall(config)#access-list 110 deny tcp
      10.300.4.0 0.0.0.255 host 192.168.100.21 eq ftp time-range Mrktgrp
   Firewall(config)#time-range Mrktgrp
   Firewall(config-time-range)#periodic saturday sunday 7:00 to 20:00
   Firewall(config-if)#ip access-group 110 in
   ```

3. What is the syntax to deny telnet access to source host 10.2.2.2 to telnet server 10.200.4.6?

   Answer: **access-list 101 deny tcp host 10.2.2.2 host 10.200.4.6 eq telnet**

4. *Why do you use the words "in" or "out" when applying an ACL to an interface?*

   Answer: The "in" ACL has a source on a segment of the interface to which it is applied and a destination off of any other interface. The "out" ACL has a source on a segment of any interface other than the interface to which it is applied and a destination off of the interface to which it is applied.

5. *What is the command to apply ACL 101 for outgoing traffic from the internal network?*

   Answer: **ip access-group 101 out**

6. *What range of numbers is used for extended IP ACLs?*

   Answer: 100 to 199 and 2000 to 2699

7. *Create an ACL to deny 192.168.10.0 255.255.255.0 network web access to web server 10.100.10.14.*

   Answer: **access-list 101 deny 192.168.10.0 0.0.0.255 host 10.100.10.14 eq 80**

8. *At a minimum, on which routers should you configure ACLs?*

   Answer: At a minimum, you should configure ACLs on your edge routers.

9. *What type of ACL would you use to prevent a particular host from accessing your FTP server?*

   Answer: Extended IP ACLs give you the added granularity to specify which type of protocol to permit or deny to your network or servers.

10. *Ryan configured the following ACL on his router:* **access-list 113 deny tcp host 10.2.2.7 any** *and* **access-list 113 deny tcp host 10.2.2.8 any**. *He then applied it to the serial interface of his router. No packets seem to passing through his router. Why?*

    Answer: There is an implied "deny" for traffic that is not permitted. Ryan must have at least one permit statement in an ACL or all traffic will be blocked.

Chapter 13

"Do I Know This Already?" Quiz

1. c
2. a, b
3. c
4. c
5. b, d

Q&A

1. *What does port-to-application mapping, otherwise known as PAM, do?*

    Answer: PAM enables you to customize TCP or UDP port numbers for network services or applications on nonstandard ports.

2. *What is the command to configure PAM?*

    Answer: **ip port-map** *appl_name* **port** *port_num* [**list** *acl_num*]

3. *Name two benefits of the Cisco IOS firewall?*

    Answer: The Cisco IOS firewall feature set protects internal networks from intrusion, monitors traffic through the perimeter of the network, and enables network commerce via the World Wide Web.

4. *What are the different ways the IDS feature in the Cisco IOS firewall can be configured to respond to an attack or suspicious activity on the network?*

    Answer: Send an alarm, drop the packet, or reset the TCP connection.

5. *What does the IDS feature use to detect and identify patterns of misuse in network traffic?*

    Answer: The IDS feature identifies 59 of the most common attack signatures to detect patterns of misuse in network traffic.

Chapter 14

"Do I Know This Already?" Quiz

1. c
2. a
3. b
4. d
5. a, d
6. a, b, c
7. b, c, d
8. b
9. a
10. a

Q&A

1. *What are the steps in the CBAC configuration process?*

    Answer: Pick an interface, configure **ip access list** at the interface, configure global timeouts and thresholds, define an inspection rule, and apply the inspection rule to an interface.

2. *Are inspection rules a requirement for CBAC configuration?*

    Answer: Yes. Inspection rules are a mandatory requirement for CBAC configuration.

3. *What are the three categories of **debug** commands that are commonly used to debug CBAC configuration?*

    Answer: The three categories for debugging CBAC configuration are generic, transport level, and application level.

4. *Can CBAC be configured to inspect all TCP, UDP, and ICMP packets?*

    Answer: No. CBAC is available only for TCP and UDP IP protocol traffic.

5. *What command enables you to show a complete CBAC inspection configured on the Cisco IOS firewall?*

    Answer: **show ip inspect config**

6. *What command do you use to turn on audit trail messages?*

    Answer: **ip inspect audit trail**

7. *What are indicators in half-open sessions that CBAC measures before it takes steps to prevent a DoS attack?*

    Answer: CBAC measures both the total number of existing half-open sessions and the rate of session establishment attempts

8. *Does CBAC block malicious Java applets that are on .jar format?*

    Answer: No. CBAC cannot block any Java applet that is wrapped in a .zip or .jar format.

9. *Name two features of the CBAC?*

    Answer: Some of CBAC features include secure per-application DoS detection and prevention and real-time alerts

10. *Name one restriction with using CBAC.*

    Answer: Some of the restrictions when using CBAC include the following:

    - Packets with the firewall as the source or destination address are not inspected by CBAC.
    - If you reconfigure your ACLs when you configure CBAC, be aware that if your ACLs block TFTP traffic into an interface, you cannot netboot over that interface. (This is not a CBAC-specific limitation but is part of existing ACL functionality.)
    - CBAC is available only for IP protocol traffic. Only TCP and UDP packets are inspected. Other IP traffic, such as ICMP, cannot be inspected with CBAC and should be filtered with extended IP ACLs instead.

Chapter 15

"Do I Know This Already?" Quiz

1. c
2. b
3. d
4. c
5. d
6. a
7. b
8. b, e
9. d, e

Q&A

1. *What happens if the user has previously authenticated and that authentication has not timed out?*

   Answer: The user is not prompted to authenticate.

2. *If you are using NAT with authentication proxy, what other feature must you also use?*

   Answer: CBAC

3. *What are the three steps for configuring authentication proxy on the Cisco IOS firewall?*

   Answer: Configure AAA, configure the HTTP server, and configure the authentication proxy.

4. *True or False: The host name is required on the HTTP login page to ensure that users log in to the correct firewall?*

   Answer: False. The **ip auth-proxy auth-proxy-banner** is disabled by default

5. *What are the three steps for configuring TACACS+ on the CSACS?*

   Answer: Network configuration, interface configuration, and group setup.

6. *Where is the Cisco IOS firewall configured on the CSACS?*

Answer: On the Network Configuration window, listed under AAA Clients.

7. *Where are dynamic ACLs configured on the CSACS for RADIUS?*

Answer: On the Group Setup window, under Cisco IOS/PIX RADIUS Attributes.

8. *What must be running on the client browser to ensure secure login?*

Answer: JavaScript

9. *What happens if you attempt authentication proxy using SSL?*

Answer: Nothing. Authentication proxy only works over port 80.

10. *How many AAA servers can you match with a single Cisco IOS firewall for authentication proxy?*

Answer: One. Authentication proxy does not support load balancing.

Chapter 16

"Do I Know This Already?" Quiz

1. a, d
2. e
3. b
4. b
5. d
6. e
7. b
8. e
9. b
10. b

Q&A

1. *How are signatures listed in the Cisco IOS firewall?*

   Answer: By number

2. *How does the Cisco IOS firewall IDS operate?*

   Answer: As an in-line IDS

3. *What are the three actions that are performed by the IOS firewall IDS when malicious traffic is discovered?*

   Answer: Alarm, drop, reset

4. *Why would you want to disable some signatures?*

   Answer: To reduce the number of false positives

5. *What is POP?*

   Answer: A Cisco proprietary protocol that allows the IDS and management to communicate

6. *What are the four steps to configuring the firewall IDS?*

   Answer: Initialize the Cisco IOS firewall IDS on the router, configure attack signatures, create and apply audit rules, and add the Cisco IOS firewall IDS to the centralized management.

7. *What must match for POP to work?*

   Answer: Both the IDS and manager must have the same organization ID.

8. *In the command* **ip audit po remote . . . timeout**, *what timeout are you configuring?*

   Answer: The heartbeat between the IDS and the Director

9. *When you configure* **ip audit po protected**, *are you configuring a subnet or address range?*

   Answer: Address range

10. *Why should you configure a maximum queue for alarms?*

    Answer: To keep from taxing your memory

454 Appendix : Answers to the "Do I Know This Already?" Quizzes and Q&A Sections

11. *Which signatures create a greater load on the router performance?*

    Answer: Compound

12. *How do you exclude a signature?*

    Answer: Use the **ip audit signature** command.

13. *What is the first step to creating an audit rule?*

    Answer: Configure the default actions.

Chapter 17

"Do I Know This Already?" Quiz

1. c
2. b
3. b, e
4. d
5. c
6. b
7. a
8. b
9. d
10. d

Q&A

1. *What is the preferred key distribution method for configuring VPN peers?*

    Answer: ISAKMP is the preferred method.

2. *What is DES?*

    Answer: Data Encryption Standard is a 56-bit symmetric encryption algorithm.

3. *Of the two hash algorithms, which is more secure?*

    Answer: SHA-1 is more secure than MD5.

4. *What are the protocol numbers for ESP and AH?*

   Answer: ESP is 50, and AH is 51.

5. *Why is it a good idea to verify connectivity before attempting to configure a VPN connection?*

   Answer: Because if you cannot establish a connection between the protected networks, you won't be able to get a VPN established."

6. *What is a policy priority?*

   Answer: The policy priority is a number between 1 and 10,000 that is assigned when the IKE policy is created.

7. *What is the first command you should input when creating an IKE policy?*

   Answer: **crypto isakmp enable**

8. *What policy priority number has greater precedence?*

   Answer: The lower number.

9. *What is the default timeout for the global IPSec SA lifetime?*

   Answer: 1 hour.

10. *True or False: Crypto access lists are bidirectional?*

    Answer: False.

11. *What must you do to activate a crypto map?*

    Answer: Apply the crypto map to the correct interface.

12. *What does Cisco recommend about manual IPSec?*

    Answer: It should not be used because it is static and could be relatively insecure.

13. *How could you find out the router host name and domain name of your peer?*

    Answer: By using the **show crypto key pubkey-chain rsa** command.

14. *What is the command for generating RSA key pairs?*

    Answer: **crypto key generate rsa**

Chapter 18

"Do I Know This Already?" Quiz

1. b
2. a
3. b
4. b
5. c
6. c
7. d
8. a
9. d
10. b

Q&A

1. *What protocols are used by SCEP?*

   Answer: PKCS#7 and PKCS#10

2. *Why is it important to configure the router host name and domain name before requesting a certificate?*

   Answer: The host name and domain name are written into the certificate.

3. *What is the best alternative to configuring the date, time, and time zone on your router?*

   Answer: Configure NTP.

4. *What does the option **usage keys** do when generating RSA key pairs?*

   Answer: It configures the router to generate two pairs of keys; one for authentication (RSA signatures) and the other for encryption (RSA nonces).

5. *How do you configure the router to accept peer certificates if the CRL is not accessible?*

   Answer: The command **crl optional**

6. *How does the router authenticate the CA?*

   Answer: By receiving the CA self-signed certificate and the CA public key

7. *What command sends out a CA/RA request?*

   Answer: **crypto ca authenticate**

8. *Why should you save the configuration after enrolling with the CA?*

   Answer: To prevent loss of the certificates if the router reboots

9. *What does the command* **show crypto key pubkey-chain rsa** *display?*

   Answer: It lists all the peer public keys on the router.

Chapter 19

"Do I Know This Already?" Quiz

1. b
2. c
3. a
4. e
5. b
6. d
7. a
8. d

Q&A

9. *How does the Easy VPN Server control VPN policies for remote clients?*

   Answer: The Easy VPN Server manages all IPSec policies centrally and pushes the policy out to the client.

10. *What is dead peer detection (DPD)?*

    Answer: DPD incorporates a series of "keepalive" messages between the IPSec peers when there is no other traffic passing through the VPN tunnel.

11. *How does the command* **aaa new model** *prepare the router for Easy VPN Server?*

    Answer: The first task is to enable AAA on the router.

12. *What must you do before selecting your IKE parameters for remote VPN clients?*

    Answer: You must ensure that ISAKMP is enabled on the router.

13. *What servers should you designate when defining the group policy for mode configuration push?*

    Answer: DNS servers and WINS servers (if applicable)

14. *What must you do to make a dynamic crypto map function?*

    Answer: Apply the dynamic crypto map to the interface.

15. *What is the difference between* **crypto isakmp keepalive seconds** *and* **retries**?

    Answer: Keepalive seconds is the time the router waits before sending a keepalive. Keepalive retries is the time the router waits before sending another keepalive after not getting a response from a previous keepalive.

16. *What is xauth?*

    Answer: Extended authentication (xauth) is a process for using AAA authentication for VPN connections.

17. *How many different remote phase II modes does Easy VPN Server support?*

    Answer: Two (client mode and network extension mode)

18. *Which remote phase II mode does not support NAT or PAT?*

    Answer: Network extension mode

Chapter 20

"Do I Know This Already?" Quiz

1. d
2. b, d
3. b, d

4. d

5. b

6. c

7. b, c, d, e

8. a

9. e

10. d

Q&A

1. *If you install CiscoWorks 2000 on any Windows platform, which additional packages are required?*

   Answer: Service Pack 2 and the ODBC Drivers (version 3.510)

2. *What is the significance of configuring the "hub" of the "hub-and-spoke" network to be located at the corporate headquarters?*

   Answer: You want all VPNs to terminate at a location that is central to the operation of the company. Also, the headquarters location most likely has the most complex network configuration, whereas the branch offices are les complex.

3. *What are some of the general settings when configuring the VPN and firewall policies on the Router MC?*

   Answer: The general settings determine routing, IPSec failover, and fragmentation parameters for the VPN connection.

4. *What is meant by "device hierarchy and inheritance"?*

   Answer: Policies that are applied at the global level are inherited by all devices that are configured on the Router MC.

5. *I have just completed deploying a job and it appears that the VPN is having connectivity issues. What steps can I take to repair the damage?*

   Answer: Rollback the job.

6. *What is the method used to capture data about existing devices and send it to the Router MC?*

   Answer: Device import

7. *What items are predefined in the Router MC?*

Answer: Device groups and policies

8. *What is the definition of IPSec?*

Answer: IPSec is a framework of open standards that provide security services at the IP layer.

9. *What additional functionality do you get by tunneling IPSec with GRE?*

Answer: You can encapsulate routing protocols within GRE to add resiliency to the VPN connection.

10. *What is defined within the "tunnel policies"?*

Answer: The authentication and encryption algorithms for the IPSec tunnel.

11. *How long can a job remain open?*

Answer: Until it has been deployed or rejected.

12. *What should you do if a job deployment doesn't "stick"?*

Answer: Redeploy the job.

13. *What CiscoWorks 2000 account has read-only permissions?*

Answer: Help Desk

GLOSSARY

3DES Triple Data Encryption Standard. A 168-bit symmetric encryption algorithm.

AAA client AAA client is the Cisco IOS firewall that is communicating with the CSACS or AAA server.

AAA server The AAA server provides authentication and authorization information to the AAA client.

access attacks An attack designed to exploit a vulnerability and to gain access to a system or a network.

access VPN An access VPN is an encrypted connection to a network from a remote location. This type of connection usually requires the use of VPN client software on the remote system.

accounting Accounting records what the user actually does and enables you to track the services that users are accessing and the amount of network resources that they are consuming.

anomaly-based IDS Intrusion detection system that detects known and unknown attacks by comparing traffic to "approved behavior" and reacting to any behavior that exceeds the approved baseline.

approver User permissions that are assigned to someone who has the authority to review and approve policy changes (activities).

atomic signature An atomic signature enables the IDS to trigger based on a single packet.

authentication Authentication provides the method for verifying the identity of users who are requesting access to network resources. However, authentication does not cover the access rights of the individuals.

authentication proxy Authentication proxy is used to proxy authentication requests to a AAA server. This allows for per-user or per-group policies.

authorization   The process of giving individuals access to system objects based on their identity.

auxiliary port   Dialup connection. The receiving modem is connected to the router auxiliary port.

block scan   A block scan is a combination of the vertical scan and the horizontal scan. In other words, it scans a network segment and attempts connections on multiple ports of each host on that segment.

CA interoperability   CA interoperability is the component that provides communication functionality between Cisco devices and CA servers.

Challenge Handshake Authentication Protocol (CHAP)   A protocol used to periodically verify the identity of the peer using a three-way handshake. The handshake is done upon initial link establishment and may be repeated anytime after the link has been established.

Cisco IOS firewall   An Cisco IOS firewall is a Cisco router that has the Cisco IOS firewall feature set installed. This allows the router to perform more complex security-related functions.

Cisco IOS firewall IDS   Cisco IOS firewall IDS compares traffic to predefined attack signatures to detect and react to malicious traffic.

Cisco Secure Access Control Server (CSACS)   AAA server developed by Cisco that runs on Windows NT/2000 and UNIX. CSACS integrates well with the Cisco IOS firewall and the Cisco PIX Firewall. The CSACS can perform as a TACACS+ or RADUIS server and can also be used to manage other AAA servers.

CiscoWorks 2000   An application that provides server-side support for the administration of PIX firewalls, SCIDSs, HIDSs, and VPN routers.

compound signature   Compound signatures require the IDS to gather a greater amount of data than an atomic signature to determine whether there is malicious activity.

console port   Direct connection from a computer to the router using a console cable.

context-based access control (CBAC)   CBAC inspects traffic up to the application layer and can affect the traffic based on the configured policy.

corporate security policy   A formal statement that specifies a set of rules that users must follow while gaining access to corporate network access.

correlation   The ability to compare log data from multiple sources.

crypto map   The crypto map is defined during the IPSec configuration and pulls together the components for the IPSec connection.

debug   Command that enables you to troubleshoot problems in a configuration.

destination   The destination is the resource that is being requested by the source.

disable   If you disable a signature, it no longer is processed by the IDS.

DNS query   A DNS query provides the unauthorized user with information such as which address space is assigned to a particular domain and who owns that domain.

DoS attacks   A denial of service attack is designed solely to cause an interruption to a computer or network.

DoS mitigation   The ability to detect and react to potential DoS attacks.

dynamic ACL   Dynamic access control lists are a form of authorization that is passed from the AAA server to the Cisco IOS firewall.

edge router   A router located at the point where the network interconnects with other networks, such as the Internet. Also known as the perimeter router.

egress   Traffic that is heading outbound.

encryption   The translation of data into a nonreadable format. Encryption is the most effective way to achieve data security. To read an encrypted file, you must have access to a secret key or password that enables you to *decrypt* it. Unencrypted data is called *plain text*; encrypted data is referred to as *cipher text*.

ESP   Encapsulating Security Payload. A protocol that provides data authentication, encryption, and antireplay protection.

event logging   The Cisco IOS firewall can be configured to log all traffic that passes through it. The firewall logs can be very helpful for troubleshooting and network forensics.

exclude   A command used when configuring the Cisco IDS. It is possible to exclude a host or network from a signature without disabling the entire signature.

extended IP ACL   Extended IP access control lists use source and destination addresses for matching operations and optional protocol type information for finer granularity of control.

extranet A network segment that is designed to provide limited access to resources for business partners and cooperative projects.

fingerprint The portion of a certificate that is returned by the CA that is used to validate the certificate.

fingerprinting Fingerprinting is the technique of interpreting the responses of a system to figure out what it is. In particular, unexpected combinations of data are sometimes sent at the system to trigger these responses

hierarchy The logical grouping of devices to facilitate efficient device management.

horizontal scans Scans an address range for a specific port or service. A very common horizontal scan is the FTP sweep. This is scanning done by scanning a network segment looking for replies to connection attempts on port 21.

hub settings Hub settings are used to configure the internal interfaces and networks on the hub side of the VPN connection.

ingress Traffic that is coming inbound.

inheritance The application of policies to an upper level affecting groups and devices at lower levels.

initial contact A feature that informs the VPN server to remove any old connection data from a connection that has died and is attempting to reconnect.

Internet Key Exchange (IKE) IKE is a hybrid protocol that implements the Oakley key exchange and Skeme key exchange inside the Internet Security Association and Key Management Protocol (ISAKMP) framework. (ISAKMP, Oakley, and Skeme are security protocols implemented by IKE.)

intranet An internal network that contains resources which have access restricted to internal users only.

IP spoofing Spoofing is the creation of TCP/IP packets using somebody else's IP address.

IPSec network security The Cisco IOS firewall supports IPSec standards and can be used to configure VPNs.

Java blocking The Cisco IOS firewall can detect and block malicious Java code.

Link Control Protocol (LCP)   PPP provides LCP to establish, configure, and test the data link connection. PPP uses LCP to automatically agree upon encapsulation format options, handle varying limits on packet size, detect a looped-back link or other common misconfiguration errors, and terminate the link. Other optional facilities provided authenticate the identity of the peer on the link and determine when a link is functioning properly and when it is failing.

Message Digest 5 (MD5)   MD5 is a one-way hash function, meaning that it takes a message and converts it into a fixed string of digits, also called a message digest. When using a one-way hash function, you can compare a calculated message digest against the message digest that is decrypted with a public key to verify that the message hasn't been tampered with. This comparison is called a hash check.

method list   A method list is a sequential list describing the authentication methods to be queried to authenticate a user. Method lists enable you to designate one or more security protocols to be used for authentication, thus ensuring a backup system for authentication in case the initial method fails.

mode configuration push   The action of pushing the policy configuration out to the remote VPN clients. This is completed on the Easy VPN Server.

NAS   Network access server.

neighbor router authentication   Neighbor router authentication is used to ensure that the Cisco IOS firewall receives updated routing information from only authenticated sources.

Network Address Translation (NAT)   The Cisco IOS firewall can translate source and destination addresses. This allows for the use of RFC 1918 addresses on internal and DMZ segments, greatly reducing the attacker's ability to route attacks across public networks.

network security   The implementation of security devices, policies, and processes to prevent unauthorized access to network resources or alteration or destruction of resources or data.

network segmentation   Segregating network resources by type and value to ensure that access to assets of greater value are restricted to more granular control.

nonce   A random or ad-hoc formation for letters or numbers.

Password Authentication Protocol (PAP)   PAP uses clear-text passwords and is the least sophisticated authentication protocol.

ping sweep   A ping sweep tells the unauthorized user the number of hosts that are active on the network. It is possible to drop ICMP at the perimeter devices, but this occurs at the expense of network troubleshooting.

PKCS#10   A standard from RSA that defines the syntax for certificate requests.

Point-to-Point Protocol (PPP)   PPP is the Internet standard for transmission of IP packets over serial lines. PPP supports asynchronous and synchronous lines.

policy priority   A number between 1 and 10,000 that is assigned to an IKE policy when it is created. The policies are checked by priority by the router, and the first matching policy is used.

port-to-application mapping (PAM)   PAM enables administrators to configure applications to pass through the firewall using nonstandard ports.

Post Office Protocol (POP)   POP is used to facilitate communication between sensors and centralized management.

preshared key   Also called the preshared secret, it is a predetermined alphanumeric "password" that can be manually configured on SA peers and used for peer authentication.

privileged EXEC   The privileged EXEC mode is entered by using the **enable** command. It is possible to view much of the router configuration, but changes cannot be made.

query url   If your CA server supports RA with LDAP, this command specifies the URL of the LDAP server.

real-time alerts   The Cisco IOS firewall can generate alerts in real time. This greatly increases the ability to react to an attempted attack.

reconnaissance attacks   An attack to search for and track vulnerabilities that can be exploited.

reflexive ACLs   Reflexive ACLs only allow access as long as the connection state remains active. Reflexive ACLs cannot be used in conjunction with CBAC.

registration authority (RA)   RA is additional functionality that acts as a proxy for the CA. It allows the systems to authenticate to the RA even when the CA is offline.

relational database management system (RDBMS)   A RDBMS is a relational database that is a collection of data items organized as a set of formally described tables from which data can be accessed or reassembled in many different ways without having to reorganize the database tables.

Remote Authentication Dial-in User Service (RADIUS)   RADIUS Database for authenticating modem and ISDN connections and for tracking connection time.

reset   One of the three audit actions is reset. The IDS is sent a TCP RESET flag to terminate the connection.

RFC 2196   The *Site Security Handbook*

ROM monitor   The ROM monitor mode is used to change the system boot configuration only.

Router MC   An application that runs on CiscoWorks 2000 or the VPM to facilitate the configuration, management, and troubleshooting of VPN routers.

SCEP   Simple Certificate Enrollment Protocol. A lightweight transaction-oriented protocol used to enroll with a CA.

security policy   A document that defines all aspects of an organization's security stance.

security server support   The Cisco IOS firewall supports the following AAA servers:

show   The **show** command displays the current system status or system configuration.

signature-based IDS   Intrusion detection system that detects known attacks by comparing network traffic to predefined attack signatures.

site-to-site VPN   A site-to-site VPN is used to connect two or more locations' networks. These encrypted connections are maintained by VPN devices on each network.

source   The source is the host that is requesting access to a resource.

split tunneling   The capability to access a VPN while simultaneously maintaining a connection to the Internet (not through the VPN). Split tunneling is normally considered to be a security risk.

spoke settings   Spoke settings are used to configure the internal interfaces and networks on the spoke side of the VPN connection.

standard IP ACL   Standard IP ACLs use source address for matching operations.

system auditing   The Cisco IOS firewall maintains an audit log of all changes made to the router.

TACACS+   Terminal Access Controller Access Control System Plus. It is a proprietary Cisco enhancement to Terminal Access Controller Access Control System (TACACS) and provides additional support for authentication, authorization, and accounting. TACACS provides a way to centrally validate users attempting to gain access to a router or access server.

TCP intercept TCP intercept is used to prevent a SYN flood attack. It cannot be used in conjunction with CBAC.

telnet A terminal emulation program for TCP/IP networks that can be used for accessing the router via the network interface.

transform set The set of IPSec configuration parameters that are used for the VPN connection.

Transport Layer Security (TLS) TLS is a protocol that guarantees privacy and data integrity between client/server applications communicating over the Internet.

Trojan horse A Trojan horse is a program that usually is masked within another program and enables an intruder to gain access to the host system.

user authentication and authorization Authentication and authorization allow for the configuration of per-user and per-group policies.

user EXEC The user EXEC mode is the mode entered by default. It is possible to view the general condition of the router in this mode.

vertical scans Scans the service ports of a single host and requests different services at each port. This method enables the unauthorized user to determine which type of operating system is running and which services are running on the computer.

virus Computer code that attaches itself to other software running on the computer.

worm A worm is a virus that exploits vulnerabilities on networked systems to replicate itself.

Index

Symbols
> (right-angle) bracket symbol, 63
? (question mark) symbol, 65

Numerics
3DES (Triple Data Encryption Standard), 312

A
AAA (authentication, authorization, and accounting), 47, 52
    accounting, 120, 128–130
    authentication, 119
        configuring, 121–124
        failed access attempts, 120
        method lists, 119
    authorization, 120, 125–127
    Cisco Secure ACS, 162
    configuring IOS firewall, 260
    configuring services, 120
    local database authentication, 406
    overview, 119
    troubleshooting, 130–132
aaa accounting auth-proxy default start-stop group tacacs+ command, 260
aaa accounting commands, 129
aaa accounting network start-stop radius command, 150
aaa authentication commands, 121, 142
aaa authentication login admins local command, 150
aaa authentication login default command, 260
aaa authentication login test radius local command, 148
aaa authentication ppp test if-needed radius command, 148
aaa authentication ppp testl radius local command, 149
aaa authorization auth-proxy default command, 260
aaa authorization commands, 126
aaa authorization exec radius command, 148
aaa authorization network radius command, 148
aaa authorization network radius local command, 150
aaa new-model command, 142, 260
access attacks, 33–34
access control (CBAC), 235
    configuration example, 245–246
    DoS detection/protection, 235
    functionality, 236
    global timeouts and thresholds, 240
    inspection rules, 241–243
    inspection rules, applying to an interface, 244
    IP access lists, 240
    memory and performance impact, 239
    protocols, 238
    restrictions, 238
    selecting an interface, 239
    verifying and debugging, 244
access control lists. See ACLs
access lists
    antispoofing, 408–409
    CBAC, 69
    Cisco IOS firewalls, 69
    creating, 290
    crypto maps, 414–415
access to commands, 83
access VPNs, 308
access-list numbers, 209

accounting, 120
    Cisco Secure ACSs, 165
    configuring, 128–130
    RADIUS, 148
    troubleshooting, 130–132
ACLs (access control lists), 207
    configuring on routers, 214
    crypto, 323
    overview, 207
    types of, 208
        extended IP, 212
        reflexive, 212
        standard IP, 209–210
        time-based, 213–214
administration
    Secure ACS, 165
    security
        configuring multiple privilege levels,
            87–88
        console access, 84
        enable password, 84–85
        enable secret command, 86
        service password-encryption
            command, 87
        warning banners, 89–90
AH (Authentication Header), 315
AH-MD5-HMAC transform, 316
AH-SHA-HMAC transform, 316
alarms (Cisco IOS firewall IDS), 288
algorithms, hash, 312
anomaly-based IDS systems, 49
antispoofing, 408–409
applications
    potential targets, 46
    weaknesses, 30
attack signatures, 288
attacks, 39
    DoS, 11, 30
    intruder motivation, 31
    potential targets, 46
    reasons for success, 28
    smurf, 196
    types of, 33
        access, 34
        DoS, 36
        reconnaissance, 34
audits
    Cisco IOS firewall IDS rules, 290
    exclusions, 291
authentication, 119
    CHAP, 110
    Cisco Secure ACS, 162, 183
    configuring, 121
        line password, 105
        login authentication, 122
        password protection, 123
        PPP authentication, 124
        TACACS+, 141
        username password, 105
    failed access attempts, 120
    method lists, 119
    methods, 104
    MS-CHAP, 111
    overview, 104
    PAP, 109
    RADIUS, 148
    remote security servers, 106–108
    routing protocols, 197
    troubleshooting, 130–132
Authentication Header (AH), 315
authentication proxy, 223, 251
    appearance, 256
    case study, 423
    compatibility with other features, 258
    configuring, 258–265
    functionality, 255

overview, 255
RADIUS, 270
TACACS+, 266–269
unidirectional function, 265
authentication, authorization, and accounting. See AAA
authorization, 120
Cisco Secure ACS, 164, 183
configuring, 125–127
RADIUS, 148
troubleshooting, 130–132
auth-proxy keyword, 260
auxiliary connection (Cisco IOS routers), 66

B

balancing business needs with security needs, 9
block scans, 34
breaches
incident response plans, 16
lack of understanding of computers or networks, 31

C

CA support, configuring (case study), 416
enrolling routers, 418–419
host/domain name, 417
NTP, 417
CAs, 343
authentication, 349
Cisco routers, 343
communicating with routers, 351
configuring, 351
declaring, 348
interoperability, 343
standards (RSA keys), 343
CBAC (context-based access control), 69, 222, 258
configuration example, 245–246
configuring
global timeouts and thresholds, 240
inspection rules, 241–244
IP access lists, 240
selecting an interface, 239
DoS detection/protection, 235
features, 235

functionality, 236
implementing (case study), 424–425
memory and performance impact, 239
protocols, 238
restrictions, 238
verifying and debugging, 244
CDP (Cisco Discovery Protocol), 199
Central Management Post Office Parameter, 286
certificate revocation list (CRL), 344
Challenge Handshake Authentication Protocol (CHAP), 110
cisco command, 325
Cisco Discovery Protocol (CDP), 199
Cisco Easy VPN. See Easy VPN
Cisco IOS
CLI, 83
RADIUS
configuring, 146–148
troubleshooting, 150–151
router, 59
TACACS+
configuring, 140–143
troubleshooting, 144–145
Cisco IOS firewall, 59
AAA server support, 73
access lists, 69
authentication proxy, 70, 255, 272–273
appearance, 256
compatibility with other features, 258
configuring, 258–265
functionality, 255
CBAC, 235
configuration example, 245–246
DoS detection/protection, 235
functionality, 236
global timeouts and thresholds, 240
inspection rules, 241–243
inspection rules, applying to an interface, 244
IP access lists, 240
memory and performance impact, 239
protocols, 238
restrictions, 238
selecting an interface, 239
verifying and debugging, 244
configuring
for AAA, 260

configuring **475**

    for an internal source and an external destination, 264
    event logging, 70
    feature set, 222
        Authentication proxy, 223
        IDS, 224
        logging and audit trail, 224
        port-to-application mapping (PAM), 225–227
    features, 72
    functioning as HTTP servers, 261
    IDS, 70, 279
        adding to centralized management, 292
        audit rules, 290–291
        case study, 420–421, 423
        Central Management Post Office parameter, 286
        clear commands, 294
        debug commands, 294
        defining the protected network, 288
        info and attack signatures, 288
        initializing on routers, 286
        maximum queue for alarms, 288
        verifying configuration, 292
    IPSec network security, 70
    Java blocking, 69
    NAT, 70
    neighbor router authentication, 70
    PAM, 70
    real-time alerts, 70
    security server support, 70
    system auditing, 69
    TCP intercept, 69
    user authentication and authorization, 70
Cisco IOS routers
    accessing CLI, 66
    configuration commands, 65
    configuration modes, 63, 71
    configuring CLI access, 68
    enabling SSH server, 67
Cisco Secure ACS (Cisco Secure Access Control Server), 157, 175
    accounting, 165
    administration, 165
    authentication, 162
    authorization, 164
    deploying, 178
        browser compatibility, 179
        hardware requirements, 178
        OS requirements, 178
    installing, 180–181
    ports requirements, 181
    troubleshooting, 182–183
    UNIX, 169–170
    Windows, 161, 166
        AAA, 162
        CSAuth, 167
        CSDBSync, 168
        CSLog, 168
Cisco Secure Intrusion Detection Sensor, 279
CiscoSecure Integrated Software, 69
CiscoWorks 2000
    Router MC, 389
    Sun Solaris installation, 384
    user accounts, 397
    Windows installation, 383
clear ip audit configuration command, 294
clear ip audit statistics command, 294
CLI (command-line interface), 59, 63, 66–68, 83
client mode (Easy VPN), 371
clock set command, 346
clock timezone command, 346
command prompts, 65
command-line interface, 59, 63, 66–68, 83
commands
    aaa accounting, 129
    aaa authentication, 121
    aaa authorization, 126
    Cisco IOS router configuration, 65
    configuring
        AAA, 260
        authentication proxy, 262
    enable password, 84–85
    enable secret, 86
    service password-encryption, 87
    verifying and debugging CBAC, 244
compound signatures, 288
computers, vulnerabilities, 27
config-if command, 64
configuration weaknesses (network devices), 29
configure terminal command, 64
configuring
    AAA services, 120
        accounting, 128–130
        authentication, 121

configuring

    authorization, 125–127
    login authentication, 122
    password protection, 123
    PPP authentication, 124
ACLs on routers, 214
authentication proxy on IOS firewall, 258–265
    AAA, 260
    HTTP servers, 261
    verifying configuration, 262
CA support (case study), 416
    enrolling routers, 418–419
    host/domain name, 417
    NTP, 417
CBAC
    global timeouts and thresholds, 240
    inspection rules, 241, 243
    inspection rules, applying to an interface, 244
    IP access lists, 240
    selecting an interface, 239
centralized manager for Cisco IOS firewall IDS, 292
Cisco IOS routers, 63
    CLI access, 68
    commands, 65
    global configuration mode, 64
    interface configuration mode, 64
    line configuration mode, 65
    privileged EXEC mode, 63
    ROM monitor mode, 63
    user EXEC mode, 63
crypto maps, 414–415
CSACS for RADIUS, 270
Director's Post Office protocol, 288
enable password, 84–86
HTTP servers, 261
IKE parameters, 411–412
IKE with RSA signatures, 353
Internet services, 29
IPSec, 324, 354
IPSec parameters, 413–414
IPSec SA lifetimes, 323
IPSec with RSA encrypted nonces, 328–330
line password authentication, 105
local database authentication, 406
manual IPSec, 328
multiple privilege levels, 87–88
port security, 93

Post Office Protocol, 287
preshared keys, 319
RADIUS, 146–147
    accounting, 148
    authentication and authorization, 148
    troubleshooting, 150–151
remote access, 359, 363–370
routers
    for IPSec, 309–313, 316–321, 326
    for IPSec with CA support, 345–349
RSA keys, 329
SNMP, 194–199
SSH parameters (Cisco IOS routers), 67
TACACS+, 140
    accounting, 143
    authentication, 141–143
    CSACS, 266–269
    encryption key, 141
    troubleshooting, 144–145
username password authentication, 105
warning banners, 89–90
xauth, 370
configuring routers for IPSec, 311–313
consistency, 13
console administration, 84
console connection (Cisco IOS routers), 66
context-based access control. See CBAC, 258
continuity, lack of leading to attacks, 28
corporate assets, 10
correlation, 50, 53
cost savings, 11
crackers, 27
creating
    dynamic crypto maps with RRI, 368
    IKE policies, 319
CRL (certificate revocation list), 344
crl option command, 348
crypto ACLs, 323
crypto key zeroize rsa command, 332
crypto maps, 324
    configuring, 414–415
    example, 325
CSACS
    configuring for RADIUS, 270
    configuring TACACS+, 266–269
CSAuth, 167
CSDBSync, 168
CSIDS (Cisco Secure Intrusion Detection System), 279

CSIS (CiscoSecure Integrated Software), 69
CSLog, 168
CSRadius, 168
CSTacacs, 168
Ctrl-Z command, 64

D

data
    fabrication, 35
    interception, 34
    modification, 35
    potential targets, 47
    vulnerabilities, 27
Data Encryption Standard (DES), 312
database authentication, 406
DDoS (distributed denial of service), 33
DDoS attacks, 35–36
dead peer detection (DPD), 363
debug aaa accounting command, 151
debug aaa authentication command, 144
debug command, 63, 130–132
debug crypto ipsec command, 326
debug crypto isakmp command, 326
debug ip audit detailed command, 294
debug ip audit ftp-token command, 294
debug ip audit function-trace command, 294
debug ip audit icmp command, 294
debug ip audit ip command, 294
debug ip audit object-deletion command, 294
debug ip audit rpc command, 294
debug ip audit smtp command, 294
debug ip audit tcp command, 294
debug ip audit tftp command, 294
debug ip audit timers command, 294
debug ip audit udp command, 294
debug radius command, 150
debug tacacs command, 145
debug tacacs events, 145
debugging CBAC, 244
debut ip audit ftp-cmd command, 294
debut ip audit object-creation command, 294
debut ip audit object-deletion command, 294
default settings (network devices), 29
defense, 46
    components used, 47
    correlation and trending, 50
    effective monitoring, 50
    host-based, 49
    identifying targets, 46
    layering, 46
    network segmentation, 49
    physical security, 51
defining Group Policy Configuration mode, 367
deploying Cisco Secure ACS, 178–179
DES (Data Encryption Standard), 312
designing networks, 403–405
devices
    configuration weaknesses, 29
    default settings, 29
Diffie-Hellman key exchange, 312
directed broadcasts, disabling, 196
Director's Post Office protocol, 288
disable command, 63
disabling
    directed broadcasts, 196
    finger services, 198
    unnecessary services, 407
disaster recovery plans, 28
distributed denial of service attacks (DDoS attacks), 33, 35–36
distributing security policies, 16
DNS whois queries, 34
DoS attacks (denial-of-service), 11, 33, 36
    Cisco IOS firewall DoS mitigation, 70
    detection and protection, 235
    ICMP, 30
DPD (dead peer detection), 363
dynamic access lists (Cisco IOS firewalls), 69
dynamic command, 325
dynamic crypto maps
    applying mode configuration, 369
    applying to interfaces, 369
    creating with RRI, 368
dynamic perimeter security, 49, 52

E

Easy VPN, 365
    configuring remote access, 364
        creating ISAKMP policy, 366
        enabling IKE DPD, 370
        group policy lookup, 366
        mode configuration requests, 369
        transform sets, 368
        xauth configuration, 370

modes of operation, 371
overview, 362
server functionality, 363
enable command, 63
enable password command, 84–85
enable secret command, 86
enabling IKE DPD, 370
Encapsulating Security Payload (ESP), 314
encryption
configuring IPSec on Cisco routers, 310–311
enable secret command, 86
end command, 64
endpoints, 307
enrollment mode ra command, 348
enrollment retry-count command, 348
enrollment retry-period command, 348
enrollment url command, 348
enterprise VPN routers
managing, 383–384
Router MC, 386–394
VMS (VPN/Security Management Solution), 385
ESP (Encapsulating Security Payload), 314
ESP-3DES transform, 316
ESP-DES transform, 316
ESP-MD5-HMAC transform, 316
ESP-SHA-HMAC transform, 316
Ethernet switches, 92–93
ethical hackers, 31
event logging, 70
EXEC mode, 83
exit command, 65
expanded IP ACLs, 209
exposed passwords, 29
extended IP ACLs, 69, 212
extended authentication (xauth), 363
extranet VPNs, 308

F

finger services, disabling, 198
firewalls, 12
Cisco IOS, 59, 255
AAA server support, 73
access lists, 69
authentication proxy, 70
event logging, 70
features, 72
IPSec network security, 70
Java blocking, 69
NAT, 70
neighbor router authentication, 70
PAM, 70
real-time alerts, 70
security server support, 70
system auditing, 69
TCP intercept, 69
user authentication and authorization, 70
IDS, 279
known hostile entities, 49
overview, 222
potential target, 46
flexibility of security measures, 15
FTP security settings, 29

G–H

global configuration mode (Cisco IOS routers), 64
Group Policy Configuration mode, 367
group policy lookup, 366
Group Setup Configuration Window, 270
guidelines (security policies), 13, 20
hackers, 31
hactivision, 33
hardware
default settings, 29
potential attack targets, 46
weaknesses, 30
hardware weaknesses, 30
hash (message integrity) algorithm, 312
hashes, 198
horizontal scans, 34
host-based defense, 49
hostile entities, 49
hosts (potential target), 46
host-specific port mapping, 227
HTTP servers, configuring, 261

I

ICMP (DoS attacks), 30
IDSs (intrusion detection systems), 49, 279
Cisco IOS firewall, 70, 224
adding to centralized management, 292

  audit rules, 290–291
  clear commands, 294
  debug commands, 294
  defining the protected network, 288
  deployment strategies, 295
  info and attack signatures, 288
  maximum queue for alarms, 288
  verifying configuration, 292
 host-based, 49
IETF (Internet Engineering Task Force), 18
IKE (Internet Key Exchange), 309–313
 CAs, 343
 configuring
  parameters, 411–412
  with RSA signatures, 353
 dead peer detection (DPD), 363
 defining policy, 310
 enabling, 319, 370
 extended authentication (xauth), 363
 polices, 319
 policy parameters, 313
 verifying configuration, 320
implementing
 CBAC (case study), 424–425
 security policies, 14, 17
  steps of, 17
  testing, 18
incident response plans, 16
info signatures (atomic signatures), 288
inspection rules (CBAC), 241
 applying to an interface, 244
 java, 243
 TCP and UDP inspection, 243
installing
 Cisco Secure ACS, 180–181
 CiscoWorks 2000, 384
 Router MC, 389–390
interactive router access, 90
interception, 34
interesting traffic, 323
interface command, 64, 142
interface configuration mode (Cisco IOS routers), 64
Internet Engineering Task Force (IETF), 18
Internet Key Exchange. See IKE
Internet Protocol (IP), 29
Internet services, configuration weaknesses, 29
internetworking, 46

interoperability, 343
intranet VPNs, 308
intruder motivation, 31
intrusion detection systems. See IDS
IOS Cisco firewall, 295
ip audit command, 292
ip audit notify log command, 286
ip audit notify nr-director command, 286
ip auth-proxy auth-cache-time command, 262
ip auth-proxy auth-proxy-banner command, 262
ip http authentication aaa command, 261
ip http server command, 261
ip inspect command, 241
ip inspect name command, 241
IPSec
 configuring, 354
  encryption on Cisco routers, 310–311
  manually, 328
  parameters, 413–414
  RSA encrypted nonces, 328–330
  SA lifetimes, 323
 configuring routers for, 309–311, 321
  enabling IKE, 319
  testing configuration, 326
  transforms, 316
  verifying connectivity, 317
  verifying current configuration, 317
  verifying IKE configuration, 320
 creating transform set, 322
 crypto maps, 324
 defining policies, 313
 overview, 309
 Router MC, 388
IPSec network security, 70
ipsec-isakmp command, 325
ISAKMP, creating policy for remote VPN clients, 366
ISAKMP/Oakley (Internet Security Association and Key Management Protocol [with Oakley distribution]), 310

J–K–L

Java applets, 29
Java blocking Cisco IOS firewalls, 69
java inspection rules, 243
Java script, 29

Kerberos, 109
keys
    preshared, 311, 319
    RSA, 329–330
legal issues (network security), 18
line configuration mode (Cisco IOS routers), 65
line password authentication, 105
login authentication, 122
login authentication admins command, 150

M

MAC address lockdown, 92
management components, 47
managing enterprise VPN routers, 383–384
    Router MC, 386–390, 392–394
    VMS (VPN/Security Management Solution), 385
maximum queue, 288
MD5 (Message Digest 5), 312
message digest, 312
message integrity (hash) algorithm, 312
method lists, 119
Microsoft Challenge Handshake Authentication Protocol (MS-CHAP) authentication, 111
mode configuration push, 367
modification of resources, 35
MS-CHAP (Microsoft Challenge Handshake Authentication Protocol) authentication, 111

N

NAT (Network Address Translation), 48, 70, 258
neighbor router authentication, 70
network extension mode (Easy VPN), 371
Network File System, 30
network infrastructure policy, 10
network security, 5, 30
    attacks, 23
        DoS, 36
        potential targets, 46
        reasons for success, 28
        types of, 33–34
    balancing needs, 9
    defense, 46
        components used, 47
        host-based, 49
    definition of, 9
    devices, configuration weaknesses, 29
    dynamic perimeter security, 49
    firewalls, 12, 59
    incident response plans, 16
    intruder motivation, 31
    legal issues, 18
    misconfigured Internet services, 29
    passwords, 29
    patches, 27
    physical, 51
    policies, 6, 9, 47
        consistency, 13
        creating, 11
        distributing, 16
        feasibility, 11
        flexibility, 15
        goals of, 12, 19
        guidelines, 13, 20
        implementing, 14
        network infrastructure, 10
        patch management, 10
        preparation for, 10
        topics to address, 10
        weaknesses of, 28
        writing direction of, 14
    process of, 20, 50
    responding to threats, 11
    sanctions for violations, 16
    security wheel, 6
    technology weaknesses, 30
    threats, 38
        categories of, 31
        curiosity, 32
        fun and pride, 32
        lack of understanding, 31
        political, 33
        revenge, 32
    theft, 32
    Trojan horses, 35
    user accounts, 10
    self-imposed vulnerabilities, 27
    worms, 35
Network Time Protocol (NTP), 199

networks
  design, 403–405
  disaster recovery plans, 28
  equipment weaknesses, 30
  interactive access, 90
  internetworking, 46
  remote access case study, 419–425
  security. See network security
  segmentation, 49, 52
  site-to-site connectivity, 409–410
  vulnerabilities, 27
NFS (Network File System), 30
NTP (Network Time Protocol), 199, 416–417
ntp access-group command options, 347

O–P

operating systems, weaknesses, 30
option, 348
PAM (port-to-application mapping), 70, 225–227
PAP (Password Authentication Protocol), 109–110
password protection, 123
passwords
  encryption, 86–87
  exposed, 29
  vty, 69
  weak, 29
PAT (Port Address Translation), 48
patch management policy, 10
patches, 27–28
peer authentication method, 312
peer command, 347
performance, CBAC's impact on, 239
perimeter security, 49
physical security, 51
ping sweeps, 34
PKCS#10, 344
PKCS#7, 344
policies (network security), 6, 47, 52
  balancing needs of business with security needs, 9
  consistency, 13
  creating, 11
  definition of, 9
  disaster recovery plans, 28
  distributing, 16
  feasibility, 11
  flexibility, 15
  goals of, 12, 19
  guidelines, 13, 20
  IKE, 319
  implementing, 14, 17
  ISAKMP, 366
  legal issues, 18
  mode configuration push, 367
  network infrastructure, 10
  patch management, 10
  preparation for, 10
  sanctions for violations, 16
  topics to address, 10
  user account, 10
  weaknesses of, 28
  workstation configuration, 10
  writing direction of, 14
political threats, 33
Port Address Translation (PAT), 48
ports (security), 93
port-to-application mapping (PAM), 70, 225–227
Post Office Protocol, configuring, 287
PPP authentication, 109, 124, 142
ppp authentication command, 142
ppp authentication pap checkin command, 150
preparing routers for, 365
preshared keys, 311
  configuring, 319
  configuring routers for IPSec, 309–310, 321
privilege levels, 83, 88
privileged EXEC mode (Cisco IOS routers), 63, 83
prompt command, 65
protocols
  authentication, 109
  CBAC supported, 238
  IKE, 310
  routing, 197
  weaknesses, 30
proxies, authentication, 70, 251
  appearance, 256
  compatibility with other features, 258

configuring, 258–265
functionality, 255
limitations, 272–273
overview, 255

Q–R

QoS (quality of service), 10
query url command, 348
query-only command, 347
question mark (?) symbol, 65
RADIUS
    authentication proxy, 270
    configuring, 146–147
        accounting, 148
        authentication and authorization, 148
        troubleshooting, 150–151
    features of, 108
    overview, 107
    responses to login attempts, 108
radius-server host command, 146–147
radius-server key command, 146
reconnaissance attacks, 33–34
reflexive access lists (Cisco IOS firewalls), 69
reflexive ACLs, 212
remote access
    case study, 419
        authentication proxy, 423
        Cisco IOS firewall IDS, 420–423
        implementing CBAC, 424–425
    configuring with Easy VPN, 359, 363–366
        creating ISAKMP policy, 366
        enabling IKE DPD, 370
        mode configuration requests, 369
        transform sets, 368
        xauth configuration, 370
    securing router access (case study), 406
remote access VPNs, 308
remote security servers
    Kerberos, 109
    RADIUS, 107–108
    TACACS, 106
    TACACS+, 108
resources
    fabrication, 35
    modification, 35
Reverse Route Injection (RRI), 368
RFC 2196 Site Security Handbook, 9

right-angle bracket (>) symbol, 63
ROM monitor mode (Cisco IOS routers), 63
Router MC
    basic concepts, 386–387
    installation and login, 389–390
    integration with CiscoWorks common
        services, 389
    job statuses, 394
    tunneling technologies, 388
    user accounts, 397
    workflows, 392–393
Router# (config) ip routing command, 65
Router# (config)hostname RouterA
    command, 65
Router# configure terminal command, 65
Router> enable command, 65
RouterA# (config) Ctrl-Z command, 66
RouterA# (config) end command, 66
RouterA# (config) interface Ethernet 0/0
    command, 66
RouterA# (config) ip address 10.10.10.254
    255.255.255.0 command, 66
RouterA# (config)exit command, 66
RouterA# (config)no shutdown command, 66
routers
    administrative acccss, 405
    CA support, 343
    Cisco IOS, 59, 63, 71
    communicating with CAs, 351
    configuring
        ACLs, 214
        host/domain names, 330
        IKE parameters, 411
        IPSec encryption, 310–311
        as SSH client, 91
    configuring for IPSec, 345–349
    disabling unnecessary services (case study),
        407
    enterprise VPN, 383–384
    initializing Cisco IOS firewall IDS, 286
    interactive access, 90
    potential target, 46
    preparing for Easy VPN servers, 365
    securing all in network (case study),
        404–405
    securing remote access (case study), 406
RRI (Reverse Route Injection), 368
RSA encrypted nonces, 328–330

RSA keys
    configuring, 329
    generating, 330
    managing, 332
    planning VPN implementation, 329
    verifying configuration, 331
RSA signatures, 311
rules (RFC 2196 Site Security Handbook), 9

S

SA lifetime, 313, 323
sanctions, 16
saving CA configuration, 350
script kiddies, 31
Secure Access Control Server. See Cisco Secure ACS
Secure Hash Algorithm 1 (SHA-1), 312
security
    access control, 235
    accounting, 120
    administration
        configuring multiple privilege levels, 87–88
        console access, 84
        enable password, 84–85
        enable secret command, 86
        service password-encryption command, 87
        warning banners, 89–90
    authentication, 119
        failed access attempts, 120
        line password, 105
        method lists, 119
        methods, 104
        overview, 104
        remote security servers, 106–108
        username password, 105
    authentication proxy, 255
    authorization, 120
    IDS, 279
    interactive router access, 90
    network design case study, 403–405
    port security for Ethernet switches, 92–93
    SSH, 91
    vty, 90
security posture assessment. See SPA
security wheel, 6, 17, 50

self-imposed vulnerabilities, 27, 37
serve command, 347
serve-only command, 347
servers (Easy VPN), 363–364
service password-encryption command, 87, 105
session keys (Kerberos), 109
SHA-1 (Secure Hash Algorithm 1), 312
show accounting command, 151
show command, 63
show crypto ca certificates command, 352
show crypto dynamic-map command, 326
show crypto ipsec sa command, 326
show crypto ipsec transform set command, 326
show crypto isakmp policy command, 317
show crypto key mypubkey rsa command, 352
show crypto key pubkey-chain rsa command, 353
show crypto map command, 317, 326
show ip audit configuration command, 293
show ip audit interface command, 293
show ip audit statistics command, 293
show running-configuration command, 317
signature based IDS systems, 49
signature disable command, 289
signatures
    Cisco IOS firewall IDS, 288
    excluding, 290
    RSA, 311
Site Security Handbook, 8–9
site-to-site connectivity (case study), 409–410
site-to-site VPNs, 307–308
smurf attacks, 196
SNMP
    securing the network, 194
        CDP, 199
        controlling interactive access, 195
        disabling directed broadcasts, 196
        NTP, 199
        protocol authentication, 197
        small server services, 198
    version differences, 194
SNMPv2, 194
SNMPv3, 194
software vulnerabilities, 27
SPA (security posture assessment), 17–18
split tunneling, 363

SSH, 91
SSH parameters, 67
SSH server, 67
standard IP access lists (Cisco IOS firewalls), 69
structured threats, 31
switches
    configuring as SSH client, 91
    Ethernet, 92–93
    potential target, 46
SYN floods, 236
system auditing (Cisco IOS firewalls), 69
system prompts, changing, 65
system-defined mapping, 225

T

TACACS, 106
TACACS+, 106
    authentication proxy, 266–269
    configuring, 140, 143
        authentication, 141, 143
        encryption key, 141
        troubleshooting, 144–145
    features of, 108
tacacs-server host command, 140–142
TCP inspection, 243
TCP intercept, 69
TCP/IP weaknesses, 30
technical documents, differing from security policy, 14
technology weaknesses, 30
telnet, SSH advantages, 91
telnet connection (Cisco IOS routers), 66
testing
    IPSec configuration, 326
    security implementations, 18
threats, 38
    categories, 31
    curiosity, 32
    dynamic perimeter security, 49
    fun and pride, 32
    intruder motivation, 31
    lack of understanding, 31
    political, 33
    profit and theft, 32
    responding to, 11
    revenge, 32

SNMP, 194
    CDP, 199
    controlling interactive access, 195
    disabling directed broadcasts, 196
    NTP, 199
    protocol authentication, 197
    small server services, 198
weaknesses
    security policies, 28
    technology, 28–30
thresholds, configuring for CBAC, 240
time-based ACLs, 213–214
timeouts configuring for CBAC, 240
traffic
    interception, 34
    interesting, 323
    signatures, 289
transforms, IPSec, 316, 322
transport input ssh command, 67
transport mode (VPNs), 313
trending, 50, 53
Triple Data Encryption Standard (3DES), 312
Trojan horses, 35
troubleshooting
    AAA services, 130–132
    Cisco Secure ACS, 182–183
    RADIUS configuration, 150–151
    SNMP weaknesses, 194
        CDP, 199
        controlling interactive access, 195
        disabling directed broadcasts, 196
        NTP, 199
        protocol authentication, 197
        small server services, 198
    TACACS+ configuration, 144–146
tunnel mode (VPNs), 313
tunnels, split tunneling, 363

U–V

UDP inspection, 243
UDP sessions, 237
UNIX, Secure ACSs, 169–170
unstructured threats, 31
crypto key generate rsa command, 348
user accounts, 10, 397
user EXEC mode (Cisco IOS routers), 63
user-defined port mapping, 227

username password authentication, 105
verifying
    CA configuration, 351
    CBAC, 244
    Cisco IOS firewall IDS configuration, 292
    IPSec configuration, 326
    RSA key configuration, 331
vertical scans, 34
virtual terminal (vty) connections, 68
VMS (VPN/Security Management Solution), 385
VPN/Security Management Solution (VMS), 385
VPNs (virtual private networks), 47
    Cisco Easy VPN. See Easy VPN
    configuration parameters, 409
    connectivity, 47, 52
    endpoints, 307
    IPSec, 309
    managing enterprise VPN routers, 383–384
    planning implementations with RSA keys, 329
    Router MC, 386–394
    site-to-site, 307–308
    transport mode, 313
    tunnel mode, 313
VPNsVMS (VPN/Security Management Solution), 385
vtys, restricting access, 90
vulnerabilities, 27, 37

W–X

warning banners, 89–90
web administration (Cisco Secure ACSs), 165
whois queries, 34
Windows
    Cisco Secure ACSs, 161, 166
        AAA, 162
        accounting, 165
        authorization, 164
        CSAuth, 167
        CSDBSync, 168
        CSLog, 168
    CiscoWorks 2000, 383
workflow, Router MC, 392–393
workstation configuration policy, 10
worms, 35
X.509v3 certificates, 344
xauth, 363, 370
xauth (extended authentication), 363
XTACACS, 106

learn

NOW
I HAVE THE POWER TO MAKE
YOU MORE PRODUCTIVE ON THE JOB.
I CAN PREPARE YOU TO MEET
NEW CHALLENGES.

I AM A CISCO CAREER CERTIFICATION.
ADD ME TO YOUR TOOLBOX WITH
AUTHORIZED TRAINING FROM
CISCO LEARNING PARTNERS...
PAY EASILY WITH CISCO
LEARNING CREDITS.

It is the power to acquire new skillsets, and expand your capabilities. Only Cisco Learning Partners can put you ahead of the curve. Visit www.cisco.com/go/learningpartners.

THIS IS THE POWER OF THE NETWORK. now.

Copyright © 2003, Cisco Systems, Inc. All rights reserved. Cisco Systems logo is a registered trademark of Cisco Systems, Inc. and/or its affiliates in the U.S. and certain other countries.

SAVE UP TO 20% OFF

Become a Preferred Member and save at ciscopress.com!

Complete a **User Profile** at ciscopress.com today and take advantage of our Preferred Member program. Benefit from discounts of up to **20% on every purchase** at ciscopress.com. You can also sign up to get your first **30 days FREE on InformIT Safari Bookshelf** and **preview Cisco Press content**. With Safari Bookshelf, you can access Cisco Press books online and build your own customized, searchable IT library.

All new members who complete a profile will be automatically registered to win a **free Cisco Press book** of their choice. Drawings will be held monthly.

Register at **www.ciscopress.com/register** and start saving today!

The profile information we collect is used in aggregate to provide us with better insight into your technology interests and to create a better user experience for you. You must be logged into ciscopress.com to receive your discount. Discount is on Cisco Press products only; shipping and handling are not included.

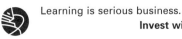

Wouldn't it be great

if the world's leading technical publishers joined forces to deliver their best tech books in a common digital reference platform?

They have. Introducing
InformIT Online Books
powered by Safari.

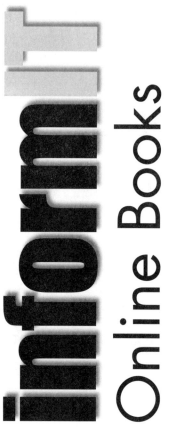

- **Specific answers to specific questions.**
InformIT Online Books' powerful search engine gives you relevance-ranked results in a matter of seconds.

- **Immediate results.**
With InformIt Online Books, you can select the book you want and view the chapter or section you need immediately.

- **Cut, paste and annotate.**
Paste code to save time and eliminate typographical errors. Make notes on the material you find useful and choose whether or not to share them with your work group.

- **Customized for your enterprise.**
Customize a library for you, your department or your entire organization. You only pay for what you need.

Get your first 14 days FREE!

InformIT Online Books is offering its members a 10 book subscription risk-free for 14 days. Visit **http://www.informit.com/onlinebooks/cp** for details.

Switching

Cisco LAN Switching
ISBN: 1-57870-094-9

CCIE Professional Development: Cisco LAN Switching is essential for preparation for the CCIE Routing and Switching exam track. As well as CCIE preparation, this comprehensive volume provides readers with an in-depth analysis of Cisco LAN Switching technologies, architectures and deployments. *CCIE Professional Development: Cisco LAN Switching* discusses product operational details, hardware options, configuration fundamentals, spanning tree, source-route bridging, multilayer switching, and other technology areas related to the Catalyst series switches. The book presents these issues at advanced levels, providing overviews of both LAN technologies and Cisco switching hardware, and covering Catalyst network design essentials not found anywhere else. CCIE candidates will gain exam preparation through the following book elements: chapter-opening overviews of objectives; scenarios that highlight real-world issues; configuration examples and case studies that help readers put the solutions presented to use; and review questions and exercises.

Cisco Field Manual: Catalyst Switch Configuration
ISBN: 1-58705-043-9

This field reference provides novice to experienced network engineers with an aid to configuring Cisco Catalyst switches during hands-on installation or troubleshooting sessions. Cisco offers two distinct operating systems in the Catalyst switch product line (the Catalyst OS COS and the traditional IOS). This book is based on the most current versions, with both COS and IOS commands appearing side-by-side throughout. *Cisco Field Manual: Catalyst Switch Configuration* is organized by like features, with sections marked by shaded tabs for quick reference. Information on each feature is presented in a concise format. This book begins with a review of how switching, then includes a comprehensive guide to configuration starting with basic design, and moves on to discuss Layer 2 and 3 configuration. Coverage then is provided on fundamental switching topics, like VLANs, multi-layer switching, multicast, accelerated server load balancing, access control, switch management, quality of service (QoS), and switching in a voice network.

Learning is serious buisiness.   **Invest wisely.**

Switching

Cisco Catalyst QoS: Quality of Service in Campus Networks
ISBN: 1-58705-120-6

Cisco Catalyst QoS is the first book to concentrate exclusively on the application of QoS in the campus environment. This practical guide provides you with insight into the operation of QoS on the most popular and widely deployed LAN devices: the Cisco Catalyst family of switches. Leveraging the authors' extensive expertise at Cisco in the support of Cisco Catalyst switches and QoS deployment, the book presents QoS from the campus LAN perspective. It explains why QoS is essential in this environment in order to achieve a more deterministic behavior for traffic when implementing voice, video, or other delay-sensitive applications. Through architectural overviews, configuration examples, real-world deployment case studies, and summaries of common pitfalls, you will understand how QoS operates, the different components involved in making QoS possible, and how QoS can be implemented on the various Cisco Catalyst platforms to enable truly successful end-to-end QoS applications.

ciscopress.com

CCNP

CCNP Flash Cards and Exam Practice Pack
ISBN: 1-58720-091-0

Available October 2003

Prepare for all four NEW CCNP exams with over 2,200 flash cards, practice test questions and quick reference sheets

- Check topic comprehension with over 1200 Flash Cards in physical cards that are also downloadable to PC, Palm OS, and Pocket PC.
- Practice for exams with an electronic testing engine with over 800 questions covering all four exams
- Review exam topics with Quick Reference cards organized by exam
- Build confidence with tools from the only Cisco authorized publisher

The CCNP Flash Card Practice Pack (CCNP Self-Study) provides final-stage preparation tools for all of the new CCNP exams that are due to be released by Cisco Systems in June 2003. These exams, 642-801 BSCI, 642-811 BCMSN, 642-821 BCRAN, and 642-831 CIT, have all been re-written with new topical coverage updated to teach networking professionals all they need to know to manage their networks. All of the elements of this title have been created to provide comprehensive coverage of all the new topics in all four of the exams.

CCNP Certification Library, Third Edition
ISBN: 1-58720-104-6

Available December 2003

Cisco CCNP Certification Library, Third Edition, is a comprehensive review and practice package for the four Cisco Certified Network Professional (CCNP) exams: BSCI (642-801), BCMSN (642-811), BCRAN (642-821), and CIT (642-821). The four books contained in this value-priced package, *CCNP BSCI Exam Certification Guide, CCNP BCMSN Exam Certification Guide, CCNP BCRAN Exam Certification Guide,* and *CCNP CIT Exam Certification Guide*, present complete reviews and ample opportunity to test your knowledge of all the topics found on the new CCNP exams.

Learning is serious buisness. **Invest wisely.**

Routing

CCNP BSCI Exam Certification Guide
ISBN: 1-58720-085-6
Available December 2003

CCNP BSCI Exam Certification Guide (CCNP Self-Study) is a revised edition of the all-time best-selling CCNP BSCI/CCNP Routing title ever! With updated technology and testing content, this book provides exceptional tutorial learning and exam preparation on advanced routing techniques and practices. It matches all the objectives of the new 642-801 BSCI exam launched in April! Written in smaller, easier to absorb chapters, this book breaks down larger concepts into manageable blocks of learning. This, combined with other new learning elements and a complete re-writing of the material, make it even easier to comprehend and retain the large amount of learning required for this essential building block of learning for a networker. As part of the CCNP, CCDP, and CCIP certifications, routing is an important building block that all networking professionals must master. This book teaches and prepares candidates for this challenging professional-level exam with chapter quizzes, foundation reviews, in-depth topical learning materials, real-world case studies, and, of course, the 200-plus question electronic testing engine on the CD-ROM included in the back of the book. This testing engine even includes simulation-based questions, just like on the actual exam. New coverage includes more on IS-IS (Intermediate System to Intermediate System), NAT (Network Address Translation), and a solid introduction to IPv6.

Switching

CCNP Practical Studies: Switching
ISBN: 1-58720-060-0
Available October 2003

CCNP Practical Studies: Switching provides networkers and CCNP candidates with an in-depth, hands-on experience in configuring Cisco Catalyst switches. This practical guide shows intermediate level networkers how to apply the theoretical knowledge they have gained through CCNP Coursework and exam preparation in a lab setting. Configuration labs performed within this book will cover all technologies tested upon in Switching exam #640-604, as well as a number of real world scenarios that will test the users overall understanding of multilayer switching. In addition to applicable labs this book also provides some general information on various switching technologies as well as tips, tricks, shortcuts, and caveats for deploying Cisco switching gear in production environments. Part of the Practical Studies series from the Cisco Press, this book provides self-study based hands-on experience. As such, it can be used in conjunction with other Cisco Press titles as well as being an excellent companion to instructor led training from a Cisco Learning Partner. This book is intended for CCNP candidates who are working on the BCMSN courseware and wish to evaluate their knowledge level or supplement existing material. A secondary audience for this book will be those who are implementing Cisco switched solutions and need configuration examples and/or a practical guide.

Learning is serious buisiness.   **Invest wisely.**

Cisco Press Security

CCNP Self-Study: Building Scalable Cisco Internetworks (BSCI), Second Edition
ISBN: 1-58705-146-X

Available April 2004

As part of the Cisco Press Self-Study series, *CCNP Self-Study: Building Scalable Cisco Internetworks (BSCI)*, Second Edition provides early and comprehensive foundation learning for the CCNP BSCI exam. This revision to the popular first edition is fully updated to include complete coverage of all important routing topics, including advanced IP addressing, routing principles, manipulating routing updates, and EIGRP, OSPF, IS-IS, and BGP configuration. In addition to the coverage of exam topics, supplemental appendices include helpful job aids, password recovery advice, and router command summaries.

CCNP Practical Studies: Routing
ISBN: 1-58720-054-6

Built upon the concepts central to the Routing portion of the CCNP certification, this practical guide shows beginning to advanced networkers how to apply the theoretical knowledge they have gained through CCNP coursework and exam preparation. The scenarios guide users through labs that can be practiced on remote-accessible networking labs, networking simulation programs or practice labs made of actual equipment. Each chapter addresses a section of the CCNP-Routing exam. For those lacking lab equipment, the book highlights the steps needed to accomplish various crucial tasks, providing the reader with concrete examples for the challenges faced in real-world configuration. In structure, this book closely follows the Building Scalable Cisco Networks course, to capitalize on existing successful topic structure and to leverage its usefulness as a supplement to a course or self-study regimen. A comprehensive reference guide that directs readers where they can purchase new and used Cisco® equipment for use in these labs is included

ciscopress.com

IF YOU'RE USING

CISCO PRODUCTS,

YOU'RE QUALIFIED

TO RECEIVE A

FREE SUBSCRIPTION

TO CISCO'S

PREMIER PUBLICATION,

PACKET™ MAGAZINE.

Packet delivers complete coverage of cutting-edge networking trends and innovations, as well as current product updates. A magazine for technical, hands-on Cisco users, it delivers valuable information for enterprises, service providers, and small and midsized businesses.

Packet is a quarterly publication. To start your free subscription, click on the URL and follow the prompts: www.cisco.com/go/packet/subscribe

CISCO SYSTEMS

CISCO SYSTEMS/PACKET MAGAZINE
ATTN: C. Glover
170 West Tasman, Mailstop SJ8-2
San Jose, CA 95134-1706

Place Stamp Here

PACKET

☐ **YES!** I'm requesting a **free** subscription to *Packet*™ magazine.
☐ No. I'm not interested at this time.

☐ Mr.
☐ Ms.

First Name (Please Print) / Last Name

Title/Position (Required)

Company (Required)

Address

City / State/Province

Zip/Postal Code / Country

Telephone (Include country and area codes) / Fax

E-mail

Signature (Required) / Date

☐ I would like to receive additional information on Cisco's services and products by e-mail.

1. **Do you or your company:**
   - A ☐ Use Cisco products
   - B ☐ Resell Cisco products
   - C ☐ Both
   - D ☐ Neither

2. **Your organization's relationship to Cisco Systems:**
   - A ☐ Customer/End User
   - B ☐ Prospective Customer
   - C ☐ Cisco Reseller
   - D ☐ Cisco Distributor
   - E ☐ Integrator
   - F ☐ Non-Authorized Reseller
   - G ☐ Cisco Training Partner
   - I ☐ Cisco OEM
   - J ☐ Consultant
   - K ☐ Other (specify): _____

3. **How many people does your entire company employ?**
   - A ☐ More than 10,000
   - B ☐ 5,000 to 9,999
   - C ☐ 1,000 to 4,999
   - D ☐ 500 to 999
   - E ☐ 250 to 499
   - F ☐ 100 to 249
   - G ☐ Fewer than 100

4. **Is your company a Service Provider?**
   - A ☐ Yes
   - B ☐ No

5. **Your involvement in network equipment purchases:**
   - A ☐ Recommend
   - B ☐ Approve
   - C ☐ Neither

6. **Your personal involvement in networking:**
   - A ☐ Entire enterprise at all sites
   - B ☐ Departments or network segments at more than one site
   - C ☐ Single department or network segment
   - F ☐ Public network
   - D ☐ No involvement
   - E ☐ Other (specify): _____

7. **Your Industry:**
   - A ☐ Aerospace
   - B ☐ Agriculture/Mining/Construction
   - C ☐ Banking/Finance
   - D ☐ Chemical/Pharmaceutical
   - E ☐ Consultant
   - F ☐ Computer/Systems/Electronics
   - G ☐ Education (K–12)
   - U ☐ Education (College/Univ.)
   - H ☐ Government—Federal
   - I ☐ Government—State
   - J ☐ Government—Local
   - K ☐ Health Care
   - L ☐ Telecommunications
   - M ☐ Utilities/Transportation
   - N ☐ Other (specify): _____

CPRESS

Packet magazine serves as the premier publication linking customers to Cisco Systems, Inc. Delivering complete coverage of cutting-edge networking trends and innovations, *Packet* is a magazine for technical, hands-on users. It delivers industry-specific information for enterprise, service provider, and small and midsized business market segments. A toolchest for planners and decision makers, *Packet* contains a vast array of practical information, boasting sample configurations, real-life customer examples, and tips on getting the most from your Cisco Systems' investments. Simply put, *Packet* magazine is straight talk straight from the worldwide leader in networking for the Internet, Cisco Systems, Inc.

We hope you'll take advantage of this useful resource. I look forward to hearing from you!

Cecelia Glover
Packet Circulation Manager
packet@external.cisco.com
www.cisco.com/go/packet

PACKET